THE
PRICE
OF
JUSTICE

Money, Morals and
Ethical Reform in the Law

RONALD GOLDFARB

FOREWORD BY
SENATOR BERNIE SANDERS

TURNER PUBLISHING COMPANY

Turner Publishing Company
Nashville, Tennessee
www.turnerpublishing.com

Cover design: Rodrigo Corral
Book design: Tim Holtz

Library of Congress Cataloging-in-Publication Data

Names: Goldfarb, Ronald L., author. | Sanders, Bernard, writer of foreword.

Title: The price of justice : the myths of lawyer ethics / Ronald Goldfarb
  ; foreword by Senator Bernie Sanders.
Description: [Nashville?] : Turner Publishing Company, [2020?] | Includes
  bibliographical references and index. | Summary: "The Price of Justice
  by Ronald Goldfarb with Foreword by Senator Bernie Sanders is a
  fascinating and edgy look at the shortcomings of our legal justice
  system and how many of them are rooted in the flawed construction of the
  ethical rules governing lawyers"-- Provided by publisher.
Identifiers: LCCN 2020029308 (print) | LCCN 2020029309 (ebook) | ISBN
  9781684425020 (hardcover) | ISBN 9781684425044 (epub)
Subjects: LCSH: Legal ethics--United States. | Lawyers--United States. |
  Justice, Administration of--United States.
Classification: LCC KF306 .G65 2020 (print) | LCC KF306 (ebook) | DDC
  174/.3--dc23
LC record available at https://lccn.loc.gov/2020029308
LC ebook record available at https://lccn.loc.gov/2020029309

Printed in the United States of America
17 18 19 20 10 9 8 7 6 5 4 3 2 1

CONTENTS

"The rich man and the poor man do not receive equal justice in our country."

—Robert F. Kennedy

From his review of *Ransom: A Critique of the American Bail System*

DEDICATION

Dedicated to my three special amigos:
Harvey Rosenwasser
Steve Rosenfeld
Hodding Carter

FOREWORD BY
SENATOR BERNIE SANDERS

In the *The Price of Justice: The Myths of Lawyer Ethics*, veteran Washington lawyer Ronald Goldfarb raises the curtain on the subject of our justice and lawyering systems—an issue that has received increased attention in recent years. In this political season some politicians have discovered criminal justice reform as if it were a new subject. But Ronald has been out front on this issue for a long, long time. Throughout his long career Ronald has written books about bail reform, jail, prison reform and farmworkers abuse, and the blurbs on the back jacket by Robert F. Kennedy, Karl Menninger, Tony Lewis, Fred Graham and Harvard scholar Robert Coles attest to Goldfarb's past contributions.

At a time when the United States has more people in jail then any other country on earth, over 2 million, it is shocking to learn how little we spend in making sure that defendants (who are overwhelmingly poor and minorities) get the legal protections that all Americans should be entitled to. In fact, as Ronald points out, the U.S. spends on justice for the poor all of $19 per client. Mind boggling.

In *The Price of Justice* Goldfarb offers powerful anecdotal stories, references to film and media, as well as his own experiences in the RFK Justice Department and the LBJ Office of Economic Opportunity task force with Sargent Shriver, and as a long time public interest lawyer. He provides analyses of interesting key cases, revealing how both the criminal and civil justice systems fail to serve poor and middle-class citizens. His underlying thesis makes a strong case for the profound systemic reform that we need.

The *Price of Justice* makes two fundamental points. One is that many of our major institutions, health and justice are prime examples, operate for the benefit of its administrators and not its clientele and users. Whether it is correctional institutions, courts or law schools that indictment often rings true.

Goldfarb's second fundamental point is that the reality of the justice system differs significantly from its rhetorical goals and purposes. The words "equal justice under law" are etched on the spandrel of the United States Supreme Court building in Washington DC and quoted in flowery speeches and legal opinions. But the reality of the justice system differs from its hortatory words. Goldfarb refers to and describes what one law professor called the manor houses of justice (courts and law schools) and their opposites, the gatehouses (police stations and the streets). Another law professor Goldfarb cites described the due process model of justice for the wealthy who lawyer up (the criminal goes free because the constable has blundered) and the crime control model for the poor (whatever it takes, "I can't breathe," get the conviction, the verdict, the civil judgment). We all cheer the tough cops on TV who capture their criminal prey at the same time our children see the noble Atticus Finch in *To Kill A Mockingbird* as their hero.

Lofty principles about equal justice are irrelevant for the poor people who are prejudiced by fines, bail, lack of adequate counsel and the widespread use of capital punishment which, among major industrialized countries, is unique to the United States. The Constitution guarantees the right to counsel in criminal cases; but the fact is that about 95% of all cases do not go to trial before a judge and jury. They regularly are plea-bargained and, in those situations, the prosecutor holds all the cards. In civil cases, the Constitution guarantees the right to trial by jury but not to lawyers, a hollow guarantee as Goldfarb's stories demonstrate. Goldfarb quotes an SEC insider who stated that the agency "polices the broken windows on the street level and rarely goes to the penthouse floors." Lawyers make the difference and money gets the legal representation you can afford.

The two myths referred in Goldfarb's subtitle are, first, that lawyers use the adversary system to justify their excessive behavior which is aimed at winning cases rather than finding truth or serving justice. And, second, that they should not be criticized for or even compared with the clients they represent and the causes they espouse that go against public interest (auto safety, bad drugs, dirty air and water, advocating torture, for examples). It is their ethics rules that require they do so, they argue. Not so, says Goldfarb. Lawyers turn away worthy clients regularly simply because they cannot pay their often exorbitant fees, and they represent scoundrels who can. Similarly, it is not uncommon for doctors to turn away patients without proof of insurance.

Despite the advent of legal services legislation, in criminal and civil cases Goldfarb describes "a chasmic justice gap." Civil legal aid and criminal public defenders are out-staffed and underfinanced to meet the challenges of well-paid lawyers, in those few cases they are retained. So much for the adversary system. You or I would not last a second in the ring with the heavyweight champ. And while pro bono representation is helpful, it is available in one percent of all the cases, an average of half an hour a week per attorney in the United States.

Legal philosophers like former Supreme Court Justice Harlan Fisk Stone and Louis Brandeis warned, a century ago, that the legal profession was becoming a business, ignoring public interests by offering an expensive menu of advice, litigation and lobbying to which only the wealthy few had access. Goldfarb's book may not make the American Bar Association happy. But if it prompts the public and his profession to pursue the reforms he concludes are necessary, his accomplishments will be very significant. Real civil and criminal justice reform is long overdue, and Goldfarb's book takes us one step closer.

INTRODUCTION

In the over half century since I became a lawyer in 1957, the profession has changed. Some changes are welcome.

I graduated two law schools, Syracuse University and Yale. There was one woman in my class at Yale Law School, two at Syracuse University Law School. No African Americans in either. Today women make up about half of most law school classes. The impressive dean of Syracuse Law School, Craig M. Boise, is African American, and the dean at Yale, Heather Gerken, is outstanding scholar, a woman. The *Washington Post* reported on February 7, 2020 that for the first time in history, the editor's-in-chief of law journals at the top 16 law schools in the U.S. are women. Barack Obama edited Harvard's Law Review; not so long before he became president.

Technological advancements have accompanied the gender and racial sociological changes in our profession. When I was a student doing research for a law review article, I would spend months in the library stacks; today my young clerk can do the same amount of work in half a day because of the internet. When I began practicing law I used carbon paper, added a fax machine, and eventually was consumed by the internet. The legal world has changed: shrunk, expanded, speeded up.

That said, not all changes are for the best. As firms grew from eight lawyers to eight hundred, from one city to many around the world, and technology spread, the corresponding emphasis on money fundamentally transformed the justice profession into a business. The modern practice resembles an internationally exclusive casino, where only the well-off are allowed a seat at the table. The scales of justice are increasingly tilted in favor of the rich, with serious consequences to us all—lawyers and clients alike.

As a result of these changes, the economics of the modern legal profession now twist the original meaning of Mr. Shakespeare's overused and often misquoted line in *Henry IV, Part II*. "First thing we do, let's kill all the lawyers." The Bard was conveying that lawyers were the guardians of justice in his time and deserved respect as the people's protectors against government misrule. Instead, today one critic suggested that in "securing justice in an efficient and affordable fashion, lawyers can in fact be the primary obstacle."[1] With fees often ranging from $200 an hour up to $1,500 an hour, most people cannot afford a lawyer, and "low and middle class families are left to fend for themselves." Even wealthier people who become enmeshed in legal processes are suffering.

If there is a major deficiency in the availability of legal services in civil and criminal cases in America—and there is!—and if lawyers are part of the problem—they are—then the marketplace fails most people in this country in providing access to fundamental justice.

In the *Federalist Papers*, Alexander Hamilton called justice "the first duty of society," and James Madison wrote that "justice is the end of government . . . of civil society."[2]

In today's capitalist system, money provides preferential access to most services and products—homes, cars, vacations, the luxuries of life. There is nothing wrong with that. But as we have witnessed in current debates about the lack of adequate health care in the United States for many people and the need for systemic social reforms—health care and equality of justice, surely—the question must be faced: How do we resolve these problems with the justice system when laissez-faire doesn't work?

Economist Katharina Pistor offers an historical analysis of this problem.[3] Lawyers, she posits, since feudal times, and now, shield, expand and protect the wealth of landowners (then), the wealthy and corporations (now), in what she labels an "empire of law." Corporate law no longer is focused on producing goods and offering services, but instead has adapted feudal land law "into a virtual capital mint." Law and lawyers have assured that the state protects these special economic interests to perpetuate inequality with the force of law.

Yale Law School professor Amy Kapczynski conducts a law and political economy blog that explores how legal doctrines enable the free market to subordinate democracy by concentrating economic and political power in dominant groups who are able to "imbed the economy in social life."[4]

Pistor's theory is supported by Oxford scholar Bernard Rudden who compares the land in feudal days with stock and bonds of today, which are abstract values that breed a "habitat of wealth."[5] As a result "law facilitates the gigantic speculative dynamic of modern finance," Pistor concludes, and the legal profession controls "the clash between capital and the people."[6]

Economic theory is not my expertise, but this book will provide examples that support this view about law, lawyers and the marketplace.

The public has a love-hate relationship with lawyers. Sarcastic lawyer jokes are common, like "Ninety-nine percent of all lawyers give the rest a bad name," and "Legal ethics is an oxymoron," and "Lawyers believe a man is innocent until proven broke." Yet popular lawyer television shows from *Perry Mason* to *LA Law* to *The Good Wife* and *Blue Bloods* portray lawyers heroically.

A paradox is at work. The public disparagement of lawyers is common, but when an individual needs a lawyer, that person's attitude changes: "I want the toughest, meanest street-fighter out there on my side." Whether it is a civil dispute, such as a difficult divorce negotiation, or a consequential criminal trial, clients want a lawyer who will aggressively pursue their private interests. If they can afford one. Most cannot. Justice has its price. Clients in these cases are self-interested and rarely looking for "justice." Too often they get neither lawyers nor justice.

In 2015, the president of the New York State Bar Association noted the need to improve legal ethical standards, to evolve a better work-life balance in what has become a "sometimes grueling profession," and to develop higher moral and qualitative standards.[7] Gallup polls of public mistrust of lawyers' honesty and ethical standards show consistently subpar results.[8] At the same time, bar studies reveal that many lawyers are distressed by their lifestyles.

The moral culture of law schools and the profession encourages students and lawyers to serve clients' interests, not the public's interest. In return, lawyers receive generous compensation. And that compensation is based on whether the client can pay the fees set by the lawyer. If a potential client cannot afford such fees, then the lawyer is likely to decline the case. Moreover, private practitioners expect to be well compensated. Lawyers at successful law firms typically receive more in salary than Supreme Court justices or US senators or law professors.

When I graduated Yale Law School in 1960, the number one member of that class began work at a well-known New York City firm at the then impressive annual pay of $16,000. According to the ABA Journal, three large New York firms are now charging over $1000 an hour for senior associates for bankruptcy work ironically.[9] In 2019, a managing partner at a major multicity law firm wrote to me that "average compensation of partners in firms of two hundred to five hundred lawyers [is] $625,000. In firms of over five hundred lawyers: $1,000,000. Starting associate compensation at top firms in major markets: $190,000 plus bonus. Senior associates in top firms: $350,000 plus bonus. Staggering!"

The old fashioned, personal law firm has been replaced by the mega-firms. A Bloomberg article[10] about changes in law firms in the 2010's provided several examples. One D.C. anti-trust firm at its peak had $573 million in revenue, $1.3 million for partner profit. It had 700 lawyers in 8 offices round the world. Then, "the firm collapsed," due to overexpansion and lax management. After the merger of two big New York City firms into a 1000 member firm, the new firm went $300 million into debt. It went bankrupt and some managing partners were indicted. A Boston firm that earned $860 million in 2009, with partners earning $1.4 million had to cease operations. Several years later over 200 lawyers moved to another firm, and that former firm went out of business. Comparable stories of firms in Richmond, VA and San Francisco were told.[11]

Bloomberg News also reported that "at most law firms today, partners are primed to compete with each other for clients,"[12] especially in their areas of expertise. And as more businesses become more complex and reinvent themselves, the world of outside counsel in private firms must adapt with their clients. One change noted is the evolution of "swarm intelligence" where attorneys collaborate within firm special units and outsource to smaller firms and alternate legal service providers. The law firm of the future reflects the business model of their large international business clients, focused on economics—not a bad idea—but different from the image and culture and as a result value systems that prior generations of lawyers foresaw.

These high income levels do not improve the lives of law firm employees, only the lawyers themselves. According to one study, "In the mid-1960's, profits per partner at elite law firms were less than five times a secretary's salary. Now they are over 40 times."[13] Former head of the Legal Services Corporation, the largest funder of civil legal services in America, James J. Sandman left a successful and profitable corporate law practice because, "I came to feel as if I were devoting myself to making rich people richer, and I'm not talking about clients; I'm talking about my colleagues."[14]

With the growth of the number of students graduating law school, many neophyte lawyers graduate in debt and have difficulty finding rewarding jobs, despite what would seem to be a perfect needs match of lawyers and clients.

How did our profession get to this place? The late US Supreme Court justice Harlan Fiske Stone, a member of the pantheon of our profession, stated a century ago that the mission of law schools should be to teach its students "how to live rather than how to make a living."[15] That notion of social responsibility for how work is performed is what distinguishes professionals from other occupations. Justice Stone instructed us to measure what we do by personal ethical standards along with our public professional responsibilities. Yes, we work to earn a living, and there is no virtue or sin to that reality—except, I would argue, if what we do in our work can be considered by reasonable standards to be virtuous or sinful. And what might these standards be? To adapt the late justice Potter Stewart's wry remark, we know that when we see it—or we ought to.[16]

Justice Stone's twentieth-century notion about the proper role of lawyers was examined a century later by retired Yale law professor Owen Fiss.[17] In 2017, Fiss wrote that lawyers "exercising the power of the law" need "to reflect on the ends of the legal system" when they do. Lawyers acting as advocates, Fiss wrote, involves more than the mere manipulation of rules to serve a client's interest. "Advocates often must define and identify just what a client's interests are, especially when the client happens to be a political group, corporation, union, government agency." While the limits on lawyers' advocacy are in criminal statutes and professional canons, Fiss continued, "The most important ones are derived from the dictates of justice or from a broad understanding of the lawyer's role in society."[18]

The American Bar Association Commission on Professionalism[19] called on lawyers to "abide by higher standards of conduct
rather than the minimum required by the Code of Professional
Responsibility and the Model Rules." Admitting that this concept
is "elastic," the report uses the phrase "in the spirit of public service,"[20] suggesting that more than formal sets of rules and regulations should guide our behavior.

The only sworn commitment I made when I was first admitted
to the New York Bar and later the US Supreme Court bar was this:
For all federal courts (including the Supreme Court):

> I, [Ronald Goldfarb], do solemnly swear (or affirm) that as an
> attorney and as a counselor of this court I will conduct myself
> uprightly and according to law, and that I will support the consti-
> tution of the United States.

For the New York Bar (which is included in the state's constitution, so it would have been the same in 1957):

> I do solemnly swear (or affirm) that I will support the constitu-
> tion of the United States, and the constitution of the State of
> New York, and that I will faithfully discharge the duties of the
> office of [attorney and counselor-at-law], according to the best
> of my ability.

Only indigent criminal defendants are entitled by constitutional
law to have counsel, and those who are assigned or choose to represent them are upholding the high standards of the bar. For that reason, the Model Rules of Professional Conduct state that representing
a client does not mean a lawyer endorses their views or activities.

But the Model Rules also state that no lawyer must take any
case, unless it is a criminal case that is assigned to him or her by

a court. Except in these unusual mandated cases, the rest of us make choices, and they are *not* based on bar ethics rules but on each of our notions about what we want to do with our time and our professional skills. If we have the right to decline a case because the fee is insufficient, why not because the client or his or her cause is repugnant?

Justice Stone's and Professor Fiss's remarks remind me of two lawyers: a fictional literary character, Atticus Finch, and a real one, Clarence Darrow. One defended an innocent man in a hostile community (Finch) and the other exposed the hypocrisy of banning the teaching of evolution (Darrow). Neither were well paid for their consuming work. They are both widely admired for what they did. Like them, I believe lawyers should be judged by what we do.

A generation of young lawyers attributes their becoming a lawyer to having read *To Kill a Mockingbird*[21] and the moral stance of Atticus Finch. A generation earlier, I was similarly lured to becoming a trial lawyer after reading about the trials of Clarence Darrow in the book *Attorney for the Damned.*[22] Few of us lawyers will be called upon to act heroically in a hostile community as Atticus Finch did or to challenge a national hero as Darrow did when he disputed William Jennings Bryan on the teaching of religion over evolution in our public schools. But many of us *will* encounter clients and causes whom we have (or ought to have) qualms about representing, or conundrums about whether our prospective behavior for a client is worthwhile and is justified by a respectable purpose. However, wealthy clients are rarely rejected, regardless of their actions in question, while many lawyers turn away potential clients, deserving ones, solely because they can't pay the fees for their work.

When it comes to criticism of the morality and professional ethics of lawyers, there is an image of cheap-suited, court-house hangers on, trolling court corridors, exploiting vulnerable poor clients. That is so, sometimes. But harder to condone are the Ivy-league clothed, large firm, mostly corporate counsel, advising rich clients in elegant offices and representing them in courts and lobbying Congress on their behalf, some of them questionable characters guilty of advancing questionable behavior and causes.

The first group fills a void, provides <u>some</u> service, often inadequate, for clients who don't have resources to do better. And, they are more readily policed by the bar and judges. Worse, morally, are the lawyers who appear to be good citizens, perform charitable services in some of their extra time, but often provide services for people and organizations who miss-serve society. This book focuses on these latter lawyers because they are influential and set the standards of our profession. When those standards are questionable, they ought to be evaluated. All professions have members who are world class citizens and others who do them no honor. In law, more than others, the consequences of their behavior are pervasive, difficult to change, and call for reforms.

How and by what standards should we manage and rationalize those moral and ethical quandaries? The traditional bar's response to this question is based on two faulty premises—myths, I will call them.

CHAPTER ONE

A TALE OF
TWO MYTHS

The ethics of the legal profession are built on two myths. The first is that lawyers do what they do because they are bound by their professional responsibility to zealously represent their clients. However, lawyers have the ability to choose their clients and causes, and they often interpret *zealously* in questionable ways.

The second myth is that they do what they do because of the wisdom embedded in the operation of the adversary system. Much like Adam Smith's metaphor of the "invisible hand" operating in the economic marketplace, the adversary system theoretically regulates the search for truth and justice in the fairest and most efficient manner possible. In this process, the lawyer's work is to be considered neutral, and a lawyer, it follows, should not be judged by his or her clients, causes, or cases.

This book takes the position that both these myths are illusory. Most lawyers make personal choices, and they do so predominantly for the financial rewards—not in furtherance of some professional principle that guarantees outcomes of justice. Thus, it is not inappropriate to characterize us by what we do. We are more than professionals behaving in a morally neutral manner; we are criminal and civil lawyers, trial lawyers, corporate or labor lawyers, civil liberties lawyers, government employees and law teachers, office lawyers and trial lawyers—solicitors and barristers, as the British label them. As such, we are correctly characterized by the social element of our work. Surely the public sees the public-interest lawyer who represents an environmental organization complaining over an oil spill differently than the big law firm partner who represents the errant oil company. *So do many lawyers.*

In fundamental ways, the lawyering we do defines us. I do not believe lawyers can justify all of their professional behavior by invoking professional guidelines or the adversary system as self-legitimizing mechanisms that supposedly bend toward justice.

The reality is that these two common justifications for the way we approach our work are misleading. Lawyers don't represent clients because all citizens are entitled to representation; they do so for financial rewards, and they leave erstwhile clients who are without money without representation. They participate in a private system that for the most part denies poor people legal representation, and a public system that does not assure funding for private or public legal service programs for poor and middle-class clients. Millions of Americans are left without private or public representation in consequential cases that have a deep impact on their lives. Justice Wiley B. Rutledge, Jr. wrote, "Poverty or wealth will make all the difference in securing the substance or only the shadow of constitutional protections."[23]

This disparity between the rich and the poor's access to professional services is compounded by the inequities inherent in the adversary system that is designed to win a dispute rather than to seek truth and justice. Saying the adversary system offers a systemic method that will produce just results, rather than a forum for combat between lawyers seeking to win whatever result they are paid to accomplish, is like putting Joe Louis in the boxing ring with a weak, unprepared opponent and declaring, "May the better man win! The system will show which one is better!" Too often, the adversarial system dictates who wins by giving one side—in civil and in criminal cases alike—vastly disproportionate power.

MYTH ONE:
FINDING LAWYERS, CHOOSING CLIENTS

I remember arguing with people when I was in law school about the traditional question from the public: How could you zealously represent someone in a criminal case you knew was guilty? The common answer is that is what lawyers are supposed to do, so they shouldn't be colored the shade of their clients. The professional rationale is that lawyers are supposed to maximize the likelihood their clients will prevail, and when doing so they are not accountable professionally or morally "for the means used or the ends achieved."[24]

Supreme Court justice Benjamin Cardozo stated that enforcing a right under the law cannot be legally wrong and may often be a moral duty.[25] Thus, if the client makes a choice the lawyer thinks is immoral, but it is not illegal, the lawyer should assist the client.[26] This approach, assisting client conduct that technically is permissible if ethically questionable, can lead to the moral ambiguity that separates lawyers from one another and from the lay public.

Representing unpopular clients can be in the best traditions of our profession. James Donovan, was assigned to defend Rudolf Abel when the federal court in New York asked him to represent the accused Soviet spy. He undertook the noble and professional assignment, which the best and most respectable lawyers do to honor their profession and our legal system's guarantee to the right to counsel under the Constitution.

Donovan must have recalled the words of Miles McDonald—a New York Supreme Court justice—who'd earlier told him: "I hope you know what lies ahead. Since John Adams defended the British soldiers for the Boston Massacre, in 1774, no defense lawyer has taken on a less popular client."[27]

Such endeavors are not the same as a mob lawyer who represents his mob boss for whom he has served as an advisor to a criminal operation, or even the lawyer who represents a commercial villain simply because the villain has money to pay a generous fee. I think every client has the right to a lawyer, but that does not mean an individual has the right to hire you or me. I retain the right to decline representation for my own reasons, including not liking the client or the cause. Doing so, I believe, is the honorable behavior of a "good person" and a "good lawyer." It is also easily distinguishable from the circumstances of James Donovan's representation of Rudolf Abel, in which money played no part and Donovan was acting as the guardian of a constitutional principle at the request of the court.

A fundamental question about the bounds of what is ethical lawyering is how much and what kind of participation private lawyers should provide for their clients. The *New York Times* published a story[28] in 2009 about a New York senator, who in her earlier career practiced corporate law for a large firm in New York City that represented a major tobacco company. The *Times* story stated that part of her work included shielding from disclosure documents that demonstrated the addictive and health hazards of smoking, which her clients, the company executives, had denied under oath before Congress. She was an active participant in defending tobacco companies, her colleagues stated, developing industry strategies and limiting what embarrassing evidence the government and plaintiff lawyers were able to gain access to. Her clients were able to "beat back the federal perjury investigation," the *Times* article reported.

She later claimed she was a junior associate with little control over the cases she handled and had limited involvement in defending that client. Her spokesman told the *Times* that her work for the tobacco company didn't reflect the range of her work or her work for pro bono clients. However, lawyers in her firm were given the right to refuse to work in tobacco cases if they had moral or ethical objections.[29] She would not discuss this matter with reporters, claiming she was prevented from doing so by the attorney-client privilege.

It comes as no surprise that tobacco companies contributed to her later legislative campaign, the *Times* reported. New York University Law School ethics professor Stephen Gillers described the practice of tobacco companies using the attorney-client privilege to prevent disclosure of "inconvenient truths" as "morally offensive."[30]

Compare that example with the experience of Marc Edell, who won the first judgment against a tobacco company for tobacco-related lung cancer. He earned his contingent share of the jury award of $400,000 to his client, after four years and thousands of hours of preparations, a four-month trial, and millions of dollars of advanced costs.[31] One source reported that tobacco companies spent "literally billions of dollars in defense . . . to discourage plaintiff attorneys . . . a strategy of intimidation." They dragged out depositions and filed diversionary motions.[32]

Edell likely earned far less for his good work than the lawyer noted earlier did for hers. He earned his client's—and the public's—respect, however.

Even when claims of public dangers are proven, there are no truly happy endings. Unnecessary harms to the public accrued, were defended aggressively by well-paid lawyers, and the eventual damages can never be truly compensatory.

Hollywood has done a good job portraying this problem, notably in the film *Erin Brockovich*, a true story dramatized by excellent performances by Julia Roberts as a paralegal and Albert Finney as her small-firm lawyer boss. The movie tells the story of

Pacific Gas & Electric Company (PG&E) in Hinckley, California and its gas pipeline which used a carcinogenic chemical compound (chromium-6) to inhibit corrosion. For twenty years the leakage contaminated water that caused cancers to users, though the company told the public the water was "suitable for both drinking and agriculture." Erin Brockovich, a clerk at the "Masry and Vititoe" Law firm found records revealing the problem that led to litigation in 1993 on behalf of 77 plaintiffs (eventually 648). After fighting the claims, PG&E agreed to pay $333 million to clean up its mess and reimburse plaintiffs—but much avoidable damage was done that the utilities lawyers had to know about.[33]

(There is a scene where the small-time lawyer and his aide are confronted in the decorous meeting room of PG&E's lawyers, and Brockovich offers her opponent a glass of water to drink from the questioned source; she, of course, declines.)

In the movie *A Civil Action*,[34] a true story based on Jonathan Harr's book, a lone attorney takes on a large corporation, W.R. Grace Company and Beatrice Foods and Unifirst Company, over its contamination of public waters. Company lawyers fought the claims of the eight plaintiff families who lost six children and one adult to leukemia related deaths. Eventually the company settled for $8 million. A Harvard law professor used that case in a course on legal ethics for first-year students. One commentator noted that "the adversary system of justice is ill-suited to deciding highly complex issues and complex cases like these . . . for every Ph.D., there is an equal and opposite anti-Ph.D."[35]

The late 2019 film *Dark Water* dealt with a young attorney who spent decades exposing the DuPont Company's negligence in a federal suit in West Virginia for dumping toxic PFOA sludge that drained into nearby properties. Animals died grotesque deaths. Seventy thousand people drank the contaminated water and many became sick. DuPont fought the claims for years, defending its chemicals as proper. Eventually DuPont paid the largest fine ordered under EPA at the time, amounting to "less than two percent of the profits earned by DuPont on PFOA that year,"[36] and dropped use of this toxic chemical. But the plaintiffs' lawyer became ill from stress; he was treated as though he had done something wrong by local press and people in the community who were beholden to DuPont. Later the lawyer wrote a book about this episode.[37] Thousands of people died or were stricken while the company fought the claims and kept the product on the market.

There are no happy endings to these stories of devoted lawyers fighting corporate wrongdoers who pay their lawyers well to keep bad products available to the public. The public has suffered death and illness from opioids, dangerous drugs, tobacco and alcohol, from faulty cars, misconduct by government agencies and corporate officials who are rarely held personally responsible for their behavior.

In his recent book about Big Pharma,[38] Gerald Posner provides case histories where teams of corporate lawyers defended major drug companies through lobbying Congress to weaken regulations, fighting FTC and FDA investigations, and defending indictments for massive wrongdoings. Class actions were "dragged through a byzantine course of discovery, procedural delays, and a seemingly endless battery of motions and appeals." Posner reports that lawyers defending OxyContin, at one point were paid $3 million a month while OxyContin was earning $30 million a week. Oxy paid millions in civil penalties while racking up billions in annual sales. Protracted legislation lasted 16 years in one case, Posner cites. He presents many depressing examples of the venality of top drug companies, aided by their high-priced lawyers.

Corporations are guilty of broad public injuries, but it is more startling when the government is responsible for questionable conduct toward its military personnel, as described in Mike Magner's *A Trust Betrayed: The Untold Story of Camp Lejeune and the Poisoning of*

Generations of Marines and Their Families.[39] Magner recounted how thousands of marines and their families were killed or poisoned by contaminated water at Camp Lejeune.

An alternative is offered by the "clawback" of the notorious Madoff Ponzi scheme by which he "made off" with about $17 billion of clients' investments.[40] Under clawback rules,[41] in certain cases courts may order representatives of defrauded victims to clawback their losses from the scheme. In the Madoff case, Irving Picard was the court-appointed trustee who oversaw monitoring the labyrinthine web of beneficiaries and victims of Madoff's shenanigans. So far Picard has clawed back $13.3 *billion* of the $17.5 billion from Madoff's investors' profits. Madoff's victims were not billed, and only they received *partial* proceeds of the clawback. Picard and his team have clawed back seventy-five cents of every dollar profited by Madoff's clients (compared to five to ten cents typical in Ponzi cases).

Here's my point: Picard and his staff were paid well ($1,000 an hour for the top two attorneys; an average of $430 an hour for hires), all reimbursed from the Securities Investor Protection Agency, a nonprofit company–created insurer (which has been reimbursed, as were the victims, from Picard's clawbacks). Good, well-paid lawyers like Picard and his team served the public and deserved their compensation for successfully fulfilling a difficult assigned task.

A century ago, Supreme Court justice Stone warned that lawyers were becoming "obsequious servants of business" guided by the "morals and manners of the marketplace and its anti-social manifestations."[42] Because of its public character, the profession, Stone thought, "must not be allowed to become the monopoly of any social or economic class."[43]

I wrote about lawyers and clients in the *Washington Post*[44] in a debate over the correctness of a Wall Street law firm's twelve associates questioning their partners about their firm's representing Swiss bank defendants in a Nazi money-laundering case brought by families of Holocaust survivors. The neophyte lawyers complained that the firm was lending its imprimatur to their clients. How could the firm do all the adversary system requires on behalf of their clients and not do injustices to their clients' adversaries? If clients define their lawyers, lawyers do the same for their clients, they argued.

The partners responded that their work was neutral; there was a legal conflict, and someone had to defend the bank's position. However, that isn't always the case. The Washington-based Covington & Burling law firm refused to represent South African Airways because of its country's racial discrimination policy, which violated our country's normative cultural policy.[45]

A spokesperson from Greenberg Traurig, a two-thousand-person law firm, stated that Rudy Giuliani's leave from the firm to assist President Donald Trump was more than a temporary leave: "He no longer worked there," the firm stated.[46] Press accounts have reported that some lawyers declined the offer to work for the controversial president. Regardless of the excitement and lucrative nature of working for a president in the White House,[47] some lawyers just say no, as a matter of principle.

Sometimes these role changes backfire. The *Washington Post*[48] described a well-known and well-regarded Washington lawyer who suffered personal anguish over hostile reactions to her representing the Trump family and campaign members. The incident raised the classic question about the relationship between attorneys and clients. Is there a difference between having an occupation and being part of a licensed profession? Lawyers are compared to doctors, whose ethics are said to require they heal all who ask for their help? Are we lawyers a kind of public accommodation like motel owners or bartenders who must serve all comers? Or do attorneys practice their profession by different rules of client selection? If so, what are they?

Mentioning her community work and her prior Democratic political ties, the respected lawyer said, "They knew who I was" when Trump family members hired her. But that is exactly the point her critics made. Did her clients pay not only to use her skills but also to exploit her popular and respected reputation? There are many excellent lawyers in Washington and elsewhere, so it is not unfair to ask why they chose her as well as why she accepted them.

Is who represents whom anyone's business beyond the individual lawyers and their clients? Press reports have noted that some successful Washington trial lawyers declined representing President Trump for personal reasons, while some firms would not permit their lawyers to represent anti-Trump clients. A famous lawyer and retired professor was shunned by some of his summertime island friends and neighbors for his remarks on television about the president, according to press accounts. [49] We do what we care to do, with our eyes wide open to the implications of our work and clients, and for our own reasons.

Lawyers represent most of their clients, most of the time, to make the most money, period. If clients don't have money, they usually don't have competent representation—no matter how high the stakes or how grave the consequences.

The morality of lawyering is filled with perplexing conflicts. It has always been so. Columbia Law School professor William Simon referred to several examples of the roles of lawyers portrayed in literature by noted writers such as Dickens, Dostoevsky, Kafka, Melville, and Sinclair Lewis to shed light on the fundamental moral components of their work.

Readers will recall Dickens's works, which insightfully fictionalized relevant themes about lawyering. While Dickens couldn't
afford to go to law school, he had worked at a law office as a young
man and filled many of his books with insights he'd gained while
there: protracted legal technicalities as in *Bleak House* in the classic
Jarndyce v. Jarndyce probate case, and in *The Pickwick Papers* dealing
with the meaning of a just society.

Samuel Johnson rationalized the justice of the adversary system
as work for judges, not lawyers: "If a lawyer had to believe in a client's case, most people would go undefended."[50] Let opposing sides
do their "tango," Johnson suggested.

Author-critic Joseph Epstein wrote that lawyers appear worse
than they may be "because the nature of their work requires them to
be better."[51] He posited, "Without our rules as officers of the court,
commissioned to uphold the grandeur of the law, we're just a used
car dealership, without the burden of inventory."

Dostoevsky wrote about coercive interrogation, mental capacity,
the difference between justice and law, and traditions of right and
wrong. Dostoyevsky himself was imprisoned and nearly executed.[52]
Kafka suffered financially when he wrote about government surveillance, the unfairness of the legal system, privacy, and closed-door
trials.[53] Herman Melville's *Bartleby: The Scrivener* is set in a Wall
Street law firm office occupied by eccentric paralegals. But the plot
deals with the growing materialism of American culture and the
importance of money in American life.[54] Readers of John Grisham
and Michael Connelly will recognize their fictionalized, but real,
descriptions of modern policing and lawyering.

According to Professor Simon's analysis, the good lawyer
emerges as one who works to remedy the imbalances of the
justice system through an awareness of the value of reaching
socially desirable outcomes. Lawyers are guided by ethical norms
beyond blind loyalty to clients. Being counsel "to a situation"

(as the late Supreme Court justice Louis Brandeis argued), lawyers must keep larger social purposes in mind, repudiate governance by categorical rules, and not sidestep truth and justice by yielding to abstract principles that exempt lawyers from moral responsibilities.[55]

The late and celebrated justice Oliver Wendell Holmes Jr. articulated the traditional viewpoint: "We are in the law business, not the justice business."[56] Those words are at the heart of the debate under discussion here. What is the difference between law and justice? A profession and a business? Should there be moral differences in people's work? Whose responsibility is it, beyond each individual, to define *justice*?

A law professor friend told me about his first day in his property class at Harvard Law School. A classmate asked their professor about the justice of a matter under discussion. Professor W. Barton Leach responded, "Justice? You want justice? This is the Law School. If you want justice, go across the street to the Divinity School!" The class laughed. Reality suggests many learned that cynical lesson from the esteemed law professor.[57]

A lawyer character in author Raymond Chandler's *The Long Goodbye* tells the iconic private eye Philip Marlowe, "The law isn't justice. It's a very imperfect mechanism. If you press exactly the right buttons and are also lucky, justice may show up in the answer. A mechanism is all the law was ever intended to be." Marlowe didn't laugh at this cynical lesson.[58]

Is evaluating a profession by a higher ethical and moral standard a quaint notion, now unrealistic?

In an art-imitates-life example that illustrates this dilemma, the character Sam Seaborn, *West Wing* actor Rob Lowe, explained to his friend and colleague Josh Lyman (portrayed by actor Bradley Whitford) why he was leaving his law firm to join the White House staff. Seaborn had prospered as did his firm helping corporate maritime clients make more money, but he admitted, "No one ever wrote a folk song about lawyers doing that."[59]

Lawyers' relationships with clients and their causes define us in fundamental ways. On a daily basis, most of us spend more time at work than we do with our families, churches, and social or political parties. In a recent survey,[60] it was reported that 72% of millennials (born between 1981–1996) and 73% of generation X'ers (1965–1980), and 77% of Boomers (1946–1964) considered their work as the central part of their lives, and an almost similar number consider their work important in finding meaning in their lives.

I accept the premise that for better or for worse, I am described by *what I do*, and that I am not guided in my professional work exclusively by professional rules I swore to abide by when admitted to the New York, California, District of Columbia, and Supreme Court bars. I am also guided by my personal values, only part of which originated during my legal training.

The characterization of lawyers begins with the nature of the work they perform for their clients, and then by the standards they live by in doing their work. When I was a uniformed lawyer in the US Air Force JAG practicing military law, my work was guided by the Uniform Code of Military Justice and by the culture of the military.

I was staff judge advocate at a small air force base near Chicago, and as such I not only tried and defended courts-martial (military trials) but also advised the base commander about legal matters. One incident challenged my ethical standards.

The commander thought too many cases had resulted in acquittals or lenient sentences, and he sent a memo to all potential hearing officers for courts-martial, stating that as commanding officer he would decide on review whether or not leniency was appropriate. The hearing officers were told to leave that job to him. When I saw the memo, I recognized that his instructions were prejudicial in all future cases I would have to review for higher authorities. With much trepidation, I wrote the commander, stating that his instructions to base officers were prejudicial and recommended that he countermand that particular instruction.

He summoned me to his office and asked for my reasoning. He defended his position, and asked: "Who would know what I wrote?"

"All reviewing authorities," I responded, because it was my obligation to send my recommendation to the same reviewing authorities he would be reporting to, much as a corporate counsel must advise his superiors about their conduct and its implications. He was upset and made his displeasure known. I knew he was the one who would write my performance reports, and that we had to maintain ongoing relations on all base matters, which I feared were now jeopardized by his obvious rancor. But I stuck to my position that he needed to rectify his instructions to base officers. He did, but our relationship was icy thereafter. Fortunately, I was assigned to another base shortly after that for reasons unrelated to this episode.

I recall this incident because military culture would have suggested to some officers that getting along or looking the other way would have been a more personally safe course of action. Because I did not plan on a military career, I had less to lose, and it was easier for me to act on principle. But what about young corporate or large law firm lawyers who don't approve of what their client—or their senior partner—is doing? The case of the Swiss banks defense mentioned earlier raised this point. Dare aspiring lawyers in large firms speak out? These types of dilemmas confront lawyers regularly. Living by your own ethical standards is not easy, especially when there are countervailing pressures against doing so. As a rule, whistleblowers usually pay a personal price.[61]

When I later became a prosecutor in the Department of Justice, investigating and prosecuting organized crime cases, I was guided by the codified ethics of a federal prosecutor. One instruction was to never comment publicly about a pending case, particularly when a government lawyer was involved in a sensational, press-saturated criminal investigation and trial. Period! That rule—which was recently violated in sensational circumstances by FBI director James Comey with serious national consequences[62]—was followed in my experience by prosecutors and by the investigators we worked with at FBI, IRS, and other law enforcement agencies. Investigative agencies do not recommend prosecutions to the public, especially in the middle of an election, nor do they add negative personal commentary about people they investigate.

The Justice Department culture differs from that of defense lawyers who operate under different principles and employ different trial practices. Using the press for the advantage of a client is a practice most defense lawyers do unless ordered not to by a judge, as was the case of Roger Stone. Defense lawyers argue that they must use all avenues to defend their clients because prosecutors have the edge in all cases: public announcements of indictments and perp walks, for example. The adversary system requires defense attorneys to attempt to mitigate that edge. Ethical prosecutors, like special prosecutor Robert Mueller, consider the public as the client they represent, and they are bound by a different set of standards—including the presumption of innocence—in their pursuit of truth and justice.

I make my choices from available clients while I practice law, as we all do. My choices do much to define me. Mostly now I represent authors, including politicians, some from another party than mine (I represented Republican Ohioan congressman John Kasich as well as Massachusetts's Republican senator Ed Brooke, Florida Democrat Claude Pepper, South Carolina Democrat James Clyburn, and Independent Vermonter Bernie Sanders); but I wouldn't represent some politicians from either party for all the money in the world (nor do I expect they'd want me). Like Thomas Jefferson's view about the First Amendment, I agree everyone should have the right to write, but I have the right not to read their books. The same type of value judgment defines lawyers and clients: the choices lawyers make of who to take on as clients and how to represent those clients are inseparable from who we are as people.

In each professional situation, we are all guided by different responsibilities, goals, clients, and operating procedures. In attitudinal and cultural ways, ACLU lawyers are different from Federalist Society lawyers, and prosecutors are different from criminal defense lawyers, though both refer to the adversary system to justify their practices. Our work on behalf of one particular kind of client—conservatives, progressives, academics—also defines us by what we do for them and how we do it. We are all lawyers, but ethically we come in various "flavors."

A classic example is Robert Jackson, who was chosen to be chief prosecutor at the Nuremberg trials after World War II. His appointment was a result of his reputation as chief law-enforcement official for the United States when he was attorney general, followed by his prestigious membership on the US Supreme Court. His jurisprudential experiences projected an image for rectitude and expertise in matters of justice that this history-making role called for. He was chosen because of what he had done. The image was earned, and it was important to his task.

How then, to return to my main point, should we characterize lawyers who represent pharmaceutical companies that sell harmful drugs, or automobile and cigarette companies that keep their deadly products available to the public, or financial organizations that bilk consumers and profit in doing so? Or insurance companies that fight honest complainants' just claims? Or government lawyers who write briefs justifying torture? Or district attorneys who sidestep constitutionally based procedures in order to secure a verdict? Different, I would think, than the James Donovans and Robert Jacksons of our profession.

When they are challenged, most lawyers claim they are merely doing what the culture of their profession calls on them to do. They argue they should not be held personally responsible for the pursuit of clients' interests.

For over a half century, I have argued against that point of view. As I stated earlier, in my judgment everyone may be entitled to a lawyer, but no one is entitled to you or to me as their lawyer. We make our own choices in clientele and subject matter of the work we undertake. Lawyers cannot claim that in defending the sale of toxic or faulty products they should not be criticized as facilitators, sometimes collaborators with their clients. Or that as overzealous government attorneys they are doing what their job description and their superiors require. The argument in those situations is that by aggressively representing their clients, lawyers are fulfilling some higher cultural and professional role. I don't agree.

A recent book on good lawyering described the exquisite lines lawyers should not cross:[63] "[Y]our client might want you to do what you, in good conscience, cannot do. No one made you take an oath that said: 'My client right or wrong.' When a little bird lands on your shoulder and whispers, 'Don't do it,' it's best to listen—even if the rules suggest it might be okay." Codes of professional ethics merely tell us what lines we should not cross over; we have to decide for ourselves how close we can get to the lines and still feel comfortable.

The notorious Panama Papers ongoing scandal involving the Panama law firm Mossack Fonseca is a classic example of lawyers profiting from what a critic described as a "dodgy world of off shore companies, where kleptocrats, drug lords and tax cheats hid their riches."[64] The firm, which grew from its start in 1986 to a staff of five hundred with affiliates around the world, claimed it didn't know it was facilitating criminal behavior or money laundering. The partners and some of their employees and affiliates were charged with money laundering by sheltering superrich clients and some notorious human rights violators worldwide in countries with amenable tax havens (the Seychelles, for example).[65]

It ought not surprise lawyers who are held responsible for being involved in money-laundering, as ethics and criminal laws make clear[66]. This subject was covered in the *60 Minutes* expose in 2016 "Lowering the Bar"[67]. The TV expose was assisted by an international organization dedicated to combating corruption, *The Global Witness*[68].

Netflix produced a movie called *The Laundromat* based on leaked papers, and was sued in federal court in New Haven, Connecticut, by the law firm whose principals argued they were portrayed as "ruthless, uncaring, unethical lawyers."[69] The film was based on Jake Bernstein's book *Secrecy World: Inside the Panama Papers Investigation of Illicit Money Networks and the Global Elite*[70] and on records of the International Consortium of Investigative Journalists.

Fonseca claimed the firm was like an auto dealership. When it sells a car to someone who has an accident, "the factory is not responsible for what is done with the car."[71] Even after the media disclosed their operation, the law firm repeatedly said "its due diligence practices were of the highest standard."[72] Justice Stone must be spinning in his cloud over this unseemly example of what he predicted about the direction of our profession a century ago.

Novelist and lawyer John Grisham described lawyering rationales this way in his novel *The Rainmaker*:

> Every lawyer, at least once in every case, feels himself crossing
> a line that he doesn't really mean to cross . . . it just happens. . . .
> And if you cross it enough times it disappears forever. And then
> you're nothin' but another lawyer joke. Just another shark in the
> dirty water.[73]

Stanford University law professor Deborah Rhode wrote, and I
agree, that lawyers cannot "market their loyalty, avert their eyes to
the consequences, and pretend that they have not made a normative
decision. To decline to take a moral stance, is in itself a moral stance."[74]

MYTH TWO:
THE ADVERSARY SYSTEM

The adversary system is the central feature of the American model
of justice. It has been considered a fundamental product of classical
liberalism.[75] It is compared favorably in the United States to the
European and other inquisitorial systems where judges rule more
actively. The essential idea of the adversary system is that opposing
lawyers present conflicting views of law and fact to a neutral judge
or an impartial jury, and the judge or jury decide who is right. The
source of this system is the constitutional due process clause.

The problem is that in criminal cases where representation is
required by the Constitution, most defendants cannot afford attorneys, and most criminal cases are not tried because the overwhelming majority of cases end in plea bargains. In contrast, in civil cases,
litigants have no constitutional right to a lawyer,[76] though they are
guaranteed a constitutional right to a jury trial.[77] A trial—even
a negotiation—without competent counsel is like a boat without
a rudder.

As the Supreme Court ruled in 1963 regarding *Gideon v. Wainwright*:

> [R]eason and reflection require us to recognize that in our adversary system of criminal justice, any person hauled into court, who is too poor to hire a lawyer, cannot be assured a fair trial unless counsel is provided for him. This seems to us to be an obvious truth.
>
> (*Gideon v. Wainwright*, 372 U.S. 335, 344 [1963]).[78]

Courts have made clear what the right to counsel means.[79] It means what its words say, and as Michigan Law professor Yale Kamisar stated, "[T]he right to counsel is the right to the effective assistance of counsel."[80] This right to effective assistance has two aspects. First, a court may not restrict defense counsel in the exercise of the representational duties and prerogatives attendant to our adversarial system of justice. Second, defense counsel can deprive a defendant of effective assistance by failing to provide competent representation that is adequate to ensure a fair trial or, more broadly, a just outcome. The right to effective assistance may be implicated as early as the appointment process. Cases requiring appointment of counsel for indigent defendants hold that, as a matter of due process, the assignment of defense counsel must be timely and made in a manner that affords "effective aid in the preparation and trial of the case."[81]

And in capital cases especially, assigned counsel must be meaningful.[82] To an argument that a state need only appoint a lawyer for indigent defendants to satisfy Sixth Amendment requirements, the Court responded that "the State's conduct of a criminal trial itself implicates the State in the defendant's conviction," and no state may proceed against a defendant whose counsel, appointed or retained, cannot defend him fully and faithfully.

Failing to meet constitutional standards may equal a "breakdown of the adversarial process."[83] As to attorney competence, although the Court touched on the question in 1970, it did not articulate a general Sixth Amendment standard for adequacy of representation until 1984 in *Strickland v. Washington*.[84] There are two components to the *Strickland* test: deficient representation, and resulting prejudice to the defense so serious as to bring the outcome of the proceeding into question.

The key difference between civil and common-law systems is the different roles played by judges and lawyers.[85] Under other countries' systems, generally civil cases are directed by judges, and the lawyers' role is residual, subordinate. In common-law countries like the United States, the judge is a passive moderator between rival advocates who become combatants before a judicial umpire. Comparative law experts have questioned "the truth-defeating distortions incident to our system of partisan preparation (coaching) of witnesses," and hired partisan (paid) experts.[86] Although the Seventh Amendment to our constitution assures the right to jury trials, in reality, most civil cases are decided pretrial by opposing parties' lawyers, if each has one, and in criminal cases by prosecutors and defense attorneys when they are involved via plea bargains.

The lawyers' role in our system is to assure a "constructive societal process" by enhancing individuals' autonomy, the late Hofstra Law School ethics professor Monroe Freedman stated.[87] But the adversarial system has been criticized,[88] even by advocates of its basic features, particularly because of lawyers' ethical and moral abuses of conduct, theoretically performed in the search for so-called truth in trials. The premium on winning can lead to "chicanery, manipulation, and deception."[89] And the disparity in the availability and quality of lawyers can undercut the philosophical foundation for the adversary system, as can the win-at-all-costs mentality of aggressive attorneys.

Under the adversarial system, checks and balances in the search for a contested truth is the ideal trial process, in which opposing partisan lawyers perform a key role. The assumption is that truth emerges that way. Proponents of the notion argue that competition is preferable to cooperation in the search for truth. But cynics argue that battling lawyers are more interested in their clients' interests than in some objective notion of "truth." Herein lies the quandary.

Defenders of the current American system argue that there is no better system, whatever the faults of ours may be. The viewpoint that lawyers also have a public interest in assisting a system that generates moral outcomes is criticized as naïve, elastic, subjective, and one that ignores the essential rationale of the adversary system in favor of more competitive realities. Civility may be a nice idea, but it's "not always the right reaction in the adversarial courtroom,"[90] one successful divorce lawyer commented.

As a result, in the criminal justice system, prosecutors have exploited the adversary system on the theory that they are carrying out their professional responsibilities, despite the fact that this system is seriously weighted against poor and middle-class people who too often have no lawyer or have inadequate representation. And as experienced judges know, 97 percent of all criminal cases are handled by plea bargains, where prosecutors hold all the cards.

In both criminal and civil cases, the fundamental questions are first, whether this process is the best way to get to the truth in issues, and second, whether lawyers should be judged by their roles with governmental or private clients and their clients' causes. Should the adversarial system shield lawyers who justify their questionable actions on the theory that only when adversaries present opposing "truths" will the actual truth prevail? Or does this rationalization explain how fidelity to client interests and not to public interests leads lawyers to "falling off the tightrope between advocacy and obstruction of justice"?[91]

Years ago I handled a civil case on behalf of a woman who was raped in her apartment. On the night of the crime, my client's husband was away; her little daughter was sleeping near her. Two men came in from the street, through her window, and raped her. We sued her landlord, who knew of the negligent state of the windows and had been warned there had been prior wrongful-entry problems.

I'll never forget the searing emotions aroused in me by the insurance company attorney who was our adversary. The insurance company lawyer dragged my client through an exacting, extended, punishing deposition that led to an emotional breakdown so bad that her therapist insisted I cease pursuing the case and take what the company offered; otherwise, her patient would be damaged further.

I understand that insurance companies must determine the facts behind the validity of claims, and that company lawyers were doing their professional duty by inquiring. But I could have strangled that lawyer who in my mind was overreaching by using his expansive and repeated attacks at my client's traumatic reaction to her horrible experience to fend off her financial claim, just to save his client some money and make some more for himself. Truth and justice had little to do with it.

I have witnessed and participated in other depositions where lawyers, without judges present to control questioning, exceeded professional standards by hammering and needling witnesses— their true goal being not to find truth but to gain advantages for their clients and run up their bills. An egregious example of this practice arises in sexual harassment and rape cases where lawyers in depositions, interviews, and trials intimidate and threaten victims.

One victim of Harvey Weinstein's many alleged sexual attacks sued him. At a meeting among Weinstein, Weinstein's attorney, the complaining victim, and her attorney, she was told by Weinstein's lawyer "that she would be painted as promiscuous if she went public with her claim against Weinstein . . .' We'll drag you through the mud by your hair."[92] She agreed to be paid off and signed a secrecy agreement. That kind of threat has foreclosed many civil sex cases where women victims were afraid to pursue their claims for fear of being victimized a second time by the flaws inherent in the adversary system. Recent civil and criminal cases have shown that this type of tactic (and result) is common.

Washington Post columnist David Von Drehle used the notorious Jeffrey Epstein case[93] to criticize millionaires using NDAs to silence their accusers in sexual assault cases, a practice called "bought silence."[94] "It is a classic case of rich man's justice," a celebrated trial lawyer stated, adding how the problem can be easily resolved: "Simply say that agreements to conceal evidence of a crime are not enforceable."[95] Crime is not solely a matter between a victim and an offender. The public has an interest in knowing about it and avoiding repeated offenses.

Columbia law professor William H. Simon made the case that "lawyers should exercise judgment and discretion in deciding what clients to represent and how to represent them" and use "ethical discretion to refuse to assist in the pursuit of some legally permissible courses of action and in the assertion of some potentially enforceable legal claims."[96] The Senate trial of President Donald Trump in 2020 was an example of a case where many lawyers would prefer not to be involved, others would jump at the chance.

Simon examined two models of lawyer ethics: the role of the lawyer as an advocate for and loyal to clients, and the lawyer as officer of the court with a duty to the public. Either approach, he wrote, provides a starting point and a strong presumption that may be in conflict with clients, third parties, and the public. Standard rules cannot be applied mechanically; they demand the use of judgment. They are rebuttable presumptions, and circumstances may arise where relevant general rules ought not apply. Lawyers do have a personal privilege to decline cases and clients they find distasteful. In pro bono cases, attorneys make personal judgments based on the merits and virtues of cases and causes they choose to represent. They could do the same when applying the "justice" criteria in accepting or rejecting certain cases they will be paid for.

Traditionalists argue that it is an arrogant, not virtuous, power for lawyers to arrogate to themselves such subjective concepts as justice on behalf of others. Simon concedes that ethical lawyers may not be able to make a living by applying exacting standards, and there will always be another lawyer happy to take the case one lawyer declines. The adversary system does not focus on assuring accurate decision making, but rather it reflects an individual's ideology about winning. The world would be a better place if lawyers were less motivated by material self-interest and more motivated by who and what is and is not worthy of their representation, and what the moral bounds of their representation ought to be.

CHAPTER TWO

THE CRIMINAL SYSTEM

A State need not equalize economic conditions. A man of means may be able to afford the retention of an expensive, able counsel not within reach of a poor man's purse. Those are contingencies of life which are hardly within the power, let alone the duty, of a State to correct or cushion. But when a State deems it wise and just that convictions be susceptible to review by an appellate court, it cannot by force of its exactions draw a line which precludes convicted indigent persons, forsooth erroneously convicted, from securing such a review merely by disabling them from bringing to the notice of an appellate tribunal errors of the trial court which would upset the conviction were practical opportunity for review not foreclosed.

To sanction such a ruthless consequence, inevitably resulting from a money hurdle erected by a State, would justify a latter-day Anatole France to add ... "The law, in its majestic equality, forbids the rich as well as the poor to sleep under bridges, to beg in the streets, and to steal bread." ... The State is not free to produce such a squalid discrimination.

—From the concurring opinion by Associate Justice Felix
Frankfurter in *Griffin v. Illinois*, 351 U.S. 12 (1956).

Historically, the criminal justice system was governed by crude practices of blood oaths and private duels and vendettas. Later systems moved adjudication and prosecution of criminal matters to the state, taking that responsibility away from private justice. The state instituted trials by peers of the people, presided over by judges and petit and grand juries. From its beginnings, that more civilized system left most of the administration of justice to lawyers, prosecutors, defense lawyers, and judges. But from the start and until modern times, poor and even middle-class people rarely have had adequate counsel, if any at all, so the system evolved into a system of justice for sale.

CRIME BY THE GOVERNMENT

Prosecutors

The case has been made that wrongdoing by public officials is more censurable than misconduct by private citizens because they represent the government with all its sovereign powers, and to that extent those officials represent the very people they sometimes prejudice. They act for us all in their work. [97]

Special Counsel Robert Mueller quoted Supreme Court justice George Sutherland in his celebrated report, [98]

> The United States Attorney is the representative not of an ordinary party to a controversy, but of a sovereignty whose obligation to govern impartially is as compelling as its obligation to govern at all; and whose interest, therefore, in a criminal prosecution is not that it shall win a case, but that justice shall be done. As such, he is in a peculiar and very definite sense the servant of the law, the twofold aim of which is that guilt shall not escape or innocence suffer. He may prosecute with earnestness and vigor—indeed, he should do so. But, while he may strike hard blows, he is not at

liberty to strike foul ones. "It is as much his duty to refrain from improper methods calculated to produce a wrongful conviction as it is to use every legitimate means to bring about a just one."

If so, why haven't most police and prosecutors whose conscious misconduct resulted in unjust convictions and imprisonments not been charged and convicted personally with an offense? How can their victims ever be compensated for the wrong done to them? Why should the public pay the fines for these wrongdoers when their misconduct does come to light? Unjustly convicting a defendant leaves the true wrongdoer free to repeat his crimes. Prosecutorial overzealousness is at the root of the problem. On the civil side, as will be shown in the next chapter, corporations have the same unfair shield of its administrators as the government does in criminal cases.

In 1940, Attorney General Robert Jackson spoke to a convention of federal prosecutors.[99] He reminded them that they had "more control over life, liberty, and reputation than any other person(s) in America." He urged them to fight crime, consistent with preserving American traditions. A spirit of fair play and decency must animate federal prosecutors, he instructed. Results are important but so is the quality of performance: "[T]he citizen's safety lies in the prosecutor who tempers zeal with human kindness, who seeks truth, and not victims, who serves the law and not factional purposes, and who approaches his task with humility." Wisely, Jackson added, "those who need to be told would not understand it anyway."

The American Bar Association (ABA) Model Rules of Professional Conduct state, "A prosecutor has the responsibility of a minister of justice and not simply that of an advocate. This responsibility carries with it specific obligations to see that the defendant is accorded procedural justice and that guilt is decided upon the basis of sufficient evidence."[100]

There are professional rules that guide lawyers in criminal cases. The Sixth Amendment to the US Constitution guarantees citizens the right to counsel in criminal cases, and states must provide counsel if that person cannot afford to have one.[101] There are three models for providing counsel in these cases: private counsel assigned by courts (fourteen states and DC) or contracted for (sixteen states), and public defender programs (slightly more than half of the states).[102] All of them are imperfect and do not cover all needs, such as funds for necessary staff, appeals, investigators, and the testimony of experts.

ABA Standards provide guidelines that govern criminal representation, including one that states lawyers are "under no obligation to act as an advisor or advocate for every person who may wish to be his client."[103] In addition, lawyers need not accept employment "if the intensity of his personal feeling . . . may impair his effective representation of a prospective client."[104] And last, lawyers may refuse an appointment "for good cause,"[105] including financial burden or repugnant causes that are false to their conscience.[106]

A twist on this problem occurred at Harvard University in 2019. Ronald Sullivan, a law professor there and dean of Winthrop House, as well as a civil rights lawyer, was criticized by students who were offended that he represented movie mogul Harvey Weinstein in sexual harassment claims against him. They called for his resignation. Professor Sullivan and his supporters at the school responded, "Lawyers are not an extension of their clients. Lawyers do law work, not the work of ideology." The right to defense is the cornerstone of justice, supporters argued. The school responded that it would take a "climate review" of student objections regarding whether the tone and culture of the students whose strong views about Weinstein were genuine or misused.[107]

The issue was not, some complained, that Sullivan and his client were assured the constitutional right to serve as counsel, but whether his student community had the right to say, "Not by one of us."

That situation took an odd turn when, after its "climate review," Harvard removed Sullivan and his wife from their positions as faculty deans of Winthrop House for residential students. Support for the Sullivans came from fifty-two members of the law school faculty. It was Sullivan's job, along with his faculty residency (the first time in the university's history that black faculty members filled this role), they argued, to represent unpopular and controversial clients. He wasn't doing his work for money but for a just cause.

Professor Randall Kennedy, Sullivan's colleague at Harvard Law School, called what Harvard University did to the Sullivans a betrayal of standards any university should follow. Students' vandalism when they protested (as opposed to their voiced opinions) should warrant *their* removal, notwithstanding the correctness of the arguments they espoused. Any worthy complaint should be up for discussion, but vandalism warrants punitive action. The students' arguments were cynical: they claimed as justification for their misbehavior that Sullivan damaged the "climate" at Winthrop and that they had a right to express themselves ideologically. But their behavior denied that very right of Professor Sullivan and his wife. [108]

Harvard's condonation of the students' behavior was inconsistent with the argument that lawyers like the Sullivans have every right to choose their cases and clients and not to be judged harshly for doing so. It is a weak university, in my judgment, that accedes to violent student protests over traditional attorney ethics. Sullivan's position was right for Sullivan; the students' arguments were correct for them. And the university taught a bad lesson by taking sides and making a decision in its role as a teaching organization which hired Sullivan to run the organization he ran (different than a private attorney who does so for a legal fee), and then took punitive action against him. What kind of lesson did the university think it was providing?[109]

POLICE

Prosecutors are not alone in managing the criminal justice system. They rely on information secured by the police. Sometimes by what insiders call "testilying," irresponsible police commit perjury or use trumped-up evidence or skirt the requirement of Supreme Court rulings such as *Mapp v. Ohio*[110] and rely on evidence that violates search and seizure laws. As a result, defendants are wrongly convicted with troubling frequency. Some police are pushed to make more arrests and obtain more convictions by their superiors, which is no excuse for the entrenched perjury that permeates the system, which a recent *New York Times* story described.[111]

Given that most cases end in plea deals, many of these injustices never come to light, and even when they do, the errant police are often protected by their institutions. The *New York Times* reported civilian review boards without enforcement powers rarely make a difference in disciplining rogue police. The New York police department has been reluctant to investigate or discipline officers for lying. The department denies this, though the article disclosed that only two of eighty-one cases reported to the department by the civilian review board were upheld.[112]

The *Time*s series on testilying ended with proposals for reforms. Body cameras on plainclothes officers would—when used—be a deterrent, as would suppression hearings by judges in the rare 2.4 percent of felony cases that don't end with a guilty plea, and publicizing not suppressing judicial findings of misconduct, even if the plea includes a no appeal provision.[113]

This problem is compounded in cases where prosecutors know they are using questionable police work practices and have exceeded their powers (a fatal choking in one notorious recent case) or worse, and their misbehavior results in injuries or wrongful convictions and long imprisonments, even capital punishment. Professor Philip M. Stinson, "since the beginning of 2005, there have been 110 non-federal sworn law enforcement officers with the general powers of arrest (e.g., police officers, deputy sheriffs, state troopers, etc.) who have been arrested for murder or manslaughter resulting from an on-duty shooting throughout the United States. Of those 110 officers, to date only 42 have been convicted of a crime resulting from the on-duty shooting (18 by guilty plea, 24 by jury trial, and none convicted by a bench trial)[114]

CAPITAL CASES

In 1985,[115] John Thompson was arrested, convicted, and imprisoned on death row at the maximum-security prison at Angola, LA, for a carjacking and murder he claimed he didn't commit.

What followed was a legal nightmare. After years of appeals, and just days before his electrocution, his lawyers discovered an undisclosed microfiche of a lab report the district attorney had obtained before the trial. It proved scientifically that Thompson's blood type provided exculpatory evidence demonstrating that he was innocent. The prosecutor didn't tell Thompson's defense about this evidence, a fact he admitted to a former colleague on his death bed years later. Not until he was dying did he reveal that he had gone into the evidence room and removed Thompson's pants with the bloodstains to keep them from the defense.

Thompson's conviction was ultimately reversed, but he was retried rather than released. The second jury acquitted Thompson after deliberating for thirty-five minutes. He had spent fourteen years isolated in a windowless cell awaiting execution, which had been scheduled six times.

Thompson sued for damages, and his case went to the US Supreme Court, which denied his $20 million claim, 5–4. Justice

Clarence Thomas, writing for the majority, denied Thompson's claim while conceding that the prosecutors failed "to see that justice is done."[116] Justice Ruth Bader Ginsburg noted in her dissent that five prosecutors had been complicit in violating Thompson's constitutional rights, along with those of other defendants over two decades. Thompson died at fifty-five, having served eighteen years in prison. He wondered why he couldn't "sue the prosecutors who nearly murdered me."[117]

The Thompson case was not unusual; sadly, it is a recurring event. And it did not have a "happy" ending. On the contrary, the extreme of the wrongness was lessened—but it was too little, too late. When Thompson was interviewed, he was asked if anyone had apologized to him; the questioner expected appreciation for the resolution but heard only bitterness. Eighteen years in prison, fourteen on death row. And he was innocent!

> "Tell me what the hell would they be sorry for. They tried to kill me. To apologize would mean they're admitting the system is broken. That everyone around them is broken. It is the same motherf-----g system that's protecting them." He said, jabbing his finger into the air for emphasis. He added, "What would I do with their apology anyway? Sorry. Huh. Sorry you tried to kill me? Sorry you tried to commit premeditated murder? No. No thank you. I don't need your apology."[118]

Thompson started a reform organization after his release called Resurrection After Exoneration to support people like him when they are released by providing housing, job, and consulting services. In 2011, Thompson wrote an op-ed in *The New York Times* titled, "The Prosecution Rests, but I Can't."[119]

The system works, one author concluded, but it is "deeply flawed."[120] On the fiftieth anniversary of *Brady v. Maryland*, the

New Orleans Innocence Project honored Thompson. The award was presented to him by Keith Plessey and Phoebe Ferguson, descendants of the infamous Supreme Court "separate but equal" decision bearing their relatives' names.

Reformer Stephen Bright wrote[121] that Brady reversals are serendipitous because most criminal defendants don't have lawyers after they appeal their convictions. "Withholding exculpatory evidence and presenting false evidence in a death penalty case is quite possibly the most serious breach for a lawyer," one insider concluded."[122]

Police and prosecutorial misconduct are inadequately monitored. Courts reviewing Brady misconduct[123] require not only exposure of hidden exculpatory evidence but proof of a reasonable probability that the jury would have reached a different conclusion had they known that evidence.[124]

Only after it is demonstrated that "a pattern or practice of abuse" took place would the Supreme Court throw out a wrongful conviction of a single innocent man.[125] As a result, many prosecution offices have remained adamant in resisting reversals based on individual misconduct. In a later case[126] Justice David Souter concluded that one district attorney office "descended to a gladiatorial level unmitigated by any prosecutorial obligation for the sake of the truth."[127] Later the Supreme Court also ruled the missing evidence must be exculpatory and material,[128] as if exculpatory alone wouldn't *necessarily* be material.

Since prosecutors are rarely charged or sanctioned for their wrongdoings in these cases, for them it is a no-lose situation. If the attorney fails to disclose and isn't caught doing so, the wrong man is convicted and the murderer is free; if the prosecutor is caught, he keeps his job and is not punished.[129]

Justice John Paul Stevens wrote to the *New York Times* in 2015, after he left the Court, regarding its editorial on the Thompson case, which the *Times* called "abominable." Stevens stated the decision was "manifest injustice." The obvious solution, he wrote, for holding prosecutors responsible was the role of *respondeat superior* holding employers (in this case the state) responsible for damages caused by an employee in the ordinary course of their business.[130]

Of six defendants in other cases that Thompson's prosecutor handled, one was sentenced to death, and five cases were reversed for prosecutorial misconduct.[131] An analysis of capital cases, clearly the most profound and consequential cases of all, demonstrates how poorly the criminal justice system works.[132]

Another controversial example of that flawed system involves San Quentin, California, death row inmate Kevin Cooper. Five people were slaughtered in their Chino Hills, California, home in 1983. Though clear and persuasive evidence pointed to three white men, police arrested Cooper, a black man. Incriminating evidence was planted on Cooper. Police lied under oath. Exculpatory evidence was hidden. Cooper had inadequate counsel. DNA evidence that became available and that would clear Cooper has not been allowed by executive authorities who could grant clemency, if not outright release.[133]

Politicians with power to correct what *New York Times* columnist Nicholas Kristof called the most outrageous failure of the justice system he'd ever known will not act.[134] The Death Penalty Information Center reported that 162 death row inmates have been exonerated—and even given their nightmarish experiences, they are the "lucky" ones.

The problem is a recurring one. Bobby Joe Maxwell was convicted in a nine-month trial for a series of ten stabbings of homeless men on Skid Row in Los Angeles in 1979. Forty years later, a California court threw out Maxwell's conviction and life-in-prison sentence, but the convict had suffered a heart attack while being incarcerated and was in a coma. A public defender worked on Maxwell's behalf for years and eventually was able to demonstrate that a notorious jailhouse snitch had testified that Maxwell confessed the crimes to him, under very questionable circumstances.[135]

An appellate court ordered Maxwell released or retried because the evidence against him was "nearly all circumstantial." The snitch was the "centerpiece of the prosecution's case." Failing to inform Maxwell of the government's deal with the snitch deprived him of due process of law, the court concluded. However, the government refused to release Maxwell and took steps to retry him if he ever woke from his coma. Maxwell will never be exonerated and was imprisoned for decades. Case closed![136]

Capital punishment expert Stephen Bright made the case, with painful examples, that "people accused of capital crimes are often defended by lawyers who lack the skills, resources, and commitment to handle such serious matters."[137] Despite two venerable Supreme Court opinions guaranteeing competent counsel in criminal cases, *Powell v. Alabama*[138] and *Gideon v. Wainwright*,[139] "the task remains uncompleted and the dream unrealized."[140]

That states are unwilling to pay for adequate defense of poor defendants is "particularly indefensible in cases where life is at stake."[141] The legal system has turned a blind eye to the fact that the death penalty is not imposed on the worst crimes, "but upon those who have the misfortune to be assigned to the worst lawyers."[142] Bright pointed out that of the approximately 20,000 homicide cases each year, the death penalty is adjudged in 250 cases. Those cases are characterized "by poor legal representation."[143]

Bryan Stevenson's work on capital punishment cases are well known. In a movie about him—*Just Mercy*[144]—his character, actually actor Michael Jordan, speaks about his client before a Senate Committee in dramatic words:

BRYAN: "This man has taught me a lot in the time I've known him . . . I came out of law school with grand ideas in my mind about how to change the world. But then I started working with people who were wrongly convicted; children who were sent to adult prisons where they were raped and abused; people with mental and physical disabilities who were thrown into cells when they should be in hospitals; vulnerable people calling me every day, begging for help. Sometimes the problem seemed so big, I felt like a fool for thinking I could do anything to fix it. (beat) But working with Mr. McMillian made me realize that we can't change the world with only ideas in our minds, we also need conviction in our hearts ... This man taught me how to stay hopeful, because I now know that hopelessness is the enemy of justice. Hope allows us to push forward, even when the truth is distorted by the people in power ... I've learned that each of us is more than the worst thing we've ever done; that the opposite of poverty isn't wealth, the opposite of poverty is justice; that the character of our nation isn't reflected in how we treat the rich and privileged, but how we treat the poor, the disfavored and condemned. Our system has taken more from this innocent man than it has the power to give back. But I believe if each of us can follow his lead, we can begin to change this world for the better. If we can look at ourselves closely, and honestly, I believe we will see that we all need justice, we all need mercy and perhaps, we all need some measure of unmerited grace."

These case histories present a chilling embarrassment to the bar and to the society that condones our practices. One scholar described our allowing grossly ineffective lawyering in capital cases as constitutionally permissible as a "lethal fiction."[145] At the trial and appellate levels, this reality undermines the adversary system in the most demanding cases. The bar, the legislatures, the courts all permit this disgrace. The late justice William Brennan wrote about death row inmates that "our treatment of them sounds no echoes beyond the chambers in which they die."[146]

BRADY VIOLATIONS

The press regularly reports reversals of convictions for Brady violations, when prosecutors have withheld exculpatory evidence, the
disclosure of which to defendants and their lawyers is a constitutional requirement. "There is an epidemic of Brady violations in the
land," a veteran federal judge stated.[147] This creates a "serious moral
hazard," he concluded. Yet "prosecutors are virtually never punished
for misconduct";[148] less than 2 percent of the time according to the
Center for Prosecutor Integrity.[149]

The idea behind the 1963 Supreme Court–fashioned Brady
rule[150] is the essence of fair play. Prosecutors should not be able
to hide exculpatory evidence. But historically many of them have
done so, despite attempts to enforce the rule.[151] Some district attorneys argue that they must protect witnesses or that they have other
decisive evidence of guilt. But that defense is one for dispassionate
judges to decide, not partisan adversaries.

Heartbreaking Brady violations are exposed regularly. When
disclosed, these miscarriages of justice make for shocking literature
like Brian Stolarz's book *Grace and Justice on Death Row: The Race
Against Time and Texas to Free an Innocent Man*,[152] about his experiences saving the life of a prisoner who had been on death row for
more than twelve years.

Stolarz worked pro bono for years, traveling from Washington,
DC, to Texas, and eventually discovered that a police investigator
had not turned over decisive exculpatory evidence to the inmate's
trial lawyer. When the prosecutor was made aware of this, she
resisted joining the death row inmate's request seeking his release.
The falsely convicted inmate spent twenty-three hours a day isolated in a six-by-six cell. Eventually the wrongly convicted inmate
was released, but only after years of daunting resistance from the
state government's lawyer.

I asked Stolarz what happened after the release. Here is his response:

> After Dewayne was released on June 8, 2015, his lawyers filed a petition for wrongful imprisonment compensation from the State of Texas. That petition was denied because the state statute requires that the individual be declared "actually innocent" by the District Attorney and Dewayne's dismissal was based on "insufficient evidence." Thereafter, his lawyers embarked on a multiyear quest to have Dewayne declared actually innocent. The newly elected ... District Attorney ... appointed a Special Counsel. ... After a 10-month investigation and over 1,000 hours of work, issued a 185-page report which declared Dewayne actually innocent, and that "It's impossible to examine the conviction of Alfred Dewayne Brown without confronting prosecutorial misconduct."
>
> The District Attorney endorsed the report, and the Judge signed an amended dismissal order declaring Dewayne actually innocent, becoming only the second defendant in Texas criminal justice history to be declared actually innocent after being sentenced to death.
>
> [In] 2019, nearly four years after Dewayne's release and over 16 years since he was arrested, the Special Counsel filed an extensive bar complaint against the trial prosecutor, alleging that he withheld critical exculpatory evidence, misled the jury, and lied to the Texas Bar. ... The bar complaint is pending. Dewayne is living a peaceful and quiet life in Louisiana. ...
>
> Dewayne was entitled by Texas law to receive compensation. Despite Texas' many faults in the criminal justice system it actually has one of the most generous wrongful incarceration statutes in the country, paying individuals $80,000 a year for every year they were wrongfully incarcerated in an annuity paid out over the individuals' life. Dewayne was entitled to just under one million

dollars . . . his attorneys filed a petition for compensation with the State Comptroller who denied Dewayne's petition. Despite the fact that the Comptroller's role in the compensation statute was "ministerial," he decided to interpret the law and decided that the amended dismissal was insufficient for compensation. The Houston Chronicle called the decision "outrageous" and "shameful." . . . Dewayne's counsel is preparing a writ of mandamus to the Texas Supreme Court to review the Comptroller's decision.[153]

Countless studies of capital punishment practices have shown that poor defendants fare worse than those with the means to defend themselves. Supreme Court justice Ruth Bader Ginsburg stated, "People who are well represented at trial do not get the death penalty. . . . I have yet to see a death case among the dozens coming to the Supreme Court on eve-of-execution stay applications in which the defendant was well represented at trial."[154]

Inept counsel is as bad as no counsel. There are shocking stories about assigned counsel in capital cases being improperly prepared, intoxicated, and falling asleep during trial.[155] In one Georgia case in 1997, an alcoholic attorney was appointed by the judge (Georgia had no public defender program). The lawyer, incompetent as well as an alcoholic, was later disbarred. The jury convicted. The clemency board refused clemency. The Supreme Court of Georgia refused to stay the execution.[156]

In a Texas case the assigned defense attorney spent four hours "preparing" the defense and fell asleep at the trial defending his client's life.[157] Prosecutors claimed the defendant had a fair trial. Texas has no public defender system. It leads the country in assigned attorneys, and since 1977 has executed 224 people.

In North Carolina, "while some capital defendants can scrape together the funds for a lawyer, more than 90% rely on a free attorney provided by the state."[158]

Supreme Court justice Thurgood Marshall said, "Capital defendants do not have a fair opportunity to defend their lives in the courtroom.... Death penalty litigation has become a specialized field of practice and even the most well-intentioned attorneys often are unable to recognize, preserve and defend their client's rights."[159]

EXONERATIONS—TOO LITTLE, TOO LATE

Injustices in capital cases are the most dramatic examples of systemic wrongs, but not the only ones. The National Registry of Exonerations reported that 43 percent of wrongful convictions result from official misconduct. The Innocence Project reports that the appellate process doesn't always know about or is not able to correct wrongful convictions.[160]

A recent book about a North Carolina man who was wrongfully convicted of rape but exonerated a quarter-century later explained how that injustice led to the first state-sponsored agency devoted to examining innocence claims.

In the last twenty-eight years, the National Registry of Exonerations reported 2102 examples of wrongful convictions.[161]

A disturbing recent book[162] by Lara Bazelon, an experienced public defender, pointed out that "the number of exonerations, the reasons for why they happen, and the people to whom they happen reveal grotesque and shameful problems with the way that we administer justice in the U.S." Her special interests and experiences are in this one corner of the criminal "justice" system that deals with the common and cruel wrongful convictions that occur each week and together these cases have led to imprisonments totaling "more than 14,750 years," according to the 2015 report of the National Registry of Exonerations.[163] Bazelon recited stories of her cases and others from the records of exoneration projects around the United States.

In 1992, Barry Scheck and Peter Neuman began the Innocence Project in New York City.[164] So far it has freed two hundred

innocent men and women wrongfully convicted. It spurred a movement in seventy other cities, states, and law schools that has revealed
systemic problems with our criminal justice system that should
embarrass and outrage the American public and its bar.[165]

In death row cases alone, the Innocence Project's DNA testing
resulted in 367 exonerations, 21 on behalf of death row inmates.
One report concluded:

> With every successive exoneration, the Innocence Project has
> been building a larger case in the court of public opinion, raising
> serious questions about the use of death penalty, casting doubt on
> the efficacy of forensic science testimony and even challenging
> the integrity of the criminal legal system itself.[166]

These cases are the tip of the iceberg, revealed only after ide-
alistic lawyers put forth tremendous personal effort for little or no
compensation to demonstrate what lawyers *can* do when motivated
to see justice done. But too often they don't. One study in Michigan
revealed that 4 percent of those on death row were falsely convicted.[167] The Federal Bureau of Justice Statistics reported that in 2017
there were nearly 1.5 million people in US prisons.[168] If just 1 percent of these people are innocent, then "on any given day, 15,300
innocent people are sitting in prison."[169] If the more likely figure,
4 percent, are innocent, then 61,200 innocent people are wrongfully
incarcerated, according to Bazelon.[170]

These wrongful convictions result from several causes: false
testimony and outright lies, good-faith mistakes, wrong eyewit-
ness testimony, cross-racial IDs, and police and prosecutor misconduct (45 percent of a documented 1,600 wrongful convictions)
that turns what is supposed to be a level playing field into "a ski
slope, with the state gliding to victory by running over the defendant's right to a fair trial."[171] Police and district attorneys are rarely

punished for their zealousness, inadvertence, or negligence, according to Bazelon.[172]

False confessions, usually caused by police coercion, are regularly revealed. The notorious Central Park jogger conviction and imprisonment (depicted in Netflix[173] and PBS[174] television series) of five teenage men for rape is an example of when truth is exposed by later DNA evidence. Those men received a $40 million settlement (from the people of New York) for their imprisonment. And they are the "fortunate" ones who suffered in prison but at least were later released.

The proof of inadequate counsel and poor defense work by assigned lawyers who have little experience and resources to defend their cases accounts for 17 percent of non-DNA exonerations, according to the 2012 Exoneration Registry. Underfunding of public defender offices and underpayment of assigned counsel for indigent defendants is systemic.

Group exonerations, often race-based wrongful convictions resulting from "a large-scale pattern of police perjury and corruption," are underreported.[175] One thousand, eight hundred and forty individuals—mostly black—across thirteen cities in the United States have been freed via 15 group exonerations, including 156 in Los Angeles alone.[176] The constitutional right to an attorney in criminal cases has been ignored by "glaring deficiencies in indigent defense services."[177] This is all in addition to the nearly 2,000 individual exonerations that have been registered since 1989.[178]

Bazelon forces us to look at the injustices in our criminal justice system, which, in her words, "speak a brutal truth that should not be ignored, both as a matter of justice and public policy."[179]

Even with the extraordinary successes of the Brian Stolarzes, Lara Bazelons, Bryan Stevensons, and Barry Schecks, there are no happily-ever-after endings. Exonerees suffered the nightmare of imprisonments, families were torn apart, victims relived their worst experiences, and health was destroyed, even though a rare savior appeared and made a miracle happen for them. The sad part of this story is that so many comparable cases never get revealed, and our system administers injustices far too often.

The notorious Wisconsin case of Stephen Avery, who was wrongly convicted and imprisoned for eighteen years for a brutal attack on a woman jogger, captured public attention as a result of a Netflix TV series. Police and prosecutors had evidence that indicated someone else was the culprit, but that evidence only came out years later as a result of a Wisconsin Innocence Project study. Not only was the wrong person imprisoned, but the guilty party remained free to commit further violent crimes. As the remorseful victim later wrote about her wrong ID, neither of the two bells of injustice could be unrung.[180]

A perverse twist came years later when Avery—then free—was convicted of a horribly brutal murder and was actually guilty this time according to the jury and a new book.[181] But he is again claiming that the conviction was wrong. You can't make up stories like this!

Whether cases like those noted here are pervasive or aberrations, ethical observers must agree at least that they should never be tolerated. Yet one carefully documented study in 2007 demonstrated that they are. A *Hofstra Law Review* article described various examples of prosecutorial misconduct that went unpunished, except in rare cases like the notorious Duke University lacrosse case where not only was the case later dismissed but the prosecutor was sanctioned and his career was ended. Sanctions against offending prosecutors like that are rare. Those defendants had lawyers.

The Hofstra study listed various common misbehaviors of prosecutors: "losing" evidence, threatening witnesses (we see that practice on all the popular TV dramas about police "detection"), misuse of the secret grand jury, and the common plea negotiation processes[182]

PLEA BARGAINING

Federal trial court judge Jed Rakoff pointed out in the *New York Review of Books* that 97 percent of federal cases are resolved by plea bargains, virtually extinguishing jury trials in the federal system.[183] With the ability to pile on charges and press for mandatory high sentences, the plea-bargaining process is stacked against defendants who run the risk of worse sentences if they elect to fight the charges and go to trial.

One Libertarian report about the vanishing jury system as a result of negotiated pleas in 97 percent of federal cases noted that the reality also precluded "government-checking and injustice preventing roles."[184] Some call this feature jury nullification or conscientious acquittals (think of OJ, as one bad example). Juries still make moral assessments about the application of strict factual or legal elements of trials, but that feature is lost in the current majority of cases that never reach a jury, the report concludes.

Defense lawyers who deal regularly with prosecutors also run the risk of antagonizing their opponents, who hold stronger cards in the continuing gamble of the adversary system. That is compounded by the old cliché that prosecutors can get grand juries to "indict a ham sandwich," since they are alone before lay grand juries and generally are able to assure that any indictment they call for will be approved. The classical notion of the grand jury as a bulwark against the sovereign is not the present reality. Denials to prosecute or to censure police or prosecutors are rarely the result of grand juries. Conservative columnist George Will criticized plea bargaining as an unfair coercive method of circumventing a defendant's right to a fair trial. It transfers sentencing from judges to prosecutors. The practice is another cause of overcriminalization in the U.S.[185]

Another eccentricity of plea bargains in criminal cases involves Alford pleas, which reportedly occur in 6 percent of all state and federal guilty pleas. These kinds of pleas are offered when a flaw in a conviction is revealed and the government concedes the verdict was flawed, but it insists that the convict plead guilty as the price of being released. Some prosecutors insist on this concession to avoid civil responsibility to the wrongfully convicted individual and to preserve their conviction record. In a 2017 case in Connecticut, the convict was released after serving decades in prison, though he always claimed his innocence. He later complained, "They knew they had to let me go, but they didn't want to let me go clean."[186]

Violation of the Brady rule is particularly troubling, and rarely comes to light because so few cases (overall, less than 5 percent) go to trial. Even when these violations are exposed, appellate courts protect prosecutors, justifying their position on the perverse ground that taking civil responsibility for their misbehavior might deter zealous prosecutions, which is the very point of these cases of overzealousness.

PROSECUTORIAL MISCONDUCT

Another old practice of district attorneys prosecuting different defendants for committing the same crime has recently been studied.[187] In twenty-nine such cases, twenty-seven of the convicts were executed, a result judges have called "deeply troubling."

In instances where several criminals attack and kill a victim, sometimes they are tried separately for committing the same homicide. While all the attackers might be guilty under conspiracy or aiding and abetting laws, they all can't have pulled the trigger, though prosecutors have taken the position that it is fair to leave that issue to a judge and jury exercising their powers. Former Supreme Court justice David Souter wrote that in these instances of multiple prosecutions, one of the results had to have been false. The appellate court in that case also had ruled that "inconsistent theories rendered convictions unreliable."[188]

State prosecutors have withheld exculpatory evidence, over-charged defendants in order to secure guilty pleas, suborned perjury, and pressured defense witnesses, a retired judge reported.[189] The Innocence Project study of four thousand California cases discovered prosecutorial misconduct on average once a week.[190] No charges against these prosecutors were brought.[191] Other studies in *USA Today*,[192] the *Chicago Tribune*,[193] and the *Yale Law Journal*[194] showed that no disciplinary action was taken in the investigations they undertook. The state (government) pays for the prosecution side of the criminal justice system, but not for the defense side.

This protection of prosecutors has provided what Innocence Project lawyers called "a gaping haven" for official misconduct. The practice is currently being challenged in federal courts in New York.[195]

Bar disciplinary sanctions of district attorneys are rare. State legislated Professional Rules of Conduct and the organizational proscriptions of the National District Attorney Association condemn the behavior that prosecutors violate regularly, such as concealing evidence, offering false evidence, manipulating witnesses (using questionable jail house snitches, for example), and using pretrial publicity to tilt public opinion (the media-saturated perp walk.)[196]

The Citizens Protection Act of 1998 requires federal prosecutors to follow relevant state ethics rules,[197] and the Justice Department has an Office of Professional Responsibility, though the independent use of its powers has been questioned.

Recent studies[198] have described the injustices of prosecutorial misconduct and the responsibility of disciplinary bodies, district attorney offices, and court officials to bring these injustices to light. While judges and scholars have bemoaned the problem, various jurisdictions have reported the problem "flows from an environment that tolerates it, oversees it, and encourages it."[199]

Courts have been hesitant to censure prosecutors, though one Louisiana case exposed the systemic vagaries that warrant judicial interventions.[200] In a 1992 prosecution for robbery, rape, and kidnapping, Robert Jones was convicted and served twenty-three years in prison, despite multiple Brady violations that would have shown his innocence.[201] Jones's lawyers described forty-five cases where systemic Brady violations resulted in improper convictions. Jones's attorneys argued that these forty-five cases are only those discovered—*many* are not. The prosecutors worked in a "culture of winning" convictions, and that culture defined their professional ethics.

Deferential to prosecutors, courts all the way to the US Supreme Court insist on proof of systemic policies of Brady misconduct, not simply specific incidents—a policy that denies individual redress in specific cases as the Constitution guarantees—before they will consider reversing a conviction. In their complaint in the Jones case, his pro bono lawyers did a mighty job of research and presented examples of many comparable incidents where this DA office denied defendants access to exculpatory evidence with impunity.[202]

The public learns of these painful injustices only occasionally, as a result of extraordinary efforts of devoted lawyers and pursuing media, and after defendants have suffered long and painful imprisonments while the real criminals are free to continue their violent activities. Until each instance of this kind of prosecutorial misconduct is punished by judges and bar associations, whenever it is proven, it will continue.

DEFENDING TORTURE

An example of federal lawyers losing their moral ways arose in 2009 when lawyers from the Department of Justice and the White House advised high executive officials about the legality of proposed torture. Federal law prohibits torture (18 USC 2340A). The lawyers went through "tortured" reasoning to sidestep the clear meaning of the statute. These lawyers advised the CIA that in its "advanced pressure phase" waterboarding would not violate that law. Reading a legal analysis that justified such techniques as wall standing, electric shock, clothing and sleep deprivation, use of insects, facial slapping, and reliance on medical and psychological experts is extremely disheartening.

A commentary in 2019 about the movie *The Report* mentions the controversial congressional investigation in 2004 into whether the CIA's "interrogation" methods constituted "torture." Former Director of National Intelligence James Clapper is quoted saying that the "implications of retroactively raising a moral standard" was "second-guessing intelligence officers who were following legal guidance at the time," the classic ticking-bomb dilemma. [203] Left open is the question of whether those lawyers were providing legal cover for their clients or good faith advice about questionable investigative techniques to guide government practices, then and now, in morally testing times.

Some prosecutors and their allies justified these practices as exigencies in the aftermath of 9/11. The *New York Times* editorialized that the government lawyers' memos justifying these techniques read like a "journey into depravity," filled with "bureaucratese favored by dungeon masters throughout history."[204] In his May 13, 2009, testimony before a Senate Judiciary Subcommittee, Georgetown University Law professor David Luban referred to these practices as "an ethical train wreck," noting that evidence extracted through torture is unreliable as well as morally repulsive. [205] (One of these government lawyers has since been awarded a federal judgeship.)

Luban continued, explaining lawyers' ethical responsibilities to clients *not* to give clients what they want to hear, but to use "unvarnished advice" and "independent judgment," and definitely not "to provide legal cover for illegal actions." He referred to the ABA Model Code of Professional Responsibility on the subject of the difference between advocating and advising: lawyers are not to shape their opinions to their clients' interests, in the case of the torture memos not to "twist and distort the law."[206]

There have been cases and commentaries dealing with prosecutorial misconduct, but rarely have the misbehaviors resulted in
punitive action.[207] The 2010 Justice Department report regarding
now law professor John Yoo and now federal judge Jay Bybee for
their legal analysis of torture recommended they be disciplined by
their bar associations.[208] No action was taken. One Justice Department report concluded that their advice was appropriate in the context of 9/11.

PROTECTING LAW ENFORCEMENT

The traditional rule that prosecutors should not be second-guessed
nor strictly policed so they can do their important work is a reasonable general policy, but it is one that has been abused in specific
cases. The US Supreme Court dealt with this issue in 1976 and
recently in 2017.

In *Imbler v. Pachtman*,[209] the Supreme Court discussed how
to measure the critical balance between vigorous and fearless performance by prosecutors with the malicious and dishonest conduct
that governs the important but qualified immunity of prosecutors.
Absolute immunity governs, the Court ruled, unless it would impede
the judicial process to permit the questioned acts of a prosecutor.

The more recent case of *Ziglar v. Abbasi*[210] dealt with harsh
post-9/11 detention of Muslim aliens by correction officials. The
Court expanded on the elements that would warrant holding
law-enforcement officials responsible for excessively carrying out
their responsibilities. Is the challenged behavior in question "the
only realistic avenue for vindication of constitutional guarantees"?[211]
Would scrutiny "unduly inhibit officials in the discharge of their
duties"?[212] Prosecutors are permitted "breathing room to make reasonable but mistaken judgments about open legal questions."[213] In
a notorious New York City case, police choked a man to death—his
last words were, "I can't breathe."[214]

These after-the-fact decisions are subjective, except in the most clear and prejudicial cases, so they are better left to trial judges and juries, or arguably the Supreme Court would be converted into a trial forum. But recent excesses by police in minority neighborhoods indicate that without a final arbiter, local juries tend to be protective of police, leaving some citizens denied the safeguards of the law.

BAD SCIENCE

Junk science (bite marks, hair ID, even DNA) often accounts for wrongful convictions when outdated theories and folklore are accepted as expert testimony. In 2017, for example, a single lab technician's misconduct necessitated the dismissal of over twenty-one thousand criminal convictions in Massachusetts.[215] Notably, this scandal occurred after the highly-publicized Annie Dookhan case revealed the need for heightened scrutiny of criminal lab results. In the latter, the court discovered that the lab chemist, Annie Dookhan, had falsified drug tests for a period of almost seven years in an effort to be viewed as the most dedicated and successful technician at work. Although Dookhan's productivity was triple that of the national average since her first year of work in 2004, her excuses were trusted, and her tests were never retried.

Only in 2011, when Dookhan was caught forging her colleagues' signatures, were substantive measures taken that to review her cases. The investigation also discovered "an inappropriately personal (albeit not romantic) relationship" had existed between Dookhan and the assistant district attorney, George Papachristos, who oversaw the operation of the lab where Dookhan worked.[216] Despite the grave injustices faced by many of the defendants affected by the scandal, the court has given the prosecutors the opportunity to retry any cases they choose. Moreover, while those wrongfully convicted as a result of the false test results were in prison for up to seven years, Dookhan was sentenced to just three years in prison; she was released in 2016.[217]

In another comparable Massachusetts case involving inaccurate drug-test findings that came on the heels of the Dookhan scandal, it was discovered that chemist Sonja Farak had been high on a range of drugs, including crack cocaine, LSD, and ecstasy, during her eight years of work at the Amherst-area crime lab. At work, Farak would use drugs from the samples she was meant to study in order to get high and would continue to conduct her experiments while under the influence. In order to cover up her indiscretions, Farak would swap samples: "[Investigators] were intrigued that the chemist had been charged with removing a substance from a case file that tested positive for cocaine and replacing it with one that did not test positive."[218]

Drug results were, as a result, not only skewed because of her mental incapacity during the tests but also because Farak was mismarking them for her own purposes. Though colleagues discovered her and reported her misconduct in 2013, the subsequent state attorney general report disclosed that "[the attorney general's office] did not believe Farak's alleged tampering would undermine any cases."[219] How could it not?

Following the state's inaction, the ACLU filed suit, and it was three years later, in 2016, that the number of cases affected by Farak was revealed. Despite the clear injustices faced by those convicted as a result of the faulty tests, prosecutors asked the court to conduct individual reviews of all cases rather than ordering a blanket amnesty, while defense attorneys claimed case-by-case analysis was impractical given the number of cases affected. Only in the spring of 2018 did Massachusetts's highest court officially dismiss more than seven thousand cases as a result of the Farak scandal.[220]

Two former state prosecutors, Anne Kaczmarek and Kris Foster, both alleged to have covered up the extent of the Farak scandal, have nonetheless been able to continue their careers. Kaczmarek is now a magistrate judge, while Foster is, somewhat ironically, the general counsel for the state alcoholic beverage commission.[221] This is despite the state superior court finding "[a] lack of moral compass ... reprehensible and magnified by the fact that it was not limited to an isolated incident, but a series of calculated misrepresentations. The ramifications from their misconduct are nothing short of systemic."[222]

Both these cases (Farak and Dookhan) were explored by Netflix's 4-part series, *How to Fix a Drug Scandal*[223], which highlighted systemic problems, 35,000 cases in these two instances. Bad lab work and prosecutors' failure to disclose what they knew about it, were compounded by the fact that among the prejudiced defendants most were probably guilty. The TV series concluded: "the vast majority of police-seized narcotics that make it to their lab desks were legitimate drugs."

The *ABA Journal* described comparable problems in St. Paul, Minnesota ("major flaws in nearly every aspect of the lab's operation"), West Virginia, Oklahoma City, Nassau County, New York, and North Carolina ("withheld or distorted evidence in more than 230 cases over a 16-year period, including three cases that resulted in executions"). In 2013, the *ABA Journal* issued a report on this phenomenon of bad and fraudulent science. It mentioned the cases cited earlier, and others. In New York City, eight hundred rape cases over ten years were mishandled by a lab technician who resigned. In St. Paul, Minnesota, a police crime lab's operation was found to have "major flaws in nearly every aspect of the lab's operation, including dirty equipment, a lack of standard operating procedures, faulty testing techniques, illegible reports, and a woeful ignorance of basic scientific principles."[224]

In Oklahoma City, a police department chemist nicknamed "Black Magic" who testified in twenty-three death penalty cases (twelve defendants were executed) was fired for sloppy work and false or mishandled evidence. She was not prosecuted. In North

Carolina's state crime lab, 230 cases over sixteen years involved "systemically withholding or distorted evidence."[225] Even the FBI, the nation's premier forensic lab, has had its problems with faulty science.[226]

California's US senator Kamala Harris, then an early candidate for president who called herself a "progressive prosecutor," has been criticized by law professor Lara Bazelon,[227] who pointed out that Harris fought to uphold wrongful convictions caused by official misconduct, evidence tampering, false testimony, and suppression of evidence. In one case when she was San Francisco district attorney, her department knew of a lab technician's misconduct and covered it up. More than six hundred cases were thrown out, even after Harris contested that ruling. As state attorney general, she took conservative stances on capital punishment as well.

In her book *The Truths We Hold*,[228] Senator Harris called those kinds of prosecutorial misconduct "a deep dark history of people using power of the prosecutor as an instrument of injustice." Before taking credit for her good works as a prosecutor, she should, one critic argued, "apologize to the wrongfully convicted people she has fought to keep in prison."[229]

Not every crime lab fraud or incompetence can be blamed on prosecutors, though it's difficult to imagine a prosecutor preparing a case and not knowing about his or her experts' work when they are called to testify under oath. At the North Carolina lab, the *ABA Journal* stated, "overwhelming evidence of a pro-prosecution bias" was found, including "training materials advising analysts on how to improve their conviction rates and instructing them to be wary of defense experts."[230] The *ABA Journal* review concluded with a proposal to assure that law-enforcement procedures "are grounded in science."[231]

All of the injustices reported here, and others like them, might not have happened if the defendants had competent counsel. Though the Constitution guarantees defendants in criminal cases the right to counsel, it wasn't until 1963 that the Supreme Court breathed life into that promise. Clarence Gideon was tried in a Florida state court for breaking and entering. He had no lawyer and asked the court to appoint one for him. At that time in Florida, the right to counsel was only provided in capital cases. Gideon represented himself, was convicted, and appealed to the US Supreme Court.

> In a unanimous opinion authored by Justice Hugo L. Black, the Court held that it was consistent with the Constitution to require state courts to appoint attorneys for defendants who could not afford to retain counsel on their own. The Court reasoned that the Sixth Amendment's guarantee of counsel is a fundamental and essential right made obligatory upon the states by the Fourteenth Amendment. The Sixth Amendment guarantees the accused the right to the assistance of counsel in all criminal prosecutions and requires courts to provide counsel for defendants unable to hire counsel unless the right was competently and intelligently waived. [232]

New York Times editorial writer Anthony Lewis wrote a popular book about this historic case, *Gideon's Trumpet*. It became a made-for-TV movie aired by CBS.

ECONOMICS AND DOUBLE STANDARDS

How did such a system evolve in our democratic, constitutional government? There are cultural reasons, along with economic ones.

Michigan Law professor Yale Kamisar perceptively wrote about the differences between what he called "the manor house" of justice (courtrooms and classrooms) and "the gatehouse" (police stations and the streets), cynically suggesting there is a fundamental difference between hortatory principled notions of how our justice system *should* work and a more realistic assessment about how it actually *does* work. [233]

Kamisar's article brilliantly examined the realities of the right to counsel in the early stages of criminal justice system in respect to confessions and waiver of counsel. He asked rhetorically, what does society owe the poor arrestee?

> [B]asic legal services are not of the same order, in our theory of government, as basic medical services . . . applied justice is an essential function of the state even under the most conservative political theory. . . . It should be understood that governmental obligation to deal effectively with problems of poverty in the administration of criminal justice does not rest or depend upon some hypothetical obligation of government to indulge in acts of public charity. [234]

It wasn't until 1963 that this constitutional guarantee was enforced. Later cases dealt with the question: When does that right to counsel begin? Arrest? Plea? Trial? Kamisar paraphrased Justice Robert Jackson [in an earlier (1949) case]: [235]

> There is no more effective practical guaranty against arbitrary and unreasonable government than to require that the poor and the stupid and the ignorant be subjected to police interrogation in no greater measure than the rich and the bright and the educated; that the protections extended to the favored few be imposed generally. Conversely, nothing opens the door to arbitrary action so effectively as to allow officials to pick and choose only the less fortunate and the less endowed to be the subjects of secret and persistent police interrogation and thus to escape the political retribution that might be visited upon them if all segments of society were so affected. [236]

Professor Kamisar compared how arrestees are treated when they do or don't have counsel, drawing from Justice Hugo Black's opinion in 1956 in *Griffin v. Illinois.*[237]

> Both equal protection and due process emphasize the central aim of our entire judicial system—all people charged with crime must, so far as the law is concerned, "stand on an equality before the bar of justice in every American court."[238]

Kamisar also referred to Justice William Douglas's opinion a few years earlier:

> [T]he evil is the same: discrimination against the indigent. *For there can be no equal justice where the kind of an appeal a man enjoys "depends on the amount of money he has."* [...] There is lacking that equality demanded by the Fourteenth Amendment where the rich man, who appeals as of right, enjoys the benefit of counsel's examination into the record, research of the law, and marshalling of arguments on his behalf, while the indigent, already burdened by a preliminary determination that his case is without merit, is forced to shift for himself.[239]

How far must poor men receive the same justice as a rich man? Kamisar answered:

> Amid all the sound and fury one point is plain: in the absence of judge and jury, law-enforcement officers can—and without hesitation do- resort to methods they would never consider utilizing at the trial; the case for the prosecution is stronger—much stronger—if what was done to the defendant was done away from the restraining influence of a public trial in an open courtroom.... In the courtroom, the conflict of interest between the accused and

the state is mediated by an impartial judge; in the police station, although the same conflict exists in more aggravated form, "the law" passes it by.[240]

Kamisar expanded on his telling metaphor, analyzing several key practical procedures:

> The courtroom is a splendid place where defense attorneys bellow and strut and prosecuting attorneys are hemmed in at many turns. ... Before an accused reaches the safety and enjoys the comfort of this veritable mansion ... he must first pass through a much less pretentious edifice, a police station with bare back rooms and locked doors.... Here ideals are checked at the door, "realities" faced ... he leaves the "gatehouse" and enters the "mansion"—if he ever gets there—the enemy of the state is repersonalized, even dignified, the public invited, and a stirring ceremony in honor of individual freedom from law enforcement celebrated ... so much that society knows and approves of the show in the gatehouse, but that society does not know or care.[241]

Quoting Associate Justice Potter Stewart in *Massiah v. US*,[242] Kamisar continued, "Constitution which guarantees a defendant the aid of counsel at ... trial could surely vouchsafe no less to an indicted defendant under interrogation by the police in a complete extrajudicial proceeding."

Kamisar pressed his metaphor, "Must the old gatehouse be razed or is only a bit of renovation needed before business may proceed there as usual?"[243]

Developing this point about the disparate treatment of rich and poor defendants in the criminal justice system, the late Stanford law professor Herbert Packer wrote about what he called the Two Models of the Criminal Process.[244] There is the due process model and the crime control model, Professor Packer wrote, citing studies of the criminal justice system that found that rich defendants are commonly judged under the former model (that they have good lawyers helped), while poor defendants were judged by the latter. From the darkest extreme of the criminal justice system in capital cases to the earliest pretrial stages, the justice people receive depends upon their financial status.

While Professor Packer's important article was written in 1964,[245] its message is relevant and contemporary today. For example, he reminded us that the minimal assumption that defendants are subject to a system conducted by judges and juries is not a fact presently when most criminal cases are plea bargained. That defendants are represented by counsel, Packer pointed out, is an unrealistic promise of the adversary system: "We may smile indulgently at such claims; they are rhetoric and no more."[246] We overuse the criminal sanctions, he concluded, for too wide a spectrum of antisocial behavior, like nonviolent drug cases today that can be better diverted out of the criminal justice system. Diversion, however, is usually reserved for defendants with means for representation and private restitution.

Packer's crime control model often compromises the adjudicative process ... Under the due process model, "the criminal is to go free because the constable has blundered."[247] That rarely is the case when a litigant can't afford a good lawyer, and the sooner in the process the better. The differences between the crime control model and the due process model follow defendants from arrest, through bail, pleas, trials and appeals, and at every phase the lack of counsel prejudices the defendant.

The old view of the late justice Oliver Wendell Holmes Jr. that it is better that one hundred guilty people go free than one innocent person is found guilty is a puristic goal, but it is not the working premise nowadays when law enforcement–oriented appellate courts look for ways to skirt rules with elastic rationales.

THE PREJUDICIAL FEATURES OF
MISDEMEANOR SYSTEM

Alexandra Natapoff, a University of California at Irvine law professor and a former public defender in Baltimore, Maryland, spoke about the prejudicial features of our misdemeanor system on the Terry Gross radio program *Fresh Air*[248]. Misdemeanors are usually minor crimes, where the punishment is less than a year. But 13 million of them occur annually (80 percent of the criminal docket), and the system punishes the poor, for example, when a defendant cannot afford a fine for a minor, say traffic offense, and can be jailed if they can't afford the fine. Their financial struggle is later compounded because then they are charged for their court costs and incarceration. It is "assembly line" justice, or "McJustice," she states in her book *Punishment Without Crime: How Our Massive Misdemeanor System Traps the Innocent and Makes America More Unequal.*[249]

She offered the example of Gail Atwater, who while searching for a lost toy in a local park allowed her children to remove their seatbelts so the kids could better see through the truck window to find it:

> They were stopped by a police officer, who pulled them over and hollered at Gail that she would be arrested for the seatbelt violation for not having her children in the seatbelt restraints. Her children started to cry. Atwater asked if she could take her kids to the neighbor's house. [the] Officer . . . said, no, they're going to come to jail with you. A neighbor happened to walk by and took care of the kids, but Gail Atwater went to jail.
>
> She was booked, fingerprinted, spent a couple hours in the lockup and eventually pled guilty to and paid the fine for the seatbelt violation. The most she could have been punished for that

violation was $50. It's a traffic misdemeanor. She could not have gone to jail for the seatbelt violation, but nevertheless spent time in jail as a result of the arrest.

Atwater brought a lawsuit asking the Supreme Court to hold that it's unreasonable for police officers to effectuate what we call full-fledged custodial arrest. . . . It was a fine-only traffic offense. The Supreme Court ruled against her.

The Supreme Court said no matter what the crime, no matter how minor the misdemeanor . . . the police have the power to effectuate a full-fledged custodial arrest—that is, take you to jail, book you, lock you up. . . .

The case . . . opens a gateway into the kinds of arrests and intrusions and jail stays that characterize this low-level world of misdemeanors and minor offenses. . . .

Misdemeanors come in all kinds of shapes and sizes. Sometimes we call them petty offenses. Sometimes . . . violations or ordinance violations.[250]

The fine system creates a regressive tax policy where fines leveled against poor defendants fund the public defender, court, parole, and police systems that incarcerated the offender. Using fines, fees, bail, and monetary penalties they can't afford but must pay ought to be considered unconstitutional.

Natapoff stated,

Their fees can include jail fees, supervision fees, fees for applying for the public defender, fees for using the public defender, fees for drug testing, fees when they swab your cheek to put your DNA in the database. They'll charge you a fee if you don't show up to court, and they issue a warrant, they'll issue a fee. If you're late paying your fees, they'll charge you a fee . . . the list of fees, ranging from a few dollars here to $10, $20, $30 or a hundred dollars there, can add up to hundreds, even thousands of dollars on top of whatever punitive fine the court decides to impose.[251]

THE BAIL SYSTEM

Associate Justice Robert Jackson defined the philosophy behind the American bail system:

> The practice of admission to bail, as it has evolved in Anglo-American law, is not a device for keeping persons in jail upon mere accusation until it is found convenient to give them a trial. On the contrary, *the spirit of the procedure is to enable them to stay out of jail until a trial has found them guilty.* Without this conditional privilege, even those wrongly accused are punished by a period of imprisonment while awaiting trial and are handicapped in consulting counsel, searching for evidence and witnesses and preparing a defense. To open a way of escape from this handicap and possible injustice, Congress commands allowance of bail for one under charge of any offense not punishable by death.... "A person arrested for an offense not punishable by death shall be admitted to bail ..." before conviction.[252]

The bail system, like the issues examined above in misdemeanor and capital punishment cases, is an example of the impact of wealth on justice. The Eighth Amendment to our Constitution prohibits "excessive" bail. What is excessive for individuals is economic based, thus dependent on their financial status. *Ransom*, my book about the bail system—which, in the United States has been a multi billion-a-year private business—detailed how the private bail bond industry functions.[253] *Ransom* described how the system can be manipulated by many prosecutors and judges, resulting in poor defendants being jailed *before* trial, which is prejudicial to the preparation of their defense, and often for prolonged periods of time. The poor plead guilty more frequently and fare worse at trial than defendants who are free before trials because they can afford bail.[254] Emily Bazelon described the current bail system as "the first domino in a series of decisions affecting guilty pleas" that "shape the outcome of a criminal case."[255] She added, "Jails serve as plea mills."

The inequities of the bail system, particularly involving poor people, have been rediscovered recently, though in 1964, Attorney General Robert F. Kennedy convened a national conference on bail reform (I worked on it and wrote about the subject then[256]) that exposed the problems. That led to the passage of the Bail Reform Act of 1966 that attempted to revise the governing emphasis of bail from assuring a defendant's presence at trial to finding a way to assure their release. Unfortunately, that moment of reform has passed. Half a century later, it has become a political issue again today.

The late justice William O. Douglas best described the confounding dilemma:

> The fundamental tradition in the country is that one charged with a crime is not, in ordinary circumstances, imprisoned until after a judgment of guilty.... This traditional right to freedom during trial ... has to be squared with the possibility that the defendant may flee or hide himself. Bail is the device which we have borrowed to reconcile these conflicting interests.... It is assumed that the threat of forfeiture of one's goods will be an effective deterrent to the temptation to break the conditions of one's release. But *this* theory is based on the assumption that a *defendant has property. To continue to demand a substantial bond which the defendant is unable to secure raises considerable problems for the equal administration of the law.* We have held *that an indigent defendant is denied equal protection of the law if he is denied an appeal on equal terms with other defendants, solely because of his indigence. Can an indigent be denied freedom, where a wealthy man*

would not, because he does not happen to have enough property to pledge for his freedom?

It would be unconstitutional to fix excessive bail to assure that a defendant will not gain his freedom. Yet *in the case of an indigent defendant, the fixing of bail in even a modest amount may have the practical effect of denying him release.* The wrong done by denying release is not limited to the denial of freedom alone. That denial may have other consequences. In case of reversal, he will have served all or part of his sentence under an erroneous judgment. Imprisoned, a man may have no opportunity to investigate his case, to cooperate with his counsel, to earn money that is still necessary for the fullest use of his right to appeal.[257]

Further reflection has led me to conclude that *no man should be denied release, because of indigence.* Instead, under our constitutional system, a man is entitled to be released on personal recognizance where other relevant factors make it reasonable to believe that he will comply with the orders of the court.[258]

The use of bondsmen as unofficial officers of courts is a disgrace. Because courts don't have adequate resources to monitor and administer the inherent economic inequity of the bail judge's order, bondsmen are available to put up bail—for a price to the defendant, usually 10 percent of the cost of the bail ordered, which many defendants cannot afford. So the system incarcerates those who can't afford either the bail itself, which is returned if they show up for trial, or even the 10 percent, which is not returned. Bondsmen make money on the judicial system and poor defendants. They aren't unofficial "law officers," but they act as police when they capture defendants who flee in order not to forfeit the bail they provided. It is a system that should be replaced by more releases and court-administered supervision administered by private agencies like Vera, in New York City, which is run by socially minded people, not pseudo-sheriffs.

VERA currently works on nearly 60 projects in 47 states. According to the latest report, conducted in partnership with leaders in the public sector, our projects drive change by advancing new knowledge about justice reform and implementing solutions on the ground. *VERA* is motivated by three missions: (1) to end mass incarceration; (2) to ensure equal justice is realized in the legal system; and (3) to strengthen families and communities. In doing so, *VERA* works a range of issues, from immigration to mental health and substance abuse.

Vera's Center on Sentencing and Corrections (CSC)

focuses on developing and supporting balanced, fair and humane sentencing and corrections policies to reduce the overall use of incarceration; to transform the in-custody experience into one that can improve the lives of those incarcerated so that they return home to support their families and communities; and to ensure that prisons and jails are safe for those incarcerated and as well as those who work there.[259]

A 2015 report conducted by the Prison Policy Initiative disclosed the current extent of this $2 billion bail bond business.[260] In the last half century, the number of prisoners in the United States grew by 700 percent. In the past 15 years, 99 percent of this increase came from the growth of the pretrial prisoner population—individuals who cannot afford to pay bail and thus remain in jail before they are formally found guilty.[261] The bail bond business is backed by insurance companies who underwrite this process, and losses are passed on to the poor defendants who sign "predatory contracts" they are offered by the bondsmen. The median amount of bail bonds is eight months of income of the defendants who reside in poor urban areas, mostly people of color. This report urged prosecutors to lead reforms abolishing cash bail, though that is unlikely to occur after centuries of the practice being institutionalized.

Even when attempts are made to relieve the prejudicial economic reasons leading to defendants being incarcerated before trial, similar problems continue. A recent study in St. Louis, Missouri, described a private program where defendants who couldn't afford bail, or the 10 percent they would have to pay bondsmen to put up their bail, could be diverted into another private system where they could be released with an ankle brace to provide community-based supervision while they were awaiting trial.[262]

But because black people make up 67 percent of those wearing these monitors, though they compose 24 percent of the population,[263] critics view it as the latest example of racial discrimination, "a new form of oppression under the guise of progress."[264] Author Michelle Alexander criticized "virtual bars and walls—walls that are invisible to the naked eye but function nearly as effectively as Jim Crow laws."[265]

The ankle monitor is visible, awkward to wear, and prejudicial to defendants looking for work before their trials. What was meant to be a relief of economic discrimination of poor defendants turned out to exacerbate the very problem it was intended to relieve, and in addition added an element of Big Brother surveillance.

Average detention periods are 291 days, so the defendants pay the private company more than they would have paid the court system if they'd had the money in the first place. And ultimately they may not be found guilty or sentenced after their trials.

In a New Orleans trial court, judges' (magistrates) bail requirements funded judicial expenses like secretaries, clerks, and travel. The practice was challenged on the grounds that the pretrial releases on bonds by a commercial surety presented a conflict of interest that violated due process because 1.8 percent of the bond paid went to the judicial expense funding, 20 to 25 percent of that fund in recent years.[266]

By the middle of the 20th Century, the US bond system was
skewed in favor of commercial bondsmen who profited through the
judicial practice of requiring bonds be paid upfront and in full prior
in order for an individuals to be released on bail. Reform efforts,
however, sought to reverse this alarming trend: the Justice Department's 1964 National Bail Conference, my book *Ransom, A Critique
of the American Bail System*, and the passage of the Bail Reform
Act of 1966. Later in the 1987 case *United States v. Salerno*,[267] the
Supreme Court upheld in the Bail Reform Act of 1984, which states
that in cases where an individual's release before trial would endanger the community, pretrial detention is warranted and appropriate.
This reflects the bail system's original and intended function, and
aligns with my own recommendation as noted in a piece I wrote for
the *New York Times Magazine* in 1970.[268]

The Supreme Court ruled in Salerno that permitting detention
before trial for public safety reasons was not "facially unconstitutional." In doing so, the Court dealt with a pressing community and
societal problem. Chief Justice Rehnquist wrote for the majority of
the Court that government regulatory interest in community safety
may outweigh an individual's liberty interest, so long as the decision
is supported by facts, is immediately reviewable, the detention time
is limited, and the defendant is kept apart from convicted prisoners
(a small percentage of most "jail populations").[269]

There have been recent hopeful signs that some prosecutors are
reforming their local practices.[270] In Houston, Chicago, Philadelphia, Kansas City, and Brooklyn, excessive practices on bail, stack-
ing charges, indicting young offenders, and modifying sentencing
demands are evolving and complemented by calls for criminal justice reform in the US Senate.[271]

The Pennsylvania Supreme Court is launching an inquiry into
Philadelphia's bail system. In response to a class action lawsuit

filed last March 2019 by the Pennsylvania ACLU, the state
Supreme Court appointed a special master to investigate the
operation of the cash bail system in one district. The question:
Did Philadelphia's magistrate judges violate due process, failing
to consider alternatives to cash bail.[272]

Volunteers sat in on 2,000 arraignments over the past year.
The suit named all six bail magistrates, claiming they hold hearings that are on average less than two minutes, with minimal discussion about a defendant's ability to pay.... One of the plaintiffs
in the case, said, "At the age of 16, I was locked up, charged as an
adult and held in prison for 18 months."[273]

PUBLIC DEFENDERS

Legal aid in civil cases and public defenders in criminal cases are
meant to address the issue of a lack of counsel for poor people.
Both are well intended but seriously inadequate because of lack of
funding. The public funds prosecutors' offices and expenses. It does
not fund the other side in criminal cases, the public defenders.

A recent press study of public defender practices reported about
one Louisiana public defender's workload on one randomly chosen day. In his office, lawyers handled five times the workload that
prevailed, including serious felonies and capital cases. He had no
clerk, no paralegal, and no investigator. When he met new clients
in court, he spent one to five minutes talking to them about their
cases. Since 94 percent of state cases are plea bargained, "terrible
things happen," and do.[274]

The American Bar Association conducted a national study of this
situation to assess how many cases public defenders can ethically handle before their clients are denied the constitutional right to effective
counsel.[275] In Colorado, Missouri, Rhode Island, Texas, New Mexico,
and Oregon, the ABA study found comparable data to Louisiana's,

showing public defenders had "outlandishly excessive workloads" that resulted in mockery of the constitutional right to counsel.[276]

Three out of four of all public defender offices have what nationally recognized criteria deem excessive caseloads. Fifteen statewide defender systems surveyed exceeded national Justice Department standards governing proper caseloads.[277] In 2007, "73% of all county-based public defender offices exceeded the maximum recommended limits of cases received per attorney," and the active attorneys often had no investigators, according to US Department of Justice Bureau of Justice Statistics.[278]

ASSIGNED COUNSEL

Four of every five criminal cases involve court-appointed lawyers or public defenders, according to a *New York Times* report,[279] and the latter are appointed by the judges who must approve their bills. The emphasis is on resolving cases quickly, a "phenomenon that pervades the entire legal system," according to DC's Civil Rights Corps.[280]

Even then, the system prejudices assigned counsel. When there is an attorney for indigent defendants, the court system can manipulate the degree of that attorney's work on their defense. One example from Galveston, Texas, made this point. There, a young attorney's attempts to thoroughly represent his court-appointed indigent clients was chastised by a local judge who told him, "You overwork cases."[281] That attorney's efforts allowed his client to plea to lesser charges than the prosecutor had asked for in plea negotiations, yet the very judge who appointed him reduced his legal fees due to allegedly "excessive out-of-court hours."[282] An appellate court later reinstated the original payment request.

In 2007, the *New York Times* reported a study demonstrating that attorneys paid by the hour are less qualified and get worse results than overworked public defenders.[283] "Appointed lawyers also cost taxpayers $61 million a year more than salaried public defenders would"; this money would be better spent elsewhere in the justice system.

The problem gets compounded. In a report about Tennessee, the prosecution spent $130 to $139 million, while public defenders had only $56.4 million, impacting their staffing, investigation efforts, and compensation of attorneys. Two percent of all federal defendants represent themselves, while three-quarters of federal defendants rely on attorneys evenly divided between salaried public defenders and appointed ones paid by the hour, the latter of which are less successful and cost $5,800 more per case to taxpayers.[284] The public defender system, which serves millions of people, is in "a state of chronic crisis."[285] In Missouri, the "chronically underfunded public defender system" even faces punishment by courts for failing to keep up with their workloads.[286]

Because plea bargains are the overwhelming conclusion of criminal cases, and many defendants are not represented, one critic referred to the practice as "the 'black box' of America's criminal justice system . . . steeped in racial inequalities and slash and burn justice."[287]

The public defender problem is not one of corruption or incompetence. It is one of inadequate and thus prejudicial funding. The competing defense attorneys do not have resources equal to the prosecutors. A double standard results, prejudicing poor litigants.

LAW ENFORCEMENT MISCONDUCT

There are cases where law enforcement goes off the rails because "bad" public officials, cops, prosecutors, and even judges are racist and prejudiced, and as a result, they abuse their powers. Those cases warrant no explanation, only condemnation. But there are also psychological and social reasons the public condones excessive systemic misbehavior by police and prosecutors—subtle ones, difficult to document, but troubling nonetheless.

Watching entertaining television police shows through the years—*Hill Street Blues*, *NYPD Blue*, and *Blue Blood*—I rooted for the tough cops when they forced confessions from the antisocial low-life characters they encountered in their work. They performed their "dirty work" on all our behalf, and I cheered them on, relaxing at home after a day's work on "serious" matters. But spoilsport that I am, that "serious work" reminded me that much of what I applauded or at least passively condoned while relaxing on my couch would not pass muster under the constitutional law that fills the rest of my life—at least my working hours.[288]

Police officers who are excessive in performing their work rarely are charged for doing so; and when they are charged, they are rarely convicted by juries. While the public may be shocked by some of the things we learn about, especially in urban and cross-racial law enforcement, the public appreciates that law enforcement works in dangerous situations and on our behalf, and that they must act under extreme provocation in making split-second, life-and-death decisions. For these reasons, it is hard for the public to second-guess them when they are later forced to justify what they did. Except in the case of Robin Hood, we all cheer for "the good guys" (and women), not the robbers. At least, all of us except those people who are the victims of these systemic injustices.

The same is the case with prosecutors who are also perceived as protecting us. For that reason, they too generally are given the benefit of any doubts that what they do is proper, legal, and justified. Jurors are people, and they prefer to stay on the good side of police and prosecutors (who, by the way, may run for office and are indebted to their supporters, who are prone to preferring popular verdicts). Prosecutors are human beings, as the police are, and as such they are governed by their private predilections, prejudices, fears, and backgrounds. We must consider that reality when we judge their specific behavior, if and when it is brought to public attention.

Emily Bazelon examined the work of prosecutors in her new book *Charged*, concluding they are responsible for many problems in the criminal justice system. Bazelon quotes Brooklyn district attorney Eric Gonzalez: "It's all about discretion. Do you authorize the arrest, request bail, argue to keep them in jail or let them out, go all out on the charges or take a plea bargain? Prosecutors decide, especially who gets a second chance."[289]

Considering that prosecuting lawyers fill two thousand offices around the country, many extensively staffed, their influence is major. "The study of criminal justice is the study of power,"[290] Bazelon pointed out.

CLEMENCY

Clemency occurs in the late stages of the criminal justice system. Its purpose is to correct or modify earlier procedures. There are four types of clemency.

Pardons, the most common one, remove civil disabilities—the right to vote, for example—and exempt further punishment. It is "an act of grace," Chief Justice John Marshall wrote,[291] mostly used by an exiting president in the final days of an administration. The idea is to recognize rehabilitation and modernize the justice system, as President Barack Obama did for minor nonviolent convicts sentenced for drug offenses, or occasionally to rectify an invalid sentence. It forgives the offense, but it does not necessarily eradicate it. The president has the federal power, and state governors have the corresponding power for state offenses, mostly after convictions or fulfilled sentences. In my book *After Conviction*,[292] I interviewed relevant officials and reported the rigorous procedures governing federal and state pardons.

Commutation is the reduction of convictions, sometimes used to reduce questionable death sentences, for example. Reprieves are postponements of sentences, used to give the president time to decide about a requested pardon or commutation. Amnesty is rarely used, though sometimes it is applied for groups after a war (Civil War, Vietnam) to bring about national harmony.

Only in about 25 percent of all clemency cases are petitioners represented by counsel—which gets to my point about the influence of money, which is an issue even in this late stage of the criminal justice system. The system seeks to avoid political considerations and the influence of money. Only in England under Richard II were pardons purchased (1377–99), but in most countries it is now the chief executive who has this power. Questions have been raised about the recent applications of this power by the current president who sidesteps regular procedures of the system and acts on his own.

In the Clinton administration, there were more than 2,000 pardon applications, of which 396 were granted (just under 20 percent). Of 5,488 commutation requests, 61 were granted (1.1 percent).[293]

In one notorious pardon case, a very wealthy fugitive from justice, Marc Rich, received a pardon from then president Bill Clinton. The full clemency process is detailed and is followed in most cases—though it was not in this one. Poor defendants may apply for clemency such as pardons, and when they do they go through a long and specific procedure that starts with the pardon attorney, then goes to the Justice Department for further review, and then is passed on to the president.[294] Rarely is a prisoner represented in this process. But it was not the case in the following situation.

The *New York Times* reported[295] about this notorious matter involving Eric Holder, then a popular Justice Department official in the Clinton (and later Obama) administration, and Marc Rich. Rich had been indicted for tax evasion, wire fraud, racketeering, and trading with the enemy, and he faced life in prison. He was living luxuriously in hiding in Switzerland while on the FBI's Most Wanted list. At the urging of a politically connected lawyer-lobbyist, Holder sidestepped pardon procedures under questionable circumstances and "brokered one of the most unjustifiable pardons that an American president has ever granted," an op-ed article by a veteran journalist concluded. After the pardon was granted, Holder reportedly reminded the lobbyist that he had referred department aides to his firm and hoped he'd consider hiring them. The details described in the *Times* were an embarrassment, a blemish on but not a hindrance to Holder's long and continuing career in Washington. Along with the influence of wealth of clients, there is a subtle culturing of lawyering that arises from their government-private roles.

Justin Peters also reported in *Slate*[296] about President Clinton's pardon of fugitive of justice Marc Rich at the final hour of his presidency. A House Committee on Government Reform reported that the Justice Department opposed the pardon but was finessed when the Holder report went directly to Clinton, who later claimed, as Holder admitted, that he was distracted and used poor judgment. The House Report concluded that Rich "bought his pardon with money and access."

> The President abused one of his most important powers, meant to free the unjustly convicted or provide forgiveness to those who have served their time and changed their lives. Instead, he offered it up to wealthy fugitives whose money had already enabled them to permanently escape American justice. Few other abuses could so thoroughly undermine public trust in government.[297]

CORPORATE CRIME

Professor Brandon L. Garrett in his book quoted one Lord Chancellor of England's remark that corporations "have no soul to be damned.... Prosecutors fail to punish the most serious corporate crimes ... holding real people accountable, not corporate persons."[298]

Once money is available to pay for legal services, the story changes, and ethical and moral questions emerge. The recent Epstein scandal is a classic example[299] of the differences in results when able lawyers are employed to defend cases. There, the lawyers and prosecutor caused the injustice by agreeing on favorable terms of Epstein's sentence.

Recent popular books demonstrate that the cultural problem noted in that notorious case remains. *The Chickenshit Club: Why the Justice Department Fails to Prosecute Executives*, by award-winning journalist Jesse Eisinger,[300] and *Too Big to Jail: How Prosecutors Compromise with Corporations* by University of Virginia law professor Brandon Garrett,[301] detailed the problem and suggested an unprovable suspicion.

The notion is that because many prosecutors and private law firm lawyers come from the same culture, many of them switch career positions regularly. They may be subconsciously protective of certain kinds of potential defendants (most notably corporate executives). Their past and future partners and colleagues are sometimes on the opposite side in these cases, suggesting the subtle corruption of the law-enforcement process.

We learned in law school that corporations are legal fictions, but we never were told that the real people who run these legal fictions are not punishable for committing crimes on their behalf. Yet that has too often been the case. When a corporation commits security or tax or any other offense, particularly in product liability cases where many people are hurt, often critically, some person or people ought to be personally responsible, civilly and criminally. They invariably are high officials in the corporate hierarchy, or hired lawyers or accountants. These people ought to be held personally responsible if these offenses are to be deterred and punished in meaningful ways. Mostly they are not.

"Corporate convictions can have terrible collateral consequences on innocent people, employees, shareholders, and the public," Professor Garrett noted.[302] But, he wrote, "a few unlucky individuals—celebrities such as the sympathetic Martha Stewart or truly notorious white-collar criminals such as the unsympathetic Bernard Madoff—receive the brunt of enforcement and the vast majority of corporations and executives get off scot-free."[303]

Professor Garrett dealt with the inconsistencies in the legal treatment of corporations as individuals. The notorious Citizens United case raised public consciousness about treating corporate officials like people, which is pertinent. There, the Supreme Court accepted the notion that corporations should be treated as people for First Amendment speech considerations. That conclusion is inconsistent with the notion that corporate officials should not be treated as individuals when criminal offenses are committed.

Fictions can't commit crimes; only people can! Professor Garrett analyzed constitutional cases where the courts do and don't apply individual rights to corporations. He reminded readers that "the central purpose of corporate criminal liability . . . is to make sure individual people are accountable while corporations as a whole are accountable for the crimes of their employees."

Professor Garrett pointed out that new techniques have been tried whereby prosecutorial agreements were negotiated for deferred prosecutions of corporate misconduct if it is reformed. Corporations may be monitored as part of such agreements, replacing prosecution. The idea is that it is preferable for a company to be rehabilitated, its cultures and policies reformed, than for its offenders to be imprisoned. In 25 percent of these cases of deferred prosecutions, monitors were provided. The remaining 75 percent lacked some

form of monitoring by courts or their designees, a key requirement
if reforms are to be assured.

There have been more than 250 such agreements in the last
decade, Professor Garrett reported, and he made them public in
his book so they can be seen and replicated. In two-thirds of these
cases of deferred prosecutions, the company was punished, but no
employees were prosecuted. The result was that the shareholders
were prejudiced for the misconduct of their agents, who themselves were shielded from consequences for their wrongdoing. There
have been "a handful" of cases where high-level corporate officials
were convicted, "but not many," Professor Garrett reported, leaving
the wrongdoers in office while the public and shareholders suffered.

Eisinger quoted a cynical SEC insider critic who complained
the agency "polices the broken windows on the street level and
rarely goes to the penthouse floors."[304]

How prosecutors exercise their powerful discretion on corporate
criminal cases "largely remains a black box,"[305] Professor Garrett
concluded. He posited that it is the prosecutors who compromise
treatment of white-collar crimes of business executives, suggesting
questionable cultural causes as possible reasons for such practices;
the revolving door of employment of lawyers, for example.

Professor Garrett's appendix includes data about corporate
prosecutions, including more than three hundred deferred prosecutions and two thousand guilty pleas. They fill a gap of knowledge
about these practices, showing, for example, that fines have gone up
steadily on average, documenting which regulatory agencies are
active regulators, and reporting the types of the corporations that
have been sanctioned, and the societal benefits resulting from the
use of qui tam whistleblowers.

He also recommends useful reforms regarding securing convictions, judicial supervision of deferred prosecutions, detailed struc-
tural reforms to assure compliance, use of serious, proportionate

fines, more transparency, and the requirement that shareholders be informed of the violations and agreements going forward.

Professor Garrett argues that most convicts are typically denied rehabilitation as a goal of criminal justice, though it is offered to justify finding alternatives to imprisonment for white-collar criminals, a cultural divide emphasized by sentencing guidelines (encouraging prospective ethical conduct). That is the reason "the largest and most serious corporate protections did not result in prosecutions."

In addition, there is inadequate victim restitution in many cases of corporate wrongdoing. Even the blockbuster fines in notorious cases amount to modest financial punishment to superrich companies, like BP for example. They "pale in comparison to company profits or the losses caused by the crimes," the US Sentencing Commission reported.[306] No company has been fined to death, the civil equivalent of capital punishment or lifetime imprisonment. Therefore there is "a surprising amount of recidivism in white-collar offenses," according to Professor Garrett. Prosecutors monitor convictions and sentences rather than judges, and monitoring is rarely made public, though there is a public interest in doing so.[307]

What the US Supreme Court did to the political process in Citizens United, they did again to organized religion in the Hobby Lobby case. It tortured notions of the corporate fiction to reach a politically desired conclusion: for its desired extra-legal purposes, the high Court ruled, corporations should be treated like people. In criminal cases, courts seem to torture the same fiction to protect white-collar wrongdoers by deeming corporate wrongdoing different from other offenses committed by real people.

The other side of the issue of prejudicial lack of counsel for poor people in the criminal justice system is where wealthy clientele are able to misuse the system through their high-priced lawyers. Restitution makes more sense in many criminal cases, but with poor defendants it is not used because it isn't feasible.

WHITE-COLLAR CRIMES

In 1949, Indiana University sociologist Edwin Sutherland first wrote about "white-collar crime," economic offenses by respectable people, a category of wrongdoing that went relatively unpunished in the early laissez faire years of our business-oriented country. By the middle of the twentieth century, corporate excesses led to regulatory legislation, but "prosecuting corporate crime was not a priority."

Some notable critics—Supreme Court justice Louis Brandeis, Stanley Sporkin, who later became the SEC's enforcement tiger, and federal prosecutor Jed Rakoff, who would go on to become a trial judge—were exceptions. Federal Judge Henry Friendly warned, "In our complex society the accountant's certificate and the lawyer's opinion can be instruments for inflicting pecuniary loss more potent than the chisel or the crowbar."[308]

But white-collar crime, particularly misconduct by business corporations, continues to be treated more with empathy, employing economic sanctions rather than the harsher personal prosecutions that are used in crimes by individuals. We imprison someone for smoking marijuana or stealing relatively small amounts of money, but not executives, professionals, and organizations that commit acts that injure vast numbers of victims?

The highly respected, conservative US Supreme Court justice Harlan Fiske Stone, former Columbia Law School dean and US attorney general, was a critic of law and lawyers and of the ascendance of corporate power in the United States. He blamed the legal profession for this "descent into corporate tyranny." Stone advocated as law school dean at Columbia that the purpose of law was not to "maximize corporate profits," and the role of lawyers was "not supposed to be the guardians of corporate power." And he called on the courts to "protect the tyranny of corporate elites."

The progressive Justice Louis Brandeis made the same point in 1905:

> "It is true that at the present time the lawyer does not hold as high a position with the people as he held seventy–five or indeed fifty years ago; but the reason is not lack of opportunity. It is this: Instead of holding a position of independence, between the wealthy and the people, prepared to curb the excesses of either, able lawyers have, to a large extent, allowed themselves to become adjuncts of great corporations and have neglected the obligation to use their powers for the protection of the people."[309]

This was the case in the 1960's with the drug thalidomide, never approved by our FDA but marketed in the U.S. by two drug companies—Richardson-Merrell and Smith, Klein, and French. Pregnant women who used the drug gave birth to disfigured babies. Litigation in Australia was settled for hundreds of millions of Australian dollars. An article in *The New York Times* examined records of thalidomide (brand name, Kevadon) showing that a Justice Department investigation resulted in no prosecution of company officials despite FDA evidence that "company lawyers appeared to have cleaned records of incriminating internal memos."[310]

More recently, author Jesse Eisinger criticized the Justice Department for failing to prosecute white-collar criminals. CEOs have received relative immunity, he argued, and Wall Street executives particularly are rarely held personally responsible for pervasive, profoundly consequential wrongdoings. Corporate defendants have the resources most individuals do not have to go to litigation war with the government by empowering expensive lawyers, experts, lobbyists, and media employees to act on their behalf.

Eisinger cited depressing instances of the Justice Department being overwhelmed by powerful law firms armed by their clients' resources ($700 million in one case he mentions). In the obstruction of justice case against Enron, its accounting firm, Arthur Andersen, earned "more than $50 million in billing revenue."[311] A key employee pleaded guilty, but the company's conviction was overturned because of disputed statutory language. The company was put out of business, a rare example of corporate capital punishment.

Eisinger's collection of major investigations of financial misconduct—their heroes and villains—explain the adage: "Give white-collar defense attorneys time, and they can muddy any investigation."[312] While Bernie Madoff's banker, J.P. Morgan, paid almost $2 billion in fines, Madoff's investors lost $20 billion, even after extensive clawback action.[313]

In the Lehman Brothers investigation of the 2008 subprime credit crisis regarding alleged accounting fraud and misleading markets, a large law firm was paid to examine and investigate (130 lawyers for fourteen months, ending in a 2,200-page report), but ultimately none of the several government agencies involved "brought civil or criminal charges against the company or any Lehman executive."[314]

Eisinger's story of federal trial Judge Jed Rakoff's actions in the Bank of America–Merrill-Lynch merger and the accompanying government bailout explains how a judge can make a serious difference in puncturing and curing a charade of law enforcement.[315] Presented with a proposed deal that had been blessed by the government and the parties, Rakoff was abashed that the deal defrauded shareholders and absolved executives. He refused to sign off on it. ("As U.S. District Judge Jed S. Rakoff has pointed out . . . plea deals . . . result[] in corporate executives being treated better than other offenders, even though their misconduct hurts not only individual victims, but also shareholders, society, and the economy."[316]) A much-improved resolution followed.

A PBS *Frontline* broadcast, wryly titled "Small Enough to Jail,"[317] told the story of one mortgage bank whose leadership was indicted and acquitted after five years and $10 million of legal fees. Abacus was a bank in Chinatown, New York City, that catered to the local ethnic population there. Some mid-level employees engaged in fraudulent dealings, but Fannie Mae testified that the bank's foreclosure record was better than most others, few mortgages failed, and the owners were not part of the fraudulent loans. They were not offered a deferred prosecution agreement. Cultural bias by prosecutors, not fraud by the owner, the *Frontline* documentary suggested, was at the crux of the case.

The provocative title of Eisinger's book, *The Chickenshit Club: Why the Justice Department Fails to Prosecute Executives*, comes from a speech then US attorney in New York City James Comey gave to his staff. If you haven't lost a case, Comey told his hotshot lawyers, you need to ask yourself if you are subconsciously staying away from tough cases for fear of losing, when seeking justice should be your exclusive standard. Comey's guideline has not been followed in recent years, Eisinger pointed out in engaging exemplary stories (including an instance where Comey himself failed to meet his own test), demonstrating how top lawyers, accountants, and corporate executives often have avoided personal responsibility for corporate frauds.

In Eisinger's view, "Today's Department of Justice has lost the will and indeed the ability to go after the highest-ranking corporate wrongdoers ... from pharmaceuticals, to technology, to large industrial operations, to retail giants."[318] Even the Justice Department of liberal darling President Obama "took little concrete action on the prosecution of white-collar crime."[319] For fear of driving corporations out of business, the emphasis has shifted to "settlements over charges," or deferred prosecution agreements.

Tough, aggressive litigation in complex cases has often been replaced by negotiated settlements. The first DPA in 1994 became a model for requiring corporate actions to police themselves rather than prosecuting any individuals for their misconduct. Currently, the Department of Justice prefers using deferred prosecution agreements requiring corporations to correct their past misconduct and submit to being monitored, rather than prosecuting and imprisoning individuals for their corporate misbehavior.

The idea behind DPAs is that public prosecutions are expensive, time-consuming, and uncertain, and they can cause collateral damages by wreaking havoc on capital markets, prejudicing creditors and innocent employees and shareholders. Thus, it is considered preferable that companies be rehabilitated, their cultures and policies reformed, than that individual offenders be imprisoned. The DPA provides a "middle ground between dropping charges and a draconian sanction," Eisinger explains. There have been multimillion-dollar mega-fines, to be sure, from which the public profits indirectly, but that course prejudices the corporate stockholders and creditors and does not punish the individual wrongdoers.[320]

Eisinger's explanation of this current culture shift is fascinating. Transactional lawyers began to replace activist litigators, and the government began "to turn away from prosecutions of individuals, becoming obsessed with changing corporate cultures through their regulation and enforcement."[321] It was easier to obtain corporate pleas than convictions of individuals. The prosecutorial saying was "Big cases, big problems. . . . Little cases, little problems, and no cases, no problems."[322] As a result, deferred prosecutions, while sounding reformative, "became stage managed, rather than punitive."[323] Major fines became a cost of doing business. Prosecutions of top executives decreased, "and most of these prosecutions covered small-time white-collar crime and criminals." As the PBS documentary noted about the big banks, "[C]ut a check and make it all go away."[324]

Eisinger speculated that possibly "young prosecutors want their adversaries to imagine them as future partners." Prosecutors and defense attorneys speak a common language and negotiate for a living. Big law firms' partners sometimes serve temporarily in high government offices where their firms' clients cases may come before their agencies. Even cases where monitors were appointed (and paid very well) created a further money-making specialty for the big law firms (which government attorneys aspire to join).

"Executives make more money than ever. Corporate profits are at record highs ... injustice threatens American democracy," Eisinger concluded.[325] He offered persuasive examples, intriguing trial stories, and anecdotes, naming names and suggesting that under modern corporate law enforcement, for the most part, the rule of law corrodes, prosecutors have become lazy, and the public suffers as a result.

Garrett's and Eisinger's books both allude to the current prosecutorial "culture" that favors deferred prosecutions of corporate misconduct if the corporations agree to make reforms and be monitored (by big law firm lawyers). The goal is rehabilitation of corporate culture and economic savings for prosecutorial offices.

The only way to cure these failures and discriminating practices of the criminal justice system is to lessen, if not eliminate, the element of money and access to legal representation in a system in which it should have no place but does. The empathy provided to corporate defendants needs revisiting, as does the lack of it in individual cases predominately involving poor and minority litigants. The scale of justice is heavily weighted in favor of the prosecution; the defense is the much weaker part of the adversary system.

CHAPTER THREE

THE CIVIL SYSTEM

"Due process refers to deprivations of life, liberty, and property, therefore to civil proceedings.... There is no valid reason why the basic concepts of due process which have been introduced in criminal proceedings should not also be incorporated in civil proceedings.... In Douglas v California, the Court squarely held 'there can be no equal justice where the kind of an appeal a man enjoys depends on the amount of money he has.' The Court could as well have substituted the word 'trial' for 'appeal.'... Once one accepts the equal protection argument for a right to free counsel there is again no logical reason for limiting its scope to criminal proceedings."[326]

There is a common misconception, especially among non-lawyers, that litigation is what most lawyers do. However, only about 10 percent of what lawyers do is in courts; most of their work is in offices on transactional matters, both mundane and critical. This chapter will show that in civil matters, lawyers typically spend most of their time handling contracts, torts, leases, divorces, financial matters, and a wide swath of non-litigation work, and that in these aspects of our everyday office work, poor and middle-class people are not represented at all or are underrepresented because they cannot afford fees for the matters that fill most lawyers' time.

In his speech given to the Harvard Ethical Society in 1905 entitled "The Opportunities in the Law," Louis Brandeis pointed out what lawyers know but the public may not realize, that "by far the greater part of the work done by lawyers is not done in courts, but in advising men on important matters."[327] But the average citizen usually cannot afford legal representation in or out of court. The scales are not balanced. They weren't then, and they aren't now.

Whether it is transactional work in law offices or trial work in courts, poor and middle-class citizens generally are without legal representation. Other countries have historically provided comprehensive free counsel in civil cases—in England since 1495, Germany since 1871, France since 1851, Sweden since 1919, and Italy since 1923.

The leading authority on the American civil legal system is Earl Johnson, once my colleague at the Justice Department, later head of the Office of Economic Opportunity's Legal Services Corporation, law school dean, appellate court judge in California, and author of the definitive three-volume treatise on civil legal aid.[328] In reviewing the historical background of the present American system in a dissent to a California case, then Judge Johnson wrote:

> It is now some seven centuries since the barons of England extracted the Magna Carta from King John, including the pledge: "To no one will we sell, to no one will we refuse or delay, right or justice." ... It is nearly five centuries since King Henry VII guaranteed poor Englishmen the right to free counsel in civil cases. And it is nearly 70 years since our own California Supreme Court reminded us, "[I]mperfect as was the ancient common-law system, harsh as it was in many of its methods and measures, it would strike one with surprise to be credibly informed that the common-law courts ... shut their doors upon ... poor suitors.... Even greater would be the reproach to the system of jurisprudence

of the state of California if it could be truly declared that in this twentieth century, . . . it had said the same thing. . . ." No one seriously contends poor Californians have the slightest chance in our civil courts unless they are given lawyers free of charge. Yet at present a poor person has to commit a crime before society cares enough to guarantee him a fair shake in our judicial system. Poor people can no longer be expected to bear and our state should no longer tolerate the continued denial of counsel in civil cases nor the injustice this denial guarantees.[329]

Until the late nineteenth century, in the United States people were on their own regarding their legal civil rights. Article Seven of the US Constitution gives all citizens the right to a civil trial, but it doesn't guarantee anyone a lawyer. That trial guarantee turned out to be a hollow one. Without a lawyer on one side of any dispute, the other side has a huge advantage.

Reviewing this history, Judge Earl Johnson sarcastically wrote, "It is difficult to escape the conclusion that in the field of civil litigation California's indigents are entitled to the same in forma pauperis right as English serfs have enjoyed since medieval times and this right includes appointment of free counsel."[330]

He then compared California state law to the more recent federal law. The US Supreme Court finally construed the Sixth Amendment to create a constitutional right to free counsel for indigents in federal felony prosecutions. It took another twenty-five years before the Court applied this requirement to states.[331] He continued, "There can be little doubt but that in *both civil and criminal* cases the right to a hearing includes the *right to appear by counsel*, and that the arbitrary refusal of such right constitutes a deprivation of due process."[332]

Johnson concluded: "Denying the assistance of a free lawyer to indigent civil litigants invokes the suspect classification of poverty to deprive poor people of their fundamental interests in 'like access to the courts' and to a 'hearing where they have the assistance of counsel.'"

Johnson wrote that an indigent litigant—proceeding on his own (in *forma pauperis*)—should have counsel at both trials and appeals. He relied on California's due process and equal protection laws to make this argument. He criticized a system in which impoverished litigants—in this case with mental problems as well—"remain naked of legal assistance in California's civil courtrooms." Johnson cited *Massey v. Moore*[333] as authority for applying the United States and California common-law constitutional due process clause to civil as well as criminal cases. Not doing so, he wrote, "is tantamount to sanctioning legalized robbery-using the coercive power of the state to force defenseless people to surrender their property without a meaningful hearing."[334]

The first attempt to organize legal aid in civil matters for needy people was in 1876 in New York City. It provided legal assistance to poor immigrants from Germany. That program led to a Legal Aid Society in New York City for all poor people. Johnson traced the development of free legal aid in civil cases from those early experiments to the twenty-first century, considering both its successes and shortcomings.[335]

Led by Reginald Heber Smith, a Boston attorney, the organizing of free lawyers for poor people grew in other cities in America.[336] Bar associations contributed to the movement, as did law schools' clinics. But the impact was minimal, even if the model has expanded through the twentieth century into a national network of legal aid offices. Smith was a twenty-eight-year-old Boston aid lawyer who was so impressed with how this system worked there that he wrote a book about it called *Justice and the Poor*, published in

1919. It inspired former presidential candidate and future chief justice Charles Evans Hughes to make this issue the focus of the 1920 American Bar Association meeting, which resulted in the ABA voting to create a Committee on Legal Aid Work that year with Evans serving as the committee's first chair. The committee led the efforts to open legal aid societies across the country. [337]

Johnson wrote to me:

> With endorsement from the American Bar Association, by mid-century, there were 236 legal aid offices, most with unpaid staff members. Their budgets were less than 10% of what the country spent for private legal services; and at that 20% of the population was unable to afford lawyers. Those who did work for poor clients handled caseloads from 1000-2500 while private attorneys' caseloads were 50. Cases were rarely tried, and almost never appealed. Until 1962, only one case brought by any legal aid lawyer went to the U.S. Supreme Court.... In 1965, the year before OEO Legal Services Program began making federal grants for the legal aid, the combined budgets of all legal aid societies in the country totaled $5.3 million at a time when the legal profession was grossing billions of dollars ... legal aid's cut was less than one-tenth of a percent of what lawyers received for their services.

At that, there was a powerful undertow to this meager start. Many private donors balked at free legal services going to underwrite suits against local businesses, banks, landlords, and merchants. Equal justice for all was an empty bromide essentially unavailable for poor people needing legal services.

In the mid-1960s, under the leadership of President Lyndon Baines Johnson and Sargent Shriver, the OEO was created in a war against poverty in America (I was on the interagency task force that set it up), and the idea of an office of legal services was a notable part of it. President Lyndon Baines Johnson wrote in 1968, announcing the program:

> To a great many poor Americans, the law has long been an alien force—the ally of unscrupulous men who prey on their weaknesses and brutalize their rights as citizens. . . . The Legal Services Program was created to give the poor the same access to the protection of the law that more fortunate citizens have. It is more than a legal aid program. It is a weapon in our comprehensive attack on the root causes of poverty . . . . It is this enormous task that the American Bar and the Office of Economic Opportunity have undertaken these past three years. I commend you all for all you have done, and for what you have resolved to do. [338]

The idea of an office of legal services was not in the original plan. It was proposed to draftsmen of the act by former justice Arthur Goldberg and was rejected, but it did become part of the war on poverty. Yale Law School graduates Edgar and Jean Cahn wrote in an influential *Yale Law Journal* article about the need for legal services. That article came to Shriver's attention and led to its adoption as a part of the historic programs. [339]

The Cahn's negotiated on behalf of OEO with the ABA, and under the leadership of its then president, future Supreme Court justice Lewis Powell, the ABA unanimously endorsed the creation of the OEO Legal Services Program. In its first seven years, lawyers employed by OEO funded legal services programs argued 110 cases in the US Supreme Court and won 64 percent of them, while in the entire history of charitably funded legal aid, only one case had made it to the US Supreme Court before then.

The OEO spread offices around the country, not without constant political controversy, but with ABA and community action and law school encouragement. From 1965 to 1971, it became for some young lawyers a mission, not a career, as Earl Johnson has chronicled. But its critics were powerful, arguing ominously that the legal profession would become socialized and that a federal dictatorship over legal assistance would result. Sound familiar, doctors?

As the evolution proceeded, participants argued over the goal of the movement. Should the focus be on handling as many individual cases as possible, or trying to bring about systemic changes through class actions, appellate litigation, legislation, and administrative rule making? Of course, there was a need for both but resources were limited. Public-interest programs blossomed during this relatively brief period, and the accomplishments of legal services programs were impressive, working with tenants organizations, social welfare programs, and farmworkers. [340]

Setbacks came in the Nixon and Reagan administrations. Politics had changed, and the idea of the government paying lawyers to sue institutions and governments themselves was challenged. Test cases led to developments of civil rights, which the Warren Court recognized as "fundamental interests" that the states could not deny classes of people. [341] A key case involved poor individuals who couldn't get welfare because they hadn't lived in the state the minimum time to be eligible—typically a year, but in some states six months.

Most public interest programs that blossomed were funded by OEO, although some that emphasized middle-class issues were funded by foundations. That history is fully developed in Johnson's three books. [342]

While legal services for the poor offices were busy all over the United States, the national political temperature was changing, and politics played a growing negative role in frustrating the energetic, high-minded young lawyers who were making waves of reform and providing meaningful legal assistance to poor people for the first

time. Advocacy on behalf of the Legal Services Corporation, arguing that underrepresented parties in civil proceedings were denied
equal protection of the law, fell on too many deaf ears.[343]

In early 1971, an ABA study group recommended creation
of an independent nonprofit corporation similar to the Corporation for Public Broadcasting that had started a year or two before.
Meanwhile, the Nixon administration had decided to apply the
same solution. What emerged was a Legal Services Corporation
(LSC) bill that was closer to the version the ABA backed than the
administration version, and Nixon vetoed it. But finally, in 1974,
Congress passed a compromise version, and in July 1974, two weeks
before resigning the presidency, Nixon signed the Legal Services
Corporation Act of 1974. It took a year for LSC to be organized
and begin operations. During President Gerald Ford's administration, the corporation made its first grants.

But its glory years came during Jimmy Carter's tenure, when its
appropriation reached $321 million (the equivalent of over $1.1 billion
in 2019 after correcting for inflation and a 25 percent increase in the
poverty population since 1981). The key to this dramatic expansion
of funding was the LSC's so-called "minimum access" strategy, which
allocated most of its funds based on the numbers of poor people in
the county or counties served by a given LSC-funded program. This
meant some funding went to every congressional district in the land
and thus increased congressional support for a larger LSC budget.

LSC funding has decreased by two-thirds since that FY 1981
peak. But some of that difference has been made up by state government funding in some states, along with *Interest on Lawyers
Trust Accounts* (IOLTA) funding and some targeted federal funding from other federal agencies—for domestic violence—and more
generous private donations from large law firms and foundations.
Notably, the state government funding and the more generous private donations have been concentrated in relatively few states, with

New York leading the way. The DC government and law firms have been generous on a per capita basis. But many state governments and law firms haven't appropriated anything. As a result, in those states, LSC remains virtually the only source of legal aid funding. This is especially true in the South and much of the non-industrial Midwest. A recent head of Legal Services Corporation, James J. Sandman compared a recent LSC budget $385 million, with how much Americans spent annually that year on their pets' Halloween costumes, $74.34 per person, in 2015, totaling $350 million.[344]

One anecdote makes the point about the political undertow LSC faces. When Berkley, California, state legislator Bill Bagley was made chairman of the California Assembly Judiciary Committee, he retained me to devise and present to his committee an omnibus law reform bill for California. My colleagues and I traveled around the state talking to professors, politicians, legal services lawyers, and other folks who were involved in state legal affairs. My assistant went to Governor Ronald Reagan's office to discuss our work and seek comments. His executive assistant told her: "You tell Goldfarb if he wants to reform the California justice system, he should do two things: cancel legal service lawyer organizations and abolish habeas corpus." Not everyone was happy with reform.

HOW DOES THE SYSTEM WORK?

Stanford Law School professor Deborah Rhode has pointed out that "we are over-lawyered and under-represented and what passes for justice in the justice system falls far short of aspirations." She reports that in the United States, "over 4/5 of the legal needs of the poor are unmet and half of the legal needs of people of modest means are estimated to be unmet."[345]

To our shame, the United States lags behind most developed countries in providing civil legal aid, "tied for 99th in terms of access and affordability of civil justice." As a result, in 75 percent of the cases that come into civil justice state courts, one or both parties is not represented. And this figure does not include transactional, non-court work, where legal representation is less.

One study concluded:

> An indigent seeking legal counsel must begin his search through either private legal aid or some form of public legal service. Only if this fails should he be permitted to request counsel from the private bar. It has become almost accepted fact that neither private legal aid, depending as it must upon charitable contributions, nor legal assistance programs, such as those under the federal Economic Opportunity Act, are capable of administering to the requests from poor persons for assistance in litigating civil matters. Despite the current flood of lawyers being graduated by law schools throughout the country, the demand for legal aid to indigents still continues to exceed the available supply. The consequences of this shortage are apparent.[346]

The Stein report continued,

> First, the number of cases that must be handled by the available attorneys is excessive, with the result that the time available for the preparation of individual cases is lessened. The attorney faced with this predicament may have no choice but to compromise the case of one client for another. Any attempt to strike a balance among cases is made all the more difficult by the uncertain nature of judicial proceedings in general. Much time must initially be spent on a particular matter before the attorney can even conjecture the amount of time that must ultimately be devoted to it.[347]

The second consequence concerns selection among the different classes of cases. To illustrate, most of the civil litigation embarked upon by poor persons is in the area of domestic relations. Yet many legal aid programs have selectively chosen to refuse to provide counsel for divorce actions because of the lack of available attorneys. "In fact, it has recently been held to be an abuse of discretion for a court to appoint an attorney when the particular legal assistance program involved has objected to such assignment because of certain limitations on the program's authority to render legal aid."[348]

As is true with all issues, the politics of legal services has suffered from political ups and downs. But legal services are a constitutional right, explicitly in criminal cases and by implication in civil cases.

As Judge Johnson described in his authoritative collection, from 1965 to 1981, when OEO came into being and replaced private donations as the chief source of funding legal services, expenditures jumped from $5.4 million to $321 million under LSC—only 1.4 percent of what was spent nationally on lawyers. US civil legal aid was funded by less than 7/1,000 of our GDP in 2012, less than a half of a percent of our national expenditures on lawyers.

IOLTA programs by bar associations that fund legal services and pro bono volunteerism by law firms grew (over 2.5 million hours in services to low-income clients). But the 6,500 civil legal aid lawyers represented 6/10 of a percent of the nation's 1.1 million lawyers, while serving 20 to 33 percent of the nation's population.

Judge Johnson pointed out that two large civil law firms received $2 billion in legal fees recently to serve their clients, twice as much as all legal aid needs of 64 million people! "The bottom 20% of the population gets 3.4% of the nation's income, but only a half percent of its legal resources."[349] Two firms earned over $3 billion, nine earned from $2 to $2.9 billion, and nineteen earned from $1 to $1.9 billion. And all or nearly all of these mega-firms have numerous offices in cities around the country and often around the world—many with thirty offices or more.

When I entered the profession, a firm with fifty lawyers was considered a big law firm. And virtually all of them were local law firms with one office in one city. If a client needed a lawyer in another city, the local firm would farm out that work to a firm in that other city. Over the years, however, many firms expanded by opening offices in other cities—becoming national and in many cases international firms.

The practice of law became more of a business and less of a profession, as critics had feared. Clint Bamberger, the first director of Legal Services Program within the Office of Economic Opportunity (OEO-LSP), was recruited for that position while he was a partner at Piper and Marbury, a successful, modest sized firm in Baltimore. When he joined the firm as a new associate, he was the thirteenth lawyer in the firm. When he left to take the OEO job, the firm still had fewer than thirty lawyers, all of them in Baltimore. The firm, now known as DLA Piper, has some three thousand lawyers and more than thirty offices all over the United States and in several foreign countries. [350]

Johnson continued,

> Ignoring competition from other societal priorities, it is apparent that by comparison to other jurisdictions from which we have data, the U.S. justice system is out of balance—failing to allocate nearly as much of its total justice system resources to subsidizing counsel for those who cannot afford their own in civil cases as our fellow common law countries do. [351]

In his third volume, Justice Johnson suggested "promising developments to improve our civil justice system." [352] He described how some courts adjudicate some disputes (family court matters, for example) without lawyers, more like the inquisitorial systems where judges have a significant, active control of court proceedings by offering forms of self-help when parties don't have lawyers. Lay advocates are cost-effective and are used in welfare hearings and in mediation before trials. Through evolving technologies—computerized kiosks, e-filings, internet assistance—governments provide help to citizens and lay parties on common matters like will probate, that enables working through the court system without lawyers.

Last, Johnson suggested that class actions and legislation can help initiate systemic changes, though modern law does not find such work to address common problems such as domestic violence, housing, consumer problems, and child custody.

As I will recommend in my conclusion, rulings by high courts in our state and federal systems could solve the problem by assuring the right to counsel as an inherent part of the right to trials. Rights without lawyers to enforce them are ideas, not realities. In order to provide adequate legal assistance to indigent civil litigants, the courts must go beyond the existing private and public legal aid programs and turn to the private bar for some relief. But, as a critic wrote: "While this may seem to be a simple solution to a difficult dilemma, there is a multitude of problems that must be resolved before such a practice can be put into operation, not the least of which is the problem of compensation."[353]

According to law professors Benjamin H. Barton and Stephanos Bibas, our civil legal system needs rebooting. "In a country built on justice for all and the rule of law, we have created a legal system so expensive and unwieldy that most Americans cannot afford it."[354] This observation of the realities of our justice system applies to civil as well as criminal cases—in trials and transactional office assistance. Still, no one has the constitutional right to counsel in civil cases,[355] under either the due process of law or equal protection of the law's provisions. Yet.

Though the Seventh Amendment assures a jury trial in civil cases, but not legal assistance, no state constitution provides funded legal assistance for indigents in civil cases. There are public and private agencies that do provide legal assistance in civil cases, but they are inadequately financed and oversubscribed, or focus exclusively on specific categories of litigants—veterans, elderly, disabled, etc.[356]

An outgrowth of President Lyndon Johnson's war on poverty, the LSC currently funds 132 programs. States and local governments fund programs, as do private organizations and foundations, bar associations, and law schools. Litigants can search for programmatic assistance on hotlines and websites. But these programs are scattered, not coordinated, and inadequately funded.

Bottom line: potential low-income litigants in civil matters—trials or general practice—are often not represented. There is for them a chasmic justice gap.[357]

A 2013 study of legal aid in the United States concluded,

> [T]he basic legal aid system has not closed the justice gap ...
> there are not enough active staff lawyers, paralegals, lay advocates,
> law students, and private attorneys available to meet the huge
> needs of low-income persons for on-line, brief service and full
> representation.[358]

There are deep but different moral-ethical problems in cases where lawyers are employed by wealthy clients. On the civil side, many controversial cases arise in the lucrative practice of corporate law, as inside counsel, or in private practice centered on counseling corporations. Two recent books made the point that corporations and their officials rarely are charged for crimes, though the offenses some commit are far more damaging to society than some crimes that individuals commit and for which they are imprisoned.[359] Corporations are fined, hurting innocent stockholders, while corporate wrongdoers are often safely steered through the criminal-law minefields by their well-paid lawyers.

A broader question about cultural distinctions arises in civil cases.[360] I wrote of one incident quite telling of the incestuous culture of lawyers in and out of government in a *New York Times* op-ed[361] about a high Justice Department official and a well-known lawyer lunching at a private Washington, DC, club. A lawyer who overheard the dialogue shared that they were there to discuss the government attorney's future plans when he left government, and incidentally, about that pending antitrust case against his host's client. The incident reminds me of the facetious song, "We met in the revolving door, and we've been going around ever since."

CONFIDENTIALITY AND NONDISCLOSURE AGREEMENTS

Confidentiality issues are another area that is particularly prejudicial to poor people because they usually do not have the assistance of lawyers in these situations. Akin to the attorney-client confidentiality privilege's general applications is the frequent reliance on confidentiality agreements in civil settlements where lawyers, blessed by judges, make it a condition of a civil settlement that the matter in question be held secret, thus avoiding responsibility while permitting comparable accidents to reoccur. Usually the sued party is wealthy and well represented. Often the opposite is true of the complainants, like altar boys in church cases or women in workplaces molested by superiors in sexual harassment cases. But times have changed. The subject arose in a 2020 Democratic candidates debate concerning former New York City Mayor Michael Bloomberg.

Confidentiality agreements have surfaced in recent years in the notorious sexual harassment cases that have been widely covered in the press where the harasser has continued to violate women long after a settlement has been reached. In cases involving powerful men, entertainers, movie and TV network stars, the alternative of open and honest litigation in a public courtroom would have been a more effective deterrent than a secret financial settlement. The leverage of money for litigation usually tilts the scale of justice.

Critics have asked why courts are complicit in secrecy agreements that shield perpetrators and enhance the likelihood of more victims. Some courts now refuse to facilitate these agreements. The essential point is that courts are public institutions and the public is entitled to know what goes on in them, especially when wrongful conduct is involved in a case and knowledge of it may provide a deterrent to future repeated misbehavior. If case resolutions pertain to matters that affect more than the litigants, those matters should be exposed. They won't be if both sides of any negotiation are not represented by lawyers.

A standard clause lawyers add in most settlements of civil disputes states that the parties agree to maintain the confidentiality of the terms of the settlement. Court records are sealed, and the parties are gagged. However logical it may be to sanction such practices that benefit a litigant, doing so raises troubling questions of public policy. Should courts allow the parties to hush facts about people or things that endanger others?

Without such confidentiality agreements, the argument goes, parties sued would lose a crucial reason for settling cases, and the judicial system would lose a way to reduce the volume of litigation. When the pop entertainer Michael Jackson was indicted (he was ultimately acquitted) for child molestation in California in 2002, his earlier settlement of a civil suit involving comparable charges was leaked to the press. Jackson cried foul; that 1993 settlement contained a confidentiality agreement. Jackson claimed that avoiding negative publicity was a major reason for his willingness to agree to the multimillion-dollar settlement.

People who agree to settlements to avoid negative publicity understandably share Jackson's feeling of betrayal. But is it good law in cases that involve child abuse and/or rape? Does the public deserve

protection from serial predators? Isn't publicity as a deterrent the justification for sex offender registrations published on the internet?

As common as confidentiality and non-disparagement agreements are, their social utility is debatable. One writer concluded that
the dearth of insightful information about the quality of civil justice
is due to the ubiquity of civil settlement agreements in courts and
in mediation, which typically contain confidentiality clauses.[362] This
problem is not limited to salacious sex and celebrity cases. Confidentiality clauses are also used to hide corporate malfeasance and
white-collar crime.

Proponents of confidentiality agreements point out that they
foster settlements, which cut the litigants' costs, as well as the public
costs, of the trial process. Secrecy facilitates compromise: "[T]he
lubricating effects of the protective order . . . would be lost if [it]
expired by the end of the case."[363] Frivolous (baseless but embarrassing) and time consuming and expensive to win nuisance claims
common to all professions can be bought off for the price of secrecy.

The counterargument is that these confidentiality agreements
allow public misconduct to go undetected, allowing the improper
conduct to be repeated. When a highly ranked professional tennis
player from Argentina, Guillermo Coria, tested positive for steroid
use, he was suspended from the pro circuit for two years, but on
appeal his suspension was reduced to seven months.[364] He lost
two seasons of potential prize money, endorsements, and appearance fees, worth millions, he claimed, in addition to being labeled a
cheater. He said that the supplement he used was contaminated and
sued the manufacturer. Terms of the settlement were not released.
Nor were the settlement terms of a similar suit by a swimmer. The
public remained uninformed. Who was really responsible in general—the supplement manufacturer or the athlete?

Similar lawsuits relating to allegedly steroid-laced vitamins and
supplements have been settled through nondisclosure agreements

(NDAs) in a spectrum of sports. In 2012, former Phillies pitcher J. C. Romero settled with a number of drug manufacturers, including GNC, over a positive drug test that had resulted in a fifty-game suspension.[365] Such drug-related settlements occur globally. In 2015, two Jamaican sprinters, Asafa Powell and Sherone Simpson, settled their own lawsuits against a drug company whose supplement allegedly was the cause of their failed drug tests.[366] Neither Romero's nor Powell's and Simpson's settlements were disclosed. When such cases are settled with secret agreements, others similarly situated had no idea of potential problems they might avoid if the findings were public.

The public has an interest in full and open adjudication when private disputes have important public implications—exposing safety problems, medical malpractice, product defects, human and civil rights violations, or government misconduct, for example. When cases involve more than private wrongdoing, the public has no way of preventing repetition of such conduct if the result of the case is hidden. Courts can perform public watchdog roles in such instances by insisting on making the facts of these settlements a matter of public record.

Yale law professor Owen Fiss is cynical about the public consequences of confidential settlements. He calls them "a capitulation to the conditions of mass society" that encourage private parties to "settle while leaving justice undone."[367] When that happens, he points out, "society gets less than what appears, and for a price it does not know it is paying."[368] In civil rights cases, such settlements "might secure the peace, but not racial equality."[369] Community peace is not the same as justice. "To settle for something means to accept something less than ideal."

In environmental disputes, confidential settlements may mask the true cost to society, allowing polluters to settle without alerting nonparties whose health and well-being is affected, shielding producers of harmful products from public scrutiny, and allowing repeat offenders to avoid adverse precedents against them. The bigger the business interest, greater may be the need for confidentiality, and also greater may be the corresponding need for public disclosure.

A related problem arises from the concealment of judicial decisions by judges and court officials. In April 2007, the Florida Supreme Court adopted a rule forbidding court insiders from secreting dispositions from public scrutiny. Under a common practice, judges, lawyers, politicians, and businesspeople regularly concealed files and records of sensitive cases—"super-sealing," it was called. Under the new rule, openness replaced secrecy unless litigants demonstrated a legitimate reason for shielding information (for example, to protect trade secrets or avoid identifying confidential informants).

There may also be private reasons for disclosing settlements. An attorney who represented many victims of sexual abuse by church officials refused to muzzle his clients. "The victims were entitled to talk to who they wanted to," he wrote to me, "as part of the healing process." He added, "Confidentiality agreements for victims of sexual abuse can become very traumatic after the fact. Almost invariably, the victim at some point begins to feel that the defendants . . . bought their silence and [victims] beat themselves up severely . . . I resist confidentiality."[370]

The use of confidentiality agreements in settlements is governed by court rules or statute, or is left to the discretion of judges. About a dozen states—including Florida, North Carolina, Oregon, Texas, and Rhode Island—have "sunshine in litigation" rules requiring the publication of settlements unless there is an overriding demonstrated public interest in secrecy. Some states forbid confidentiality clauses in cases involving public officials.

There is a discernable trend—judicial and legislative—toward disapproving secret settlements. The South Carolina Supreme

Court, for example, amended its court rules to require a balancing of public and private interests before courts approve secret settlements. Judges are required to consider the public harm caused by keeping settlements secret and the public interest in open settlements. And "under no circumstances shall a court approve sealing a settlement agreement which involves a public body or institution."[371]

Several federal circuit courts have articulated the policies behind disclosure of settlement agreements. They have noted the "presumptive common-law right of access to court documents,"[372] the need for public access to court records, the public interest in court matters. It is the secondary nature of the private litigants' interests in settlements involving public issues, and the need to protect the integrity of the judicial process by not allowing courts to be implicated in keeping public information hidden.

Recent cases have decreed that the public's right to know should outweigh the private parties' interest in secrecy for personal or business reasons when public interests are involved. When settlements are kept secret, the public is deprived of a valuable asset. Duplicate litigation is necessitated. To require repetitive litigation is economically inefficient and in cases where public interests are involved can be a hazard to public health and safety. Secrecy can conceal corruption and should not be sanctioned by courts unless strong reasons require it. Secret settlements are unethical and dangerous to the public.

Compromise should not be difficult. In cases involving trade secrets or personal intimacies, there are clear reasons to protect secrecy. In false charges that most doctors and attorneys face and settle solely and reluctantly to be rid of the nuisance, expense and public aggravation, secrecy is the only reason for settling. On the other hand, in commercial cases involving public misconduct, secret settlements are mischievous and against the public interest, amounting to no more than hush money.

When the US Senate passed the $2 trillion CARES ACT, corona virus stimulus bill in March 2020 (which passed 96-0), the capital was awash with lobbyists advancing the First Amendment rights of businesses to redress their grievances before legislators who were there to represent the public which had only them to advance them.

One expert concluded that "courts should accommodate the various competing interests, both public and private, in determining whether and when to override the litigants' mutual desire or need for privacy and the strong, institutional policy favoring settlement."[373]

Because most cases are settled, often the administration of justice is carried out quasi-privately regardless of the public interest involved. These situations generally are followed by litigants with lawyers; they are not always used by unrepresented civil complainants. The impact of secret justice can be profound. A case-by-case, issue-by-issue balancing approach would weigh the need for public monitoring of the judicial system and its core adjudicative product against the competing value of private and confidential settlements. But many settlements are conducted before trial in courts—and for that reason.

Until there is a uniform balanced policy, well-paid private lawyers will exploit secrecy agreements, rationalizing them on the basis of their duty to their client and ignoring the public ramifications that result. Critics point out that litigation is not for the litigants alone and courts are publicly funded and have a public role.[374]

There is real conflict between the duty of plaintiffs' lawyers to their clients and the duty many lawyers would feel to assure that an unsafe product does not continue on the market. That kind of conflict must be resolved in favor of the client unless there is a supervening rule of law that not only allows but encourages lawyers to do what is their public duty.[375]

As public interest lawyer and law professor Alan Morrison has written: "The public interest lies elsewhere than in secrecy when public safety is at stake."[376]

SECRECY AND THE CATHOLIC CHURCH

The classic example of anti-public results from secrecy is the thousands of cases the Catholic Church has settled. The church's protecting their offending clergy through secret settlements not only prejudiced young congregants and their families but also led to other church members being molested by the same offenders.[377] Hidden misconduct often leads to repeated offenses, just as hidden defects in a product may damage others using the same product. All institutions, public or corporate, worry more about their institution than the people the institution is created to serve. Should lawyers in these historically one-sided negotiations who use secrecy agreements to settle cases that risk future public harm be considered complicit with their clients for subsequent injuries to the public?

This issue raises a church-state conflict, where ironically the state fills the high moral ground. It is an article of faith in the Catholic religion that confessions are sacrosanct requirements for the confessor's salvation. Priests would be subject to excommunication and disgrace, to eternal damnation, if they were to reveal confessions. The clergy privilege covers members of the clergy who have a religious duty to keep confessions secret.

The sanctity of confession is based on the notion that confession soothes "the torments of a wounded conscience" and that it would be iniquitous to fail to protect the confidentiality of the confessional. The assistance to justice that might be lost by protecting confidentiality would be minimal, whereas the conflicts caused by violating this trust would be harmful to practitioners of their faith. Confessions may prevent mischief rather than hide it, advocates of privilege point out. Even the prominent opponent of privileges, the influential legal philosopher Jeremy Bentham, argued that it would be an unjust persecution to punish Catholics for following their religion's essential dictates.[378]

According to Catholic dogma, what a priest knows from confession, he knows as a "representative of God, and not through human knowledge," that he is detached from it "as if he knows nothing." In the view of the Catholic Church, that information is beyond the control of the temporal courts.[379]

One high-ranking Catholic Church official remarked that "the good of religion prevails over the good of justice."[380] Priests are subject to an inviolable sacramental seal of silence. But what is the responsibility of church lawyers who shield these injustices by frustrating exposure and using nondisclosure agreements to keep the church secrets that endanger church members? Shouldn't our duty as lawyers be defined by the state supersede church rules of secrecy?

Courts have followed the Wigmorean approach in judging when confidential communications between clergy and their parishioners is privileged. Wigmore's four criteria for permitting the privilege are (1) that the communication originated in confidence; (2) that confidentiality is essential to the religion; (3) that the community fosters that relationship; and (4) that, on balance, the injury to the relationship caused by disclosure would be greater than any benefit to the litigation. It is this fourth criterion that raises a question about the appropriateness of an absolute privilege to protect all priestly confessions.

Most states now have statutes sanctioning the privilege for confessions of sins to religious ministers (of all faiths). The extensive and dramatic litigation against the Catholic Church for predatory behavior by priests, particularly sexual crimes against children, reveals the awful abuse of that privilege.

The morality and wisdom of church confidentiality rules aside, courts and legislatures now mandate exceptions in cases involving crimes. Historically, the church protected the institution and its priests from charges of misconduct by fighting claims, moving offensive priests to different places, and demanding confidentiality agreements where claims were settled and victims and their families were paid. Surely the lawyers representing the church in these cases were aware that protecting the offending priests was equivalent to releasing a moral virus on the playground.

After centuries of nondisclosures, the dike broke late in the twentieth century. Then, the Catholic Church was forced to settle three thousand civil cases around the country regarding known patterns of abuse, usually settling the complaints confidentially. More than thirteen thousand minors were known to have been abused by priests; three hundred priests were convicted of crimes, and one thousand were severed from the ministry. Litigation revealed that the church's sins had been long concealed.[381] Still, abuses by Catholic priests have steadily continued. More than one thousand children have been so abused in Pennsylvania alone, according to a 2018 grand jury report.[382]

When the Catholic Church set up a panel to look into its far-flung and historic sexual-abuse scandal, bishops refused to provide requested information. The panel chairman resigned, stating that the clergy "turned to their lawyers when they should have looked into their hearts."[383]

In recent decades, the Roman Catholic Church in the United States has paid more than $2.6 billion to thousands of victims of predatory priests, causing some archdioceses to go bankrupt and sell their property. The Boston archdiocese paid $85 million to settle more than 550 claims; the Los Angeles diocese paid $650 million to settle 500 claims. In San Diego, the diocese paid 144 people nearly $200 million for sexual molestations of children occurring between 1938 and 1993.[384]

While all these disclosures were revealed early in the twenty-first century, painfully, slowly, and reluctantly, the problem persisted. A Bridgeport, Connecticut, high church official Archbishop William Lori fought a seven-year battle while in West Virginia "to keep secret thousands of pages of court documents" from lawsuits accusing local priests of abuse. The accused official told the press that the public was not interested "about what happened in the past, tragic and reprehensible as that was." An investigation concluded "the coverups have been facilitated by our acquiescence to a culture of clericalism that has pervaded our Church."[385]

In Greenwood, Mississippi, in 2019, Franciscan priests paid $15,000 to two poor black men who were assaulted as children by priests at their school. "We don't have lawyers. We felt we had to take what we could," one survivor stated, though the traumatic events scarred their lives.[386] They agreed to a confidential nondisclosure agreement. An earlier claim in 2006 in Jackson, Mississippi, settled for $250,000, and others elsewhere (St. Paul, Minnesota, for example) for $500,000 a claim. The AP report stated that the American church "continues efforts to limit fallout and keep sexual abuse under wraps," despite a 2002 American Council of Bishops charter outlawing nondisclosure agreements. "The lawyers put it in there," a church official claimed. The devil made me do it, he might have added. In the Santa Barbara and Los Angeles dioceses in 2006, twenty-two victims were paid an average of $1.3 million.

A major investigation in 2018 by a team of AP reporters[387] disclosed that after the exposes and the initial wave of clergy abuse settlements early in the twenty-first century, their research found 1,700 priests and other Catholic clergy who eluded supervision or punishment by law enforcement officials or church authorities. These 2018 disclosures came after 5,100 clergy were identified as offenders. In state after state, exposure of predatory priests continued: one thousand children in six dioceses in Pennsylvania alone, according to one grand jury report. These sheltered offenders continued to work in schools and childcare centers, "ticking bombs" under the radar that inevitably exploded. The institution continues to protect itself over its followers.

Despite public exposure, the problem persists, most recently in Colorado. After decades of international revelations, state study commissions, and church payoffs to revealed victims, on October 23, 2019, the *New York Times* reported that a state attorney general investigation disclosed that 166 children had been abused by 43 priests, incidents that had been hidden for decades. That didn't include misconduct with adults, church personnel, religious sisters, or seminary students. The reason for this late revelation: "A strong culture of reluctance" that would harm the "reputation of the Church or a fellow priest."[388]

In November 2019, "AP interviews with more than a dozen lawyers and clergy abuse watchdog groups offered a wide range of estimates but many said they expected at least 5,000 new cases against the church in New York, New Jersey and California alone, resulting in potential payouts that could surpass the $4 billion paid out since the clergy sex abuse first came to light in the 1980s."[389]

The Vatican recently abolished its high-level secrecy policy that shielded priests, including the cloak of confidentiality, leaving the church "no longer a hiding place." Hereafter, having altered its policy of pontifical secrecy, abuse cases will be reported to civil authorities. However, guilty priests are still allowed to remain in the ministry.[390]

The clergy privilege is interdenominational and applies to all clergy, rabbis, imams, and established Christian ministries. Even lay associates of religious clergy—a Muslim brother acting as a spiritual adviser, nuns, jailhouse "reverends" in some cases—occasionally have been covered by the privilege if they are acting for recognized religious officials and offering sacramental guidance.[391] But if the executive privilege relents for the president of the United States in situations involving misconduct and the public need for access to otherwise privileged information, as it did in the Nixon tapes case, how dare it not when the privilege claim is based on a church's doctrines?

CONFIDENTIALITY AND SEXUAL HARASSMENT

Perhaps the notorious stories of repressed settlements of sexual harassment claims will lead to changes. Reported use of public money by state and federal legislators to settle cases against them and stifle complaints should lead to systemic reforms to deter the disgraces that have been publicized. Trickier is the question about the use of confidential settlements, and the propriety of claimants taking the money and then violating the secrecy they promised in return for their private, often luxurious, payments.

The *TIME* Magazine Person of the Year 2017 was, instead of one individual, the "Silence Breakers," noting the many women who spoke out about their experiences of being sexually harassed. Openly or anonymously, some under the hashtag #MeToo, the women publicized the details of their complaints.[392] Some had signed non-disparagement, confidentiality, and nondisclosure agreements required in many industries and businesses. The moral consideration regarding the need to speak out and deter further misconduct after receiving compensation predicated on silencing these complaints is a conundrum policy makers will be addressing as reform measures are debated and designed.

News stories reporting the Harvey Weinstein saga told of famous, well-regarded trial lawyers advising Weinstein employees that their complaints could lead to tough private investigations that would seek embarrassing information about them.[393] If accusers were muffled by such tactics, then Weinstein would not be held accountable for his many sexual assaults—as was the case until the outbreak of the "Me Too" movement.

Eventually the seal of secrecy was broken, and while the public applauded the exposure of Weinstein's wrongdoing, we are left wondering about the future ground rules for confidentiality agreements, which are common and can be useful ways for contesting parties to avoid the vagaries of the trial system. The most notorious example of the potential impact was the current president's challenge by a woman who claimed she earlier had sex with him, was paid to be silent about it, and signed a nondisclosure agreement that her lawyer tried to circumvent.

Recent articles reported how the #MeToo movement surged for a while, then met "a crackling backlash."[394] Hundreds of prominent men lost their jobs after public allegations of sexual harassment, as did many major media stars and well-known government and entertainment celebrities.[395] If an alleged wrongdoer pays a claimant and demands a secrecy agreement to protect his marriage, for example, is it fair to take the money and breach the NDA?

An example of possible overkill is the forced resignation of Senator Al Franken over complaints from a senate colleague for what many thought was juvenile fun-making and not sexual harassment, like one recent president bragged about doing. Indeed, one New York City lawyer has had great success defending male clients who denied charges of misconduct. He described the feminist movement as unfair because "firms are shooting people without doing a fulsome investigation."[396]

The common ingredient in all these cases is whether the accuser is represented in the negotiated settlement—usually lawyers negotiate these agreements for corporate or celebrity parties.

ETHICS IN THE PRACTICE OF LAW

In his introduction to Mark Green's *The Other Government: The Unseen Power of Washington Lawyers*, consumer crusader Ralph Nader wrote, "What is at issue is not the right of corporations to counsel but the duty of outside counsel to independently and professionally decline to serve a nefarious cause."[397] And I would add, not to rationalize one's method of representation by arguing that the ethics rules demand it. The issue has roiled media as well as other businesses, as continuing exposes have shown.

LOBBYING

Corporate lawyer-lobbyists fighting to keep their clients' hazardous products on the market and unregulated is another practice that needs to be addressed.[398] Every reformative proposed law releases cadres of well-paid lawyers leading the battle to frustrate passage. Indeed, the term "Washington Lawyer" has come to describe a post-New Deal breed of legal work, much as local lawyers as lobbyists pursue city and state government members on behalf of privileged clients. While legislators are supposed to be representing the public, some of these corporate lobbying lawyers have claimed a First Amendment right to seek redress of their clients' grievance via legislation. Lobbyists inundate legislators with their clients' causes in effective ways that the public cannot match.

Lawyers turned lobbyists are another breed of lawyer. In Mark Leibovich's book *This Town*, he stated, "Now 50 percent of senators and 42 percent of congressmen" become lobbyists upon leaving office. One of Leibovich's examples is lawyer and lawmaker Dick Gephardt, who switched his support for the Armenians while he was in Congress to the Turks when he left public office, and became a lobbyist "to work on i$$ues he was pa$$ionate about." A generous monthly stipend changes one's view of genocide, Leibovich posited.[399]

Again, the late justice Harlan Stone's words resonate on this question of lawyer ethics. Big business, he wrote, "made the learned profession of an earlier day the obsequious servant of business, and tainted it with the morals and manners of the marketplace in its most anti-social manifestations."[400]

These cases raise questions about the majoritarian view among lawyers that everyone is entitled to a lawyer, therefore lawyers are not to be judged by the views or actions of their clients. We are not supposed to sit in judgment of the people who come to our offices to seek legal advice. But accepting or rejecting clients and cases is not governed solely by legal strictures. These decisions are *personal* choices.

Lawyers' responsibilities are *not* the same as those of doctors. Medical ethics relieve doctors of being associated with their patients. They may operate on a criminal or treat a political enemy without being associated with those patients. The majoritarian view compares lawyers and doctors: "Zealous advocacy requires subordinating all other interests—ideological, career, personal—to the legitimate interest of the client. You are the surgeon in the operating room whose only goal is to save the patient, whether the patient is a good person or a bad person, a saint or a criminal."[401]

I disagree with the comparison. Doctors have different professional guidelines, and saving the patient in surgery—like him or not—is not the same as serving a questionable client in court on a mercantile matter. Physicians are guided by professional rules that instruct them to treat all patients equally, without making moral judgments about them. But even that proposition is not absolute. Some doctors do not treat patients if they don't have the right insurance, and this is an economic door, not a professional one to which they keep the key.

The late Dr. Arnold Gold, a noted pediatric neurologist, remarked, "You're only half a physician if you're just good at your craft. Unless it's coupled with patient centered care and humanism, its suboptimal care."[402] Dr. Gold had a humanistic approach to the Hippocratic Oath that doctors swear by, as I would think good lawyers should have in interpreting our professional guidelines governing the practice of our profession. Our professional rules are not meant, surely shouldn't be meant, to provide cover to morally repugnant behavior.[403]

How we balance a modern doctor's right to deny treatment and a patient's right to receive it is not so black and white as the public believes. Patients may refuse treatment and doctors may refuse to provide it. One cardiologist reminded doctors that the American Medical Association's code of ethics requires them "to place patients' welfare above the physician's own self-interest."[404] It also allows doctors "considerable latitude to practice in accord with well-considered, deeply held beliefs that are central to their self-identities."[405] Federal law permits doctors to opt out of care that is incompatible with their religious or moral beliefs ... but not when self-determination (AIDS cases, for example) is a cover for rank prejudice. The Thirteenth Amendment to the Constitution does prohibit involuntary servitude.[406]

A *New York Times* columnist recently shamed Trump attorney and "fixer" Michael Cohen for his past actions, adding, "An uncle provided medical services to the Luchese family." Unless his uncle was aiding their criminal acts, it was not misconduct to provide medical services to them, though I would argue that legally representing a "crime family"—depending on the nature and extent of that representation—may well say something about a lawyer's reputation.[407] Is the doctor or lawyer an employee of a criminal enterprise?

I conducted a panel on this question on a public television show, *Devil's Advocate* (WETA), that I hosted years ago. I invited successful Washington trial lawyers to argue the case against my point of view that was, and remains, that clients should have equal access to legal representation but they are not entitled to any specific lawyer. They may ask, but we lawyers may accept or reject their requests on personal, political, or ideological grounds (so long as one's rejection does not discriminate against a protected class—like gender or race). All of us choose whether to represent our clients and their causes. One of the panelists—later a TV "pundit"—cynically criticized my notion, saying, "You *shoulda'* gone to medical school."

It is a respected business practice of a majority of lawyers who represent objectionable clients that "the constitutional right to representation" is the proper professional ethic. But that right does not bind an attorney in making his or her personal choices. No one believed that ACLU lawyers advocating on First Amendment grounds that Nazis should have the right to march in Skokie, Illinois, meant the ACLU was a Nazi front. Despite the outrage from some of their supporters, the ACLU lawyers were raising an important constitutional point. Public commentary is not limited to agreeable people.

I don't think I should have gone to medical school. I think that while lawyers may choose who they represent, and may choose what they do when they represent them, they can't be surprised if they are chastised or characterized negatively for their choices and their behavior in exercising their choices. We all are, to one important extent, what we do. I am not claiming that there are agreed-upon client candidacy tests that all lawyers apply and must follow and all clients must pass before acceptance. But I do think there are personal standards each lawyer must adopt *for themselves* in deciding which people and issues they decide to represent and how far this representation goes before it is deemed beyond the required duties of lawyer advocacy. This is a different question than why poor potential clients are rarely represented by lawyers.

Consumer advocate Mark Green wrote that it is not a "neutral principle that lawyers will represent those who can pay and not represent those who cannot." Rather, it is a value choice that excludes a large class of clients. He suggested a "new ethic of conscientious refusal. As the concept of a good German has changed, so will the concept of a good lawyer."[408] He criticized lawyers who lack "a sense of consequence"[409] when they rationalize their behavior by referring to the tradition that "lawyers assume that anything goes in legal combat—as the judge and jury decides the winner."

Lawyers who claim that all clients are entitled to legal representation to explain their motives for representing clients whose work may be viewed as against public interests make a specious case. Lawyers represent this category of clients not for professional ethical reasons. If it were simply because all clients are entitled to legal representation, how come so many rich scoundrels have extensive and expensive legal representation while so many poor people with legitimate needs don't have any needed legal representation?

The fact is that rich clients get better "justice" than poor ones, the best justice their money could buy. In 2005, a lawyer wrote about the two worlds of law practice he experienced when he moved from working as a litigator in a large firm to a neighborhood legal aid office. He described the differences between the experiences of his former wealthy clients and those low-income people in adjudications and alternative administrative proceedings where the stakes were vital, often involving "food and shelter, life and death."[410] His change of professional lives was a "leap from a professional precipice."[411] He wrote, "It is astonishing that the principle enshrined in virtually every articulation and embodiment of civic virtue and pride in our democracy, from courthouse facades, to the Pledge of Allegiance, to the iconography of 'blind justice'—remains so obviously and utterly hollow and illusory."[412]

THE DEARTH OF LEGAL AID

As of 2018, there were 1,338,678 attorneys in the United States, according to the ABA. The most recent study on the practice-area breakdown for lawyers was conducted in 2005: 75 percent of lawyers were in private practice, and the rest were mostly practicing in the government or private industry. Only 1 percent of lawyers were legal aid providers or public defenders.[413] From the approximately one million in private practice, consider how many potential clients have no or inadequate representation, and who they are. These data apply to the disparities in the criminal justice system mentioned earlier, as they do in the civil justice arena.

Low-income litigants in America received inadequate or no professional help in 86 percent of their civil legal problems, according to a 2017 report of the Legal Services Corporation (LSC).[414] In 2015, 60 million Americans, one in five, qualified for free legal aid based on their income according to the US Census Bureau.[415] Yet LSC studies[416] have found that approximately half of those seeking legal aid are turned away because of limited public resources. LSC found that for every client who was served by an LSC-funded program, at least one eligible person seeking help was turned down. That fact should come as no surprise, since each legal aid attorney serves a potential client base of 6,415 low-income people, while private attorneys serve a base of 429 people.[417]

Roughly 15 percent of the US population reside in rural counties; many of those counties are without any attorneys, so residents must travel hundreds of miles to meet with an attorney, if they can get there, and if they can afford their fees.[418] More broadly, low-income Americans—regardless of where they lived—received inadequate or no legal aid for 86 percent of their civil legal issues. This data only reflects issues for which legal aid was sought. The number is likely far greater, because only 22 percent of all low-income Americans even seek out legal aid for such issues in the first place—and this number drops to 19 percent when the only low-income individuals considered are those with no more than high-school educations are considered.[419]

If there is a need for legal aid to poor defendants in ordinary times, when extraordinary events occur those problems are exacerbated.[420] One example occurred during the Coronavirus pandemic of 2020. While civil legal aid attorneys could manage "only a fraction of the needs for those in poverty" the epidemic was overwhelming for them . . . "when it comes to basic needs such as shelter, safety, or economic security," in categories of cases especially relevant to poor people—evictions, foreclosures, joint custody agreements.

The cost of an attorney for civil matters is often out of reach even for those who are comfortably in the middle class, according to the National Center for Access to Justice at Fordham Law School. In New York, there are fewer than three civil legal aid lawyers for every 10,000 people who live under 200 percent of the federal poverty guidelines, the center's Justice Index data shows. That level is $25,520 a year for one person and $52,400 for a family of four in 2020.[421]

Because many poor defendants cannot afford lawyers or find them in government programs, many represent themselves. But while pro se representation is a democratic notion, studies have shown that they mostly result in prejudice against those citizens who try it.[422] Federal judge Richard Posner concluded after his long, distinguished career that most judges "treat these people as kind of trash not worth the time of a federal judge."[423]

No subject has had more attention in recent years than the disparity between rich and poor Americans in their access to health care insurance. Even after the passage of the Affordable Care Act a decade ago, about 20 percent of our population still has no health care coverage. By comparison, we offer $1 billion for public funding of civil legal aid compared to $351 billion for nationwide health care. The United States spends on justice for the poor less than one-third of 1 percent of what it spends on health care for the poor—only $19 per eligible client compared to $7,000 per eligible patient.[424]

If the solution to uniform health care scandal still eludes the richest country in the world, consider the status of legal assistance in the United States. The recent data indicates that only a small fraction—less than 15 percent—of low-income Americans have adequate—or any—legal representation for civil issues.[425]

A related class question is the role and reputation of lawyers who handle contingency and class-action cases. They are sometimes criticized as plunderers, ambulance chasers, shysters, hired guns in search of high fees. There continues to be a classist perspective to this criticism. First, those big firm lawyers who make snide remarks about these members of the bar themselves earn enormous fees, paid by the hour by their rich, usually corporate, clients for fighting the very same class actions against companies who often have been found at fault, after protracted and aggressive defenses of their wrongdoing. And these class actions wouldn't have been necessary if the government agencies and their publicly paid lawyers created to regulate such wrongdoing had done their job in the first place.

How did our country get to this point? Our motto is "Equal Justice for All," but our reality is that "Justice Is for Sale," and very few can afford it. The data here is offered to challenge the common thesis that lawyers represent clients because they have a professional duty to do so. If that is so, our profession has failed for a great many people in need of legal assistance.

There is nothing wrong with some people having more money than their neighbors, and as a result having more buying power for their homes and clothes and vacations. But justice in our legal system (like health care) ought to be available to and work for all people regardless of their wealth. Legal representation has an impact on *all* issues of life. Without it, too many Americans cannot compete in the present marketplace.

CHAPTER FOUR

PERSONAL CHOICES

Lawyers sometimes cross lines and become confederates with their clients in their strategies and the implementation of them. Lawyers who cross ethical lines are not honorable professionals; they are facilitators of behavior that goes against public interests. There are important distinctions between advice and participation.

When a lawyer represents only one client, is his work truly as an attorney? Remember the Robert Duvall consigliere character in *The Godfather*? Was he acting as a lawyer or a tactical confederate with a criminal group? If a person who happens to be a lawyer is a participant in a criminal organization, is he not a criminal or conspirator? If so, how does he differ in degree or in kind from the white-shoe, big law firm attorney or in-house corporate counsel who spends all or most of her time representing a tobacco or opioid company besieged with litigation about its deleterious products, knowing the product is the cause of a major health problem worldwide? Does the expression "hired gun" apply to these attorneys, with all its negative connotations?

It is not pseudo-moralistic for us to make personal choices in the use of our professional skills. We have options. For our income and personal enjoyment and fulfillment, lawyers can join businesses that need their skills, or government agencies, NGOs, charitable organizations, unions, media, and other public service organizations.

In my long practice of law, I practiced what in the 1960s and later was called public interest law. I made a point of touching all the bases of general law practice—writing wills and contracts, arguing in courts, trial and appellate, from small claims to the US Supreme Court, dipping into some unknown areas and intentionally exploring unfamiliar law practice, like a churning case where a friend's stock account was wrongfully depleted. It was not my specialty, but my outrage at the situation led to my client's successful compensation. What most intrigued me were assignments that came my way and led me to involvements of public service. There is no one way to practice law, but my experience demonstrates that one can practice widely, generally, with public interests at the center, without taking an oath of poverty or succumbing to strictly commercial values.

My career started with three years in the Air Force JAG trying courts-martial. Following that, I worked at the US Department of Justice prosecuting criminal cases for about four years. But gradually, and more interestingly in my long private practice, I consulted and worked with academic institutions like Princeton's Woodrow Wilson visiting teaching program, the Brookings Institution, the California Assembly Judiciary Committee, the National Advisory on Civil Disorders (also called the Kerner Commission), a House of Representatives Special Committee investigation as one of its special outside counsel, and several Senate and presidential committees. I was special counsel to a congressman who was appointed, reluctantly, to the House Un-American Activities Committee (HUAC). He assigned me the enviable task of writing his dissents to its mischief. I wrote books, created and was counsel to a writer's organization and an ex-convicts group. I wrote books and contributed to other books, and wrote op-eds, reviews, and articles on legal subjects of public interest.

Two telling experiences especially stand out in my recollections. Both demonstrated how poor people are shortchanged by the legal system.

In the first, I investigated our prison system, with the financial help of the Ford Foundation, and wrote about what was inaptly referred to as the "correction system" that in many ways worked counterproductively as a poor house for minority people.[426] The Twentieth Century Fund later underwrote my research regarding jails[427] which unlike prisons, house unconvicted defendants awaiting trial when they are unable to afford bail.

I was able to apply these ideas in a precedential case in the federal trial court in the District of Columbia. Along with the Public Defender Service, we brought a class action lawsuit against the DC jail claiming—successfully and for the first time—that conditions at that jail violated the cruel and unusual punishment guarantee of the Eighth Amendment for jailed defendants who are not yet tried or convicted, poor people who could not afford bail. Defendants with means make bail and await their trials living their normal lives. Jailed defendants live isolated for protracted periods of time (months, sometimes years) in unhealthy conditions, eat poor food, lose their jobs, and are not free to assist their lawyers in their defense. Jailed defendants generally fared worse at their trials than those defendants who awaited trial free on bail. I wrote about that subject, again with foundation help and served as an expert witness in a New Orleans jail case on the same subject.

Robert Ardrey, anthropologist and author of *The Territorial Imperative*, visited the jail and explained our theory to the court. Housing pre-trial detainees in overcrowded, isolated, and prejudicial conditions causes demonstratable physiological and psychological damage comparable to physically abusing them. It amounts to cruel and unusual punishment prohibited by the Eighth Amendment.

Dr. Karl Menninger, the noted psychiatrist, also visited the jail and testified, at his expense, as did Ardrey, to that same conclusion. So did Dr. John Calhoun from the National Institute of Health, whose animal studies showed the damaging effect of isolation and overcrowding on those inhabitants. These and other architectural and psychological experts testified similarly, until the judge said sufficient evidence had been provided.

After hearing the testimony of experts I brought to see the jail and to court to testify about what they saw, the federal court in Washington, DC, required no further evidence or testimony from inmates than our experts provided and found in our favor, ordering drastic changes in the DC jail that were backed by a court order if they failed to perform.[428] I petitioned the court for legal fees; the judge denied my request. Sanctions and remuneration comes in other forms. It wasn't why I did my work.

During that period I was called by three ex-offenders who had been imprisoned at the DC prison in Lorton, Virginia. They had read about my work in a magazine article and asked for my help setting up an organization they would run called EFEC—Efforts from Ex-Convicts. I organized that group and was its general counsel for several decades. I proudly watched them successfully provide correctional services the government agencies in DC were performing inadequately. Eventually the city contracted with EFEC to run a halfway house, which they did with award-winning success. I was paid modestly for my EFEC work for many years.

EFEC's African American director, Randolph Yates, himself an ex-offender, took me for a tour of the neighborhoods in DC that most of Lorton's inmates came from. As we walked the dirty streets, I noticed stares from passersby and others near alleys and on porches of shabby buildings. Yates nodded toward them subtly, and there were no incidents. When we were done, Yates stepped into a busy street to hail a taxi for us to go back to EFEC's building nearby. No cabs stopped to pick us up. I entered into the street, and the next cab that came by picked us up.

I wrote an op-ed[429] for the *Washington Post* about this revealing experience, concluding metaphorically that without Yates I never would have gotten out of that neighborhood and that without me, neither would he.

Another experience could not have concerned a more different subject, though it did provide another example of institutional failure to serve poor people. In 1975, a federal judge in the District of Columbia issued a decision in a major lawsuit filed by multiple farmworker and related civil rights organizations against the Department of Labor. He ruled that farmworkers had been historically discriminated against in the application of our nation's labor laws. He ordered enforcement of existing labor laws governing their lives—work, health, housing, education, and more. I was appointed by the court to chair a seven-member special review board (this time paid for by the defendant Department of Labor), composed of three designees of the Department of Labor and three from representatives of farmworker organizations. We held hearings for two years in the three migrant streams in the United States that revealed a world I knew little of beyond dramatic documentaries and books about the lives of migrant workers—*Grapes of Wrath* and *Harvest of Shame* among the more well-known.

I traveled and observed the lives of migrant farmworkers and met representatives of the players in that world. One conversation with a young woman who worked for the farmworker union particularly touched me. She said as we talked over collards, crackers, and iced tea in her spare union hall in Avon Park, Florida, "I know you wrote about prisons. I hope you will write about the lives of migrant farmworkers. You will see that they too exist in prisons, even if you don't see the bars that lock them up. Their prisons are servitude, lack of decent living conditions, exploitation of their lives—all as they harvest the food for our tables."

Her remarks stayed with me. I repeated them in the book I later wrote about those experiences with the aid of a Ford Foundation grant,[430] and I think of this conversation now looking back at my

professional life in law and courts. That devoted young woman had a
wise insight into a world few people know about but all profit from.

Because she had asked to have one of my books, I sent her a
copy of my most recent one (about jails) along with a note thanking
her for her hospitality. A short time later I received a friendly letter
from her. She thanked me for sending the book and said she looked
forward to reading all my books, "including the one I hope you'll
write someday about farm workers." Then she wrote:

> This note was really prompted by my thinking about the possibility
> of such a book and my wondering how people write books about
> very different subjects, and know enough about all of them to write
> a book. Then, I thought, maybe you—being pretty expert on pris-
> ons—are already an expert on farm workers. There are all kinds of
> cages, maybe. Some have stones or bricks for walls and some have
> iron bars. Some have only systems and prejudices and traditions
> (like slavery) to hem folks in. But, like all cages, you can't get out
> except for an occasional and unique escape. It would really be neat
> to read about those cages and how we might tear down the walls.

The lawyers who served those workers and won that class action
lawsuit were doing the public's work in seeking enforcement of
Congress's laws that the Department of Labor should have enforced
but did not. Their organizations paid them less than the department representatives earned, no doubt. Our transitory efforts during
the tenure of our years doing the court's oversight and enforcement
work made a ripple of improvement in the lives of hardworking
laborers who systemically were not protected by the agencies of government that we taxpayers paid to administer our laws. Today still,
those labor laws do not provide this class of workers in America
with the quality of life and justice they deserve. They continue to
live in prisons without bars, as my guide to that world advised me.

The rich-poor distribution of justice these workers received as compared to the people they served was demonstrated in the active decades (1950–1970) of the farmworker labor movement instituted by Cesar Chavez and his colleagues. When the farmworker union fought for laws to protect their workers, the local churches at first supported the growers, whose money supported the church, but not the workers, whose lives failed to receive the aid their churches preached about.

Eventually church leaders realized "the heresy that churches and synagogues are to be concerned only with so-called 'spiritual matters,'" and that the farmworkers' grievances were "a fundamental injustice which we dare not evade." [431]

This inherent crosscurrent in all institutions—correctional, labor, churches, military, media—between doing what sustains the administrators of the institution above its constituents it is there to serve was observed in the movie *The Two Popes*. It concerned the replacement of conservative, traditionalist Pope Benedict XVI in 2015 by the current progressive, Pope Francis. They discussed their differences in one scene where Francis argued to Benedict, "We have spent these last year's disciplining anyone who disagrees with our line on divorce, on birth control, on being gay, while our planet was being destroyed, while inequality grew like a cancer. . . . All the time the real danger was inside us, inside with us," alluding to the scandal of the church protecting clerics who preyed on children under their supervision. The contrite Benedict suggested he was suffering a crisis of faith by his inadequate response to the church sex scandal that should disqualify him, and this led him to resign. [432]

Among the involved citizenry I met during my work was Chris Hartmire, director of an ecumenical council of churches that was concerned about the social lives of farmworkers. The predicament Hartmire described was a classic example of institutionalization, a process in which all institutions must make fundamental decisions on whether to preserve themselves or to work for the constituents they were created to serve when a situation arises in which doing both is impossible. Church activists in California were accused by their critics of involving themselves in an economic war aimed at reforming the distribution of power to secure social justice for a poor and weak group. The church's social activists argued that to do less would be dishonest; it would be no more than "salving the conscience while hanging onto an unjust social system that benefits 'our kind of people' at the expense of the poor."

After entering all-out warfare over the union, the boycott, and the strikes, there were fears that the CMM might be pressured out of existence by influential members of the church who either were growers or sympathetic to them. Hartmire wrote about their struggle:

> The most important thing that can be said about this "churchly" support is that it helped; it helped keep a very brave people alive and strong in an important struggle for social justice. These Christians did not come with sermons or admonitions or membership cards. They did not need to identify themselves because farm workers knew who they were. Farm workers knew better than we do what it is that God's people should be doing. The ministry of Jesus is highly visible and easily identified when it is in fact done—and not only talked about. [433]

In his recapitulation of these exciting days, Hartmire eloquently articulated the excruciating balance that was in play during those times. In assisting the underdog in a major confrontation, the church was painfully aware that the very power interests who had to be reformed sat in the same pews with those who sought change. The church really was being asked to put up or shut up—to help one group of constituents attain the kind of justice the church preached for all at a time when doing so would conflict with those members with more power.

The farmworkers were militant and aggressive, but they were motivated by nonviolence and had strong ties to the church. They persisted in operating within the system, though it was one that had denied them justice for so long and to which they had none of the access their opponents had. They had to depend on the institutions of society that concern themselves with justice. Public interest organizations and lawyers helped them seek justice, and in doing so, they forced an agonizing decision on the church. In Hartmire's words, the farmworkers forced the church to think "not only in terms of what is institutionally possible, but first and foremost in terms of what is truly helpful." Hartmire said, "We were driven by the circumstances of our work to put the highest priority on the needs of the people and only a secondary priority on the needs of the institution."[434]

The church could not preach a dogma it did not practice in the real world, one compassionate church figure told me. The local growers were active in their churches in areas where agribusiness was prominent in government and churches. "We could no longer ignore the people our institution existed to serve, even when it conflicted with the custodians of the established power order."[435]

These two experiences are classic examples of law professor Kamisar's insightful distinction between the manor houses (courts and legislative halls) and gatehouses (jails and agricultural fields) of justice. Justice cannot be served for the rich but not the poor, and for powerful elders of religious institutions and not the poor congregations of those same institutions.

These two examples demonstrated systemic failures of our institutions—the correction system and the Department of Labor to aid poor constituents they were established to aid. Every day individuals who need legal assistance in carrying out their lives and dealing with society's institutions also learn that justice (the legal system) is for sale and does not serve those who cannot pay for it. Such a system cannot include the word *justice*.

I learned doing these assignments that our institutions, sadly, work for the administrators of these institutions more so—with exceptions—than its consumers. The Catholic Church's dealings with young congregants who were abused that was noted earlier provides another example of an institution serving itself over its consumers, as does the "correctional" system and our Labor Department that were responsible to execute prison and farmworker laws.

We lawyers are trained and licensed to conduct and administer justice. That system need to assess the legal system's failures in this regard. A columnist recently wrote about her first seminar years ago at Harvard Law School. Her professor asked the class, "Where does your morality come from?"[436] She concluded, "Your actions are your morality. Your morality comes from what you do."

I agree with her that our personal morality derives from what we do, as opposed to what we believe, what we learn, and what we espouse. In the case of farmworkers, a classic example, the churches preached on Sundays that it is important to help your fellow citizens. In reality, the rest of the week influential members of that church initially supported the very growers who were exploiting the farmworkers.

Of course, we lawyers can only do what we are asked to do. I've been fortunate. Opportunities like my work for Representative John Culver gave me the chance to comment on HUAC's work. But he did recruit me because of my reputation, about which I had something to do.

In one instance, I sought out a position that the Holocaust Museum was seeking to fill in its planning stage. Key staff set up a lunch to see if I would like to help get their books published. I was their first interview. I went to that lunch to assure there would be no second, nor third interviewee. I wanted to do that work, made it clear I did, and I was hired when lunch ended. We did over a dozen books together through the years, and television documentaries as well. It was an education for me.

Like the associates in the New York City firms that represented the Swiss banks mentioned earlier, and the DC attorney early in the Trump era, we are what we do, we do what we want to do if we have any control over it; and our clients characterize us, as we do them.

Columnist Molly Roberts made the point that it is hypocritical to cloak one's "words and deeds in philosophy as if we are playing around with hypotheticals." Her view reflects that of Chris Hartmire, who worked on behalf of his organization of local churches in California to aid farmworker causes—in the name of what those churches stood for. And what lawyers like Earl Johnson, organizational heads like Bryan Stevenson (Equal Justice Initiative), and Barry Scheck (Innocence Project), educators like Owen Fiss and Yale Kamisar and Herbert Packer, and judges like Skelly Wright, Jed Rakoff, and Louis Brandeis exemplified.

LAW AND HONOR

A question haunts the profession: *Does being a good lawyer require being a good person?* Don't most young college graduates entering law school aspire to live moral lives and to participate in a justice system that "makes the world a better place"? I've never heard a young law student say, "I want to represent corporate polluters so that I can help hasten the pace of global warming." Or, "I want to protect corporate executives responsible for releasing toxins into the water and air because that's where the big money is to be made!" When we are good, we can be very good, as in Innocence Project criminal cases or notable class action civil cases (like those mentioned earlier). But when we are bad, we can be very bad figures taking part in antisocial actions.

I do not suggest that there is one true, honorable way to practice our profession. One lawyer may care deeply about the wrongness of capital punishment and spend a career fighting it by handling Eighth Amendment cases. Others might question devoting one's professional life to helping criminals who committed the most vile offenses, violating the social contract citizens must follow in any decent society. They prefer to prosecute those same people and never would represent them. Those are personal choices lawyers make, and no right and wrong should be associated with the choice. But a lawyer's work in both instances is not neutral. It defines what they do, how we do it, and who we are.

Whether one prosecutes or defends an oil spill says something else about a lawyer. Even corporate lawyers who claim their representation should not suggest some relation to some of their clients' actions would not make the same case for, say, a Michael Cohen, a lawyer who was labeled a "fixer."

Others may simply enjoy quieter, undramatic transactional work—solving tax puzzles, designing patent applications—and they decide to do that in their careers for reasons of personal predilection. There is no moral element in their choice. Some lawyers may want to make the most money and will practice near the largest honeypot, probably corporate law. That work probably leads them to representing rich clients seeking to enhance their riches. Rich people get the biggest cars and homes and the best services, as a rule, so of course they get talented legal services as well.

The purpose of this book has been to examine the culture of my profession, the models I applaud and those I abhor. I do not mean to posit that big law firms and corporate practices are better or worse than small ones and those that focus on commercial affairs. I have worked with lawyers who were examples of the best of our profession, such as Sargent Shriver and Stuart Eizenstat, whose public works were most admirable, and who between public assignments worked in large law firms.

That milieu as a work culture never appealed to me. It did to many of my contemporaries and friends whose professional lives seemed appealing but whose fortunes were based on questionable clients' affairs like those noted in this book. I hope this book suggests to the next generation that there are other options.

It would be arrogant for me—or anyone—to define what other lawyers may or may not do. Our regulations and the criminal laws determine the outer limits of what we *cannot* do—mingle clients' money with our own or counsel commission of crimes, for example. But the point that Justice Stone made, and others have made more recently, is that there *is* a difference between selling shoes, running a restaurant, and lawyering. Too often the public interest is lost in our calculations about what clients or issues we represent and how far we should go in our representation. At a minimum, consciousness-raising about the obligations licensed professionals have to the public and the degree to which public interests should play some part of what we all do is needed.

Not every matter that comes to any lawyer is loaded with social import. Consider lawyers who specialize in their practice in careful, prudent drafting of documents, for example. Surely lawyers who work for the government—federal, state, or local—are performing public service, usually underpaid for doing so, which itself is a statement about the values governing our public policies. The same can be said about teachers. But the practice of law requires, I would argue, a more sensitive implementation of the moral and ethical aspects of what we do in our offices and in courts or other adjudicative proceedings.

Most clients and clients' work does not raise inherent questions of morality or ethics. Drafting a contract or will, offering matrimonial or tax advice, securing a copyright, or incorporating a company, or any of the various matters that regularly come to attorneys' attention, rarely require a moral assessment (so long as what specific conduct we are asked to perform does not raise such issues).

But even mundane matters may raise ethical issues. Years ago my partner asked me to try a contentious divorce case she couldn't settle. She didn't handle trials, and I didn't handle divorces. We represented the wife, a sophisticated and successful businesswoman. Her husband was a high government official.

It became clear to me that mediating their rancorous arguments was not what they wanted from their lawyers. Who pays the dentist and summer tennis camp had nothing to do with the operative issue of what was in the best interests of the children, which was getting lost in their personal battles. Rather than allowing my "meter" to run out, along with my interest in their angry battles, I moved the court to appoint a separate counsel to represent solely the interest of the children, and the court did. I could then pursue my clients' interests without prejudicing the children or allowing the father to. I enjoyed feeling Solomonic and fair, rather than exacerbating the rancorous positions of the parties., and being paid more for it.

There is also a personal, humanistic element to providing legal services, as another incident in my experience demonstrated. A woman I knew professionally came to me to write her will. As she spoke, I had a concern she was considering suicide. I am no psychiatrist, and I might well have been wrong, and yet I didn't know how to respond to her. By chance, that weekend I visited a friend, a doctor in Philadelphia, and he was talking to another doctor friend about someone they knew who had been killed in a traffic accident. "That was no accident," his friend said. "I was treating him and I believe it was suicide." I asked them both what I should do about my client, and they both said to intervene, deftly but immediately. I asked a friend back home, also a psychiatrist, what he thought, and he said the same.

When my client came back to my office for her will, I did tell her that if I was out of line or wrong she should please understand that it was my care for her well-being that prompted me to ask if our conversation about her will might be related to any mental-health concerns, and I suggested that if so she should seek help from an appropriate professional. I worried how she would take my non-legal advice, but she acknowledged that she did have a problem and thanked me for my thoughtfulness. She did see a doctor, and all was well thereafter. I was relieved to have taken that course, but I was also aware it was a risky step. My genuine human concern might have been wrong and hurtful to her. However, I felt I would be remiss to do nothing.

Law students' consciousnesses need to be raised about those kinds of ethical elements of our work. There are few guidelines in situations like this, but when dealing with clients, lawyers no doubt encounter comparable dilemmas that require resorting to insights we don't develop in law school.

Attorneys are in unique positions, because of their intimate private relations with their clients, to advise them in matters beyond the expertise they gain in law schools. Such was my experience with the woman whose will I wrote who had appeared suicidal, and the rape victim whose therapist asked me not to pursue her valid claim for personal therapeutic reasons. It is part of what we encounter occasionally, often in trial contexts. People seek our advice (even more than bartenders and taxi drivers), and these situations come with an element of undefined personal responsibility. Like this note in the *Washington Lawyer* of the DC Bar to its ethics expert by a sensitive member who reached out for advice in such a case.

Question: My client, whom I believe to be emotionally unstable, announced yesterday that if he receives one more piece of bad news, he will "take action to relieve [his] pain, once and for all."

This morning, I received notice that summary judgment had been entered against him, and I fear what he might do if I tell him that he has lost his case. What are my responsibilities here?[437]

Returning to Justice Stone's remark about the importance of how we live as lawyers rather than how we earn our livings as lawyers, the conclusions and examples I have offered are meant to provide useful ethical guidance and consciousness raising for the next generation of lawyers. When Justice Stone spoke at the University of Michigan in 1934 (*Harvard Law Review* printed his remarks[438]), he spoke of the "durable satisfactions which are to be found in a professional service more consciously directed toward the advancement of the public interest," as well as to his clients. The justice's observations about lawyering is the same point poet-essayist Elizabeth Hardwick made in an essay in 1963: "Making a living is nothing; the great difficulty is making a point, making a difference."[439] Stone spoke to lawyers, Hardwick to writers. Both offered profound insights into the universal questions of personal ethics and morality.

Stone wrote years after becoming a Supreme Court justice "that my work as a teacher will be far more influential and lasting than anything I ever do as a judge."[440] He advocated throughout his career that lawyers should be "the primary instrument for bringing about social justice."[441] He criticized the drift of the legal profession away from making "law more readily available as an instrument of justice to the common man,"[442] rather than pursuing the "morals and manners of the marketplace in its most antisocial ramifications."[443]

It is not empty elitism to practice law as a "learned profession" rather than as a business, though large modern law firms with offices in many cities and countries can operate like big commercial businesses. Given the options provided by the internet, the practice of law has changed in ways not likely to disappear. Conveniences are gained but costs escalate, and as a result, our work styles are changed. Economics becomes the overriding motive.

These advances have altered the nature of law practice and can be expected to continue to do so. Some of these innovations have improved law practice—faster research, for example. But the relative speed of the internet and its related privacy challenges have changed the culture of lawyering. Who really believes that the privileged nature of attorney-client communications is protected by adding words through an email instructing so? "Or that there might be digital trials?"[444] Will there be a new definition of public trials? How can huge law firms operate ethically when partners don't personally know each other?

Many have predicted that further revolutionary changes lie ahead. One example is the new practice of seeking funding for litigation from outside investors for a share for the profit, if any. *Big Money Is Betting on Legal Industry Transformation* by Mark Cohen spelled out this phenomenon.

> If "Money makes the world go 'round," then the legal world is spinning as never before. Law has been big business for decades, but only recently has significant venture capital, private equity, and entrepreneur money been pumped into the legal sector. Last year saw an eye-popping 718% increase in legal industry investment, and this year's capital infusion ... surpassed last year's $1 billion total and could well double it.[445]

That author, a lawyer and legal business consultant, concluded that

> Legal practice may have its own practice rules, but legal delivery is now operating by business standards.... Law is a trillion-dollar global industry.... Law has long been inward-facing. Its focus has

been on input—hours and billing—not output—results and customer satisfaction. So too has profit-per-partner, not net promoter score been law's Holy Grail. Lawyers, not clients, long called the shots.... Clients were generally compliant because law firms had a uniform *modus operandi*. Law was a guild.... Legal practice is no longer synonymous with the delivery of legal services ... peripatetic partners ("laterals") have swapped firms for decades. That means that money—not the firm—is the glue that binds.[446]

Of major legal providers, Cohen reports:

Their annual revenue is approximately twelve times that of the largest grossing law firms.... The recent infusion of capital into the legal industry is the best evidence that a tipping point has been reached.[447]

TEACHING ETHICS

Justice Stone's goal for the legal profession was "placing the public interest above the particular interests they represented and from which they gained their livelihoods."[448] That hortatory instruction is in conflict with the prevailing ethic of our profession that our work is "neutral," required of us by our rules. Stone's colleague at Columbia Law, the eminent law professor Walter Gellhorn, agreed with Stone that there was a deplorable "fundamental disharmony between the lawyer's work and the public interest."[449]

Justice Stone stated that for a new morality to evolve within the profession, a "moral readjustment" would be necessary. Law schools and professional organizations must not ignore inculcating the social responsibilities of practitioners of a vital public profession. As he wisely preached, they must reach beyond mere "platitudinous exhortation."[450] In more modern times, Associate Justice Stephen Breyer told a girls' school audience that if they pursued work that "you are happy doing and that you feel is worthwhile . . . and you do it well, that's a success."[451]

There is a public element to law practice. My college alma mater took notice of changing cultural positions of the New York State Bar.[452] One of its earlier (1905) graduates was refused admission to the bar on the basis of his race and could not practice law despite his exceptional scholarly record. Law firms refused to hire him. This year, more than a century later, he was admitted posthumously to the bar on motion of his family, local bar and judicial organizations, and the law school to correct that egregious earlier discrimination.[453]

When a major respected New York City law firm posted a photo of twelve of their new partners (144 out of that 1,000 member multicity law firm are partners), all but one of the twelve was a white male, the *New York Times* noted. The *New York Times* referred to this image as a "blind spot" and quoted one critic remarking about the firm's "commitment to the white in white shoe."[454] Prospective clients reportedly called on the firm to add more diversity in the legal community or face losing their business.

African American partners are becoming an endangered species, one of the firm's African American partners commented. The percentage of women and African Americans who make partner is far less than Caucasians in large, high-paying law firms. In fact, the reputation of the firm at the center of the *Times* article was widely considered better in these respects than many of its competitors. For social and cultural reasons, minority lawyers may be welcomed by recruiters but then they may be sidelined in their progress at the firms. Studies report that "people prefer to associate with others they perceive to be like themselves."[455] It follows, then, that lawyers at firms tend to promote associates who look like them. Or those who bring in prosperous clients.

In *The Good Lawyer: Seeking Quality in the Practice of Law*, the authors approached the question of how to find a good quality of life in the law from an interesting perspective. Law school, they thought, had too narrow an approach: suppress feelings, develop facts and rationality. "Law school cannot be made into something it is not," they wrote. "It is not a playing field that tilts toward humanistic values." Lawyers need more than "justice, empathy, humility, and courage," they stated; yet their interviews of hundreds of lawyers showed that they were happiest "when they accomplished great results for clients they cared about."[456]

No one anecdote can define or reveal a complex and nuanced issue such as a lawyer's ethics. But at the risk of over simplifying, I would offer this one, from a fictional television storyline in 2001 in the series *The Practice*, written by David Kelley, about a small trial lawyer firm in Boston. The firm represented a client insurance company in a tort case involving a ten-year-old boy who was struck and injured by an automobile. The lawyers from both sides were on the verge of negotiating a settlement when the firm learned that a relevant medical report included a fact not disclosed or known about before. The boy had an aneurism, not caused by the accident, but potentially fatal if it was not dealt with immediately. The client didn't want the lawyers to reveal this fact. It might cost the insurance company a multimillion-dollar fortune, and a half-a-million-dollar settlement was about to be reached.

One of the lawyers agonized about his duty under the circumstance. He went to the family that night and urged them to take the boy to the hospital immediately, before the settlement conference the following morning. He feared the boy might die of the aneurism if it was not treated, and he couldn't live with that. Nonetheless, in revealing the information, the firm could be sued for his violation of the ethical rule against breaching the attorney-client privilege, which is sacrosanct.

One partner reported his colleague for his act, because it jeopardized his firm's financial position and violated the professional canons of ethics. A hearing was called before the bar ethics committee.

At the hearing, and among the partners privately, the characters debated the propriety of the partner's disclosure, which turned out to have saved the boy's life. Under general ethics rules, if a lawyer learns his client is about to commit a crime, bar rules of privileged communications may be circumvented in the public interest. In civil cases where an attorney learns something that would prejudice his client, he need not reveal that fact against his client's instruction under prevailing ethical rules that make sense, generally. The lawyer's critics pointed out that if every lawyer could make exceptions to the rule of client confidentiality whenever his moral compass directed him to do so, there would be no client protective rule, which is essential to law practice.

What should be the case where doing something wrong according to one's professional ethical obligations is a humane life-saving act? The lawyer, in his defense, argued that the adversary process in that situation stopped being about finding the truth, fairness, and due process, but rather became about winning, even over matters of life and death.

The program concluded with the initially hostile bar committee ruling that the lawyer had breached an essential rule of legal ethical process under a system that permitted him no choice, and that the violation could not be ignored nor not enforced. Balancing the competing values, however, the lawyer was suspended for two weeks because, as the stringent judge stated, the profession will be better served with such a lawyer in it. One of his partners and his client disagreed.

Another dramatic example of the painful, if not unjust, implication of a rigid rule governing client confidentiality arose in 1973, in what became known as the "Lake Pleasant Bodies" case. Robert Garrow stabbed and killed an eighteen-year-old student who was camping in the Adirondacks. A statewide manhunt resulted in Garrow's arrest. Police suspected that Garrow had also killed three

other campers who were missing. Frank Armani, a local attorney
with no criminal law experience (and a former classmate of mine),
was assigned by the court to defend Garrow. Armani recruited a
successful criminal defense attorney, Francis Belge, to work with
him on the case.

Garrow told his attorneys that he had killed all three of the
other victims and raped the two who were young women, and he
told his lawyers where the bodies were hidden. They went to the
sites and found the three remains, but they left them there and told
no one—neither the law-enforcement authorities nor the families
of the deceased. Student hikers eventually found the bodies.

Armani and Belge put Garrow on the witness stand during his
trial, and he confessed to the three other murders and two rapes as
part of his insanity defense. Garrow was convicted and sentenced to
twenty-five years to life in prison. He escaped from prison and was
shot and killed.

The attorneys publicly admitted that they had known about the
bodies for six months, but they argued that they were constrained
from taking any action—such as advising law-enforcement authorities or the families of the victims—because of the rules of confidentiality. They were harshly judged by the involved parties and vilified
by the general public because they withheld information about the
corpses and protected the murderer (they had offered the information as part of a plea bargain that was rejected).

Belge was indicted for violating public-health laws requiring
a decent burial for dead bodies and for obstructing justice. Attorney organizations pleaded in his defense, arguing that a judgment against him would destroy the attorney-client privilege and
force attorneys into a Hobson's choice. Which social institution is
owed an attorney's duties—the legal system or the public? Should
the rules of evidence overwhelm rather than aid the search for truth
and justice?

The New York court dismissed the charges against Belge, reasoning that "the effectiveness of counsel is only as great as the confidentiality of the client-attorney relationship."[457] Belge had, the court decided, "conducted himself as an officer of the Court ... to protect the constitutional rights of his client."[458]

Armani was torn by his ethical dilemma, understandably, and felt ashamed, even though most of his professional colleagues supported him. He said in a television interview, "To me it was a question of which was the higher moral good ... the question of the Constitution, the question of even a bastard like him having a proper defense, having adequate representation, being able to trust his lawyer. ... It's a terrible thing to play God." Armani anguished over the agony of the victims' parents: "Your mind screaming one way. Relieve these parents! ... One sense of morality wants you to relieve the grief."[459] His torment, as well as the families', must have been unbearable; any sensitive attorney would feel that way.

Legal theorists have debated the dilemma created by this case, and there is no totally acceptable answer. "One expert even questioned whether a decent ethical person can ever be a lawyer."[460] The law elevates the adversary system, the presumption of innocence, the right to counsel, and rules of confidentiality. Does this create a separate commercial morality while ignoring the corresponding ethical one? If so, might there be exceptions?

How do we decide? Who strikes a balance between common morality and professional or legal morality, and by what standards? Who teaches lawyers what their responsibilities are as "officers of the court"?

When I was a rookie lawyer in private practice, I experienced the phenomenon all lawyers encounter. A total stranger walks into our office, sits down and talks to us about the most private, personal, intimate, embarrassing, sometimes incriminating events that brought them to us for advice and assistance on these private

matters. This is not the same as conversing in other comparable set-
tings. One often feels like a psychiatrist or doctor or priest in these
instances. We are not trained on how to deal with delicate conundrums like those mentioned here.

What makes the situation work is the cultural understanding
that to receive the best counseling, that stranger must believe that
our conversations are completely confidential. They have to trust a
stranger with their secrets, and they do because of this understanding, one that often goes unsaid, as both parties operate on this cultural ground rule with a total stranger. For the sensitive attorney,
this can be a profound experience, different from our other habits,
necessary for our work, yet wondrous and troubling too.

This special relationship between client and lawyer rarely
takes place for the majority of people with legal problems. Are the
assigned counsels or public defenders who meet their poor clients
and read their file minutes before dealing with their cases in courts
practicing a profession or lending their names to an unjust system?
Or the inadequate legal aid client in the civil law system who is
alone with his or her problem because the agency designed to help
is distant and understaffed. The whole culture of lawyering has
drifted to the place critics like Stone and Brandeis predicted about
the dangers of marketplaces for justice.

More and more in our times, critics are asking: What is a "good
lawyer,"[461] a "human" one"?[462] Does the legal system contribute to
a society that preserves the distribution of economic wealth and
social control? Is the legal system, like the prison system and the
farmworkers system I described, working for those who administer the system and have a stake in its continuation? Is the system
a reflection of prevailing cultural, racial, economic values? As this
critic wrote, "People working within the system become dependent on its perpetuation for their livelihoods and even for their
identities."[463]

That insight need not always lead to bad behavior. When Reverend Martin Luther King, Jr. was killed in April 1968, Washington, DC erupted into violence, as did many other cities. As arrests piled up, the criminal justice system collapsed—the courts and the jails and public defender systems were overrun. I knew the Chief Justice of our trial courts and asked him how I might help, and we worked together through the night doing what we could. The Bar Association and media helped recruit voluntary lawyers who could represent these burgeoning thousands of defendants whose volume had overrun the system. Many lawyers volunteered and served throughout the night, and without payments. They proudly performed a public service doing so.

A local philanthropist, Phil Stern approached me in the deserted street peopled by National Guard troops at 4:00am as I was leaving the courthouse. He asked what we were doing. I explained that I was helping the chief judge develop a contingency plan for criminal justice emergencies of this sort, and he said, "When this is all over, would you write a report about these problems? I'll have it printed and distributed."[464] I did.[465] As a consultant to the Kerner Commission I wrote about comparable efforts by lawyers in the many cities where the rioting continued.[466]

A similar event arose at a prison riot in DC when inmates held the head of the corrections department hostage during a frightening night. With Congresswoman Shirley Chisolm and other local leaders, we negotiated a settlement in a midnight court hearing where the inmates were promised that each of their complaints would be dealt with by court appointed attorneys who volunteered to do so, pro bono. Our intervention saved lives.[467]

My point is that lawyers can be public spirited when they are motivated to do so. That motivation should not be limited to emergency situations. If the legal profession fails to include the public's interest in more common everyday matters we work on, as some lawyers did in these two extraordinary events, our profession is no better than the agricultural farm owners, or the prison administrators, or the church officials whose silence and participation undercut those institutions by failing to serve their users.

CHAPTER FIVE

CONCLUSION

WHAT ARE THE ANSWERS?

Where do we go from here? The next generation, I suspect, is not entering law school to help make a better world. New law students are looking for respectable jobs to make a good living. There is nothing wrong with that, except when it becomes the germ of what else might follow. Once the goal of work is to make a good living, the need to make money can overcome all else and lead to choices of clients, fields of practice, and lifestyles. These priorities compound the initial perspective that being a lawyer is the same as other work where the riches go to the most driven and the rest is charity.

How does an ethical change in lawyering come about as more than a rhetorical editorial? How can reforms like those mentioned in this book become reality? What can sympathetic observers do?

To start, all the change agencies in and out of our profession must participate in the direction of reform. In 2019, the influential and conservative American Bar Association endorsed Justices Stone's and Brandeis's notion that our profession has changed to a business model over the last century and needs reform. Its Standing Committee on Professionalism instructed lawyers to enhance and promote "the fundamental tradition and core values of the legal profession in the 21st Century ... the lawyer's role in society as a whole."[468] This book examined that idea, and offers some steps in that direction.

LAW SCHOOLS

A shift in ethical perspectives within the profession can begin in law schools. To start, law schools must teach and encourage ethical options in their specialized legal practice and ethics courses, and in the traditional substantive courses—property, evidence, corporations, and criminal law—as well. The ethics of lawyering ought to be more than a passing requirement in law school curriculum.

In *Failing Law Schools*, law dean Brian Z. Tamanaha made the case that law schools are failing for several reasons. The cost of attendance is exorbitant, leaving 90 percent of graduates in debt. Law professors do a poor job of training law students. Matriculation is too long; perhaps we'd do better with two years than three. Professors are stressing theory over fundamentals of law practice. As a result, law schools are graduating a new crop of forty-five thousand indebted lawyers who will be entering a marketplace with twenty-five thousand new openings annually.[469]

Many law professors have had little or no practical experience to draw from in analyzing legal ethics. They are, according to Dean Tamanaha, scholars, theoreticians. Even the conservative current Supreme Court chief justice John Roberts has complained about "the tremendous disconnect between the legal academy and the legal profession." He said in 2007, "They occupy different universes. What the academy is doing, as far as I can tell, is largely of no use or interest to people who actually practice law." [470]

Law schools need to add courses on law practice taught by experienced practitioners and ethicists. I found that the bright, young law graduates of top law schools who worked for my firm were equipped to be appellate judges, but they didn't know much about handling day-to-day office and client protocols, let alone the moral dilemmas lawyers encounter.

The escalating costs of law schools contributes to the problem. Too many neophyte lawyers graduate heavily in debt. The extent of law student debt is striking. According to a *U.S. News & World Report* study covering 186 schools, 100,000 students in Florida and Louisiana graduated with debt totaling from $61,000 to $94,000. The fewest indebted grads were in North Dakota (34 percent, with an average of $68,000). The lowest debt totals on average were in Georgia, New Jersey, and Utah. The highest indebtedness averages were in big cities—Los Angeles, Washington, DC, San Francisco, and San Diego (ranging from $166,000 to $212,000).[471] On average, in 2018 only about 13 percent of law students graduated with no debt;[472] the rest have debts sometimes of $100,000 or more. That debt pressures graduates to seek jobs with commercial specialties rather than lower-paying jobs in government (such as in legal aid or as public defenders) or with private public interest organizations that cannot pay what large law firms do, not by a long shot.[473]

Dean Tamanaha's suggestion that law school matriculation be two years with a voluntary third for specialties if students prefer prompts me to think of another idea. Why not have all the essential courses in years one and two, like property, torts, contracts, constitutional law, procedure, as Tamanaha recommended? Stanford law Professor Deborah Rhode also recommended several levels of legal education—each involving either one, two, or three years of training.[474] And more readily accessible.

Apprenticeships have worked in many businesses and as an alternative to formal education in law. Today, California and a few other states offer a four-year non-academic alternative to gaining entrance to the legal profession as licensed attorneys. This alternative tier to becoming a professional should appeal to students who don't want to run up huge debts, as most law students do now. The hope is that those with clinical training may work in communities where minorities are especially in need of legal counseling.[475]

Seven states allow individuals to participate in apprenticeships in lieu of at least one of the three years of law school. In four of these states—California, Vermont, Virginia, and Washington—three to four years of apprenticeships completely negate the need to attend law school. The remaining three states—Maine, New York, and Wyoming—require individuals to attend at least one to two years of law school, but create an option to receive the rest of one's legal education via apprenticeship.[476]

I suggest in place of a third year for specialization, as Dean Tamanaha suggested, requiring a third year of public service in the profession working with organizations, public or private, that serve unserved citizens with their legal needs. The students would gain monitored clinical experiences and perhaps discover interests in fields that engage them. Then, better prepared, they would be free to work wherever they want. That system might also reduce their school debts.

Like the idea of national public service, this experience in legal education would accomplish several goals: training new lawyers in practical work in their fields of interest, developing a sense of professional pride in fulfilling public service, and assisting needy citizens by providing them with supervised legal services.

This time of training and public service might be combined with the idea of pairing retired lawyers who want to serve pro bono in fields in which they have expertise with charitable legal services programs in need of lawyer assistance, including mentoring the fledgling law students doing their third year of law training.

Lawrence Mirel, one of my former professional colleagues, started such an organization in Washington, DC.[477] His Emeritus Foundation did this kind of pairing of retired, experienced professionals (not exclusively lawyers) with organizations doing public services without adequate staffing funds to service their clients. Mirel's smart idea was that many healthy retirees want to slow down but not stop working, while many rookie lawyers have energy and are looking to have experienced mentors like these retirees.

The District of Columbia Bar has a Pro Bono Center, Advocacy and Justice Clinic that reeducates retirees, enabling them to work in new areas of law in which clients have unmet needs. One volunteer retiree who worked there in an area different from her professional experiences told an interviewer that she volunteered "when I had a midlife crisis and realized that I wanted to be both professionally fulfilled and give back to others using my professional skills." She added, "It helps my pro bono clients survive."[478]

Other jurisdictions could follow this model, with bar or other organizations or pro bono or free legal services providers, to match retirees and law students' requiring experiences doing clinical work.

College faculty members, judges, and diplomats regularly continue work in emeritus roles. Matching experienced lawyer retirees with the emerging class of law graduates for a year is a win-win-win situation, with the public as the third winner. The movie *The Intern* with Robert De Niro offered an entertaining but impressive example of the emeritus idea. Everyone came out ahead.

Using the Peace Corps and National Public Service as examples, the program—a Law Corps run by state bars—could train neophyte lawyers in local public service jobs, filling the needs of both the rookie lawyers and agencies doing good work for economically deprived clients. The military draft was a version of the same idea. My three years in the Air Force JAG educated me in the practicalities of law practice, and provided me with useful experiences, along with a respect for uniformed public service.

In his passionate book *Unusual Cruelty: The Complicity of Lawyers in the Criminal Justice System*, Alec Karakatsanis, a young reformist lawyer, asked, "How the culture of elite law schools produces professionals who tolerate a legal system that is profoundly unjust?" He questioned the differences between how law is written and how law is lived, much as Professor Kamisar did decades ago. "We advertise the law with beautiful inscriptions on our public monuments or lofty words in judicial opinions taught in law schools," Karakatsanis wrote, and then "crush poor people and people of color in our streets, our prisons, and our courtrooms."

As a former public defender in Washington and Alabama who now runs a civil rights organization, he asked if we lawyers are living our lives in accordance with how our moral values impact other people. He called for law schools to "create better models for legal careers" and for a new vanguard of lawyers to make their livings creating a system that does not victimize marginalized people.[479]

THE FALLOUT FROM THE CHANGED NATURE OF LAW PRACTICE

Law practice has changed in recent years. Law schools receive fewer applications for admission. A third of law school graduates can't find legal work. Average salaries have dropped 15 percent, and associates are told to bill more than two thousand billable hours a year. Moral values change when the profit motive governs economic, moral, and social values.

The results are negative. Denise Perme directs the DC Bar's lawyer assistance programs staff. It assists lawyers, students, and judges by providing them with mental-health counseling.[480] This active program is voluntary, confidential, and free. It deals with addiction, anxiety, depression, and stress, endemic problems for lawyers for whom mental stresses, billing long hours, and constant conflicts balancing work and life are common. The group provides evaluations, interventions, counseling, and referrals in the world's largest bar association, many of whom have deep dissatisfactions with their lives. "I would like to find something else to do that would satisfy me on a deeper level than practicing law" is their common complaint.

This problem is attributed, studies demonstrate, to the inhuman climate created by law schools and law firms. "Rather than build on the students' standards and moral compasses, law schools wipe the slates clean and discourage students' emotional side, sometimes resulting in depression and substance abuse."[481] In a legal education that tends to dehumanize people, rookie law students are trained to "think like lawyers" and set aside their sense of morality and fairness by adopting the adversarial system's external awards, which do not necessarily bring them happiness.[482]

One public interest lawyer wrote of his frustrations at not being able to "remake the system," unable to do for his tenant's clients what he wanted to do.[483] MacArthur Foundation "genius grant" awardee Rebecca Sandefur stated, "During law school, students' commitment to work for the public good is either crushed, or its meaning is changed to encompass more mainstream aspirations."[484] Law schools focus on fundamental skills through the case method but fail to teach law students about their civic duties and social responsibilities.

> I think being a public interest lawyer brings with it an internal conflict between feeling powerless to make change and feeling the great responsibility for the outcomes of our cases.... We toil as cogs in legal machines but also desire to dismantle them. We uphold the rule of law while questioning its foundations. We work within systems such as courts, corporations and governments while developing a deep knowledge of the flaws, cracks and hypocrisy within them.
>
> Ultimately, there can be no skill or superpower under the law. There is no solution in a whirlwind of power and force. We must seek incremental change, one case at a time. And we must look beyond our limited and ill-defined roles as lawyers to seek solutions.[485]

Why is the desire of law students to work for the public interest ignored or crushed? Why don't lawyers have a better understanding of their civic duties and social responsibilities? Obviously law school debt and other financial burdens make pursuing public interest careers a sacrifice. But there are other factors.

THE PRO BONO SYSTEM

The pro bono publico system, in which some lawyers and firms offer free legal services, is important and commendable. But it is a very small part of what our profession does (as small as 1 percent, one author posited[486]), and it is insufficient to meet the needs of the large number of people who cannot afford legal services. The rich get as much lawyering as they can afford, and they get better results. The Jeffrey Epstein sex scandal demonstrated that fact. He received a token sentence with the help of expensive star lawyers, and he obtained NDAs from his young victims.[487] Other less wealthy defendants get what is left over, which is not much, so most people do not get justice unless by fortuitous good fortune.

Lawyers' work, like their clients' behavior, is not neutral. And performing part-time pro bono work for charitable causes does not compensate for lawyers doing every day work that is arguably antisocial. Valuable and needed and laudable as it is, pro bono work by some lawyers may be cynically scorned as *noblesse oblige* in some instances, and in a harsher view, as social reparations. Is it unfair to criticize a lawyer who makes a private fortune keeping faulty cars or drugs on the market, who in his spare time provides legal help to a good government organization?

While the pro bono practices by lawyers and law firms offer one valuable and worthy relief to a legal system in need of lawyering, it is not a systemic solution to the problem of justice for sale. As Stanford Law professor and legal scholar Deborah Rhode reported, "A wide gap persists between professional rhetoric and professional practice." About 10 to 20 percent assist only causes they encourage (clean air, for example), not necessarily involving services to low-income clients. The average time lawyers perform pro bono work is less than half an hour a week. Pro bono contributions can be remarkable, providing "purpose and meaning to their professional lives." Yet Rhode's study demonstrated that, favorable examples aside, "most students do not have public service in law as part of their educational experience."[488]

The pro bono system can be expanded in meaningful ways—by law schools, bar groups, and special interest and not-for-profit organizations. Fifteen states allow pro bono work to count toward CLE credits. The ABA's Model Rule 6.1 urges every attorney to consider it a professional responsibility to provide legal services (fifty hours a year) to clients unable to pay. Most states have adopted similar guidelines, though none require it. Many law schools require pro bono work in order to graduate.

The DC Bar, for example, has actively promoted pro bono activities by members and was awarded for its championing these efforts in its offices around the country. Some law firms promote their recruiting by noting their pro bono work. While they remain inadequate, these advancements are indeed valuable. The question going forward is how to systematize a hospitable alternative for needy clients, one that is fair to lawyers. Perhaps the answer is licensing authorities—bar associations—requiring a set level of pro bono legal work to lessen the economic gap, if not close it.

Access to competent legal services must be provided for those other than rich people who already have that access, along with the other entitlements of their lives. Lawyers have a monopoly on providing legal services, and arguably that warrants imposing special obligations on them.[489] Professor Rhode argued persuasively that pro bono is more than philanthropy—it has moral significance, an essential part of professional responsibility. It needs to be institutionalized through the bar associations in each state.

PROFESSIONAL ORGANIZATIONS

Special interest bar associations, such as groups for women, minority groups, and other specialized law associations, could better monitor the current ethical excesses noted in this book. So could related professional organizations, prosecutorial agencies, legislatures, and courts that have supervisory powers over the issues discussed here. The National Association of Criminal Defense Lawyers, for example, advocates for decriminalization of some drug offenses, abolition of the death penalty, and broadening of legal aid—reforms that are against their economic interests. [490]

Courts could better monitor depositions, civil and criminal settlements, NDAs, and arbitrations as they do mediations. Judges mostly work hard and mean well, but they cannot be unaware of the charades they participate in and confirm with plea bargains in criminal cases and procedures in the civil adversary system like NDAs and closed records.

The National Association of State Trial Judges conducts summer seminars for its members. I taught one on legal writing for many years. The organization should add to its continuing education agenda some of the ethical subjects in this book—NDA and Brady oversight, for example. [491]

Poor people don't have expensive lobbyists, and law firms are unlikely to lobby, pro bono, for changes against their private economic interests. Interestingly, the largest and richest law firms have fewer ethics claims made against them than small firms and solo practitioners, perhaps suggesting a cultural prejudice? [492]

An increased sense of institutional responsibility could do much to further a shift in ethics. A dramatic example of this is the judge's role in sanctioning and overseeing the inherent flaw of prosecutorial misconduct. One exoneree aptly asked, how come when a prosecutor acts wrongly and knowingly in a Brady situation, the innocent defendant is convicted and executed, and that district attorney isn't indicted? Only when professional prosecutorial organizations and judges in their own courts move in the direction of responsible monitoring of these lawyers will this hypocrisy be eliminated.

The need for judicial and prosecutorial responsibility over the excesses of the criminal justice system was displayed in the Mississippi case of Curtis Flowers. He was a black man prosecuted by white prosecutors and judges for the 1966 murders of four people in a Winona, Mississippi, furniture store. Black people were peremptorily challenged excessively during jury selection, so the last jury empaneled was 11–1 white. Flowers's six convictions were reversed on appeal or ended in hung juries, but Flowers was imprisoned for more than twenty years. In 2019, he was finally released on bail after 23 years in prison.[493] Eventually the US Supreme Court sent the case back for a seventh retrial. Justice Brett Kavanaugh wrote that the government had violated the Constitution in its jury selections. "We cannot ignore that history," he wrote after reviewing Flowers's saga,[494] which was the subject of an award-winning podcast *In the Dark*, on American Public Media.[495] Flowers is now represented by able capital punishment counsel from the Mississippi Center for Justice.[496]

As of December 2019, Flowers is out of prison, released on bail provided by an anonymous donor, and free after twenty-three years. After three convictions were dismissed by the state supreme court, and two ended with hung juries, DA Doug Evans recused himself from trying any further prosecutions of Flowers.[497] Supreme Court justice Samuel Alito wrote this case was "one of a kind."[498] Would that it be so.

In 2008, veteran Alaska senator Ted Stevens was convicted of making false statements in his financial disclosure forms. Stevens was represented by impressive counsel but was still convicted.

After the conviction, the Justice Department conducted a review of the evidence and found egregious Brady examples of exculpatory evidence that had not been turned over to defense counsel by the department prosecutors. The court appointed an independent investigator to look into the matter. He found "systemic concealment of significant exculpatory evidence"[499] by the experienced prosecutors.

If that kind of prosecutorial abuse occurred in a high-visibility, politically potent case when top DC trial lawyers represented the defendant—no doubt for a very expensive (well-earned, but not available to most people) representation—imagine what the situation is with a poor defendant, like Flowers, with inadequate funds and thus more limited representation. Or in the 97 percent of cases that are plea bargained, in which defendants would not even know about such misconduct.

The Justice Department's report recommended that Rule 16 of Federal Rules of Criminal Procedure be amended to make the Brady rule of court a specific and unqualified federal law with enforcement procedures. The proposed amendment to Rule 16.1 was introduced to Congress in December 2019. Ordinarily the process—when successful—takes three years from a rule's formal amendment proposal to its enactment.

About sixty district attorney offices around the United States have established conviction integrity units to review wrongful convictions, resulting in six hundred exonerations. A group of thirty-six prosecutors around the United States have supported prosecutors' efforts to reopen cases where justice demanded it. "Elected prosecutors should not be expected to wait or rely on the action of others to correct legal wrongs; indeed they are ethically required to proactively address these concerns."[500]

As we know from the many popular cop shows on television, and from Michael Connelly books about homicide detective Hieronymus "Harry" Bosch and his lawyer relative in the *Lincoln Lawyer*, most police officers have cold case files where unsolved cases may be brought to light by new evidence. Why not have comparable offices in real-life state and local attorney general offices where those excessive police and prosecutor crimes and Brady violations by overly aggressive police and prosecutors could be "policed"? Current complaints as well as past, overlooked ones could be reviewed when the circumstances warrant.

New York now is second in the nation (Texas is first) in convictions of innocent people. New York State has created a State Commission on Prosecutorial Conduct to provide independent oversight and accountability over prosecutorial misconduct. Existing institutions must sanction egregious misconduct like witness perjury, using fraudulent evidence, and hiding exculpatory evidence.

The Commission on Prosecutorial Conduct is modeled after the New York State Commission on Judicial Conduct ("Judicial Commission") that reviews allegations relating to the misbehavior of judges. Before the Commission on Judicial Conduct was established, state judges were regulated by "a patchwork of courts and procedures" that proved blatantly inadequate: only twenty-three judges were disciplined in the *century* before the Judicial Commission's creation. By contrast, since the Judicial Commission's creation in 1975, "1,124 complaints involving 848 judges have resulted in disciplinary action," including 169 judicial removals. An additional "1,721 complaints resulted in cautionary letters to the judges involved."[501] These numbers do not account for the more than one thousand other matters that ended preemptively due to voluntary resignations or court vacancies. Unfortunately, the Commission on Prosecutorial Conduct is *not* yet in force, nor may it ever be.

Not only does prosecutorial misconduct ruin the lives of many innocent people, but it also costs the public money to relitigate cases and pay off faulty convictions that do come to light. It also lowers public confidence in the criminal justice system.

Court interventions have led to diversion programs as an alternative to incarceration in appropriate cases. Some judges have monitored settlement agreements to assure that nondisclosure agreements and plea bargains, which are potentially unjust, are not mindlessly rubber-stamped. Judges should exercise more active control over these situations. When a gross Brady violation occurs, the presiding judge—or the appellate court—should refer that case to an appropriate prosecutorial official and grand jury. Judges should better monitor excessive civil depositions that exploit the adversary system. Governors can exercise their clemency powers more broadly to correct correctable injustices. Police authorities should better monitor their own officers, and when they are charged with misconduct, an independent review agency should be the judge.

We all should appreciate the public service that police and prosecutors perform and the need not to second-guess their dangerous actions. But that does not mean that courts and juries should always take the side of those officers when their worst behavior is demonstrated. There are regular cases of excessive police brutality that led to civil unrest because police generally are exonerated. The Eric Garner "I can't breathe" case is a classic example; there federal prosecution was halted following an order to do so by Attorney General William Barr himself.[502] George Washington Law professor Paul Butler wrote in his book *Chokehold: Policing Black Men* that the word *chokehold* has become a metaphor for police violence against black and brown men.[503]

Anyone who has followed the news in recent years is aware of highly charged cases where police conduct generated civil unrest and litigation. In 2018, 992 people in the United States were shot and killed by members of law enforcement, and a disproportionate number of those victims were minorities. Rarely are police disciplined.[504] An independent review agency (not part of the system being investigated) should oversee these cases.

The media has a critical responsibility to highlight these problems and push for appropriate changes. I have often observed that a highly motivated investigative reporter often wins a press award for revealing awful jail or prison conditions, employer excesses of the crudest criminal variety, and inequities of police and bar and court procedures where economics governed access to justice. The journalism is valuable and commendable, but the necessary follow-up reforms do not automatically follow. Rachel Carson's *Silent Spring*, Ralph Nader's auto safety book, Marjorie Stoneman Douglas's book about the despoiling of the Everglades, my books about bail and prison reform and farmworker exploitation have all promoted reforms. But the institutions themselves need a self-cleansing apparatus to clean house before public scolding exposes their problems.

Most institutions are run for the benefit of the administrators of their institutions, not their clientele or consumers. They have a built-in focus on their own well-being, not on what the institution is created to accomplish. The Catholic Church cases mentioned earlier offer one extreme example of an institution protecting itself over its users. So, too, do the professional sports organizations, media groups, and government agencies that punish legitimate whistleblowers. The legal profession must do more to professionalize and equalize access to justice for the public.

The bar associations are experimenting with new models for law firms.[505] Some alternatives, like using technology to make certain legal forms available to low income clients, present helpful opportunities. Non-profit sliding scale legal services have been tried in Utah to address the gap in legal services for those who aren't offered lawyers under traditional fee models.[506] The ABA named the founders of this model (tried now in 30 other places) Legal Rebels of 2015.

The expansion of using non-lawyers in law firms—lobbyists, consultants, technological experts, for example—raise questions to traditionalists. Using outside experts where necessary makes sense. But including such non-lawyers in the firm itself takes lawyering further into the business model rather than the professional model. The experiments in the United Kingdom, Germany and Australia are gaining popularity there. Some states here (Arizona, California, Utah, District of Columbia) do, too. This idea can lead to further commercializing law practice and diminishing the ethical and moral aspects of our profession, all the more. Some large firms already provide nursery care, restaurant services, useful, expensive, and typical of the business model.

State and federal governments—judicial and legislative—must ensure that in *all* civil and criminal cases, the basic right to adequate legal assistance is available. That is not the case today, and the situation denies basic fairness and justice to the public. Courts can expand their controls over the majority of cases that do not go to trial. Legislators and courts should have officials or supervisors to oversee equal justice matters.

Our civil justice system can and should require, legislatively and judicially, counsel to indigents, and it should provide adequate funds to make their representation real and comparable to what wealthy users of the legal system have available.

Judge Johnson made the case for such a proposition in his extensive opinion in *Quail v. Municipal* Court for the Los Angeles Judicial District of Los Angeles County. "It is difficult to escape the conclusion that in the field of civil litigation California's indigents are not entitled to the same in forma pauperis right as English serfs have enjoyed since medieval times and this right includes appointment of free counsel," he wrote.[507]

The United States Supreme Court finally construed the Sixth Amendment to create a constitutional right to free counsel for indigents in federal felony prosecutions. It took another twenty-five years before the Court applied this requirement to the states.[508]

Denying the assistance of a free lawyer to indigent civil litigants allows poverty to deprive poor people of their fundamental interests in "access to the courts" and to a "hearing where they have the assistance of counsel." Fears about "intolerable burdens" on the legal system cannot justify ignoring the common law or constitutional rights to counsel in civil cases. Most other Western democracies have lived for decades, even centuries providing comprehensive legal entitlement to free counsel in civil cases.

Legal Aid in civil cases and public defenders organizations in criminal cases must be adequately funded, to a level at least equal to prosecution offices and civil justice organizations. All other suggestions are unlikely alone to change the justice system, welcome improvements as they are. It comes down to the governments, state and federal, to make civil legal aid and criminal public defenders systems a fair competitive system, as the present system is for clients who are well represented. That is far from the case, and will remain so with the justice system until the hortatory words we use to describe it are a reality. Creating a fair system is not socialism, nor is it a replacement of the current capitalistic system, but an improvement of it. As with health care, it is essential that the government step in to make equal justice in civil and criminal cases a right of all citizens.

The police and prosecutorial misconduct cases that were eventually discovered and reported demonstrate a systemic police and prosecutorial problem, beyond the occasional inevitable mistake. The drug test labs described earlier made this point. Experts who are critical of this situation have called for accreditation, hiring, monitoring and management reforms, and background checks of hires. One knowledgeable academic wrote, "We can't delegate to a private organization what should rightfully be a function of government."[509] The National Academy of Sciences 2009 study of forensic science issued its report urging thirteen reforms of staffing, funding, certification, accreditation, training, and continued education. Bills governing forensic science crime labs are pending in Congress, demanding better science and management.

Federal judge Jed Rakoff added an important and authoritative article on bad science.[510] Crime shows of the *CSI* format have convinced the public that science captures criminals, playing into our prejudices in favor of police and prosecutors. False confession and convictions result when defendants do not have the economic resources to hire lawyers and technological experts to dispute government witnesses, paid for by the government.

Through the last century, Judge Rakoff reported, forensic evidence involving hair, fibers, paint, clothing, bloodstains, bite marks, handwriting comparisons, and firearms evidence have had a major influence on wrongful convictions. One-quarter of scientific evidence in 2,400 cases analyzed in 1989 by the National Registry of Exonerations proved false and misleading. The advent of DNA, far more scientifically sound, has resulted in many convictions *and* exonerations.

Judge Rakoff suggested, among other reforms, that trial judges do a better job examining offered scientific evidence and better supervision of Brady violations. The 1993 case *Daubert v. Merrell Dow Pharmaceuticals* made the argument for better supervision to weed out junk science.[511] That ruling has been applied in thirty-eight states in civil cases, but rarely in criminal cases.

In 2009, the National Academy of Sciences issued a lengthy report critical of junk science and urging reforms. In 2013, a National Commission on Forensic Science reached the same conclusion and made forty recommendations for reform measures calling for rigorous testing and eliminating subjectivity favoring preferred conclusions. Court-appointed experts make sense; independent scrutiny of police and prosecutors evidence does too. The report also recommended an Independent National Institute of Forensic Science to promulgate standards and oversee reform of this problem. Rakoff concluded, "Crime shows can live with these lies (of so called experts) . . . but our criminal justice system should not."[512]

Bottom line: most criminal defendants are indigent and unable to afford forensic experts, even when counsel are provided.

CIVILITY IN THE PRACTICE OF LAW

We might also consider the role of civility, meaning professionalism, modeled by those polite but crafty English barristers, in an expanded ethics of law practice. Civility, behavior for the good of the community, is a private virtue and a public necessity. Philosophically speaking, it is more than affability and politeness and manners, though surely they are a part of the idea. Lawyers must see themselves as aspiring to dual loyalties, both to the public legal system and in their role of advocates for clients.

An example where manners and fair precedent may go out the window is in depositions where no judges are present and only the transcripts provide witnesses. Lawyers can behave like participants in a World Wrestling Entertainment program. One study complained that "the gradual degradation of the practice of law" has led to perverse, uncivil lawyer conduct and a resulting rise in "mental illness and substance abuse."[513] Some state court systems, South Carolina for one, have required pledges of civility by attorneys.

Keith Bybee, a legal scholar at Syracuse University Law School, wrote about *How Civility Works*,[514] describing it as "a foundational form of good manners," a code of conduct in public behavior. It is, Bybee wrote of civility, "a species of morality." He quoted Benjamin Franklin: "Do the right things and in time you will learn to want to do the right thing."[515] Philosopher Ruth Grant added, "It is impossible for people to permanently set aside moral principles for the sake of interactions anchored solely in self-interest."[516] And Bybee added, apropos of what this book suggests, "We need not wait for moral transformation in order to exploit the rules for appropriate conduct."[517] This point returns to law schools, which have the opportunity to inculcate a culture of civility consistent with the competitive style of legal representation consistent with the adversarial system.

MIDDLE GROUNDS OF REFORM

Some reasonable ripples of reform are happening. Current interest in mediation, a more humane dispute-resolution alternative to the adversarial system with its surprises, tricks, and concealments, is a result of modern criticisms of adversarial justice.[518]

Court administrators, noting the increasing volume of cases coming to courts, have sought and successfully used alternative techniques for settling disputes by modifying the adversary system.[519] Using magistrates, special masters, hearing officers, and simplified procedures, traditional trials have been replaced in categories of civil cases by arbitration, mediation, and conciliation. The costs and stress of litigation have been reduced, and the parties' satisfaction with results has risen.

Under arbitration, disputing parties choose a neutral arbitrator with expertise in the matters in question. A less combative atmosphere prevails, relaxed and more informal procedures are followed, and the time and costs of the dispute are lessened. The practice is now common in matrimonial cases, and it is required in many business disputes.

In a recent case, employees challenged their employment contracts' mandatory arbitration clauses, which some critics claim favors employers who are lawyer staffed and funded. The matter reached the United States Supreme Court in 2017, and in 2018, the Court reached a decision upholding the clauses, which required workers and their employers to resolve their conflicts in arbitration rather than in court.[520]

But without legal representation, claimants may find this requirement unfair or onerous. Plaintiff lawyers may have come up with a technique that turns the tables on employers who relied on enforced arbitration as a deterrent to small claims, averaging $700. Some law firms have organized mass common arbitration claims against some large companies. Now, "companies are trying to weasel their way out of the system they created," it has been reported.[521]

Conciliation and mediation seek to clarify issues and assist parties to arrive at a mutually agreeable resolution in a more amicable setting, presided over by non-judicial experts. Parties must agree to any result, or to bring in the lawyers and go forward with litigation if they cannot. Sometimes binding arbitration clauses are required, though they are usually disadvantageous to the weaker party.

Finally, some firms are experimenting with various alternative fee arrangements (AFAs)—a 2019 survey found that "88 percent of respondents' law departments" have done so. Up to 71 percent say they are more cost-efficient than hourly rates, according to recent surveys.[522] These alternative fee arrangements include flat fees, caps, and discounts with bonuses. However, their rationale is not increasing accessibility to low- and middle-class prospective clients. AFA reform should deal with the fundamental problem this book focuses on: access to legal assistance for poor and middle-class clients.

I organized and represented a writer's organization for many years, and my firm provided a discounted legal services at reduced rates program for members. Other organizations might pursue this idea for providing discounted legal assistance for clients with limited means.

HOW TO CHANGE THE SYSTEM

There was a short-lived period half a century ago when public-interest law practice compelled law students and young and high-minded lawyers, and private and government agencies evolved to harness

their interests. Law firms, then and now, have contributed significant pro bono services to worthy clientele, even if it didn't make
systemic changes. But the basic culture of law practice remained
money-driven, the public interest work an incidental interest.

I think being a public-interest-minded lawyer brings with it an
internal conflict between feeling powerless to make change and the
feeling of disappointment with outcomes out of their control.

Toward what ends are the skills we are taught to be used? Justice Stone asked. Nearly a century later, I suggest again that lawyers question ourselves and reexamine our personal and professional
codes of conduct. We ought not need formal legal education to
know not to abuse the adversary system in depositions, or not to
assist clients in laundering money. But cases reported here suggest
we do need consciousness- raising in these ethical standards.

The legal system is a human one, and it will never be perfect or
flawless. But the problems discussed in this book can be improved
in major, systemic ways. Unless they are, we will never see the true
national reform that is necessary if we are to claim to be a real democratic government.

Money is a central part of the problem, as it is with most national
problems. The reforms discussed here do not mean all people must
have everything that other people have. Cars, homes, vacation favor-
ites are everyone's hope and dream. But food, clothing, shelter, health
care, and legal assistance are in another category of rights that should
be available to everyone, at least by minimal human standards. "The
right to a decent education was declared a constitutional right in a
federal case in Detroit in 2020." [523] Money as the critical factor in
having legal assistance, in paying for bail and fines, to the extreme of
capital punishment, should have no place in the justice system.

As essayist David Brooks wrote, apropos of the extraordinary
impact of the corona virus, ". . . the inequality in the world seems more
obscene when the difference between rich and poor is life or death." [524]

The government, the private sector, and the media, the academic, and the charity worlds must join forces to even the balance of the scales of justice.

The culture of our profession can only change with the speed of an ocean liner making a mid-ocean turn. Many parts must function at the same time—the law schools, the bar and professional organizations, the courts, and the legislators. It will be a long but necessary turn of events, but a necessary one to begin.

We are what we do, I wrote at the start of this book. We lawyers need to keep that thought in mind as we pursue our professional lives and determine what our roles are and what we seek to do with our brief opportunities in our profession.

According to the United Nations' Universal Declaration of Human Rights, Article 2.5:

> Everyone has the right to a standard of living adequate for the
> health and well-being of himself and of his family, including food,
> clothing, housing, and medical care and necessary social services. [525]

Airey v. Ireland [526] dealt with the European Community's human rights guarantee that civil litigants are to receive a "fair hearing" in civil as well as criminal cases. If a "fair hearing" requires governments to provide free counsel to indigent litigants in Europe, why didn't "due process" and "equal protection" require the same in the United States?

Georgetown law professor Peter Edelman has written about the American welfare system's failures. In his recent book *Not a Crime to Be Poor: The Criminalization of Poverty in America*, he demonstrated that the bar, the courts, police, and our justice and social agencies haven't improved in the past half century. We know what the problems are, Professor Edelman wrote, but "we lack the will to act as a nation to rectify these problems." [527]

The nation has struggled in recent years to agree upon the application of the term "and necessary social services" to health care. This book presses the same question about our country's access to justice in and out of courts, in civil and criminal affairs. Our profession advertises "equal justice under law" in its rhetoric and on its edifices. But this book demonstrates that the goal is not met for most people in this uniquely prosperous country.

Does the responsibility to right this social wrong fall on the executive branch, which emphasizes and deemphasizes the problems of the poor cyclically for political reasons? That was the case with the promising war against poverty in the LBJ era and after. He and we thought we had defined a problem and offered solutions. Congress passed appropriate laws and determined it had done what it could. The problem was in fact not solved by the executive or legislative branches. In the farmworker case, Congress had passed laws that the executive branch (the Department of Labor in that case) did not enforce. When the court became involved, attention was paid and action was taken, but courts are the weakest branch in assuring rights as they have limited enforcement powers.

Voices like those mentioned in this book have identified the problem and offered paths to reform. Critic Lincoln Caplan reported that "poverty in America is a product of the combination of capitalism and a limited welfare state. No amount of creative lawyering can eliminate poverty."[528] Political voices have raised this question in the 2020 presidential campaign. New legal technologies need to develop accessible applications to offer alternatives to poor and illiterate people.[529] The corporate and internet world have a role to play in this national effort.[530]

It is not only the trial courts, where most cases begin and end, that could provide the reform of excesses such as those pointed out in this book. In its ability to systematically reform nationwide laws, the U.S. Supreme Court can make a huge difference, as lawyer-journalist Adam Cohen demonstrated in his new book *Supreme Inequality* [531]. Cohen makes the case, and offers examples, how the U.S. Supreme Court under Earl Warren (1953–1969) moved from judicial activism favoring minorities to recent times when the current Court moved the opposite way politically. Cohen cited voter registration cases that prejudiced poor voters,, along with three strikes laws that imprison poor people for life for minor crimes, as well as campaign finance and class action laws that lessened the powers of the poor and civil matters that prejudiced litigants without lawyers. Changing this present political leaning of the U.S. Supreme Court is a route which seems unlikely in the immediate future. We can hope, and vote.

The legal profession, and each of us in it, along with the public, government agencies, the press, and academics must be guided by our own lights and values and responsibilities. The public should insist upon it.

The late Edmond Cahn, a wise and inspiring law professor at New York University Law School, wrote this passage 60 years ago; it should edify us all today:

> If, by way of a metaphor, we imagine the ancient stronghold of Jericho as a citadel of injustice, then no wonder its walls collapsed—not, however, as some have thought, when the priests blew their trumpets but, as the Scripture makes clear, when the people shouted in unison with a great and mighty voice. [532]

ACKNOWLEDGEMENTS

Alan Morrison and Earl Johnson read my manuscript and offered wise suggestions,

Gerrie Sturman and Madeline Greathouse were constant colleagues and invaluable helpers throughout.

My thanks also to Stephanie Beard and her team at Turner Publishing—Heather Howell and Kathleen Timberlake.

NOTES

1 Jonathan H. Adler, "Why We Need Fewer Lawyers," *Wall Street Journal*, September 7, 2017 (commenting on Benjamin Barton and Stephano Bibas, *Rebooting Justice* [New York: Encounter Books, 2017]).

2 Nathan L. Hecht, "The Twilight Zone," *Daedelus*, Winter 2019, 148 (1). Also, James Madison, "The Structure of the Government Must Furnish the Proper Checks and Balances between the Different Departments," The Federalist Papers, No. 51 (1788).

3 Katarina Pistor, *The Code of Capital: How the Law Creates Wealth and Inequality*, Princeton University Press, 2019.

4 Adam Tooze, "How 'Big Law' makes Big Money," New York Review of Books, p. 25, February 13, 2020

5 IBID at p. 26

6 IBID p. 27.

7 David P. Miranda, "President's Message: Influencing the Future," *NYSBA Journal* 22 (2015).

8 "Honesty/Ethics in Professions," Gallup (2019).

9 Debra Cassens Weiss "At least 3 BigLaw firms charge more than $1K per hour for top associates," *ABA Law Journal*, May 27, 2020.

10 Megan Tribe, *Decade of Dissolution: The Top Law Firm Failures of the 2010s*, Bloomberg L. (Dec. 23, 2019).

11 *Id.*

12 Bosman, Jaap "INSIGHT: Fundamental Changes Coming to the Legal Industry this Decade", BloombergLaw.com, Feb. 5, 2020

13 Daniel Markovits, *The Meritocracy Trap*,, noted in David Brooks, "Who's Driving Inequality?", NY Times, Apr. 24, 2020., p. A-23.

14 Debra Bruno, "James Sandman Goes Back to School", *Washington Lawyer*, June 2020, p. 30.

15 Alpheus Thomas Mason, *Harlan Fiske Stone: Pillar of the Law* (New York: Viking Press, 1956); see also, Chris Hedges, *The Corruption of the Law*, Truthdig, August 20, 2017. Various sources have stated the adage that it is better "to teach a youth how to live rather than how to make a living." Examples date back to Dr. Everett Clark Sanford in a 1910 volume of *the Journal of Pedagogy* (pp. 122–23), and continue to the modern day with the words of Samuel Hazo in an August 9, 2015, article in the *Pittsburgh Post-Gazette*: "The effect on 'accommodating' universities is that the ideal of the liberally educated student (he or she who is primarily concerned with learning how to live rather than how to make a living) becomes secondary."

16 Jacobellis v. Ohio, 378 U.S. 184, 197(1964) (Stewart, J., concurring) (defining porn: "I know it when I see.").

17 Owen Fiss, *Pillars of Justice: Lawyers and the Liberal Tradition* (Cambridge, MA: Harvard University Press, 2017).

18 Ibid., 96.

19 American Bar Association Commission of Professionalism, ". . . In the Spirit of Public Service: A Blueprint for the Rekindling of Lawyer Professionalism" 15 (1986).

20 See Timothy Terrell and James Wildman, "Rothenberg Professionalism," 41 *Emory Law Journal* 403 (1992).

21 Harper Lee, *To Kill a Mockingbird* (Philadelphia, PA: J. B. Lippincott & Co., 1960).

22 Irving Stone, *Clarence Darrow for the Defense: A Biography* (New York: Doubleday, 1941).

23 Foster v. Illinois, 332 U.S. 134, 142 (1947) (Rutledge, J., dissenting).

24 Thomas L. Shaffer and Robert F. Cochran Jr., *Lawyers, Clients, and Moral Responsibility* (Eagan, MN: Thomson/West, 2009), 10.

25 Ibid., 117.

26 Ibid., 25.

27 James B. Donovan, *Strangers on a Bridge: The Case of Colonel Abel and Francis Gary Powers* (New York: Scribner, 2015, 1964), 13.

28 Raymond Hernandez and David Kochieniewski, "As New Lawyer, Senator Was Active in Tobacco's Defense," *New York Times,* March 26, 2009, A1.

29 Dorothy Samuels, "Smoke and Politics: Considering Senator Gillibrand's Tobacco Past," *New York Times*, April 8, 2009, A22.

30 Ibid.

31 Douglas O. Linder and Nancy Levit, *The Good Lawyer: Seeking Quality in the Practice of Law* (New York: Oxford University Press, 2014), 68–69, 70.

32 Ibid., 70.

33 "Groundwater Contamination with Chromium-6 in Hinkley, California," *Environmental Justice Atlas*, April 9, 2018.

34 *A Civil Action*, directed by Steven Zaillian, Touchstone Pictures, 1998; Jonathan Harr, *A Civil Action* (New York: Vintage Books 1996). Daniel J. Fitzgibbons, "A Decade After the Woburn Toxic Waste Case, Chemist Still Ponders Truth, Justice," *Campus Chronicle*, August 25, 2000.

35 *A Civil Action*, directed by Steven Zaillian, Touchstone Pictures, 1998; Jonathan Harr, *A Civil Action* (New York: Vintage Books 1996).

36 Nathaniel Rich, "Rob Bilott v. DuPont," *New York Times Magazine,* January 10, 2016, 36.

37 Robert Bilott, *Exposure: Poisoned Water, Corporate Greed, and One Lawyer's Twenty-Year Battle against DuPont* (New York: Atria Books, 2019).

38 Gerald Posner *PHARMA: Greed, Lies, and the Poisoning of America,* (New York: Avid Reader Press, 2020).

39 Mike Magner, *A Trust Betrayed: The untold Story of Camp Lejeune and the Poisoning of Generations of Marines and Their Families* (Cambridge, MA: Da Capo Press, 2014).

40 Tunku Varadarajan, "The Amazing Madoff Clawback," *Wall Street Journal*, November 30, 2018.

41 Picard and his partner in this effort, David Sheehan, continued their work collectively as co-leaders of the Madoff Recovery Initiative. The Initiative was funded by the Securities Investor Protection Corporation, the entity through which individuals could file their recovery claims. Madoff Recovery Initiative.

42 Alpheus Thomas Mason, *Harlan Fiske Stone: Pillar of the Law* (New York: Viking Press, 1956), 383.

43 Ibid., 95.

44 Ronald Goldfarb, "Lawyers Should Be Judged by the Clients They Keep," *Washington Post*, April 6, 1997, C3.

45 Thomas L. Shaffer and Robert F. Cochran, *Lawyers, Clients, and Moral Responsibility* (Eagan, MN: Thomson/West, 2009), 89.

46 Michael S. Schmidt and Maggie Haberman, "To What Giuliani Said, His Former Firm Objects," *New York Times*, May 11, 2018, A18.

47 Jill Abramson, "Lawyers, Lawyers Everywhere. And None to Represent Trump," *Guardian*, March 28, 2018).

48 Marc Fisher, "True to the Law's Principles or Betraying Her Own?," *Washington Post*, June 12, 2017.

49 Niraj Chokshi, "Alan Dershowitz Says Martha's Vineyard is 'Shunning' Him Over Trump," *New York Times*, July 3, 2018.

50 Joseph Tartakovsky, "Dickens v. Lawyers," *New York Times*, February 6, 2012, A23.

51 Ibid., quoting Joseph Epstein, *In a Carboard Belt!: Essays, Personal Liberty, and Savage* (New York: Houghton Mifflin Co., 2007), 94.

52 Steven Grosby, "Lawyers Should Read Dostoevsky," *Law & Liberty*, January 29, 2016.

53 Matthew Reisener, "Does Kafka's 'The Trial' Have Lessons for Today?," *National Interest*, February 23, 2018.

54 Jane Desmarais, "Preferring Not To: The Paradox of Passive Resistance in Herman Melville's 'Bartleby,'" 36 *Journal of the Short Story in English* (2001).

55 William Simon, "Ethics, Professionalism and Meaningful Work," 26 *Hofstra Law Review* 445 (1997).

56 Alan Dershowitz, *Letters to a Young Lawyer* (New York: Basic Books, 2001), 65.

57 Correspondence with Alan B. Morrison, Lerner Family Associate Dean for Public Interest & Public Service Law, George Washington University Law School.

58 Raymond Chandler, *The Long Goodbye* (Vintage Books, First Vintage Crime/Black Lizard Edition, August 1992), 56.

59 *The West Wing*, "In the Shadow Two Gunmen: Part I," NBC, broadcast October 4, 2000.

60 Indiana Lawyer Staff "Study: Millennial law partners share common values with older generations" THE INDIANA LAWYER, April 2, 2020.

61 Sheelah Kolhatkar "The Personal Toll of Whistleblowing," *New Yorker*, January 28, 2019.

62 Ronald Goldfarb, "James Comey's Conflicted Loyalty," *Washington Lawyer*, August/September 2018.

63 Douglas O. Linder and Nancy Levit, *The Good Lawyer: Seeking Quality in the Practice of Law* (New York: Oxford University Press, 2014), 210.

64 Nicholas Nehamas, "'A Mickey Mouse Operation': How Panama Papers Law Firm Dumped Clients, Lost Miami Office," *Miami Herald*, June 21, 2018.

65 US Attorney's Office Sourthern District of New York, *Four Defendants Charged in Panama Papers Investigation*, US Department of Justice, April 4, 2018.

66 *In re Koplik*, 168 A.D.3rd 163 (1st Dept. 2019); *In re Jankoff*, 165 A.D.3d 58 (1st Dept.2018). Lawyers like Koplik and Jankoff who provided information effectuating the minister's aims violated Rules 1.2(d) (counseling a client in conduct known to be illegal or fraudulent) and 8.4(h) (conduct adversely reflecting on a lawyer's fitness).

67 https://www.cbsnews.com/news/hidden-camera-investigation-money-laundering-60-minutes/

68 Si Aydiner, "Money Laundering, Lawyers, and Escrow: The Case for Voluntary Due Diligence".Law.com (NY Law Journal) Apr. 1, 2020.

69 Julia Jacobs, "Firm at Center of Panama Papers Sues Netflix Over 'The Laundromat,'" *New York Times*, October 17, 2019, C-3.

70 Jake Bernstein, *Secrecy World: Inside the Panama Papers Investigation of Illicit Money Networks and the Global Elite* (New York: Henry Holt & Co., 2017).

71 Kirk Semple, et al., "Panama Papers Cast Light on a Law Firm Founded on Secrecy," *New York Times*, April 6, 2016, A1.

72 Nicholas Nehamas, "'A Mickey Mouse Operation': How Panama Papers Law Firm Dumped Clients, Lost Miami Office," *Miami Herald*, June 21, 2018; *Miami Herald*, McClatchy, and an international consortium of investigative journalists based in Washington, DC.

73 John Grisham, *The Rainmaker* (New York: Doubleday, 1995).

74 Deborah L. Rhode, "Ethical Perspectives on Legal Practice," 37 *Stanford Law Review* (1985) 589, 623.

75 For articles detailing interesting studies on this subject see Monroe H. Freedman's articles, "Our Constitutionalized Adversary System," 1 *Chapman Law Review* 57 (1998), and "Professionalism in the American Adversary System," 41 *Emory Law Journal* 467 (1992).

76 See Monroe H. Freedman, "Professionalism in the American Adversary System," 41 *Emory Law Journal* 467 (1992); Lassiter v. Department of Social Services., 452 U.S. 18 (1981).

77 See Sartor v. Ark. Nat. Gas Co., 321 US 620, 627 (1944).1944)

78 Earl Johnson, Jr. "50 Years of Gideon, 47 Years Working Toward a 'Civil Gideon,'" 47 *Clearinghouse Rev. Journal of Poverty Law and Policy* 47 (2013)

79 "Amendment 6.8.1.4: Effective Assistance of Counsel," *Constitution Annotated*.

80 Powell v. Alabama, 287 U.S. 45, 71–72 (1932).

81 Ibid.

82 Amendment 6.8.1.4: Effective Assistance of Counsel," *Constitution Annotated*.

83 Amendment 6.8.1.4: Effective Assistance of Counsel," *Constitution Annotated* (quoting *United States v. Cronic*, 466 U.S. 648, 657–59 (1984)); see also, Strickland v. Washington, 466 U.S. 668 (1984).

84 466 U.S. 688 (1984).

85 Geoffrey C. Hazard and Angelo Dondi, 2006, Faculty Scholarship-Series, Paper 2329.

86 John H. Langbein, "The German Advantage in Civil Procedure," 52 *University of Chicago Law Review* 823, 825 (1985).

87 Monroe H. Freedman, "Our Constitutionalized Adversary System," 1, *Chapman Law Review* 57, 63 (1998).

88 Judge Marvin Frankel, *Partisan Justice* (New York: Hill & Wang, 1980).

89 "The Adversary System: Who Wins? Who Loses?," JRank.

90 Douglas O. Linder and Nancy Levit, *The Good Lawyer: Seeking Quality in the Practice of Law* (New York: Oxford University Press, 2014), 108.

91 Mark J. Green, *The Other Government: The Unseen Power of Washington Lawyers* (New York: W.W. Norton & Co., revised edition 1978) (1975).

92 Ellen Gabler, Megan Twohey, and Jodi Kantor, "New Accusers Expand Harvey Weinstein Sexual Assault Claims Back to ⊠70s," *New York Times*, October 30, 2017, A9.

93 Julie K. Brown, "How a Future Trump Cabinet Member Gave a Serial Sex Abuser the Deal of a Lifetime," *Miami Herald*, November 28, 2018).

94 David Von Drehle, "Von Drehle: An Appalling Tale of Bought Silence," *Press Democrat*, June 16, 2019.

95 David Von Drehle, "Jeffrey Epstein's Scandal of Secrecy Points to a Creeping Rot in the American Justice System," *Washington Post*, June 14, 2019.

96 William H. Simon, "*Ethical Discretion in Lawyering*," 101 *Harvard Law Review* 1083, 1083 (1988).

97 Edmond Cahn, *The Predicament of Democratic Man* (New York: Macmillan Co., 1961).

98 "Transcript of Robert S. Mueller III's Testimony Before the House Judiciary Committee," *Washington Post*, July 24, 2019 (quoting, in part, *Berger v. United States*, 295 U.S. 78, 88 (1935)) .

99 Robert H. Jackson, Attorney General of the United States, Address at the Second Annual Conference of United States Attorneys: The Federal Prosecutor, April 1, 1940.

100 Model Code of Professional Conduct rule 3.8 comment (American Bar Association, 1983).

101 Robert L. Spangenberg and Marea L. Beeman, "Indigent Defense Systems in the United States," 58 *Law & Contemporary Problems* 31 (1995).

102 Suzanne M. Strong, U.S. Dep't of Justice Bureau of Justice Statistics, State Administered Indigent Defense Systems, 2013 18, 23 (2017).

103 Model Code of Professional Responsibility EC 2-26 (American Bar Association, 1983).

104 Model Code of Professional Responsibility EC 2-30 (American Bar Association, 1983).

105 Model Code of Professional Conduct rule 6.2 (American Bar Association, 1983).

106 Stephen Jones, "A Lawyer's Ethical Duty to Represent the Unpopular Client," 1 *Chapman Law Review* 105 (1998).

107 Jan Ransom and Michael Gold, "Harvard Dean Criticized for Representing Weinstein," *New York Times*, March 6, 2019, A21.

108 Randall Kennedy, "Harvard Betrays a Law Professor," *New York Times*, May 17, 2019, A29.

109 Kate Taylor, "Harvard Drops Weinstein Lawyer as a Faculty Dean," *New York Times*, May 12, 2019, A27.

110 367 U.S. 643 (1961).

111 Joseph Goldstein, "'Testilying' by Police: A Stubborn Problem," *New York Times*, March 18, 2018.

112 Joseph Goldstein, "Promotions, Not Punishments, for Officers Accused of Lying," *New York Times*, March 19, 2018.

113 Joseph Goldstein, "Police 'Testilying' Remains a Problem. Here Is How the Criminal Justice System Could Reduce It," *New York Times*, March 22, 2018.

114 Philip M. Stinson, Sr., J.D., Ph.D. "On-Duty Shootings: Police Officers Charged with Murder or Manslaughter, 2005-2020", Bowling Green State University, Revised: March 22, 2020

115 Sam Roberts, "John Thompson, Cleared After 14 Years on Death Row, Dies at 55," *New York Times* October 4, 2017.

116 Connick v. Thompson, 563 U.S. 51.

117 Sam Roberts, "John Thompson, Cleared After 14 Years on Death Row, Dies at 55," *New York Times*, October 4, 2017.

118 Radley Balko, "John Thompson, an Exoneree and Relentless Voice for Criminal-Justice Reform, Has Died," *Washington Post*, October 4, 2017.

119 John Thompson, "The Prosecution Rests, but I Can't," *New York Times*, April 9, 2011.

120 Andrew Cohen, "Prosecutors Shouldn't Be Hiding Evidence from Defendants," *Atlantic Monthly*, May 13, 2013.

121 Maurice Possley, "Prosecutor Accused of Misconduct in Disputed Texas Execution Case," *Washington Post*, March 18, 2015.

122 Ibid., quoting Innocence Project staff attorney Bryce Benjet.

123 Brady v. Maryland, 3737 U.S. 83, 87 (1963)("We now hold that the suppression by the prosecution of evidence favorable to an accused upon request violates due process where the evidence is material either to guilt or to punishment, *irrespective of the good faith or bad faith of the prosecution*" [emphasis added]).

124 United States v. Bagley, 473 U.S. 667 (1985)

125 Radley Balko, "John Thompson, an Exoneree and Relentless Voice for Criminal-Justice Reform, Has Died," *Washington Post,* October 4, 2017.

126 Ibid.

127 Radley Balko, "New Orleans's Persistent Prosecutor Problem," *Washington Post*, October 27, 2015 (quoting the majority opinion in Kyles v. Whitley, 514 U.S. 419, 439 [1995]).

128 Radley Balko, "John Thompson, an Exoneree and Relentless Voice for Criminal-Justice Reform, Has Died," *Washington Post*, October 4, 2017.

129 Andrew Cohen, "Prosecutors Shouldn't Be Hiding Evidence From Defendants," *Atlantic Monthly*, May 13, 2013.

130 Jesse Wegman, "John Paul Stevens Dissented Until the End," *New York Times*, July 18, 2019, A26.

131 Jesse Wegman, "An Innocent Man Who Imagined the World As It Should Be," *New York Times*, October 6, 2017, A26.

132 Bryan Stevenson, *Just Mercy* (New York: Spiegel & Grau, 2014).

133 J. Patrick O'Connor, *Scapegoat: The Chino Hills Murders and the Framing of Kevin Cooper* (Rock Hill, SC: Strategic Media Books 2012).

134 Nicholas Kristof, "Framed For Murder?," *New York Times*, December 9, 2010, A47.

135 Pamela Colloff, "He's a Liar, a Con Artist and a Snitch. His Testimony Could Soon Send a Man to His Death," ProPublica, December 4, 2019.

136 Bill Blum, "Bobby Joe Maxwell and the Life-Destroying Danger of Prosecutorial Misconduct," Truthdig, August 13, 2018.

137 Stephen B. Bright, "Counsel for the Poor: The Death Sentence Not for the Worst Crime But for the Worst Lawyer," 103 *Yale Law Journal* 1835 (1994).

138 287 U.S. 45 (1932).

139 372 U.S. 335 (1963).

140 Stephen B. Bright, "Counsel for the Poor: The Death Sentence Not for the Worst Crime but for the Worst Lawyer," 103 *Yale Law Journal* 1835, 1837 (1994).

141 Ibid., 1881.

142 Ibid., 1883.

143 Ibid., 1840.

144 From the script of the movie Just Mercy, p. 161-162, Warner Brothers 2020.

145 Stephen B. Bright, "Counsel for the Poor: The Death Sentence Not for the Worst Crime but for the Worst Lawyer," 103 *Yale Law Journal* 1835, 1863 (1994) (quoting Bruce A. Green, "Lethal Fiction The Meaning of 'Counsel' in the Sixth Amendment," 78 *Iowa Law Review* 433, 491–99 [1993]).

146 McCleskey v. Kemp, 481 U.S. 279, 344 (1987).

147 The Editorial Board, "Rampant Prosecutorial Misconduct," *New York Times*, January 4, 2014 (quoting the Ninth Circuit's then chief judge Alex Kozinski).

148 Ibid.

149 Center for Prosecutor Integrity, "An Epidemic of Prosecutor Misconduct" 8 (2013).

150 Brady v. Maryland, 373 U.S. 83 (1963).

151 Alan Feuer and James C. McKinley Jr., "Rule Pushes Prosecutors to Disclose Evidence Favorable to Defense," *New York Times*, November 9, 2017, A18.

152 Brian W. Stolarz, *Grace and Justice on Death Row* (New York: Skyhorse Publishing, 2016).

153 Correspondence with the author.

154 Pat Schroeder, "The Adversarial Legal System: Is Justice Served?," *Law Insider*, September 3, 2010.

155 Bryan Stevenson, *Just Mercy* (New York: Spiegel & Grau, 2014).

156 "Execution Set for Man Whose Drunk Lawyer Botched His Defense," *Time*, December 9, 2015.

157 Henry Weinstein, "A Sleeping Lawyer and a Ticket to Death Row," *L.A. Times*, July 15, 2000.

158 Andrea Neal, United Press International, "Death Row Inmates Point to Poor Quality of Lawyers Who Defend Them," *L.A. Times*, October 29, 1986.

159 Ibid.

160 Dr. Emily M. West, Innocence Project, Court Findings of Prosecutorial Miscon-
     duct Claims in Post-Conviction Appeals and Civil Suits Among the First 255
     DNA Exoneration Cases (2010).

161 Benjamin Rachlin, *Ghost of the Innocent Man: A True Story of Trial and Redemption*
     (New York: Little, Brown & Co., 2017).

162 Lara Bazelon, *Rectify: The Power of Restorative Justice After Wrongful Conviction*
     (Beacon Press 2019), 36.

163 Ibid., 36.

164 Innocence Project, www.innocenceproject.org.

165 Ibid., 214–15.

166 Amy Costello, "How One Nonprofit Helped Change a Nation's Thinking about
     Criminal Justice," *Nonprofit Quarterly*, October 29, 2019.

167 Dina Fine Maron, "Many Prisoners on Death Row Are Wrongfully Convicted,"
     Scientific American, April 28, 2014.

168 Bureau of Justice Statistics, "Prisoners in 2017" (2019).

169 Lara Bazelon, *Rectify: A Story of Healing and Redemption After Wrongful Conviction*
     (Boston, MA: Beacon Press, 2018), 21.

170 Ibid.

171 Ibid.

172 Associated Press, "Massachusetts High Court to Examine Drug Lab Misconduct
     Case," WBUR, January 31, 2018.

173 *When They See Us*, Netflix May 31, 2019.

174 *Central Park Five*, PBS, November 23, 2012.

175 Samuel R. Gross et. al, "National Registry Exonerations, Race and Wrongful Con-
     victions in the United States" 20 (2017).

176 Ibid.

177 "Repairing New York's Justice System," *New York Times*, June 2, 2008, A18; see
     also, Samuel R. Gross, "National Registry of Exonerations, Race and Wrongful
     Convictions in the United States" (2017); Edwin Montefiore Borchard, *Convicting
     the Innocent: Sixty-Five Actual Errors of Criminal Justice* (New Haven, CT: Yale
     University Press, 1932).

178 Samuel R. Gross et. al, "National Registry Exonerations, Race and Wrongful
     Convictions in the United States" 20 (2017) (based on exonerations recorded in
     the National Registry of Exonerations).

179 Lara Bazelon, *Rectify: A Story of Healing and Redemption After Wrongful Conviction*
     (Boston, MA: Beacon Press, 2018), 37.

180 Michael Griesbach, *The Innocent Killer: A True Story of a Wrongful Conviction and
     Its Astonishing Aftermath* (American Bar Association, 2014).

181 Michael Griesbach, *Indefensible: The Missing Truth about Steven Avery, Teresa Hal-
     bach, and Making a Murderer* (Fayetteville, NY: Pinnacle, 2017).

182 Angela J. Davis, "The Legal Profession's Failure to Discipline Unethical Prosecu-
     tors," *Hofstra Law Review*, 2007 (providing extensive documentation of unpun-
     ished instances of prosecutorial misconduct.).

183 Jed S. Rakoff, "Why Innocent People Plead Guilty," *New York Review of Books*,
     November 20, 2014, 16; Jed S. Rakoff, "Plea Bargains & Prosecutors: An
     Exchange," *New York Review of Books*, December 18, 2014, 95 (replying to letter

written by Robert Swartz and Michael M. Baylson critiquing Rakoff's *Why Innocent People Plead Guilty*).

184 Neily Clark, "Our Broken Justice System," CATO Institute, May/June 2019.

185 George Will, "Coercive Plea Bargaining is a National Shame," *Washington Post*, May 21, 2020. *A-23*.

186 Alan Feuer, "After 28 Years in Prison, a Rare Deal Frees a Connecticut Man," *New York Times*, November 24, 2017, A20.

187 Ken Armstrong, "Conflicting Convictions," *New Yorker*, November 13, 2017, 40.

188 Stumpf v. Mitchell, 367 F.3d 594, 613 (6th Cir. 2004).

189 Radley Balko, "Chief Judge for 9th Circuit Cites 'Epidemic' of Prosecutor Misconduct," *Huffington Post*, December 11, 2013 (detailing Alex Kozinsky's dissent in United States v. Olsen, 737 F.3d 625, 626–33 [2013]).

190 Kathleen M. Ridolfi and Maurice Possley, "N. Cal. Innocence Project, Preventable Error: A Report on Prosecutorial Misconduct in California 1997–2009," 2–3 (Veritas 2010) (noting the one-a-week average "undoubtedly understates the total number" because the calculation only included "cases in which courts *explicitly* found that prosecutors committed misconduct" [emphasis added]).

191 Ibid., 3. ("In the vast majority—548 of the 707 cases [considered]—courts found misconduct but nevertheless upheld the convictions, ruling that the misconduct was harmless—that the defendants received fair trials notwithstanding the prosecutor's conduct. Only in 159 of the 707 cases—about 20 percent— did the courts find that the misconduct was harmful; in these cases they either set aside the conviction or sentence, declared a mistrial or barred evidence.").

192 See Christian Watson, "Prosecutors Wield Way Too Much Power. And Their Misconduct Brings Far Too Few Consequences," *USA Today*, April 4, 2019) ("[A] chilling 44% of defendants thought guilty pleas were inherently involuntary.").

193 Ken Armstrong and Maurice Possley, "Part I: The Verdict: Dishonor," *Chicago Tribune*., January 11, 1999.

194 David Keenan et. al, "The Myth of Prosecutorial Accountability After Connick v. Thompson: Why Existing Professional Responsibility Measures Cannot Protect Against Prosecutorial Misconduct," 121 *Yale Law Journal* Online 203 (2011).

195 Alan Feuer, "Holding Prosecutors Accountable is Hard. It Could Get Harder," *New York Times* October 8, 2017.

196 See National District Attorneys Association, "National Prosecution Standards" (3rd. ed. 2009); see also Dist. Attorneys Association of the State of N.Y., "The Right Thing: Ethical Guidelines for Prosecutors" (2015).

197 Citizens Protection Act, Pub. L. No. 105-277, §801, 112 Stat. 2681 118-119 (1998).

198 Thomas P. Sullivan and Maurice Poseley, "The Chronic Failure to Discipline Prosecutors for Misconduct: Proposals for Reform," 105 *Journal of Criminal Law & Criminology* 881 (2015); Anthony C. Thompson, "Retooling and Coordinating the Approach to Prosecutorial Misconduct," 69 *Rutgers University Law Review* 623 (2017).

199 Anthony C. Thompson, "Retooling and Coordinating the Approach to Prosecutorial Misconduct," 69 *Rutgers University Law Review* 623 (2017).

200 Michael Wines, "Lawsuit Cites 45 Cases of Prosecutor Misconduct," *New York Times*, January 18, 2018, A18.

201 Ibid.

202 Complaint at 11, 31–39, Jones v. Cannizzaro, No, 2:18-cv-00503 (E.D. La. January 16, 2018 (citing Giglio v. United States, 405 U.S. 150 (1972), United States v. Agurs, 427 U.S. 97(1976), and Kyles v. Whitley, 514 U.S. 419 (1995).).

203 Mark Mazzetti and Scott Shane, "The Senate-CIA Clash That Hollywood Left Out," *New York Times,* November 16, 2019, C1, 6.

204 "The Torturers Manifesto," *New York Times,* April 19, 2009, WK9.

205 "What Went Wrong: Torture and The Office of Legal Counsel in the Bush Administration Before the S. Subcomm. on Admin. Oversight & the Courts of the S. Judiciary Comm.," 111th Congress (2009) (Testimony of David Luban, Professor of Law, Georgetown University Law Center).

206 Ibid.

207 Bill Blum, "Prosecutorial Misconduct Reaches Epidemic Proportions," Truthdig, March 26, 2018.

208 David Margolis, U.S. Department of Justice Office of Deputy Attorney General, "Memorandum of Decision Regarding the Objections to the Findings of Professional Misconduct in the Office of Professional Responsibility's Report of Investigation into the Office of Legal Counsel's Memoranda Concerning Issues Relating to the Central Intelligence Agency's Use of 'Enhanced Interrogation Techniques' on Suspected Terrorists," January 5, 2010; see Eric Lichtblau and Scott Shane, "Report Faults 2 Who Wrote Terror Memo," *New York Times,* February 10, 2010, A1.

209 Imbler v. Pachtman, 424 U.S. 409 (1976).

210 Ziglar v. Abbasi, 137 S. Ct. 1843 (2017).

211 Harlow v. Fitzgerald, 457 U.S. 800, 814 (1982).

212 Anderson v. Creighton, 483 U.S. 635, 638 (1987).

213 Ashcroft v. al-Kidd, 563 U.S. 731, 743 (2011).

214 Jonathan Blitzer, "Waiting for the Garner Grand Jury," *The New Yorker,* December 3, 2014.

215 Associated Press, "Massachusetts High Court to Examine Drug Lab Misconduct Case," WBUR, January 31, 2018.

216 Mark Hansen, "Crime Labs Under the Microscope After a String of Shoddy, Suspect and Fraudulent Results," *ABA Journal,* September 1, 2013.

217 Katie Mettler, "How a Lab Chemist Went from 'Superwoman' to Disgraced Saboteur of More Than 20,000 Drug Cases," *Washington Post,* April 21, 2017.

218 Tom Jackman, "Mass. Crime Chemist Admits Daily Drug Use in Lab, Sparking a Second Scandal," *Washington Post,* May 5, 2016.

219 Ibid.

220 Nate Raymond, "Thousands of Massachusetts Cases Tied to Drug Chemist Get Dismissed," Reuters, April 5, 2018.

221 Tom Jackman, "Prosecutors Slammed for 'Lack of Moral Compass,' Withholding Evidence in Widening Mass. Drug Lab Scandal," *Washington Post,* October 4, 2017.

222 Ibid.

223 Nick Schager, "Netflix Takes You Inside the Massive Drug Scandal That Freed 35,000 People" *DailyBeast* Apr.1, 2020.

224 Mark Hansen, "Crime Labs Under the Microscope After a String of Shoddy, Suspect and Fraudulent Results," *ABA Journal*, September 1, 2013.

225 Ibid.

226 Ibid.

227 Lara Bazelon, "Kamala Harris Was Not a 'Progressive Prosecutor,'" *New York Times*, January 17, 2019.

228 Kamala Harris, *The Truths We Hold* (London: Penguin Press, 2019).

229 Lara Bazelon, "Kamala Harris Was Not a 'Progressive Prosecutor,'" *New York Times*, January 17, 2019.

230 Mark Hansen, "Crime Labs Under the Microscope After a String of Shoddy, Suspect and Fraudulent Results," *ABA Journal*, September 1, 2013.

231 Ibid.

232 "Gideon v. Wainwright," *Oyez* (summarizing Gideon v. Wainwright, 372 U.S. 335 (1963)).

233 Yale Kamisar, "Equal Justice in the Gatehouses and Mansions of American Criminal Procedure," in *Criminal Justice in Our Time* 1 (University of Virginia Press, 1965).

234 Bertram F. Wilcox and Edward J. Bloustein, "The Griffin Case Poverty and the Fourteenth Amendment," 43 *Cornell Law Quarterly* 1, 16 (1957).

235 Yale Kamisar, "Equal Justice in the Gatehouses and Mansions of American Criminal Procedure," in *Criminal Justice in Our Time* 1 (University of Virginia Press, 1965).

236 Ry. Express Agency, Inc. v. New York, 336 U.S. 106, 112-13 (1949).

237 351 U.S. 12 (1956).

238 Ibid., 17.

239 Douglas v. California, 372 U.S. 353, 355 (1963).

240 Yale Kamisar, "Equal Justice in the Gatehouses and Mansions of American Criminal Procedure," in *Criminal Justice in Our Time* (University of Virginia Press, 1965), 1, 13.

241 Ibid., 19–20.

242 377 US 201, 204 (1964).

243 Yale Kamisar, "Equal Justice in the Gatehouses and Mansions of American Criminal Procedure," in *Criminal Justice in Our Time* (University of Virginia Press, 1965), 1, 55.

244 113 *University Pennsylvania Law Review*, 1, 1964.

245 Herbert L. Packer, "The Two Models of the Criminal Process," 113 *University of Pennsylvania Law Review* 1 (1964).

246 Ibid., 9.

247 Ibid., 26 n. 26 (quoting Justice Cardozo in People v. Defore, 242 N.Y. 13, 21 (1926)).

248 "'Punishment Without Crime' Highlights the Injustice of America's Misdemeanor System," *Fresh Air,* National Public Radio, January 2, 2019.

249 Alexandra Natapoff, *Punishment Without Crime: How Our Massive Misdemeanor System Traps the Innocent and Makes America More Unequal* (New York: Basic Books 2018).

250 "'Punishment Without Crime' Highlights the Injustice of America's Misdemeanor System," *Fresh Air*, National Public Radio, January 2, 2019.

251 Ibid.

252 Stack v. Boyle, 342 U.S. 1, 7-8 (1951), emphasis added.

253 Ronald Goldfarb, *Ransom: A Critique of the American Bail System* (New York: Harper & Row Publishers, 1965).

254 Ronald Goldfarb, *Ransom: A Critique of the American Bail System* (New York: Harper & Row Publishers, 1965) (foreword by Justice Arthur J. Goldberg of the US Supreme Court.).

255 Emily Bazelon, *Charged: The Movement to Transform American Prosecution and End Mass Incarceration* (New York: Random House, 2019), 37.

256 Ronald Goldfarb, "The Bail Scandal," *New Republic*, June 6, 1964, 14–17.

257 Bandy v. United States, 81 S. Ct. 197, 197-98 (1960), emphasis added.

258 Lee v. Lawson, 375 So. 2d 1019, 1022 (1979) (quoting Circuit Justice Douglas in Bandy v. United States, 82 S. Ct. 11, 13 (1961)), emphasis added.

259 Vera Institute of Justice,

260 Peter Wagner, "Jails Matter. But Who is Listening?" *Prison Policy Initiative*, August 14, 2015.

261 Kayla James, "How the Bail Bond Industry Became a $2 Billion Business," *Global Citizen*, January 31, 2019).

262 Ava Kofman, "E-Jail," *New York Times Magazine*, July 7, 2019, 36.

263 Ibid.

264 Ibid.

265 Michelle Alexander, *The New Jim Crow: Mass Incarceration in the Age of Colorblindness* (New York: New Press, 2010), 12.

266 Caliste v. Cantrell, No. 18-30954, 2019 U.S. App. LEXIS 26288 (5th Cir. August 29, 2019).

267 United States v. Salerno, 481 US 739, 1987.

268 Ronald Goldfarb, "A Brief for Preventive Detention," *New York Times Magazine*, March 1, 1970.

269 18 USC 3142 (e).

270 Emily Bazelon and Miriam Krinsky, "A Wave of New Prosecutors Means Justice," *New York Times*, December 13, 2018, A29.

271 Jennifer Gonnerman, "Acts of Conviction," *New Yorker*, October 29, 2018, 28.

272 Cherri Gregg, "Pa. Supreme Court Grants Inquiry into Alleged 'Systemic Failures' of Philly's Bail System," KYW News Radio, July 9, 2019.

273 Cherri Gregg, "ACLU Sues Philadelphia Courts Over Cash Bail System," KYW News Radio, March 12, 2019.

274 Richard A. Oppel Jr. and Jugal K. Patel, "One Lawyer, 194 Felony Cases, and No Time," *New York Times*, January 31, 2019.

275 Rubin Brown, "The Missouri Project: A Study of Missouri Public Defender System and Attorney Workload Standards," American Bar Association, 2014.

276 "Public Defender Caseload Tracking Shows How Systems are Overburdened, Panelists Say," American Bar Association, September 17, 2014.

277 Lynn Langton, Donald J. Farole Jr., and US Department of Justice Bureau of Office Statistics, State Public Defender Programs, 2007 1 (2010).

278 Donald J. Farole Jr., Lynn Langton, and US Department of Justice Bureau of Office Statistics, County-Based and Local Public Defender Offices, 2007 1 (2010).

279 Richard A. Oppel Jr., "Preferring a Quick Guilty Plea to a More Thorough Defense," *New York Times*, March 31, 2018, A10.

280 Ibid.

281 Ibid.

282 Ibid.

283 Adam Liptak, "Gap Seen Between Court-Appointed Lawyers and Public Defenders," *New York Times*, July 13, 2007.

284 Gerhard Falk, *The American Criminal Justice System: How It Works, How It Doesn't, and How to Fix It* 91 (2010)

285 Justice Policy Institute, "System Overload: The Costs of Under-resourcing Public Defense" 2 (2011).

286 Dan Margolies, "*Many Missouri Public Defenders Decline New Cases After State Supreme Court Disciplines Lawyer,*" KCUR, October 6, 2017.

287 Liane Jackson, "Change Agents: A New Wave of Reform Prosecutors Upends the Status Quo," *ABA Journal*, June 1, 2019.

288 John Fram, "How Crime Writers Justified Police Brutality", New York Times, June 8, 2020, p. A25.

289 Emily Bazelon, *Charged: The New Movement to Transform American Prosecution and End Mass Incarceration* (New York: Random House 2019).

290 Ibid.

291 U.S. v. Watson 32 US 150 (1832).

292 Ronald L. Goldfarb and Linda R. Singer, *After Conviction: A Review of the American Correction System* (New York: Simon & Schuster, 1973), 36.

293 Office Pardon Attorney, "Clemency Statistics: William J. Clinton," US Department Justice.

294 Ronald L. Goldfarb and Linda R. Singer, *After Conviction: A Review of the American Correction System* (New York: Simon & Schuster, 1973).

295 George Lardner Jr., "A Pardon to Remember," *New York Times*, November 24, 2008, A21.

296 Justin Peters, "How Eric Holder Facilitated the Most Unjust Presidential Pardon in American History," Slate, July 2, 2013.

297 Ibid.

298 Brandon L. Garrett, *Too Big to Jail: How Prosecutors Compromise with Corporations* (Cambridge, MA: Belknap, Harvard University Press, 2014).

299 Julie K. Brown, "How a Future Trump Cabinet Member Gave a Serial Sex Abuser the Deal of a Lifetime," *Miami Herald*, November 28, 2018.

300 Jesse Eisinger, *The Chickenshit Club: The Justice Department and Its Failure to Prosecute White Collar Criminals* (New York: Simon & Schuster, 2017); *see* Ronald Goldfarb, "No Big-Game Hunting at Justice," *American Prospect*, February 14, 2018.

301 Brandon Garrett, *Too Big to Jail: How Prosecutors Compromise with Corporations* (Cambridge, MA: Belknap, Harvard University Press, 2014); see also, Ronald

Goldfarb, *Books in the Law*, DC Bar, May, 2015 (reviewing Garrett's book, *Too Big to Jail*).

302 Ibid.

303 Ibid.

304 Jesse Eisinger, *The Chickenshit Club: The Justice Department and Its Failure to Prosecute White Collar Criminals* (New York: Simon & Schuster 2017), 267.

305 Jed. S. Rakoff, "Why Innocent People Plead Guilty," *New York Review of Books*, November 20, 2014.

306 Ronald Goldfarb, "Books in the Law," *DC Bar*, May, 2015, (reviewing Garrett's book, *Too Big to Jail*).

307 Brandon Garrett, *Too Big to Jail: How Prosecutors Compromise with Corporations* (Cambridge, MA: Belknap, Harvard University Press, 2014), 165.

308 United States v. Benjamin, 328 F.2d 854, 863 (2d. Cir. 1964).

309 Justice Louis D. Brandeis, Supreme Court of the United States, Address at Phillips Brooks House Before the Harvard Ethical Society: "The Opportunity in the Law," May 4, 1905.

310 Katie Thomas, A Treatment Was Flawed, as Was the Investigation", NY Times, Mar 24, 2020, also see The Unseen Survivors of Thalidomide Want to be Heard by Katie Thomas.

311 Stephan Landsman, "Death of an Accountant: The Jury Convicts Arthur Andersen of Obstruction of Justice," 78 *Chicago-Kent Law Review* 1203, 1209 (2003).

312 Jesse Eisinger, *The Chickenshit Club: Why the Justice Department Fails to Prosecute Executives* (New York: Simon & Schuster 2017), 234.

313 Ibid., 236.

314 Ibid., 237, 243.

315 Ibid., 202–28; see also, Ronald Goldfarb, "No Big-Game Hunting at Justice," *American Prospect*, February 14, 2018.

316 Ronald Goldfarb, "No Big-Game Hunting at Justice," *American Prospect*, February 14, 2018).

317 "Abacus: Small Enough to Jail," PBS, September 12, 2017.

318 Jesse Eisinger, *The Chickenshit Club: Why the Justice Department Fails to Prosecute Executives* (New York: Simon & Schuster, 2017), 17.

319 Ibid., 58.

320 Perry Zinn Rowthorn and George Jepsen, "Opioid 'Negotiation Class Action' Under Consideration in Cleveland Court Should Be Rejected," Cleveland.Com, July 15, 2019 (criticizing unequal power dynamic between drug manufacturers and local prosecutors in the ongoing litigation over the opioid crisis); Ronald Goldfarb, "No Big-Game Hunting at Justice," *American Prospect*, February 14, 2018.

321 Jesse Eisinger, *The Chickenshit Club: Why the Justice Department Fails to Prosecute Executives* 267 (New York: Simon & Schuster, 2017), 214.

322 Ibid., 197.

323 Ibid.

324 "Abacus: Small Enough to Jail," PBS, September 12, 2017.

325 Jesse Eisinger, *The Chickenshit Club: Why the Justice Department Fails to Prosecute Executives* (New York: Simon & Schuster, 2017), 21.

326 J. Earl Johnson Jr., "50 Years of Gideon, 47 Years Working Toward a 'Civil Gideon,'" 47 *Clearinghouse Review: Journal on Poverty Law & Policy* 47, 48–49 (2013) (quoting himself from a March 1968 speech to the Jacksonville Bar Association).

327 Louis D. Brandeis, from "The Opportunities of the Law" speech delivered to the Harvard Ethical Society at the Phillips Brooks House, May 4, 1905.

328 Earl Johnson Jr., *To Establish Justice for All: The Past and Future of Civil Legal Aid in the United States* (Santa Barabara, CA: Praeger, 2013).

329 Quail v. Mun. Court, 171 Cal. App. 3d 572, 577–93 (Cal. Ct. App. 1985) (Johnson, J., dissenting).

330 Quail v. Mun. Court, 171 Cal. App. 3d 572, 577–93 (Cal. Ct. App. 1985) (Johnson, J., dissenting).

331 Quail v. Mun. Court, 171 Cal. App. 3d 572, 577–93 (Cal. Ct. App. 1985) (Johnson, J., dissenting).

332 Mendoza v. Small Claims Court, 49 Cal.2d, 668, 673 (1958) (emphasis added).

333 348 U.S. 105 (1954).

334 Quail v. Mun. Court,171 Cal. App. 3d 572, 577–93 (Cal. Ct. App. 1985) (Johnson, J., dissenting).

335 Earl Johnson Jr., *To Establish Justice for All: The Past and Future of Civil Legal Aid in the United States* (Santa Barbara, CA: Praeger 2013).

336 Reginald Herber Smith, *The Carnegie Found. For the Advancement of Teaching, Justice and the Poor: A Study of the Present Denial of Justice to the Poor and of the Agencies Making More Equal Their Position Before the Law with Particular Reference to Legal Aid Work in the United States* (Boston, MA: Merrymount Press, 1919), 195.

337 Earl Johnson Jr., *To Establish Justice for All: The Past and Future of Civil Legal Aid in the United States* (Santa Barbara, CA: Praeger 2014), 898.

338 Earl Johnson Jr., "Fifty Years Ago on January 8th, America Declared a War on Poverty—Without Mentioning the Denial of Justice to the Poverty Population," Georgetown Law Library, January 7, 2014.

339 Edgar S. Cahn and Jean Camper Cahn, "The War on Poverty: A Civilian Perspective," 73 *Yale Law Journal* 1317 (1964).

340 Ronald Goldfarb, *A Caste of Despair* (Iowa State University Press, 1981).

341 Shapiro v. Thompson, 394 U.S. 618, 658-63 (1969) (providing illustrative list of fundamental rights, which included the rights to "pursue a particular occupation," to "receive . . . wages," and to "inherit property.")

342 Earl Johnson Jr., *To Establish Justice for All: The Past and Future of Civil Legal Aid in the United States* (Santa Barbara, CA: Praeger 2014), 898.

343 Ibid.

344 Lou Carlozo "Americans Will Spend $350 Million on Halloween Costumes. For Their Pets." Christian Science Monitor, October 14, 2015.

345 Deborah L. Rhode, *Stanford Law's Deborah Rhode on the Access to Justice Challenge in U.S.*, Stan. L. Sch. (November 18, 2019) (Transcript from Q&A moderated by Sharon Driscoll).

346 Alan Jay Stein, *The Indigent's "Right" to Counsel in Civil Cases*, 43 Fordham L. Rev. 989, 1001-02 (1975).

347 Alan Jay Stein, "The Indigent's 'Right' to Counsel in Civil Cases," 43 *Fordham Law Review* 989, 1001 (1975).

348 Ibid.

349 Earl Johnson Jr., *To Establish Justice for All: The Past and Future of Civil Legal Aid in the United States* (Santa Barbara, CA: Praeger 2014), 879.

350 Correspondence with Earl Johnson, Jr.

351 Earl Johnson Jr., *To Establish Justice for All: The Past and Future of Civil Legal Aid in the United States* (Santa Barbara, CA: Praeger 2014), 922.

352 Ibid., 898.

353 Alan Jay Stein, "The Indigent's 'Right' to Counsel in Civil Cases," 43 *Fordham Law Review* 989, 1001–02 (1975).

354 Benjamin H. Barton and Stephanos Bibas, *Rebooting Justice: More Technology, Fewer Lawyers, and the Future of Law* (New York: Encounter Books 2017).

355 Monroe H. Freedman, "Professionalism in the American Adversary System," 41 *Emory Law Journal* 467 (1992); Lassiter v. Dep't of Soc. Servs., 452 U.S. 18 (1981).

356 Rebecca L. Sandefur and Aaron C. Smyth, "Access Across America: First Report of the Civil Justice Infrastructure Mapping Project," American Bar Foundation, 2011.

357 Ibid., 8.

358 Alan W. Houseman, "*Civil Legal Aid in the United States: An Update for 2017* (2018), 77-78.

359 Jesse Eisinger, *The Chickenshit Club: The Justice Department and Its Failure to Prosecute White Collar Criminals* (New York: Simon & Schuster, 2017); Brandon L. Garrett, *Too Big to Jail: How Prosecutors Compromise with Corporations* (Cambridge, MA: Belknap, Harvard University Press, 2014).

360 Jesse Eisinger, "The Fall Guy," *New York Times*, May 4, 2014, 34.

361 Ronald Goldfarb, "First the Filet. Then Integrity for Dessert," *New York Times*, January 11, 1977.

362 Ronald L. Burdge, "Confidentiality in Settlement Agreements Is Bad for Clients, Bad for Lawyers, Bad for Justice," American Bar Association, November 1, 2012.

363 Laurie Kratky Dore, *Secrecy by Consent: The Use and Limits of Confidentiality in the Pursuit of Settlement*, 74 Notre Dame L. Rev. 283, 336 n. 216 (quoting Poliquin v. Garden Way, Inc., 989 F.2d 527, 535 [1st Cir. 1993]).

364 John Hurdle, "Coria Sues U.S. Vitamin Firm over Doping Ban," Reuters, June 19, 2007.

365 Christian Red, "J.C. Romero, Former Phillies Reliever Suspended for Performance Enhancing Drugs, Settles Lawsuit, Says 'Justice is Served' After Supplement Is Tainted," *New York Daily News*, January 10, 2012.

366 Kayon Raynor, "Powell, Simpson Settle Case with Nutrition Company," Reuters, September 8, 2015.

367 Owen M. Fiss, "Against Settlement," 93 *Yale Law Journal* 1073, 1075, 1085 (1984).]

368 Ibid., 1085.

369 Ibid.

370 Ronald Goldfarb, *In Confidence* (New Haven, CT: Yale University Press, 2009), 171.

371 Ibid.

372 Ibid.

373 Laurie Kratky Dore, "Public Courts Versus Private Justice: It's Time to Let Some Sun Shine In on Alternative Dispute Resolution," 81 *Chicago-Kent Law Review* 463 (2006).

374 Alan B. Morrison, "Protective Orders, Plaintiffs, Defendants and the Public Interest in Disclosure; Where Does the Balance Lie?," 24 *University of Richmond Law Review* 109, 123–24 (1989).

375 Ibid.

376 Ibid.

377 Ronald Goldfarb, "Secrets of the Catholic Church," *Hill*, April 12, 2010.

378 Ronald Goldfarb, *In Confidence* (New Haven, CT: Yale University Press, 2009), 8.

379 Ibid., 9.

380 Ronald Goldfarb, "Secrets of the Catholic Church," *Hill*, April 12, 2010.

381 Ronald Goldfarb, *In Confidence* (New Haven, CT: Yale University Press, 2009), 132. The movie *Spotlight*—which won two Academy Awards, including Best Picture, in 2016—dramatizes this problem. *Spotlight* (Participant Media et al. 2015).

382 Laurie Goodstein and Sharon Otterman, "Church Hid Abuse of 1,000 Children, Grand Jury Finds," *New York Times*, August 15, 2018, A1 ([T]he Roman Catholic Church in Pennsylvania covered up child sexual abuse by more than 300 priests over a period of 70 years . . .").

383 Frank Keating, "Finding Hope in My Faith," *New York Times*, June 19, 2003.

384 Laurie Goodstein, "Deal Reported in Abuse Cases in Los Angeles," *New York Times*, July 15, 2007, A1; see also Randal C. Archibold, "San Diego Diocese Settles Lawsuit for $200 Million," *New York Times*, September 8, 2007, A8.

385 Michelle Boorstein, "W.Va Scandal Muddies Legacy of Vatican's Longtime Fixer from Baltimore," *Washington Post*, September 3, 2019, A14.

386 Michael Rezendes, "In Mississippi Delta, Catholic Abuse Cases Settled on Cheap," Associated Press News, August 27, 2019.

387 Claudia Lauer and Meghan Hoyer, "Unsupervised Accused Priests Teach, Counsel, Foster Children," Associated Press News, October 4, 2019.

388 Liam Stack, "Colorado Report Accuses 43 Catholic Priests of Child Sex Abuse," *New York Times*, October 23, 2019.

389 Bernard Condan and Jim Mustian, "Surge of New Abuse Threatens Church Like Never Before," Associated Press News, December 2, 2019.

390 Elisabetta Povoledo, "Pope Francis Ends Secrecy Rule in Abuse Cases," *New York Times*, December 18, 2019, A12.

391 Christopher B. Mueller and Laird C. Kirkpatrick, *Evidence Under the Rules: Text, Cases, and Problems* § 211 (3rd. ed. 2007) (citing various examples); see also Claudia L. Catalano, *Who Are Clergy?* 101 A.L.R. 5th 619 (2006); David M. Greenwald et al, Testimonial Privileges § 6.14 (3rd. ed. 2005).

392 Nicole Karlis, "How Non-Disclosure Agreements Silence Victims," *Salon*, December 10, 2017.

393 Megan Twohey et al., "Weinstein's Complicity Machine," *New York Times*, December 5, 2017. Also see Jodi Kantor and Megan Twohey, *She Said, Breaking the Sexual Harassment Story that Helped Ignite a Movement* (London: Penguin, 2019).

394   *See* Rachel Louise Ensign, "Meet the lawyer Representing Wall Street's #MeToo Men," *Wall Street Journal*, August 27, 2018; Audrey Carlsen et al., "Me Too Brought Down 201 Powerful Men. Nearly Half of their Replacements Are Women," *New York Times*, October 29, 2018.

395   See Anastasia Tsioulcas, "The Allegations Against R. Kelly: An Abridged History," NPR, January 11, 2019 (R&B singer R. Kelly); Yohana Desta, "Disturbing Details of Matt Lauer's Alleged Sexual Misconduct," *Vanity Fair*, November 29, 2017 (former *Today Show* co-host Matt Lauer); John Frank and Jesse Paul, "Colorado Rep. Steve Lebsock Faces Expulsion After 10 Sexual Harassment Allegations Against Him Are Deemed Credible," *Denver Post*, February 27, 2018 (Democratic member of the U.S. House of Representatives, Steve Lebsock).

396   Rachel Louise Ensign, "Meet the lawyer Representing Wall Street's #MeToo Men," *Wall Street Journal*, August 27, 2018.

397   Mark J. Green, *The Other Government: The Unseen Power of Washington Lawyers* (New York: W.W. Norton & Co. rev. ed. 1978).

398   *See* Ralph Nader and Wesley J. Smith, *Collision Course: The Trust About Airline Safety* (Blue Ridge Summit, PA: Tab Books, 1993) (describing how influential lawyer-lobbyists' work was prejudicial to the public); Mark J. Green, *The Other Government: The Unseen Power of Washington Lawyers* (New York: W.W. Norton & Co., 1978).

399   Ronald Goldfarb, "This Town," *Washington Independent Review of Books*, August 19, 2013, (reviewing Mark Leibovich, *This Town* [2013]).

400   Harlan F. Stone, "The Dubious Influence of the Bar," 48 *Harvard Law Review* 1, 6–7 (1934).

401   Alan M. Dershowitz, *Letters to a Young Lawyer* (New York: Basic Books 2005), 50.

402   Richard Sandomir, "Dr. Arnold Gold, 92, a Pediatric Neurologist Who Made Compassionate Care a Cause," *New York Times*, February 5, 2018, A20.

403   Ibid.

404   Code of Med. Ethics 1.1.1.

405   Code of Med. Ethics 1.1.7.

406   Sandeep Jauhar, "Should Doctors Refuse to Treat a Patient?," *New York Times*, May 14, 2019, A23; Sandeep Jauhar, "When Doctor's Slam the Door," *New York Times*, March 16, 2003, 6–32 ("The Fifth Circuit Court of Appeals . . . rul[ed] that doctors can refuse to treat violent or intransigent patients as long as they give proper notice so that the patient can find alternative care. Forcing doctors to treat such patients, the court said, would violate the 13th Amendment, which prohibits involuntary servitude.").

407   David Brooks, "Trump's Lizard Wisdom," *New York Times*, May 11, 2018, A27.

408   Mark J. Green, *The Other Government: The Unseen Power of Washington Lawyers* (New York: W.W. Norton & Co., rev. ed. 1978, 1975), 291.

409   Ibid., 275–76.

410   Robert Rubinson, "A Theory of Access to Justice," 29 *Journal of the Legal Profession* 89 (2005).

411   Ibid., 96.

412   Ibid., 156.

413   *"ABA National Lawyer Population Survey,"* American Bar Association, 2018 (reporting the number of attorneys in the United States in 2018); "Lawyer

Demographics," American Bar Association, 2013 (noting how many lawyers practiced in the various legal sectors in 2005. The ABA has not published a more recent study of this kind.). "New ABA Data Reveals Rise in Number of U.S. Lawyers, 15 Percent Since 2008," American Bar Association, May 11, 2018.

414 Legal Services Corp., "The Justice Gap: Measuring the Unmet Civil Legal Needs of Low-Income Americans" 6 (2017).

415 Ibid.

416 Ibid., 6–7.

417 Legal Services Corp., "The Justice Gap in America: The Current Unmet Civil Legal Needs of Low-Income Americans" 1 (2009) [hereinafter 2009 Justice Gap Report].

418 "New Census Data Show Differences Between Urban and Rural Populations," U.S. Census Bureau, December 8, 2016; see also, Lisa R. Pruitt et al., "Legal Deserts: A Multi-State Perspective on Rural Access to Justice," 13 *Harvard Law & Policy Review* 15, 120–21 (2018) (Noting many rural counties only have one attorney for several thousand rural residents, a problem that is amplified because many such counties neighbor one another); Jessica Pishko, "The Shocking Law of Lawyers in Rural America," *Atlantic*, July 18, 2019 (providing examples, including that "[i]n Minnesota, counties can span hundreds of miles . . . requiring . . . lawyers to drive an hour each way.").]

419 Legal Services Corp., "The Justice Gap: Measuring the Unmet Civil Legal Needs of Low-Income Americans" 6, 29 (2017).

420 Tod Ruger "Coronavirus Could Overwhelm Legal Help for America's Poor," *Roll Call*, Mar.31, 2020.

421 *Id.*

422 Benjamin H. Barton and Stephanos Bibas, *Rebooting Justice: More Technology, Fewer Lawyers, and the Future of Law* (New York: Encounter Books, 2017).

423 Debra Cassens Weiss, "Posner: Most Judges Regard Pro Se Litigants as 'Kind of Trash Not Worth the Time,'" *ABA Journal*, September 11, 2017.

424 Earl Johnson Jr., *To Establish Justice for All: The Past and Future of Civil Legal Aid in the United States* (Santa Barbara, CA: Praeger 2013).

425 Legal Services Corp., "The Justice Gap: Measuring the Unmet Civil Legal Needs of Low-Income Americans" 6 (2017).

426 Ronald L. Goldfarb and Linda R. Singer, *After Conviction: A Review of the American Correction System* (New York: Simon & Schuster, 1973).

427 Ronald L. Goldfarb, *Jails: The Ultimate Ghetto* (New York: Anchor Press/Doubleday 1975).

428 Ibid.

429 Ronald Goldfarb, "A Clear Message from a Ghetto Walk," *Washington Post*, June 24, 1970, A18.

430 Ronald L. Goldfarb, *Migrant Farm Workers: A Caste of Despair* (Iowa State University Press, 1981).

431 Father James Vizzard et al., "Remarks Prepared By a Team of Interfaith Leaders at the Invitation of the California Migrant Ministry: Religious Leaders' Statement," December 14, 1965, quoted, in part, in the January 29, 1966, issue of the national Catholic weekly *Ave Maria*, 18.

432 Daniel J. Wakin, "A Discordant Duet," *New York Times*, December 21, 2019, C1, 4.

433 Ronald Goldfarb, *A Caste of Despair* (Iowa State University Press, 1981), 195.

434 Ronald L. Goldfarb, *Migrant Farm Workers: A Caste of Despair* (Iowa State University Press, 1981), 196.

435 Ibid, 194.

436 Molly Roberts, "Your Actions Are Your Morality," *Washington Post*, August 4, 2019, A23.

437 Saul Jay Singer, "Can I Delay Informing My Client?," *Washington Lawyer*, July/August 2019, 44.

438 Harlan F. Stone, "The Dubious Influence of the Bar," 48 *Harvard Law Review* 1, 6–7 (1934).

439 Elizabeth Hardwick, "Grub Street: New York," *New York Times Review of Books*, February 1, 1963.

440 Alpheus Thomas Mason, *Harlan Fiske Stone: Pillar of the Law* (New York: Viking Press, 1956), 90.

441 Ibid., 97.

442 Ibid., 378.

443 Ibid., 379.

444 William Roberts, *Digital Justice*, Washington Lawyer, May 2020.

445 Mark A. Cohen, "Big Money Is Betting on Legal Industry Transformation," *Forbes*, October 7, 2019.

446 Ibid.

447 Mark A. Cohen, "Big Money Is Betting on Legal Industry Transformation," *Forbes*, October 7, 2019.

448 Alpheus Thomas Mason, *Harlan Fiske Stone: Pillar of the Law* (New York: Viking Press, 1956), 381.

449 Ibid., 382.

450 Harlan F. Stone, "The Dubious Influence of the Bar," 48 *Harvard Law Review* 1, 6–7 (1934).

451 Victoria Kwan, "SCOTUS Map: December 2017," SCOTUSblog, December 28, 2017).

452 Paula C. Johnson, "NYS Bar to Admit Syracuse's First Black Law Graduate, Correcting Century-Old Injustice (Commentary)," syracuse.com, October 16, 2019.

453 Paula C. Johnson, "William H. Johnson, Class of 1903: The First African American Graduate of Syracuse University College of Law," 55 *Syracuse Law Review* 429 (2005).

454 Noam Scheiber and John Eligon, "12 White Faces Reflect Blind Spot in Big Law," *New York Times*, January 28, 2019, A1.

455 Jean M. Phillips and Stanley M. Gully, *Organizational Behavior: Tools for Success* (Cengage Learning, 2010), 53.

456 Douglas O. Linder and Nancy Levit, *The Good Lawyer: Seeking Quality in the Practice of Law* (New York: Oxford University Press, 2014).

457 People v. Belge, 83 Misc. 2d 186, 189 (N.Y. Cty. Ct. 1975).

458 Ibid., 191.

459 276 Paul W. Mosher and Jeffrey Berman, *Confidentiality and Its Discontents: Dilemmas of Privacy in Psychotherapy* (Fordham University Press, 2015), 302.

460 Ronald Goldfarb, *In Confidence* (New Haven, CT: Yale University Press, 2009), 72. Griffin, *The Lawyer's Dirty Hands*, 8 Geo. J. *Legal Ethics* 219 (1995)

461 Douglas O. Linder and Nancy Levit, *The Good Lawyer: Seeking Quality in the Practice of Law* (New York: Oxford University Press, 2014).

462 Alec Karakatsanis, *Unusual Cruelty: The Complicity of Lawyers in the Criminal Justice System* (New York: New Press, 2019).

463 Ibid., 63.

464 Ronald Goldfarb, "Phil Stern's Gifts," *Washington Post,* June 2, 1992.

465 Ronald L. Goldfarb "The Administration of Justice in Washington, DC During the Disorder of April 1968" (unpublished manuscript, 1968).

466 *Report of The National Advisory Commission on Civil Disorders,* by Otto Kerner, John V. Lindsay, Fred R. Harris, I.W. Abel, Edward W. Brooke, Charles B. Thorton, James C. Corman, Roy Wilkins, William M. McCulloch, Katherine Graham Peden, and Herbert Jenkins (1968) ["Kerner Report"].

467 C.J. Ciaramella, "How Not to Build a Jail," *Reason,* December 2016.

468 Ronald C. Minkoff, "Access to Justice and a New Definition of Professionalism," *New York Legal Ethics Reporter.*

469 Brian Z. Tamanaha, *Failing Law Schools* (Chicago: University Chicago Press, 2012) (reviewed in February 2013 issue of *Washington Lawyer).*

470 Joan Biskupic, *The Chief: The Life and Turbulent Times of Chief Justice John Roberts* (New York: Basic Books, 2019), 278.

471 "Which Law School Graduates Have the Most Debt?," *U.S. News & World Report,* 2019.

472 Sandy Baum and Patricia Steele, "Graduate and Professional School Debt: How Much Students Borrow," AccessLex Institute & Urban Institute, 2018.

473 Ronald Krotoszynski, "Bigger Is Not Better at Law School," *Washington Post,* June 12, 2019, A23.

474 Deborah L. Rhode, "Legal Education: Rethinking the Problem, Reimagining the Reforms," 40 *Pepperdine Law Review* 437, 455-56 (2013).

475 Farah Stockman. "Apprenticeship a Growing Alternative to College (and Debt)," *New York Times,* December 11, 2019, A23.

476 *State-by-State Guide to Apprenticeships,* Like Lincoln (accessed December 11, 2019); see also, Sean Patrick Farrell, "The Lincoln Lawyers," *New York Times,* August 3, 2014, Education Life–22.

477 Lawrence H. Mirel, "Giving Purpose to Retirement," *Washington Post,* May 1, 1977.

478 John Murph, "Lee Ann Watson: 'We Have the Time to Be Zealous Advocates,'" *Washington Lawyer,* October 15, 2019.

479 Alec Karakatsanis, *Unusual Cruelty: The Complicity of Lawyers in the Criminal Justice System* (New York: New Press, 2019).

480 "A Conversation with Denise Perme, DC Bar," *Washington Lawyer,* March 2008.

481 Kathryn Alfisi, "Escaping the Trap of Job Dissatisfaction, DC Bar," *Washington Lawyer,* April 2014.

482 Ibid.

483 Sateesh Nori, "Public Interest Attorney Takes Cue from Man of Steel, Aspires to Be Super-Lawyer," *ABA Journal,* December 18, 2018.

484 Sateesh Nori, "Public Interest Attorney Takes Cue from Man of Steel, Aspires to Be Super-Lawyer," *ABA Journal*, December 18, 2018.

485 Ibid.

486 Latham & Watkins LLP, "Pro Bono Practices and Opportunities in the United States of America" 689 (2015).

487 Julie K. Brown, "How a Future Trump Cabinet Member Gave a Serial Sex Abuser the Deal of a Lifetime," *Miami Herald*, November 28, 2018.

488 Deborah L. Rhode, "The Pro Bono Responsibilities of Lawyers and Law Students," 27 *William Mitchell Law Review* 1201 (2000).

489 Ibid.

490 "Drug Law Reform Overview," National Association of Criminal Defense Lawyers.

491 Ronald L. Goldfarb and James C. Raymond, *Clear Understandings: A Guide to Legal Writing* (New York: Random House, 1982).

492 Dan Mills, "How to Avoid Becoming an ODC Statistic," *Washington Lawyer*, July/August 2019, 8.

493 Parker Yesko, "Curtis Flowers Released on Bail," *APM Reports*, December 16, 2019.

494 Mihir Zaveri, "Curtis Flowers's Conviction Tossed by Mississippi Supreme Court," *New York Times*, August 29, 2019.

495 "In the Dark: Season Two", *APM Reports*.

496 Parker Yesko, "All Things Considered," Northern Public Radio, October 3, 2019.

497 Mihir Zaveri, "Prosecutor Recuses Himself for 7th Try at Murder Trial," *New York Times*, January 8, 2020, A12.

498 Rick Rojas, "Out on Bail after 6 Trials for Murder Over 3 Years," *New York Times*, December 17, 2019, A12.

499 Bennett L. Gershman, "Subverting Brady v. Maryland and Denying a Fair Trial: Studying the Schuelke Report," 64 *Mercer Law Review* 683 (2013).

500 Richard A. Oppel Jr., "Review of a Murder Case in Missouri Casts its Shadow," *New York Times*, December 26, 2019, A13.

501 Bennett Gershman, "How to Hold Bad Prosecutors Accountable: The Case for a Commission on Prosecutorial Conduct," *Daily Beast*, April 14, 2017.

502 Katie Benner, "No U.S. Charge Against Officer in Garner Case," *New York Times*, July 17, 2019, A1.

503 Paul Butler, *Chokehold: Policing Black Men* (New York: New Press, 2018).

504 "What Happened in Ferguson?," *New York Times*, August 10, 2015.

505 Sarah Kellogg, « Revolutionizing the Business of Law," Washington lawyer, May 2020, noting ABA Model Rule 5.4 concurring use of non-lawyers by law firms.

506 Lyle Moran "Hope for Nonprofit Law Firm Model Remains Despite Closing of Open Legal Services," *ABA Law Journal*, May 12, 2020.

507 Quail v. Mun. Court, 171 Cal. App. 3d 572, 577–93 (Cal. Ct. App. 1985) (Johnson, J., dissenting).

508 Gideon v. Wainwright (1963) 372 U.S. 335 [9 L.Ed.2d 799, 83 S.Ct. 792].

509 Mark Hansen, "Crime Labs Under the Microscope After a String of Shoddy, Suspect and Fraudulent Results," *ABA Journal*, September 1, 2013) (quoting Paul

Giannelli, law professor at Case Western Reserve University). Also see p. 81 where this subject was treated in the Netflix series, *"How to Fix a Drug Scandal"* from *Daily Beast* article by Nick Schager, Apr. 1, 2020.

510 Jed S. Rakoff, "Jailed by Bad Science," *New York Review of Books*, December 19, 2019.

511 509 U.S. 579 (1993).

512 Jed S. Rakoff, "Jailed by Bad Science," *New York Review of Books*, December 19, 2019.

513 Jayne R. Reardon, "Civility as the Core of Professionalism," American Bar Association, August 22, 2019.

514 Keith J. Bybee, *How Civility Works* (Redwood City, CA: Stanford University Press, 2016), 25–26.

515 Keith J. Bybee, *How Civility Works* (Redwood City, CA: Stanford University Press, 2016), 50.

516 Ibid., 55.

517 Ibid., 64.

518 "Alternative Dispute Resolution," 9 *Ohio State Journal on Dispute Resolution* 203 (1994) (detailing jurisprudential surveys of historical literature on this subject).

519 Kenneth J. Rigby, "Alternative Dispute Resolution," 44 *Louisiana Law Review* 1725 (1984).

520 Epic Sys.Corp. v. Lewis, 138 S. Ct 1612, 1616 (2018).

521 Michael Corkery and Jessica Silver-Greenberg, "New Tactic in Arbitration: Raise Volume," New York Times April 7, 2020, p B1, 6.

522 Brad Blickstein, "The Price You Pay—And How You Pay It," *Above Law*, January 29, 2019.

523 Corey Turner, "Court Rules Detroit Students Have Constitutional Right to an Education" NPR, April 27, 2020.

524 David Brooks, "The Moral Meaning of the Plague," NY Times, pg A-26, March 27, 2020.

525 Universal Declaration of Human Rights, General Assembly Resolution 217A article 25 (December 10, 1948); see also Peter B. Edelman, "The Next Century of Our Constitution: Rethinking Our Duty to the Poor," 39 *Hastings Law Journal* 1 (1987).

526 2 European Court of Human Rights, Report 305 (1979–1980).

527 Peter Edelman, *Not a Crime to Be Poor: The Criminalization of Poverty in America* (New York: New Press, 2017). Reviewed by Ronald Goldfarb in *Washington Lawyer Magazine*, April/May 2018.

528 Lincoln Caplan, "The Invisible Justice Problem," *Daedalus*, Winter 2019, 19.

529 Rostain, Techno -Optimism and Access to the legal system, Ibid, 93; Chambliss, Marketing Legal Assistance, Ibid., 98; Hagan, Participatory Design for Innovation in Access to Justice, Ibid., *120*.

530 Wallace, Corporate Support for Legal Services, Ibid., 136; Frazier, Why Big Business Should Support Legal Aid, Ibid., 150.

531 Adam Cohen, *Supreme Inequality*, Penguin Press, 2020.

532 Edmond Cahn, *The Consumers of Injustice*, quoted in *The World of Law II: The Law as Literature* (Ephraim London ed., Simon & Schuster, 1960), 590.

INDEX

ANCIENT ROMAN RELIGION

The Library of Liberal Arts

ANCIENT
ROMAN RELIGION

Edited, with an Introduction, by

FREDERICK C. GRANT

Edward Robinson Professor of Biblical Theology
Union Theological Seminary

PREFACE

It is a pleasure to record my indebtedness to the following persons for their counsel, suggestions, and criticism in the course of preparing this volume: *in primis* to Professors A. D. Nock of Harvard, F. R. Walton of Florida State University, and Agnes K. Michels of Bryn Mawr College; to Professors H. L. Friess and Gilbert Highet of Columbia University; to Professors Robert M. Grant and H. R. Willoughby of the University of Chicago, Robert H. Pfeiffer of Harvard, and Francis R. Beare of Trinity College, University of Toronto; and to Dean Sherman E. Johnson of the Church Divinity School in Berkeley, California.

The development of cults and beliefs under the Empire cannot be ignored—it also is a part of the history of Roman religion; but for fuller and further illustration I refer the reader to my earlier volume, *Hellenistic Religions: The Age of Syncretism,* published in this series in 1953. Other aspects of the syncretistic movement and of the independent religions of the time are illustrated in other volumes of the series.

The translations are my own, though naturally I have consulted other translations in the long tradition of the English rendering of the classics. Most translators have paid primary attention to literary values; but I have been more concerned with the religious significance of the selected passages, and have not hesitated to introduce, within square brackets, the Latin or Greek terms used, and even explanatory phrases, where either will make the meaning clearer to the student. For example, the term *expiare,* or *expiatio,* is usually rendered "atone" or "atonement" or "make atonement," or even "offer sacrifice" or—remoter still—"placate" (i.e., angry gods). In reality it means "restore the broken connections or relations with the divine powers, of which the evidence is clear from some portent or portents which have been observed." It is not necessarily or first of all a matter of placating angry gods: men

v

spoke of "expiating" the prodigy itself. And the rites used were often older than the belief in personal gods, at least gods of the Olympic or Capitoline order, and came down from a time when the ancient Italians believed that every forest dell, every spring and grove, was inhabited by some numen, friendly or otherwise. The oldest idea of expiation was the longest to survive, and practices found in far later centuries, even post-Christian, prove the depth and reality of the religious feeling involved. It will not do at all, then, to translate the word by some such highly theological term as "atone" or "reconcile" or "propitiate."

The student should read the classics, the inscriptions, and the papyri for himself. A useful method is to insert simple markings in the margin (of his own copies!), *R* for religion, *P* for philosophy, *E* for ethics, *T* for theology, *S* for sociology (or the social element in religion), and so on. When the marked passages are gathered together, he will have a collection of sources far ampler than the present volume, and one that will be priceless to him because it is his own—discovered, understood, and interpreted by himself as a student of ancient religions, perhaps one who is on the way to becoming a historian of ancient religion.

F. C. G.

CONTENTS

LIST OF ABBREVIATIONS

AFA   W. Henzen, *Acta Fratrum Arvalium* (1874).

BL   Bohn Library.

CAH   *Cambridge Ancient History* (1923–39).

CIL   *Corpus Inscriptionum Latinarum* (1863–).

Dessau   *See* ILS.

DT   A. Audollent, *Defixionum Tabellae* (1904).

ERE   J. Hastings (ed.), *Encyclopaedia of Religion and Ethics* (12 vols., 1908–21; Index vol., 1926).

GGR   M. P. Nilsson, *Geschichte der Griechischen Religion,* Vol. II, *Die Hellenistische und Römische Zeit* (1950).

HR   F. C. Grant, *Hellenistic Religions* (1953).

HRK   P. Wendland, *Die Hellenistisch-Römische Kultur* (2nd ed., 1912).

HRR   F. Altheim, *History of Roman Religion* (Eng. tr., 1938).

IGR   *Inscriptiones Graecae ad res Romanas pertinentes* (1906–).

ILS   H. Dessau, *Inscriptiones Latinae Selectae* (3 vols., 1892–1916).

LCL   *Loeb Classical Library* (1912–).

LGRM   W. H. Roscher, *Ausführliches Lexikon d. griechischen u. römischen Mythologie* (1884–).

OCD   *Oxford Classical Dictionary* (1949).

OGIS   W. Dittenberger, *Orientis Graeci Inscriptiones Selectae* (1903–05).

PW   A. Pauly, G. Wissowa, and W. Kroll, *Real-Encyclopädie d. klassischen Altertumswissenschaft* (1893–).

RC   N. Lewis and M. Reinhold, *Roman Civilization: Selected Readings,* Vol. I, *The Republic* (1951), Vol. II, *The Empire* (1955).

RERP   W. W. Fowler, *The Religious Experience of the Roman People* (1911).

RGVV   *Religionsgeschichtliche Versuche und Vorarbeiten* (1903–).

RKR   G. Wissowa, *Religion und Kultus der Römer* (1902; 2nd ed., 1912).

RO   F. Cumont, *Les Religions orientales dans le paganisme romain* (4th ed., 1929; Eng. tr. of 1st ed., 1911; German tr. of 4th ed., 1931).

ROL   E. H. Warmington, *Remains of Old Latin,* Vol. IV, *Archaic Inscriptions* (LCL, 1940).

RR   K. Latte, *Die Religion der Römer und der Synkretismus der Kaiserzeit* (1927).

RRA   N. Turchi, *La Religione di Roma Antica* (1939).

SP   A. S. Hunt and C. C. Edgar, *Select Papyri,* Vol. I, *Private Affairs* (LCL, 1932).

INTRODUCTION

Crowning the heights of beautiful, historic Taormina, in northeastern Sicily, lie the ruins of a Roman theater which had been built upon the foundations of an earlier Greek or Hellenistic one; this older theater had been built over what was once an early Greek shrine or small temple, erected, perhaps, by the founders of Naxos, the city at the foot of the cliff, when they arrived from their Aegean island in the year 735 B.C. The scene and its history are a parable of Roman religion, and they illustrate the remark of J. A. Hartung: "It is an ancient temple which was covered up by a later building, after which both buildings were destroyed, and we must now excavate the ruins of the earlier beneath the debris of the later."[1] The ancient Roman religion was overwhelmed by the Greek —and by the Greek not at a comparable early stage, but in its later, developed, mythological, even skeptical form, to which the old Roman rites, the names of gods, and the general preconceptions were all accommodated. Our information about the early Roman religion is thus both confused and extremely fragmentary.

1. Sources

The ancient literary sources are interesting but inadequate. Ovid's *Fasti* (*Festivals*), for example, covering the festivals from January to June (the rest of his book was probably never published), is overlaid with poetic and mythological fancies and interpretations which cannot be old and authentic, though his descriptions of the actual rituals are often profoundly illuminating. Varro, whose book on ancient Roman religion, *Antiquitates rerum divinarum* (*Sacred Antiquities*), survives in fragments quoted by St. Augustine, acknowledged that he could only guess the meaning of much of the primitive ritual.

[1] *Religion der Römer* (1836), I, 9; quoted in Wissowa, RKR, p. 1.

Livy's *History of Rome* gives us stories, legends, and traditions, often told with later conceptions read into them. Other ancient writers, like Dionysius of Halicarnassus and Aulus Gellius, give us fragmentary bits, though they themselves did not possess the key to their original meaning. Plutarch, for example, wrote a whole monograph on *Roman Questions,* and dealt with unexplained and problematic details of the old religion.

Nevertheless the main features of the ancient Roman religion can be made out with fair assurance. As Theodor Mommsen and Georg Wissowa believed—and all later experts accept their view—our best clue to the reconstruction of the ancient cults is the pre-Julian calendar, which survives in fragments but can be pieced together. We possess, more or less complete, the fragments of more than twenty copies of this calendar, which tradition ascribed to King Numa, and which, in its main features, was left unaltered by Julius Caesar when, in 46 B.C., he revised the calendar and added ten days to the year. Each of these pre-Julian copies distinguishes certain days by the use of large capital letters in inscribing their names and in marking the eight-day "weeks" (A–H) and indicating the character of most of the days in the year: F = *fastus,* "legally available"; NF = *nefastus,* "not legally available"; NP = *nefastus parte,* "unavailable in part"; EN = *endotercisi,* or *intercisi,* when the business part of the day came in the middle; C = *dies comitiales,* when political assemblies could be held.[2] In contrast to these days named in large capital letters are a whole series of other names and of notes in smaller capitals, apparently added later, and so numerous that only smaller letters made their inclusion possible.[3] The obvious explanation of this difference in the size of the letters is that the festivals named in large capitals are the older, those in smaller capitals the ones added later. We shall come back to this explanation below.

2 See Wissowa, RKR, e.g., §§ 1, 3, 63, and Appendix I.
3 See the illustrations in Turchi, RRA, Plates VII and VIII, pp. 46, 65.

2. *General Character*

As reflected in this ancient calendar and also in the literary sources, the old Roman religion was a system of religious
observances, agricultural for the most part, without myth,
theology, statues of the gods, or temples. Indeed, it has been
argued by some scholars that it was originally a religion without gods, during the "predeistic" age before Greek or Etruscan
influence led to the importation or creation of personal, an-
thropomorphic deities; instead of gods there were only vague,
mysterious, impersonal forces, *numina,* local powers or spirits
in control of various activities of daily life and the forces of
nature. But the argument is precarious; Jupiter and Mars
were personal gods from the beginning. It was a religion centered in various cult practices, many of them so old that their
original meaning had been long forgotten—if indeed they ever
had possessed a fully thought-out meaning. For they represented no rational application of specific media to recurrent
situations in primitive agricultural or social life, but were
rooted in age-old tradition; these things had been found to
work, whatever the reason. Piety even forbade a too curious
inquiry into the reasons. Thus it was not in theology, myth,
or sculpture—i.e., in art—that the old Roman religion excelled: all these were lacking, in the earliest period, and when
they came to be adopted were only borrowed from the Greeks
and others, chiefly from the Greeks. Instead, it was in its ritual
that the old Roman religion was pre-eminent. As Cicero said
with true Roman pride: "If we wish to compare our people
with foreigners, we find that although we are only their equals
or even their inferiors in other matters, in religion—i.e., *in
the cult of the gods* [*id est cultu deorum*]—we are far superior."[4]

It was a religion in which ritual reigned supreme, since ideas
were secondary; but it was not a ritual performed for its own
sake—it was a ritual which produced certain results, a ritual

[4] *De natura deorum,* II. 8.

which was guaranteed (by long usage) to achieve the practical ends which men desired. Sacrifice was the fundamental principle of most of its rites, though a few beans or flowers might suffice for an offering, and the ritual often included a procession or a dance, while games were a regular part of public religious festivals. The fundamental conception is reflected in the common liturgical phrase used in this ancient cultus, *Macte esto,* "Be worshiped, be honored." Some of the rites have been compared with those of the Old Testament, but the difference between the old Roman religion and that of the Old Testament is more marked than the resemblance. The Old Testament retains only a few traces of a genuinely primitive stage of religion; most of the ritual has been rationalized and refined under the influence of the prophets, especially their teaching of the oneness of God and of Israel's responsibility to Yahweh alone. But Roman religion (i.e., ritual) never was revised under any such overmastering impulse: it remained static, conservative, old-fashioned to the end. Indeed, the "reforms" of Augustus were intended to be only a revival of ancient rites, not a sweeping reformation; and the purpose of the emperor was to safeguard and preserve the state, not to promote a spiritual or philosophic conception of religion. As Cicero, Varro, Virgil, and others imply or assume, the very existence of the state depended upon the proper performance of these age-old rites; accordingly, their performance was a chief function of the state itself. We can see how inevitable, therefore, was the collision between the Roman state and the early Christian church, which held a totally different view of religion. The classic statement of the divergence is to be found in the opening books of St. Augustine's *City of God.*

Another function of the ritual, though really subsidiary to the main purpose of safeguarding the state, i.e., the common welfare, was the expiation of prodigies. Primitive man had found himself in the midst of a strange, mysterious, dangerous world—like a person wandering blindfold through an electric powerhouse, where at any moment a "live" switch or wire might give him a shock or possibly destroy him. By the immemorial process of trial and error, ever since an age far back in man's prehistory, certain patterns of procedure had been firmly established: follow these, and all would be well. What these approved patterns were, the priests knew; directions could be obtained from them. But when a comet appeared in the sky, when rains flooded the fields for too long a season or when the crops failed because of drought, when an enemy threatened the very existence of the city and its gods, then special procedures were clearly required to meet the new situation. Prophets or soothsayers, augurs or haruspices, might order what was to be done; oracles might be consulted, or the Sibylline books. Some rite or other surely must be found, like an appropriate remedy, which would meet the crisis and safeguard those in danger. The oldest name for this procedure was *expiatio,* which was not "propitiation," for that implies a god who must be placated, but something needing to be done in order to restore the status quo, avert the threatened disaster, restore the broken contact with the invisible world, and reestablish right relations with the unseen powers (the *pax deorum*). The requisite procedure might be a public supplication, or a procession, or a *lectisternium.* Whatever the means of expiation, it was the prodigy itself, as a sign that something was wrong—though it was not always clear just what was wrong—which required expiation and had to be neutralized.

3. Early Stages

The ancient Roman calendar presupposes a series of successive stages in the evolution of the old Italian religion down to the end of the Republic. That is to say, the names of the gods inscribed in the pre-Julian calendar, and their functions, reflect these earlier stages. The earliest of these deities were chiefly the following (deities with flamens or other official cultic representatives are marked with asterisks):[5]

[5] To these deities Wissowa applied the name *di indigetes,* thus interpreting the ancient term as "native gods" in contrast to the *di novensides* (or *novensiles*) which he took to mean the later arrivals, some coming

Anna Perenna
*Carmenta
Carna
*Ceres
Consus
Di penates
Diva Angerona
*Falacer
*Faunus, Fauna
*Flora
Fons (?)
*Furrina
Genius and Juno
*Janus
*Jupiter
Juturna
Larenta
Lares (?)

Lemures (?)
*Mars
Mater Matuta
Neptunus and Salacia
Ops
*Pales, Palatua
*Pomona
*Portunus
*Quirinus
Robigus (?)
Saturnus
Silvanus
Tellus
Terminus (?)
Veiovis
*Vesta
*Volcanus and Maia
*Volturnus

Of these earlier deities, the most ancient of all (i.e., the earliest to be worshiped in Rome) were probably the following: Janus, Jupiter, Mars, Quirinus, Vesta, the *di penates* and the *lares,* Genius, Tellus, Consus, Ops, and Saturnus. Their relation to the conditions of life faced by the early Romans seems clear. Although some deities are older still, i.e., prehistoric, and have left no trace but their names (e.g., Falacer), and although some of them were shared with other peoples in ancient Italy, it is still impossible (though not unattempted) to write the "prehistory" of Roman religion, or to describe the cults of the various peoples which occupied the Italian peninsula during the centuries before the founding of Rome in 753 B.C. It is impossible to describe the religion of the ancient Etruscans, for example, or to appraise their influence, positive or negative, upon the religion of the Romans. The novelist D. H. Lawrence thought them a kind and generous people with a beautiful and romantic religion, who were accordingly hated by the

---

from elsewhere in Italy, others from Greece. Many present-day scholars question Wissowa's interpretation. The severest critic has been Altheim; see HRR, pp. 106–114.

warlike Romans and exterminated. But their tomb paintings seem to tell another story, or at least to echo one.

The later arrivals, according to Wissowa, were: (from Italy) Diana, Minerva, Fortuna, Castor and Pollux, Hercules, Feronia, Vortumnus, and Venus; (from Magna Graecia) Apollo, Ceres, Liber and Libera, Mercury, Aesculapius and Salus, Dis pater and Proserpina, Mens, Sol and Luna; and (from Phrygia) the Great Mother of the Gods. There is still uncertainty about this classification, but in general the distinctions are clear. The oriental gods and goddesses, especially the "mystery" deities, came later still, chiefly under the early Empire. After Julius Caesar revised the calendar there were no changes of fundamental importance but only additions: the notable events in the history of the Caesarian family were added, but they were more like the national holidays added to an ecclesiastical calendar. Other and later additions were chiefly games.[6]

As reconstructed by Mommsen, Wissowa, Deubner, Warde Fowler, and others, the earliest stages of Roman religion reflect successively (1) the most primitive conditions of life in ancient Italy, when men lived in the forest where spirits lurked, where charms and spells were potent, where every rock, tree, stream, and hill was sacred—feelings that never wholly left the ancient Italians; (2) the period of settled agricultural life, where the ritual centered in the farm, with its lar or lares, and included not only the farmhouse with its hearth sacred to Vesta, its storechamber and guardian penates, its doorway sacred to Janus, but also the fields with their boundary mark or Terminus, their annual lustration or blessing at the Ambarvalia, the religious observances connected with seedtime and harvest, at the Saturnalia, Vinalia, Consualia, and Opiconsivia; finally (3) the settled life of the city and the political constitution of the Roman people, with the memorials of the dead at the Parentalia and the worship of the common lares or guardians of the whole community (*Lares Praestites*, May 1), the organized religion of the state with Vestals and Flamens

6 See Wissowa, RKR, Appendix I.

and a Pontifex Maximus in charge of the rites, the great Latin
Festival (end of April) celebrating on the Alban Mount the
consolidation of the Latin tribes under the hegemony of
Rome. As in the Hebrew religion and in some others, the festivals in the calendar reflect the nation's history. The oldest
rites may have been "predeistic," as some maintain, at least in
the sense that the deity involved was often uncertain, always
more or less impersonal, and quite subordinate to the rite,
which was effective per se and as an *opus operatum,* an "act
done." From the time, presumably, of King Numa, the traditional founder of the national cultus, a triad of gods stands
out distinctly: Jupiter, Mars, and Quirinus.

These earliest, fundamental, creative stages in the development of Roman religion were succeeded by (4) the period of
the Etruscan kings, when real temples were built (as distinct
from groves, caves, open-air altars, and little shrines), and
when statues of the gods first made their appearance, when
indeed new gods arrived, and when Greek rites were introduced, probably by new elements in the population. It was
due to the Etruscans, apparently, that the great temple was
erected on the Capitol and dedicated (509 B.C.) to Jupiter, Juno,
and Minerva. The new gods included Mercury (Greek Hermes),
Ceres (Demeter, probably connected with the grain import
from the south, where Greeks had been settled since the
eighth century B.C.), Fortuna, Diana (from Aricia?), and
Apollo; while older Italian gods reappear in new guises—
Neptunus, for example, the god of streams, now taking over
the sea as well, and identifying himself with the Greek god
Poseidōn. The new ritual was showy and luxurious, as contrasted with the simple, old-fashioned rites of the forefathers:
it was a ritual of cities, primarily, and the old rites survived
chiefly in the country districts. In addition to the Pontifex
Maximus and the *Duoviri sacris faciundis,* who had charge of
the specifically Greek rites prescribed by the Sibylline books,
there now followed a large growth in the numbers, power, and
influence of the *pontifices,* the pontifical college associated
with and in charge of all public rites and ceremonies. It was

the *pontifices,* apparently, who drew up the *indigitamenta,* i.e., the lists of deities, each with his or her appropriate function in the life of the state and its people.

This lush growth of new cults with their temples and statuary, and with added deities partly recruited from abroad but also derived by abstraction from ordinary experience and from various human motives, was presently succeeded by (5) a period of material growth and expansion. The third century was remarkable for the great number of state temples which were erected.[7] Nevertheless, with the Hannibalic war began (6) a new era. In its effort to survive in that struggle, Rome revived the ancient *ver sacrum,* by which all the animals born in one whole springtime were dedicated to the gods and destroyed as a sacrifice,[8] and proclaimed a *lectisternium* (or public feast) to the Twelve Gods. It even went the length, after the catastrophic defeat at Cannae (216 B.C.), perhaps in imitation of powerful and victorious Carthage, of offering human sacrifice. In 205 B.C. the Sibylline books were consulted, and a mission was sent to Pergamum in Asia Minor to bring the sacred stone of Cybele from Mount Ida to Rome. The reception given the Mother of the Gods on her arrival was an event never forgotten in later history. Cybele was given a place of her own in the temple of Victory on the Palatine mount, though for two centuries and more no Roman was permitted to share in her rites. Hannibal was driven from Italy and defeated at Zama in 202 B.C.; success had crowned the innovation of the new worship and given the highest possible approval to the principle of the importation of foreign, especially Eastern, deities. Other cults followed: for example, that of Dionysus (Bacchus), identified with Liber pater, though the orgiastic private rites of the Bacchanalia were soon (in 186 B.C.) strictly regulated by decree of the Senate. Their character may be inferred from the language of the *senatus-consultum* (see pp. 54 ff.).

As the republican empire continued to expand, many more foreigners settled in Rome, bringing with them their cults—

---

[7] Forty-five in Wissowa's list; see RKR, Appendix II.

[8] Livy, *History of Rome,* XXII. 10. 3.

though these were not officially recognized, nor were the cult centers admitted to the sacred precincts of the Capitol or the Palatine; nor were the foreign festivals ever included in the calendar of the state religion. By the end of the Republic the cults of Isis, Magna Mater, Ma (Bellona), Sarapis, Mithras, and Dionysus had all gained a firm foothold in Italy. The impact of Greek thought, especially of Greek philosophy with its criticism and reinterpretation of the traditional religion, made a deep impression on the religion of the educated classes. At the beginning of the second century B.C. the poet Ennius had translated the works of Euhemerus, who explained the myths and cults of the gods as fanciful tales of deified men and rites based upon superstition. By the time of Varro (116–28 B.C.) it was possible for that eminent, vastly learned, but completely skeptical antiquarian to maintain the theory that religion was threefold: that of the poets, pure fancy; that of the philosophers, a rational explanation of the universe; that of the state, the ritual—however absurd—which was necessary to maintain law and order. By the time of Augustus the old public rites and priesthoods had fallen into neglect, and by many persons religion was valued chiefly for its political utility.

Then came (7) the reforms of Augustus, or rather his restoration of the older temples—eighty-two of them, he tells us in the inscription on the Monumentum Ancyranum—with their ancestral rites and priesthoods. It is often argued today that the motive behind this "reform" was more political than religious. But we must remember that the ancient world did not distinguish religion and politics, as the modern world does. All religious activities had a bearing upon the welfare of the state. It was an era of optimism and good feeling. After the long agony of the civil wars, after two centuries of endless warfare abroad, peace had at last returned to this troubled earth, and the temple of Janus could now be closed. The secular celebration of 17 B.C., which is recorded both in the fragmentary inscription (p. 178) and in Horace's beautiful *Carmen saeculare,* was intended to mark the beginning of this new era; while in far-off Priene and Halicarnassus, in Asia Minor, the local calendar was changed so that the year should begin with the emperor's birthday, since his birth had marked "the beginning of the good news [*euaggelion*] of safety and welfare [*sōtēria*] for mankind."

But the religious reforms of Augustus affected only the state cult. The real beliefs of men—and their unbeliefs—remained unaltered, and the cults of the oriental deities, though officially discouraged, still survived. Even as perfect a poet as Virgil could not produce a Bible for the Roman world, or instill a living faith in the hearts of men. For good or ill, the Augustan "reform" attached a system of primitive rites and sacrifices to the new imperial house and its program of unification, peace, and prosperity, promoted under the slogan "The restoration of the Republic." Men were still free to believe or not, in private, in whatever ideas were attached to these rites, in the myths imported from Greece (chiefly those of the Greek poets), and in the speculations of the philosophers. Unfortunately for religion, it was mainly the skeptical and critical trend in Hellenistic philosophy which appealed to the hard-headed Roman: Skepticism, Empiricism, Cyrenaicism, Materialism, Epicureanism, the endless suspense of judgment of the later Academy, or the "physical" theology of the Stoa. In the rural districts and villages the old rites survived, rooted deep in the soil and intimately bound up with the agricultural seasons. Here and there might be found scattered conventicles of Pythagoreans, while devotees of Isiac or other types of eastern worship mingled with the Roman populace. The religious scene under the early Empire, even in Italy, was one of conflicting cults, creeds, and philosophies, all living and competing under the formal aegis of a vast and comprehensive state cult.

Finally, (8) under the early Empire still other cults and doctrines were introduced or revived. Astrology and fatalism had not been unknown in republican Italy, but the extent of this influence increased enormously in the first and second centuries of our era. As a mode of escape or a refuge from the iron determinism of the heavenly bodies, which were in complete control of affairs here on earth, many persons resorted to magical rites. The "theurgy" of the later Neoplatonists [9] was only a rarefied form of the basic magic to which many resorted in their attempt to escape an all-embracing determinism. The mood of countless men and women, and their prayer—to Zeus, to Helios, to whatever god seemed to promise release, and eventually to the Christian God, "the Maker of heaven and earth"—is reflected in Hilaire Belloc's lines:

> Strong God which made the topmost stars
> To circulate and keep their course,
> Remember me; whom all the bars
> Of sense and dreadful fate enforce.

4. Syncretism

The popular syncretistic religion of the first century was marked by three outstanding features which were destined to be of permanent (if sometimes exaggerated) importance for the general history of religion at the beginning of our era and during the centuries that followed. These were (1) the mysteries, (2) the cults of the hero gods, the "Sons of God" or "Helpers," especially of such gods as Hercules and Aesculapius, Castor and Pollux, and (3) the imperial cultus and emperor worship.

(1) *The mysteries* had been age-old in Greece. Those at Eleusis, attached to the cult of Demeter, go back to the beginnings of agriculture (i.e., of grain-growing) in Attica. Those at Andania in the southern Peloponnese were perhaps equally old. Those of the "Great Gods" on the island of Samothrace were so old that their beginnings seemed prehistoric. In the first century, eminent Romans, even emperors, craved admission to the Eleusinia. Evidence for the popularity of the mysteries at Andania is found in the decree set up in 93 B.C., where men and women votaries were chosen from among the citizens.[10] There were strict rules governing the apparel to be

9 See F. C. Grant, HR, pp. 176 ff.
10 *Ibid.*, pp. 31 f.

worn by the initiates: it must be simple, and unadorned with gold. There was a sacred procession of the chest or chests containing the sacred objects of the cult. Tents were set up for visitors, but they were very simple. The sacrifices, on the other hand, were most elaborate—e.g., one of a hundred lambs.

The Eleusinian rites demanded purity of both body and soul: they began with a baptism in the sea near Athens. Following the preparatory initiation (or dedication) in the Lesser Mysteries in February (which may have preceded the baptism), the full initiation took place in September—really two Septembers, a year apart, the first (*muēsis*) one year, the second (*epopteia*) the next. The candidate was led into the shrine and shown certain objects. The essence of the rite was not the imparting of a secret doctrine or even of a revelation, but the inducement of a particular mental state, resulting from fasting and the excitement of the occasion; under these conditions the reception of sacred food, the handling of certain sacred objects, or the hearing and seeing of the sacred drama—whichever of these it was, and we cannot be sure—made a never-to-be-forgotten impression upon the neophyte. Indeed, some men testified that it changed their whole life and character. Contrary to the popular modern view, the purpose of the initiation was not to insure immortality—this had been taken for granted by most persons from the days of Homer and long before, though the wraith-like existence in Hades was nothing to anticipate with pleasure. Instead, the purpose of the initiation was to insure a better, more blissful, more desirable kind of immortality, in union with the life-giving powers controlled by Demeter in this world and by her daughter Korē (or Persephonē) in the world below. The Eleusinian rites were among the most famous and most ancient in the Greek world; and they were probably the most influential, other mystery cults conforming more or less to the standard set by them. The new oriental mysteries (those of Attis, Adonis, Mithras, Isis, Osiris, Sarapis, Dea Syria, and others) differed greatly in their rites, but their objects were more or less the same: to confer a more blissful kind of immortality—or at least a somewhat happier state in the life to come—or a renewal and enrichment of life here and now, as in the "rebirth" through the taurobolium which restored one to the status of childhood once in twenty years; or to guarantee a relationship on better terms with such an adorable supernatural being as Isis or Sarapis. The mode was not always "sacramental," though some modern writers use the term; the benefits of mystery initiation could be conveyed either by a deep emotional experience, the result of seeing, feeling, or hearing the mystery performance (the *drōmenon*), or by the imparting of secret, occult knowledge, or by magic ritual—any of these could, apparently, induce a state of moral and spiritual transformation or "conversion." Even the severely restricted *bacchanalia,* the rites of Dionysus (Bacchus) in his guise as god of the vine, presumably offered something more than momentary ecstasy.

As M. P. Nilsson and A. D. Nock have shown, the majority of the new oriental cults (except, of course, the Mithraic) were originally primitive vegetation rites which, under the influence of Hellenism, were reinterpreted and elaborated and made into "mysteries" of personal salvation; that is, they were not native growths of spiritual or philosophic aspiration, but were conformed to the pattern of the Greek mysteries. Modern writers have tended to read into their scanty literary records and archeological remains far more significance than they can rightly claim. To begin with, our knowledge of the mysteries is extremely fragmentary and sketchy. We can trace their spread to every part of the Roman world, but their actual content, the details of the rites, their organization and leadership, the beliefs and doctrines inculcated—all this is extremely obscure. Yet they testify, according to J. Carcopino and N. Turchi, to a spiritual fact of major importance, "the rise of personal religion, apart from and superior to the religion of the state with its lack of concern for the individual and his destiny; the souls of men had now found the way to their own personal salvation." [11] As always in the ancient world—this also was a Greek trait—salvation was conceived as achieved

---

[11] N. Turchi, *Le religioni misteriche del mondo antico* (1948), p. vii.

through knowledge, but in this case not a knowledge of the merely rational kind but mystical, supernatural, an illumination derived from the direct vision of deity, or conveyed by those who had received it from such a supernatural source. Thus the vision of God and spiritual fellowship or association with him would be, for a devout pagan, not only the supreme goal of initiation but also the guarantee of a blessed status in the life to come, since it was this, rather than immortality itself, that the mysteries promised their devotees. So, at least, the priceless account which Apuleius has given in his *Metamorphoses*, Bk. XI,[12] must probably be interpreted. Furthermore, some such type of religious experience seems to lie behind the Gnostic systems, and also Neoplatonism. It was the point even of crude magical operations, as in the *Leiden Magical Papyrus*,[13] where the devotee addresses his god, "Thou art I, and I am thou." The magical import of these words is clear from what follows: "Whatever I command must come to pass. Thy name I bear as a talisman [phylactery] in my heart, and no power of flesh whatsoever can prevail against me, no spirit oppose me, no daemon, no ghost nor other evil [being] from Hades." The whole prayer is a fascinating example of syncretism, for it contains echoes from several different quarters, including Judaism.

This mysticism—the term is a better one, as Nilsson notes, than the still popular but more fanciful one, "theology of the mysteries"—accordingly came in contact with and was influenced by the revivals of older philosophies, such as Neopythagoreanism and Neoplatonism, and the emergence of new ones, in Hermetism, Gnosticism, and the widespread theosophy which was one striking expression of the final stage of syncretism in the third and fourth centuries. Eventually, likewise, they all were confronted with the new religion of a "revealed mystery," viz., the Christian gospel, as it swept westward from Palestine after the middle of the first century. The philosophies likewise were challenged by a religion which viewed sal-

---

[12] See F. C. Grant, HR, pp. 136–144.
[13] II, col. 18; see Preisendanz, *Papyri Graecae Magicae*, II, 123.

vation not as the possession of some body of secret knowledge
about the origin of the soul or the structure of the universe
or the destiny of the material cosmos, but as the transformation of the human will into conformity with the will of God
and the consequent ethical and spiritual remaking of human
nature into the divine likeness as manifested in the person of
Jesus Christ, the incarnate Son of God. That both later Hellenistic-Roman religious mysticism and philosophy contributed to
the triumph of their rival does not minimize either the victory
or the significance of those earlier quests for salvation.

The second-century Platonic philosopher Theon of Smyrna
described five stages in the mystery initiations: (1) the preliminary purification, (2) the initiation itself, (3) a simple vision,
(4) a more solemn vision, (5) priesthood, which carried with it
the right to initiate others. To these he compared the five
stages in a scientific education: arithmetic, plane geometry,
solid geometry, astronomy, and music. Whether this outline of
the stages in mystery initiation really reflects a pattern common to the cults, or to a majority of them, or is only a bit of
scholastic theorizing (like the medieval "ladders" of prayer or
of the love of God), a theory spun by Theon himself, we do
not know. But the procedure which it summarizes (known to
Theon but not to us) must have included rites of purification,
fasting and abstinence from secular—including sexual—activities; the initiation itself probably included dances, displays,
invocations, a combination of "things done" (*drōmena*) and
"things said" (*legomena*) which had a powerful effect on the
mind and emotions of the candidate. What teaching, if any,
accompanied these rites, or just what formulas were used, we
can only surmise.[14]

The significance of the mysteries for the New Testament or
for the early Christian Church was indirect; for Judaism it
was almost *nil*. Though often assumed, there is little or no
evidence of any direct borrowing by Christianity: for one
thing the new religion was far too Jewish in its origin to permit such borrowing. The religious inheritance enshrined in

14 See F. C. Grant, HR, pp. 136–149.

the Old Testament stood in the way, even though Hellenistic syncretism had apparently influenced Diaspora Judaism to some extent, at least on its periphery. As for any borrowing by the mysteries from Christianity, though some of the apologists and Church Fathers made capital of every trace of resemblance, this seems most unlikely: the mysteries were much too old and too foreign to be dependent upon Christian rites or doctrines. Moreover, the area of contact between Christianity and the mysteries was too narrow, in the first century. As Franz Cumont has shown, the heyday of popularity for the mystery religions came in the second and third centuries, not in the first; it was also the period of the great conflict between Christianity and the mysteries. Nevertheless the mysteries are significant for the student of the New Testament. Some of their language was already in current use, especially in religious circles, and along with the language went the ideas: e.g., spiritual rebirth, immortality, hidden knowledge, and the very notion of a "mystery" itself—which was not a riddle, or a secret withheld, but a secret which had been divulged to the few, the initiates or the elect, and was to be guarded by them and kept from "those outside" (cf. Mark 4:11). But more than all this, the chief significance of the mysteries for the student of the New Testament lies in their expression of the deepening religious mood and the heightened aspirations of the period. As Theon insisted, the end of all study of the sciences, as of religious aspiration, is "the greatest possible likeness to God." In his classic *Hellenistisch-römische Kultur*, Paul Wendland described the deep undercurrent of religious feeling which flowed through the Augustan age and the century that followed. Of this phenomenon the mysteries were perhaps more a symptom than a cause, more an expression than a satisfaction.

It was this widespread religious need which Christianity, as it came forth from its Palestinian homeland and faced the broad world of Hellenistic-Roman culture, undertook to satisfy. In its effort to meet this demand, the Church naturally adopted the language of the outside world, at least to some extent; and naturally also, in the process, was influenced by what it took over. The vocabulary of the New Testament is fundamentally Semitic, Old Testament, Jewish (largely via the Septuagint and the Greco-Jewish writers); but it has added to its store many words whose primary connotation is Greek, i.e., Hellenistic, drawn from the religious or philosophical vocabulary of the already partly orientalized Mediterranean world of the early Empire. No foreign missionary can accomplish much who does not speak the language of the people whom he evangelizes or who does not "speak to their condition." There was every reason in the world why the early Church should address itself to this orientalized Greco-Roman world of the first three centuries in language which that world could understand, and should undertake to meet its deep religious needs with the message of the gospel. In fact, as some of the Church Fathers insisted, the whole history of paganism, up to and including the reign of Augustus, could be regarded as a part of the divine preparation for the Christian message.

(2) The evidence for the popularity and influence of *the hero gods* is widespread. The "Olympians" or the "Capitoline" gods might be far away, or concerned only with the state cult; these gods, the "Saviors," "Preservers," and "Helpers" of men were close at hand, approachable, patient listeners to human appeals, *epēkooi*. Indeed they had chosen to be with men: Heracles (Hercules), whose prolonged and painful series of mighty labors were now interpreted as undertaken for the good of mankind (schoolboys in the Roman Empire studied his exploits as moral examples); Asclepius (Aesculapius), who had brought to men the healing arts and whose shrines (especially the one at Epidaurus) were crowded with pilgrims in search of health; Castor and Pollux, who shared equally their mortality and immortality, and were the "saviors" of storm-tossed mariners. These "Sons of Gods" were the noblest representatives of deity which first-century paganism could conceive, and appealed most strongly to the rank and file of men, who, in spite of the skepticism of the learned and the half-learned, and the rigid determinism or the magic of the illiterate, still continued to believe in the existence and activity of

beneficent divine powers. The satirist Lucian made fun of the
Olympian gods, castigating the foibles and follies of Zeus and
his court; but he never once ventured to criticize the hero
gods, who were the saviors of mankind dear to the hearts of
the majority of men. A Son of God like Asclepius was no remote or officious deity, but a god who lived close to men,
could be appealed to directly, and was concerned for human
welfare.[15] Strange as it may seem to us, no higher title was
available for true and worthy deity than this, in the first century—as the early gentile Church proved when it adopted the
title and filled it with still richer meaning.

As a contrast to Lucian's satire on the Olympians, Horace's
lovely *Ode to Apollo,* for all its formality, expresses genuine
devotion to the god whom Augustus identified with his family
and reign.

> What prayer should one offer Apollo, even a poet,
> Pouring fresh wine from the bowl? For harvests abundant,
> Wains groaning and slow amid sunny Sardinian grainfields,
> Calabrian cattle, well nourished and sleek, or gold
> From far-away Ind, with ivories cunningly carven,
> Or fields by that beautiful stream, the smooth-flowing
>   Liris? . . .
> But grant me, O Son of Latona, thy gift of contentment,
> With soundness of body and mind, though age be
>   advancing—
> Let age be with honor, and ever the song of the lyre! [16]

Such a prayer cannot be dismissed as "merely literary." Ancient
Italian religion was not introspective—and this is one reason
why certain modern scholars, schooled in one particular theological tradition and sharing a post-Renaissance view of
Christianity, find it difficult to do justice to the religion of
Horace and Virgil. Horace is a poet all the time. His religion
is the religion of a literary man, and it is real religion. Though
in origin an Olympian, Apollo shared with the hero gods in
human vicissitudes and adventures and in rendering services

---

15 *Ibid.,* pp. 53–59.
16 I. 31.

to mankind—which George Meredith celebrated in his beautiful and classic *Phoebus with Admetus.*

(3) The growth of *emperor worship* almost reached its zenith at the end of the first century, under Domitian. But its antecedents were very old, and long antedated the Empire. (*a*) The accession of Augustus and the era of peace which he inaugurated, after the two long and bloody centuries of foreign and civil warfare, were celebrated by the poets Horace and Virgil, as in the line,

He is a god who has given us this leisure

(*Deus nobis haec otia fecit*—this peace, this quiet, this tranquillity and freedom from care).[17] The Provincial Assemblies of Asia decreed that from now on the year should begin with the emperor's birthday, September 23. The whole world rejoiced that peace had come at last; and the one through whom world peace had come—must he not be divine? This fact alone would suffice to account for emperor worship. (*b*) Nevertheless, its antecedents go back much farther in ancient history. First of all, there was the old oriental influence and example, at least as old as the rise of the Pharaohs in Egypt. For thousands of years the Pharaoh had been king in Egypt because he was a god, designated as heir to the throne by his divine father. (*c*) In time this view of Egyptian kingship was inherited by the Ptolemies, who were honored even during their lifetimes as divine beings; and the same was true of the Seleucids in Syria and the Attalids in Pergamum. Not only did they become gods after death, they were adored and had their priests even while living. Though the ancient oriental monarchs were often viewed as divine by virtue of their office, while the Hellenistic ruler cult recognized merit rather than descent—the kings were "benefactors" (Luke 22:25)—there can be little doubt that in the East it had been true for centuries that "there's . . . divinity doth hedge a king." The whole ethos and presupposition of political loyalty led to emperor worship, in the ancient Near Eastern world. (*d*) Still closer to the Christian era was

---

[17] Virgil, *Eclogue* I, line 6.

Antiochus of Commagene (98–34 B.C.), who built for himself a tomb on one of the peaks of the Taurus Mountains and set up an inscription in which he insisted with magnificent complacency upon his divine descent.[18] One of the bas-reliefs on the monument shows the king and his god, Mithras, wearing the same royal costume and grasping hands as a symbol of their alliance. When the Roman emperor Augustus came into possession of the empire of the Ptolemies and of certain smaller kingdoms in the East, he fell heir at one stroke to the divine cultus which had been paid to their rulers. It is therefore not surprising that the earliest expressions of religious veneration and worship addressed to the emperor and to the Empire came precisely from the eastern half of the Empire.

Moreover, the idea had already been taken over in later Greek thought. (e) Before launching his triumphant campaign against Darius III and the kingdoms of the East, Alexander the Great had journeyed far into the Libyan desert to consult the oracle of Zeus-Amon. Here he had been greeted by the priest as "son of Amon"—as successor to the Pharaohs he now held their title. It was a great advantage, if he was to succeed to the sovereignty of the "Great King" of Persia and also to that of the rulers of the far older monarchies of Egypt, Mesopotamia, and Hither India, that he should, like them, be descended from a god—indeed, from the highest god. (f) Following Alexander, as the political history of the period makes amply clear, the imperialistic idea now begins to supplant that of the old Greek city-state; from now on the rulers of mankind are usually men of daring and of military prowess at the head of large mercenary armies. It was not difficult for the ordinary person to acknowledge the divinity of these "strong men armed" (Luke 11:21) who ruled the nations and were given the title of "benefactors"—men like Demetrius Poliorcetes.[19] (g) All this was the easier in that it was assumed that a spirit or daemon accompanied the individual, especially the unusual individual—e.g., such a man as Brutus—and also that Roman thought assumed

---

18 See F. C. Grant, HR, pp. 20–25.
19 *Ibid.*, pp. 63 ff.

the existence of the Genius of the house, the family, the city, as well as of the individual; and it was especially so after divine honors had been given Julius Caesar, following his death. Since the survival and the welfare of the state were primary concerns of Roman religion, the unusual individual whose services had conspicuously promoted the safety and success of the nation was thought of as guided and inspired by a supernatural power. When, for example, a man like Demetrius Poliorcetes achieved what no god had done, or when the young Octavian accomplished even more than Demetrius, and brought peace to the whole world after centuries of warfare, it seemed obvious to many that such a ruler must be himself divine, the incarnation or "manifestation" not only of the Genius of his own family but also of the Genius of the state.

It was partly as a result of its collision with emperor worship and the cult of the Roman Empire that the early Christian Church came nearest to being annihilated. In the Apocalypse of John (*ca.* A.D. 95) it is assumed that the question is very real, whether or not there will be any Christians left by the time the end of the age arrives (Rev. 7). The whole book concerns the crisis which had arisen in the Province of Asia during the reign of Domitian, when membership in the Christian Church apparently came to be viewed as disloyalty to the state, and when extreme penalties were meted out to those who refused to conform to the public cultus. Only the Jews escaped—their religion had long been tolerated. For the emperor cult was anything but simple, old-fashioned idolatry. It carried with it the highest values in human culture: peace, law, order, stability, progress in the arts and in learning, public welfare, prosperity and wealth, the health and the safety of the bodies and the minds of men—of all men everywhere throughout the civilized world. All this was bound up with the worship of the Roman emperor, i.e., of his Genius, and of *Roma,* the world state which he headed. It was not because it was a depraved and superstitious rite, like some of the barbaric worships still to be found here and there on the fringes of civilization (e.g., the Druid), surviving from remote antiquity; on the contrary, this cult was one of the most refined and ennobling that men could conceive, a beautiful, humane, patriotic and public-minded cultus devoted to the common welfare. It was a "religion of all good men," and the inference was obvious that anyone must be harboring secret designs of treason or revolution if he failed to conform and share in the simple ceremony which acknowledged the divine source of the benefits enjoyed under the *pax romana!*

The struggle between the Church and the religion of imperial Rome, including the emperor cult, was surely inevitable; and no one in the first or second century, and especially from the middle of the third to the beginning of the fourth, could have predicted the outcome. Yet the improbable really occurred, and Christianity eventually became the religion of the Roman Empire: Christ ruled and was worshiped instead of the Caesars, their state or their gods. *Pontifex maximus* ceased to be the title of the head of Rome's age-old cultus, and was taken over by the leading bishop of the Christians, the Vicar of Christ on earth, the successor of the Fisherman, the "servant of the servants of God," the Christian *servus servorum Dei.*

5. Later Stages

The chief characteristics of the old Roman religion had been its formalism, its ritualism, its archaism, and its conservatism. The early Italian, unlike the ancient Greek, appears to have been extremely unimaginative. It was essentially a political or social religion, not personal; it was in general materialistic, with an exact *quid pro quo* arrangement with the supernatural world—Roman prayers included the familiar *do ut des,* "I give so that you will give," i.e., in return. And it was nonprogressive, indeed rooted in the past and incapable of spiritual development, and made a virtue of undeviating fidelity to the customs, rites, and ideas of the ancestors of the Roman people. This was a feature diametrically opposed to what we see in some other religions, notably the Hebrew. Hence when it found itself confronted by new intellectual and political conditions, as especially in the first and second centuries, it was not able to adapt itself to the new situation, certainly not in time to be effective. Incapable of accommodation, in the end it succumbed, first to the rivalry of, and later to a forced combination with, the all-embracing Hellenistic syncretism, which took over the ancient and traditional Italian rites and beliefs, and swept them into the vast medley of gods and cults with which paganism ended. In its great days of old it had supplied and supported that Roman *gravitas* and *pietas* which were the heart and sinews of the early Roman character, with its unlimited endurance of pain and hardship, its insatiable ambition, and its zeal for conquest. But it always remained essentially a religion of public cultus and in the end it proved itself incapable of understanding what an increasing number of people in the ancient world were deeply interested in, viz., a spiritual view of life, a piety born from within and characterized by renunciation and otherworldliness.

One of the most notable features in Roman religion after the second century, and especially under Aurelian (A.D. 270–275), was the growth of solar monotheism and of the corresponding cult of *Sol Invictus*. It was really the culmination of syncretism, with its "lords many and gods many" (I Cor. 8:5), and corresponded to the development of absolutism in government, with one supreme divine ruler in heaven and one supreme human ruler upon earth. Philosophers—or teachers of philosophy—like Macrobius (*ca.* A.D. 400) elaborated the speculative implications of this idea: as the other gods are "manifestations" of the one supreme deity, so the earthly potentates derive their authority from the one head of the universal empire—and so do the potencies of nature derive their strength from the sun. Nature, society, the cosmos itself are all one unified hierarchy of power, wisdom, and authority.

To cultivated pagans like Symmachus, or the emperors Aurelian and Julian, or the philosophers Plotinus, Porphyry, and Proclus, or the religious writer Sallustius,[20] it seemed utterly

20 *Ibid.*, pp. 178–196.

impossible that the vulgar cults—and among them Christianity—could provide those safeguards for the state or those satisfactions of the desire for learning, culture, art and philosophy which were the whole world's most priceless heritage from the past. The brief reaction under Julian (A.D. 361–363), and the final struggles of defeated paganism which centered in the affair of the altar of Victory, showed unmistakably both the weakness of the pagan following and the certainty of the coming triumph of their opponents. Even Hermetism with its strong strain of morality and mysticism, and the solar theology with its basic monotheism, even Neoplatonism with all its dispassionate intellectual purity, could not avail to save the old religion with its many cults. After a thousand years of unceasing observance, they were dying. Even as early as the middle of the third century, at the very time when the furious persecution under Decius was directed against the Christians, they were already dying for lack of public support.[21] They had lost their attractiveness and their power. They no longer captivated the imaginations of men, or inspired their confidence and their faith. And they could not cope with the problems of the new and darker age which was now dawning.

FREDERICK C. GRANT

21 J. Geffcken, *Der Ausgang des Griechisch-römischen Heidentums* (1920), p. 89.

ANCIENT ROMAN RELIGION

I. THE OLD AGRICULTURAL RELIGION

The old agricultural religion of Rome, "the religion of Numa," was no doubt only one among a number of different cults belonging to the early peoples of Italy. About the others we have almost no information, but we are justified in assuming that most of them bore a more or less common character. Hence the rites of expiation of a neighboring town and people in Umbria may be studied as presumably similar to those practiced elsewhere in the Italian peninsula. Only in the south where the Greeks were dominant and in the northwest where the Etruscans lived were other rites observed. What these were, among the Etruscans, we do not know; their scanty literature perished long ago, and their funerary inscriptions, still largely indecipherable, will perhaps never tell us. The earliest Roman rites, and the religious ideas connected with them, were "primitive"—i.e., prehistoric—in origin, and were not always (some would say not often) understood by later writers. But though Livy and Ovid, Cicero and Virgil *interpret* what they report, the inscriptions are first-hand records, and such an early writer as Cato writes down frankly and briefly what he believes and does.

For the earliest period in Roman religious history see: G. Wissowa, RKR, §§ 1–6, 19–37, 61–70, and Appendix I–II, and *Gesammelte Abhandlungen* (1904); F. Altheim, *History of Roman Religion* (Engl. tr., 1938), and *Terra Mater* (RGVV, 1931); E. Aust, *Die Religion der Römer* (1899); C. Bailey, *The Religion of Ancient Rome* (1907), "Roman Religion and the Advent of Philosophy" and bibliography in CAH, Vol. VIII (1930), pp. 423–465, 773 f., *Phases in the Religion of Ancient Rome* (1932); J. B. Carter, *The Religion of Numa* (1906), *The Religious Life of Ancient Rome* (1911); L. Deubner, "Religion der Römer," in C. de la Saussaye, *Lehrbuch der Religionsgeschichte* (4th ed., 1925), II, 474 ff.; S. Eitrem, *Opferritus und Voropfer der Griechen und Römer* (1914); W. W. Fowler, "Religion and Mythology," in J. E. Sandys (ed.), *A Companion to Latin Studies* (3d ed., 1921), *Roman Essays* (1920), especially Part I (see

3

the paper on the meaning of *religio*, pp. 7–15), *Religious Experience of the Roman People* (1911), chs. 1–9, *Roman Festivals* (1899), "Roman Religion," in ERE; F. Granger, *The Worship of the Romans* (1895); A. Grenier, *Les Religions étrusque et romaine* (1948); W. R. Halliday, *History of Roman Religion* (1922); H. S. Jones, *A Companion to Roman History* (1912), ch. 4, and "The Primitive Institutions of Rome: Religious Institutions," in CAH, Vol. VII (1928), pp. 425–431; N. Lewis and M. Reinhold, RC, I, ch. 1 and §§ 46–56; André Piganiol, *Histoire de Rome* (1949), with especially full bibliographies; J. S. Reid, "Worship (Roman)," in ERE; H. J. Rose, *Ancient Roman Religion* (1948), *Primitive Culture in Italy* (1926), *The Roman Questions of Plutarch* (1924), especially the Introduction, and "Numen Inest," in *Harvard Theological Review*, XXVIII (1935), 237–257; N. Turchi, RRA, Part I, and Part II. 1; see also other relevant articles in OCD, ERE, PW, LGRM.

EXPIATION OF A TOWN IN UMBRIA

Franz Bücheler, *Umbrica* (1883), VI. A, B; VII. A. Bronze tablets from Gubbio, ancient Iguvium, in Umbria, inscribed in Umbrian dialect. Gubbio, famous for St. Francis and the wolf, is a hundred miles north of Rome. The ritual described was probably typical of early Italian religion generally, including Roman. See the article "Tabulae Iguvinae" in OCD; cf. CAH, Vol. VIII (1930), pp. 443 ff. (by Cyril Bailey); and the fine edition, with plates, text, and Latin translation and commentary by J. Devoto (1940). See also a note by G. Dumézil in *Revue de l'Histoire des Religions*, CXLVII (1955), 265 ff.; K. Latte, RR, § 1. The text also appears in *Textus Minores*, Vol. XI (1949). Finally, see G. Wissowa, "Expiation and Atonement (Roman)," in ERE.

(VI. A) This sacrifice must begin with observation of the birds, when the owl and the crow are favorable [prospering], and the woodpeckers, male and female, are on the right hand [legitimizing]. The one who goes to observe the birds must sit in a fenced enclosure and call upon the priest: "Specify, that I observe favorable owls, favorable crows, a male woodpecker on the right hand, a female woodpecker on the right hand, birds on the right, voices of birds on the right, sent by the gods." The priest shall specify accordingly: "Observe there favorable owls, favorable crows, a male woodpecker on the right hand, a female woodpecker on the right hand, birds on the right, voices of birds on the right, sent by the gods for me, for the community of Iguvium, at this particular time." While he sits in his seat—the one who goes to listen to the voices of the birds—no noise [whispering] shall be made, and no one shall come between [to obstruct his view], until he has returned— i.e., the one who went to listen to the voices of the birds. If any noise is made or any person sits between [him and the birds], it shall be invalid. . . .

(16) When the voices of the birds are heard, the one sitting in the enclosure shall announce it, calling the priest by name, "[I announce] favorable owls, favorable crows, a male woodpecker on the right hand, a female woodpecker on the right hand, birds on the right, voices of birds on the right hand for thee, for the community of Iguvium, at this particular time." For all these sacred acts, for the procession about the people, for the expiation of the city, he must carry the sacred staff. The sacrificial hearth at the Treblanian gate, which is to be laid for the expiation of the city, thou shalt so arrange that fire may be kindled from fire. So likewise at the two other gates, the Tesenacan and the Veiine.

Before the Treblanian gate, three oxen shall be sacrificed to Jupiter Grabovius. At the offering shall be said: "To thee I offer prayers, O Jupiter Grabovius, for the Fisian city, for the town of Iguvium, for the names of the city, for the names of the town; be friendly, be gracious to the Fisian city, to the town of Iguvium, to the name of the city, to the name of the town. O holy one, to thee I pray with supplications, O Jupiter Grabovius, trusting in the sacred [sacrificial?] rite, I pray to thee with supplications, O Jupiter Grabovius. O Jupiter Grabovius, to thee [I offer] these fat oxen [as an expiation] for the Fisian city, for the town of Iguvium, for the names of the city, for the names of the town.

"O Jupiter Grabovius, by the effect of this [offering] . . . if in the Fisian city a fire breaks out [as a result of lightning], if in the town of Iguvium the due rites are neglected, [look upon it] as if it had been unintentional. O Jupiter Grabovius, if in thine offering [anything] is amiss, or neglected, or omitted, or [fraudulently] held back, or at fault, or if in thine offering there be any blemish, whether seen or unseen, O Jupiter Grabovius, let it be expiated by these fat oxen for an expiation, as is right. O Jupiter Grabovius, expiate the Fisian city, the town of Iguvium. O Jupiter Grabovius, expiate the names of the Fisian city, the town of Iguvium; the full citizens, the sacred rites, slaves, cattle, the fruits of the field, expiate. Be kind, be gracious with thy favor to the Fisian city, the town of Iguvium, the name of the city, the name of the town. O Jupiter Grabovius, preserve the Fisian city, preserve the town of Iguvium. O Jupiter Grabovius, preserve the Fisian city, preserve the town of Iguvium; full citizens, sacred rites, slaves, cattle, fruits of the field, preserve. Be kind, be gracious with thy favor to the Fisian city, to the town of Iguvium, the name of the city, the name of the town. O Jupiter Grabovius, with these fat oxen as an expiation for the Fisian city, for the town of Iguvium, for the names of the city, for the names of the town, O Jupiter Grabovius, I call upon thee."

[This prayer was to be repeated two or more times, over the two other sacrificial animals.]

(56) The whole prayer shall be said silently. Then lay [the parts of the sacrifice] upon the altar and announce what has been laid on, add the measured-out round cakes of meal and the morsels of the sacrifice, and offer fruits of the field. This sacrifice is to be accompanied by wine or water.

[As the rite proceeded, an offering was presented to other gods at the other gates, where perhaps their temples were located; the ritual was only slightly altered in each case, to meet the requirements of the particular cult.]

(VI. B. 47). Thus the city is expiated. If anything interrupts the sacrifice, it is invalid, the birds must be consulted; go back to the Treblanian gate and begin again as before and offer the sacrifice there.

(48) When it is intended to expiate the people by a circumambulation it is necessary first to observe the birds. The specifying shall be the same as for the expiation of the city. So likewise shall the announcing be done. The observation of the birds shall take place within the same enclosure. When the voices of the birds have been announced, [the priest] shall take his sacred staff, gird up his mantle and throw [the end] over his right shoulder. He shall lay a fire. When it is to be borne for use at a sacrifice, then he who carries the sacred staff shall bear the sacrificial hearth, on which the fire is kindled. The same person shall carry it, afire, upon his right shoulder. With him shall go two escorts, who shall carry the staff of the crier. Then he shall specify, favorable owls for itself, the town of Iguvium. In the same way announcement shall be made at the place of observation of the birds. He must not start the procession before favorable [omens] have been announced. When the favorable omens have been announced, they shall proceed along the street of the Bird Observatory to [the place for the] sacrifice, with fat oxen. When they have got beyond Acedonia and have come to the exit, they shall make a halt at the boundary stone. The one who carries the sacred staff shall [then] pronounce the ban. Thus shall he banish: "Whoever belongs to the town of Tadina, to the tribe of Tadina, to the Tadine, Etruscan, Naharcian, or Japudian names, let him depart from this people. Whoever does not depart from this people, or if anyone remains among this people, he shall be brought forward to [the place] where justice is dealt out, and [they shall] do to him what is right." Three times shall he pronounce the ban. Then he shall go to the boundary stone with his escorts, and say "Order yourselves, arrange yourselves, Iguvians." Then, accompanied by his [two] escorts he shall make the circuit with the fat sacrifices. When they have gone all the way around, and have come back to the boundary stone, he shall pray beside the boundary stone, accompanied by his escorts: "O Cerfe Martius, Praestita Cerfia [wife?] of Cerfe Martius, Tursa Cerfia

of Cerfe Martius, the Tadine town, the Tadine tribe, the Etruscan, Naharcian, Japudian names, of the Tadine town, of the Tadine tribe, of the Etruscan, Naharcian, Japudian names the eldest, girded and ungirded, the youths bearing arms and not bearing arms, [these] shall thou terrify, frighten, destroy, scatter, deafen, smite. [The language is alliterative and magical: *nomner nerf sihitu ansihitu iovie hostatu anhostatu tursitu tremitu hondu holtu ninctu nepitu sonitu savitu preplotatu previlatu*]. O Cerfe Martius, Praestita Cerfia of Cerfe Martius, Tursa Cerfia of Cerfe Martius, be friendly, be gracious with your favor to the people of the town of Iguvium, to the town of Iguvium, its eldest, girded and ungirded, its youths bearing arms and not bearing arms, its name, the names of the town." When they have thus spoken, he who bears the sacred staff shall say, "Go, Iguvians!" When he has said this, the same persons shall make the circuit a second time. When they have returned to the boundary stone, they shall pray again in the same words. They shall say the same thing, and command them to go. Then they shall make the circuit a third time.

[Then follow directions for single sacrifices to certain deities named with the appropriate prayers. After the identical final prayer as given above after the third circuit, which was to be said three times, the following sacrificial ceremony concluded the rite:]

(VII A. 51) Then the one who carries the sacred staff and his escorts shall scare away fat young heifers. Below the grain market, anyone in the town who wishes to do so may catch them. The first three to be caught, they shall sacrifice at Acedonia to Tursa Jovia for the people of the town of Iguvia, and for the town of Iguvia. And they shall speak [pray] as before the Treblanian gate. [Then follow five brief rubrics. Note the change in spelling.]

THE CULTUS OF THE BOUNDARY STONE

Siculus Flaccus, *De Agrorum Conditionibus et Constitutionibus Limitum* . . . ed. Adrien Turnebus (1554), pp. 6 f.; ed. C. Thulin, in *Corpus Agrimensorum Romanorum*, I. 1 (1913), p. 104. Siculus Flaccus wrote early in the second century, but his material was obviously old and traditional. His style is not always grammatical.

There are some who maintain that under every boundary stone must lie a sign [*signum*]. But this is left to individual preference. For if there were strict rules or customs, then a similar sign would be found everywhere under the boundary stones. But since it is left to personal preference, under some we find nothing at all, under others ashes, charcoal, broken pieces of pottery or of glass, copper coins, lime, or plaster. But, as we have said above, the practice is voluntary. The reason why we find ashes or charcoal is a very definite one—a custom which used to be observed but which later fell into neglect, so that thereafter other signs or none at all were to be found. For when they set up the stones [*terminos*], they stood them erect on firm ground, close to the place where they had dug the hole in which they were about to place it, and they adorned it with ointment, fillets, and garlands. Above the hole in which it was to be set a sacrifice was offered; an animal was slain and set afire with torches; its blood was allowed to run down into the hole, and incense and fruit [or grain, *fruges*] were thrown into it. So also honeycombs and wine and other things, which it was customary to offer to the boundary stone, were added. When the whole sacrifice [food, *dapibus*] had been burned up, the stone was let down upon the still-warm remains [of the sacrifice] and it was settled firmly in place. Pieces of stone were laid about it and tamped down hard, to hold it secure. This sacrifice was brought by the owners of the property between which the boundary ran. When the stone marked a triple boundary, i.e., a point where three properties met, all three owners offered the sacrifice. As many owners as had a share in the boundary took part in setting the boundary stone and offered the sacrifice; thus the boundary stone proved the agreement of the owners. [Such stones were set up at every corner, and also where long stretches of boundary were otherwise unmarked.]

THE PROPHECY OF VEGOIA

F. Blume, K. Lachmann, and A. Rudorff, *Die Schriften der römischen Feldmesser* = *Gromatici Veteres* (1848–52), I, 350 f. The passage is said to be from the Etruscan ritual books, which were given to Aruns Veltymnus as the teaching of the seeress Vegoia. But the prophecy probably comes from the time of Sulla; note the clear reference to the dictator's distribution of land to his troops, which fell upon the Etrurians with special severity. Cf. Deut. 19:14, Isa. 5:8–10. See also K. Latte, RR, § 2.

When Jupiter took the land of Etruria under his protection, he specifically commanded that the commons should be surveyed and the fields marked off. Since he knew the greed of men and earthly covetousness [*vel terrenum cupidinem:* the desire to possess more land?], he willed that all should be marked with boundary stones. These were some day to be purposely disregarded by men, seized and moved away through greed, toward the end of the eighth world age. But whoever lays his hands upon them and removes them, in order to increase his property and thus decrease that of another, will for this offense be condemned by the gods. If slaves do it, they will have a change of masters, for the worse. But when it takes place with the knowledge and consent of their master, his house will soon be blotted out and his whole family come to ruin. The one who has proposed it will be visited with the severest sicknesses and wounds and lose the use of his limbs. The land itself will then cave in, in many places, amid tempest or whirlwinds. The fruit will often be damaged and knocked off by rain and hail, dried up by the heat, or destroyed by blight. Much dissension among the people. Know that all this comes to pass when such offenses are committed. Therefore, do not be deceitful nor double-tongued. Safeguard the teaching in your heart!

THE FESTIVAL OF THE TERMINALIA

Ovid, *Fasti*, II. 641–662 (Feb. 23). Ovid must be read with caution and discrimination. If so read, he yields much valuable information about ancient rites and religious customs. But his explanations of their meaning and his fanciful mythology—often his own invention —are unreliable. See text and translation by Sir James G. Frazer in LCL (1931), and also his commentary (5 vols., 1929).

When the night has ended, see that the god whose mark separates your fields is given his customary honor. O Terminus, whether thou art a stone or a post sunk in the ground, thou too hast been held divine [*numen habes*] from days of old. Thee the two owners crown, each on his side; to thee they bring the two wreaths of flowers and two cakes. An altar is built. Hither the farmer's rustic wife brings on a potsherd the fire which she has taken from her own warm hearth. The old man chops wood, and neatly piles up the sticks; the branches he tries to set firm in the solid earth. Then he feeds the kindling flames with dry bark, his boy standing by and holding the broad basket in his hands. When from the basket he has three times tossed grain into the heart of the fire, his little daughter presents the pieces of honeycomb. Others hold out vessels of wine. Some of each is cast into the flames. The festive company, all in white, look on in silence. Terminus himself [i.e., the boundary stone], at the meeting of the bounds, now is sprinkled with the blood of a lamb, and offers no complaint if a sucking pig is given him. The simple neighborhood meets and celebrates a feast, chanting thy praises, O holy Terminus. Thou dost fix the bounds of people and cities and huge kingdoms. Without thee every field would be a scene of wrangling. Thou seekest no favors; thou art corrupted by no gold. The lands entrusted to thee thou dost guard in loyalty and honor.

THE INAUGURATION OF KING NUMA

Livy, *History of Rome,* I. 18. 1–10. According to tradition, Numa was the founder of the Roman religion. His example was therefore as important as his precepts and institutions. For another example of taking auspices, see pp. 4 f. Livy's dates are 59 B.C.–A.D. 17.

In those days Numa Pompilius was widely known for his justice and his piety. He lived at Cures, a town of the Sabines [east of Rome], and he was profoundly learned—as far as was possible in that age—in all laws, divine and human. [He was not a disciple of Pythagoras, as some say—how could he have been, when Pythagoras lived almost two centuries later! Instead,] it was his natural disposition, as I believe, tempered with virtues, which qualified him, rather than training in some foreign discipline: [his was] the harsh, stern discipline of the ancient Sabines, as incorruptible a race of men as ever lived. And so it was unanimously voted to offer the kingship to Numa Pompilius.

Being called to Rome, he ordered that, just as Romulus had obeyed the augural omens when he built the city and assumed the royal power, so likewise concerning himself the gods must be consulted. Accordingly an augur (afterwards, as a mark of honor, this was made a permanent public priesthood) conducted him to the citadel and caused him to sit down on the stone, facing toward the south. The augur then seated himself at Numa's left, with his head covered and holding in his right hand the crooked knotless staff which they call the *lituus.* Then looking out over the City and the country lying beyond he prayed to the gods. First marking off the sky by a line from east to west, designating as "right" the region to the south and as "left" that to the north, and fixing in his mind some object before him and as far away as the eye could reach, he next shifted the crook to his left hand and, laying his right hand on Numa's head, he prayed as follows: "Father Jupiter, if it is right [*si est fas*] that this man Numa Pompilius, whose head I hold, should be king in Rome, declare it to us by unmistakable signs [*signa certa*] within those limits which I have marked off." He then named the auspices which he wished to be sent. When they appeared, Numa was declared to be king, and descended from the augural station [*de templo*].

THE MEANING OF "TEMPLUM"

Varro, *On the Latin Language*, VII. 8–10. Varro lived in the first century B.C., and wrote on philology, archeology, and religion. See text and translation by Roland G. Kent, in LCL (2 vols., 1938). Like Greek *temenos*, the Latin *templum* is understood as a sacred area rather than a building. This points toward the original meaning of the term. See G. Wissowa, "Divination (Roman)," in ERE.

[In the sky, which is Jove's temple, there are four quarters, East, West, South, North; but on earth] *templum* means a place set apart by the appropriate specific form of words for the purpose of augury or of taking auspices [or observations of the birds]. The language of the formula is not everywhere the same. On the Citadel it runs [in Early Latin]:

"Temples and wild lands [i.e., sacred and secular areas?] shall be mine, as far as I have declared them to be such by solemn pronouncement.

"That truth-speaking [? *olla vera*] tree, whatever its kind, which I believe myself to have named [at a distant observation], let it mark off temple and wild land on the left.

"That truth-speaking tree, whatever its kind, which I believe myself to named, let it mark off temple and wild land on the right.

"Between these two regions, [temples and wild lands be mine] for observing and for interpreting, just as I have assumed that I have spoken correctly [*rite*] about them."

In making [i.e., marking off] this temple, the trees appear to form the boundaries within which the eyes are to view, i.e., to "gaze" [*theamur*], from which come the words *temple* and *contemplation*. . . .

As to the addition of "wild lands" [*tesca*], the glossators say that this means "sacred." But they are quite mistaken: the Curia Hostilia [the ancient Senate House] is not a "temple" and is not sacred [i.e., inviolable]. The idea that a temple is a consecrated *building* results from the fact that in the city of Rome most sacred edifices *are* temples, and likewise inviolable, and that in the country certain plots of ground belonging to a god are called *tesca*.

FORMALISM IN PRESCRIBED PRAYERS

Pliny, *Natural History*, XXVIII. 3. 10 ff. Pliny's *Natural History* is a vast encyclopedia of "scientific" learning in thirty-seven volumes, from the late first century. It was still in process of revision when the author died in A.D. 79. (As admiral of the fleet stationed at Misenum, he crossed the Bay of Naples to get a closer view of the eruption of Vesuvius and to rescue, if possible, the survivors at Pompeii and Herculaneum.) See the translation by J. Bostock and H. T. Riley in BL (1856). A new translation by H. Rackham and W. H. S. Jones, with Latin text, is appearing in LCL (1938 ff.). The text of the present passage will be found in the edition by F. Franzius (1788), VIII, 115 ff. See G. Appel, *De Romanorum precationibus* (RGVV 7:2, 1909); J. B. Carter, "Prayer (Roman)" in ERE; G. Rohde, *Die Kultsatzungen der Römischen Pontifices* (RGVV 25, 1936).

With reference to remedies derived from man, there arises first of all a question, one which is of the greatest importance and is always attended with the same uncertainty, viz., whether certain words, and the chanting of songs [incantations], have any efficacy or not. For if this is the case, it will be only proper to ascribe such efficacy to man himself; . . . though I should add, that the wisest of men, taken individually, refuse to credit these opinions. And yet, in our everyday life, we show practically that we do entertain this belief, though we are not aware of it. Thus for example [it is a general belief that] without [the specified *form* of] prayer it would be useless to sacrifice a victim, or formally [*rite*] to consult the gods. Moreover, there are different forms of address to the gods, one form for entreating them, another form for averting [evil], and still another form for commendation.

We also observe that our highest magistrates use certain formulas for their prayers; that not a single word may be omitted or pronounced out of its proper place; that it is the duty of one person to precede the official in reading the formula from a written ritual, of another to listen to every word, and of a third to see that silence is not ominously broken; meanwhile a musician performs on the flute in order to prevent any other words being heard. There are, in fact, memorable instances recorded in our annals of cases where either the sacrifice has been interrupted, and thus blemished, by imprecations [or curses], or where a mistake has been made in the recitation of the formula; the result was that the lobe of the liver or the heart has disappeared in a moment, or has been doubled, while the victim was standing before the altar. There is still in existence a most remarkable bit of evidence in the formula which the Decii, father and son, pronounced on the occasions when they devoted themselves. There is also preserved the prayer uttered by the Vestal Tuccia, when, upon being accused of incest, she carried water in a sieve—an event which took place in the year of the City 609 [144 B.C.]. Our own age even has seen a man and a woman buried alive in the Ox Market, Greeks by birth, or else natives of some other country with which we were at war at the time [226 and 216 B.C.]. The prayer used upon the occasion of this rite, the one which is usually pronounced first by the Master of the College of the Quindecemviri, if read by a person, must assuredly force him to admit the potency of formulas—when it is recalled that it has been proved effectual by the experience of eight hundred and thirty years.

At the present day, too, it is a general belief that our Vestal virgins have the power, by uttering a certain prayer, to arrest the flight of runaway slaves and to rivet them to the spot, provided they have not gone beyond the precincts of the City. If then these opinions are once accepted as truth, and if it is admitted that the gods do listen to certain prayers, or are influenced by set forms of words, we are bound to conclude in the affirmative upon the whole question. Our ancestors, no doubt, always entertained such a belief, and have even assured us, a thing by far the most difficult of all, that it is possible by such means to bring down lightning from heaven, as I have already mentioned on a more appropriate occasion [Bk. II, 140 f. = ch. 54].

THE NERIO OF MARS IN ANCIENT PRAYERS

Aulus Gellius, *Attic Nights,* XIII. 23. 1–11. Aulus Gellius lived *ca.* A.D. 123–165, i.e., during that brilliant period of late classical history, the age of the Antonines. After studying at Athens, he returned to Rome and practiced law, serving as a judge in the court dealing with private cases. His *Attic Nights* is a melange of criticism and comment—legal, archeological, grammatical, literary—begun during the long winter nights of his student years at Athens. See text and translation by J. C. Rolfe, in LCL (3 vols., 1927); see also W. W. Fowler, *Roman Festivals* (1899), pp. 60–62.

The prayers [*conprecationes,* worship with all the proper ritual accompaniments] to the immortal gods which follow the Roman ritual are set forth in the books of the priests of the Roman people and also in many ancient books of prayers. In these it is written: "Lua of Saturn; Salacia of Neptune; Hora of Quirinus; the Virites of Quirinus; Maia of Vulcan; Heries of Juno; Moles of Mars; and Nerio of Mars." Of these, the one which I have put last I hear most people pronounce with a long initial syllable, just as the Greeks pronounce *Nēreids.* But those who speak correctly make the first syllable short and lengthen the third. For the nominative case of the word, as it is written in the books of ancient writers, is *Neriō,* although Marcus Varro, in one of his *Menippean Satires* entitled "The Shadow Battle," uses *Neriēnes,* in the vocative, not *Neriō,* in these verses:

Thee, Anna Peranna, Panda Cela, thee Pales,
Nerienes and Minerva, Fortune and Ceres.

From which it follows of necessity that the nominative case must be the same. But *Nerio* was declined by our forefathers like *Anio:* just as they said *Aniēnem* with the third syllable long, so also they said *Neriēnem.* Furthermore, whether it is Nerio or Nerienes, the word is Sabine and signifies valor and fortitude. Hence among the Claudii who, we believe, were originally Sabines, anyone who was of outstanding and superior courage was called *Nero.* But the Sabines appear to have taken over this word from the Greeks, who called the sinews and ligaments of the limbs *neura,* from whence we also in Latin call them *nervi.* Therefore *Nerio* designates the strength and power and in a certain way the majesty of Mars. Plautus, however, in the *Truculentus,* says that Nerio is the wife of Mars, and he places the statement in the mouth of a soldier, in the line (515):

Mars, coming home, greets his wife Nerio [*Nerienem*].

THE SONG OF THE ARVAL BROTHERS

CIL, VI. 2104; H. Dessau, ILS, 5039; W. Henzen, AFA, pp. cciv, 24–36. The tablet containing this inscription was found in 1778 under the apse of St. Peter's in Rome. It is dated A.D. 218, though the song is as old, presumably, as the sixth century B.C. It is an antique chant, *Enos Lases juvate!* and was sung in procession, to some kind of three-step tune or beat. Selections from the later *Acta* of the Brotherhood are given below in ch. 5. See articles "Fratres Arvales" and "Carmen Arvale" in OCD, J. B. Carter, "Arval Brothers" in ERE. Cf. K. Latte, *De Saltationibus Graecorum* (RGVV, 13. 3, 1913).

Then the priests, the doors being closed and their robes girded up, and taking their books, danced the solemn three-step [*tripodiaverunt*] and sang as follows:

Help us, O household gods! (repeated three times)
Let no harm or danger, O Marmar, attack our people!
  (three times)
Be thou satisfied, O fierce Mars!
Leap over the threshold!
Stand still! Beat [the ground]! (three times)

In alternate chant address all [the gods] of sowing [?] three times.

Help us, O Marmor! (*sic;* three times)
Rejoice! (five times)

After the three-step dance, at a given signal, the public slaves came in and gathered up the books.

Cf. Virgil, *Georgics,* I. 338–350, which is addressed to Ceres, not to Mars. See also E. H. Warmington, ROL, pp. 250 ff.; J. E. Sandys, *Latin Epigraphy* (2d. ed., 1927), 165 f.; E. Norden, *Aus Altrömischen Priesterbüchern* (1939), esp. pp. 111 ff.; F. Bücheler, *Carmina Latina Epigraphica,* II (1895), pp. 1 f.

THE RATIFICATION OF A TREATY

Livy, *History of Rome,* I. 24. 3–9. Livy's importance rests partly upon the lack of any better history of ancient Rome, but more upon the fact that he gives the traditional lore, as it was handed down in the famous old families whose ancestors had made that history. See text and translation by B. D. Foster in LCL (1919). The *fetials* were a sacred college whose office was to represent the state in declaring war, making peace, and setting up treaties. The *pater patratus* was the leader and spokesman of the group.

Before beginning the battle, a treaty was made between the Romans and the Albans, providing that whichever people won the contest should rule the other peacefully. Treaties differ in terms, but the same procedure is always followed. On this occasion, it is said, they did as follows—and it is the most ancient treaty of which we have any record. The *fetial* asked King Tullus, "Do you command me, O King, to make a treaty with the *pater patratus* of the Alban people?" Being so commanded by the king, he continued, "I demand of you, O King, the sacred herb." The king replied, "You must take it untainted [*pura*]." The *fetial* then brought from the citadel an untainted plant. After that he asked the king, "Do you make me, O King, with my sacred emblems [*vasa*] and my colleagues, the royal

emissary [*regium nuntium*] to speak for the Roman people of
the Quirites?" The king replied, "In so far as it may be done
without prejudice [*sine fraude*] to myself and to the Roman
people of the Quirites, I do so." The *fetial* was Marcus Valerius; he made Spurius Fusius the *pater patratus,* touching
his head and hair with the sacred twig.

The *pater patratus* is appointed to pronounce the oath, that
is, to solemnize the treaty. He does this by using many words,
set forth in a long rhythmic formula which we need not quote
[*carmen* may mean an incantation]. The terms of the treaty
having been recited, he then says: "Hear, O Jupiter; hear,
pater patratus of the Alban people; hear also, ye people of
Alba! Upon these terms, even as they have been publicly read
from beginning to end without any deceit from these tables or
wax tablets, and as they have this day been clearly understood
[i.e., by both parties], the Roman people will not be the first
to depart. But if it shall be the first to depart from them, by
general consent and with wicked guile, then on that day do
thou, O Diespiter [Jupiter], smite the Roman people even as I
shall here today smite this pig; and so much the harder smite
them as thy power and might are the greater."

When Spurius had said these words, he struck the pig with
a rock of flint. In the same way the Albans pronounced their
own formula [*carmen*] and took their own oath, by the mouth
of their own dictator and their own priests.

A DECLARATION OF WAR

Livy, *History of Rome,* I. 32. 5–14. Livy credits the foundation of
the Roman religion, and all its ancient forms, to King Numa. One
of the most ancient was the ritual followed in declaring war.

In order that, having now instituted religious rites for times
of peace, he might himself set forth the ceremonies for war;
and in order that wars might not only be waged but also declared with some kind of formal ritual, King Numa copied

from the ancient tribe of the Aequicoli the legal custom, which the *fetials* now observe, of demanding redress.

When the envoy [*legatus*] arrives at the frontiers of the people from whom the satisfaction is demanded, he covers his head with a veil—the veil is made of wool—and says: "Hear, O Jupiter; hear, ye boundaries of"—naming whatever nation it is—"hear, O right [*fas*]! I am the public herald of the Roman people; I come justly and religiously commissioned; let my words be believed." Then he recites his demands, following which he calls upon Jupiter as witness: "If I unjustly and contrary to religion demand that these men and these things be surrendered to me, then let me never again see my native land!" These words he recites when he crosses the boundary line, and again when he meets the first man, when he enters the city gates, when he reaches the market place, with only a few changes in the formula and the wording of the oath.

If those [persons] whom [or things which] he demands are not surrendered, at the end of three and thirty days—this is the sacred number of days—he declares war as follows: "Hear, O Jupiter, and thou, Janus [some mss. read Juno], Quirinus, and all ye heavenly gods, and ye gods of earth, and ye of the lower world, hearken! I call you to witness that this people"—naming whatever people it is—"is unjust, and does not make just reparation. But of these matters we will take counsel of the seniors by birth in our own country, by what means we may obtain our right." Then the messenger [*nuntius*] returns to Rome for the consultation.

At once the king would consult the Fathers, in words more or less like these: "Concerning the things, the suits at law, the causes, about which the *pater patratus* of the Roman people of the Quirites has made demands on the *pater patratus* of the Ancient Latins and upon the men of the Ancient Latins, which things they have not handed over, fulfilled, or satisfied, these being things which ought to have been delivered, fulfilled, and satisfied, speak." Addressing the man whose opinion he was accustomed to ask first, he said, "What do you think?" Then the other would reply: "I am of the opinion that those

things ought to be sought for in warfare, justly and fairly
[*puro pioque*]; so I consent and so I vote." The others were
then asked the same question, one by one, and when the majority of those present arrived at the same view, war was agreed
upon.

It was the custom for the *fetial* to carry to the borders of the
other nation a bloody spear, either iron-pointed or hardened
in the fire; there in the presence of not less than three grown
men he would say: "Whereas the people [tribes] of the Ancient
Latins and the men of the Ancient Latins have done injury
and offense to the Roman people of the Quirites; and whereas
the Roman people of the Quirites has given order that war
shall be made upon the Ancient Latins, and the Senate of the
Roman people also has agreed, consented, and voted that war
should be made upon the Ancient Latins; for this cause I therefore and the Roman people declare and make war on the
people of the Ancient Latins and on the men of the Ancient
Latins." When he had said this, he would hurl his spear into
their territory. This is the way in which, at that time, redress
was sought from the Latins and war was declared, and the custom has been retained by later generations.

EVOCATIO

Livy, *History of Rome*, V. 22. 4–7. *Evocatio* ("calling out," or
"away") was the formal invitation, addressed to the gods of a besieged city, to desert and come over to the attackers, under promise
of better treatment, ampler sacrifices and gifts, or richer temples. An
early instance is described in Livy's account of the capture of Veii
(369 B.C.). Cf. PW, VI. 1153.

When the human wealth of Veii had been carried away,
they began to plunder that of the gods and to carry away even
the gods themselves—but more like worshipers than plunderers.
Youths were chosen from the whole army, clean in body and
arrayed in white, who were assigned the duty of transporting
Juno to Rome. Reverently entering her temple, they hesitated

at first to lay their hands on her, since this statue was one which, according to Etruscan custom, only a priest belonging to a certain family was allowed to touch. Then one of them, either because he was divinely inspired or as a youthful joke, asked, "Don't you want to go to Rome, Juno?"—and the rest all cried out that she had nodded her head. A further addition to the legend affirms that she was also heard to say that she was willing. One thing is certain: she was carried from her dwelling with very little effort, as if she were accompanying them voluntarily, and so was transported easily and without damage to the Aventine, her permanent dwelling place, to which the prayers of the Roman dictator had invited her. There Camillus later dedicated to her the temple he had vowed.

THE FORMULA OF EVOCATION

Macrobius, *Saturnalia*, III. 9. 7 f. Macrobius was a teacher of philosophy in North Africa at the end of the fourth century. His *Saturnalia* was a potpourri of literary criticism (chiefly of Virgil), archeology, and legend. The whole chapter (9) deals with the subject. We give only the formula which Macrobius quotes. See T. R. Glover, *Life and Letters in the Fourth Century* (1901; repr. 1924); T. Whittaker, *Macrobius* (1923); text and French translation by Henri Bornecque (1937). K. Latte, RR, § 8.

This is the formula [*carmen*] by which the gods of a besieged city are called out:

"If it is a god or if it is a goddess who has taken under his or her protection the people and state of Carthage, and thou above all who hast taken this city and this people into thy keeping: I pray, I implore, I plead with thee to grant me this favor—abandon the people and the state of Carthage, their lands, their temples, their sanctuaries, and their city; depart, and leave them. Inspire this people and city with fear, terror, forgetfulness [of religious duties? or loss of all memory of the past?]. Leave them and come to Rome, to me and my people.

Our land, our temples, sanctuaries, and city will be more pleasant to thee and dearer. To me, to the Roman people, and to my soldiers be graciously disposed, and let us know [this] and be aware of it. If thou wilt do this, I vow to thee a temple and games!"

[Macrobius adds that the prayer should be accompanied by a sacrifice and the *exta* examined to see whether or not the god will respond.]

DEVOTIO: THE SACRIFICIAL DEATH OF DECIUS

Livy, *History of Rome,* VIII. 9. 1–11. 1. This legendary incident took place, presumably, during the Samnite wars, *ca.* 340 B.C.

The Roman consuls, before they led their troops into the battle, offered sacrifice. It is said that the soothsayer [*haruspex*] pointed out to Decius that the head of the liver was on the friendly [right] side, that the victim was in other respects acceptable to the gods, and that the sacrifice of Manlius had been most favorable. "It will do," said Decius, "if my colleague has received favorable omens." In the formation above described they advanced into the field. Manlius commanded the right wing, Decius the left. At first the battle was fought with equal strength and ardor on both sides; but after a time the Roman *hastati* [spearmen] on the left, unable to resist the pressure of the Latins, fell back upon the *principes* [i.e., the heavy armed troops]. In this instant of alarm Decius the consul shouted with a loud voice to Marcus Valerius: "We need help from the gods, Marcus Valerius! Come, state [or public] pontiff of the Roman people, dictate the words, so that I can devote myself for [i.e., to save] the legions." The pontiff bade him put on the purple-bordered toga and veil his head, with one hand thrust out from beneath the toga and touching his chin, and standing upon a spear that was laid beneath his feet to say as follows: "Janus, Jupiter, Father Mars, Quirinus, Bellona, Lares, Divi Novensiles, Di Indigites, gods in whose

power are both we and our enemies, and you also, Di Manes—
I invoke and implore you, your favor I beg and beseech, that
you may prosper the power and the victory of the Roman
people of the Quirites, and visit upon the foes of the Roman
people of the Quirites terror, fear, and death. As I have pronounced the words, even so on behalf of [or, in lieu of, *pro*]
the republic of the Roman people of the Quirites, the army,
the legions, and the auxiliaries of the Roman people of the
Quirites, I hereby devote the legions and auxiliaries of the
enemy, together with myself, to the Di Manes and to Earth
[*Tellus*]."

Having uttered this prayer, he ordered the lictors to go to
Titus Manlius at once and announce to his colleague that he
had devoted himself for the good of the army. Then, girding
himself with the Gabinian cincture and leaping, armed, upon
his horse, he plunged into the thick of the enemy, a conspicuous sight to both armies and with something about him more
august than human, as though he had been sent from heaven
to expiate all the anger of the gods, and to avert destruction
from his people and turn it upon their enemies. Thus the
greatest terror and dread accompanied him, and, throwing the
Latin front into disorder, it at once spread deeply into their
whole army. This was most clearly evident from the fact that,
wherever he rode, men trembled as if struck by some baleful
star; and when he fell beneath a hail of missiles, in that instant there could be no doubt of the consternation of the
Latin cohorts, which everywhere deserted the field and took to
flight. At the same time the Romans—their spirits now set free
from religious fears—pressed on as if only then the signal had
been given for the first time, and delivered a united blow. The
light-armed men were running out between the first two ranks
of foot soldiers and were adding their strength to that of the
spearmen and the heavy-armed troops, while the troops in the
third rank, kneeling on their right knees, were waiting for the
consul to signal them to rise [and advance] . . . .

(10. 3) For the rest, among all the citizens and allies the
chief praise in that war belongs to the consuls, of whom one

[Decius] had drawn upon himself above all the threats and dangers belonging to the gods above and the gods below, while the other had shown such courage and skill in battle that of those Romans and Latins who have handed down a report of the conflict all agree that whichever side was led by Titus Manlius would surely have won. The Latins fled to Minturnae. After the battle their camp was captured and many men—mostly Campanians—were seized and put to death there. The body of Decius could not be found that day, and night fell while the search continued. On the following day it was discovered in a great heap of enemy dead, covered with missiles, and was given burial by his colleague in a manner befitting his death.

It seems appropriate at this point to add that the consul, dictator, or praetor who devotes the legions of the enemy need not also devote himself, but may instead devote any citizen he chooses from an enlisted Roman legion. If this man is killed, it is proof that all is well. If he does not die, then an image [*signum*] of him is buried seven feet or more beneath the ground and a sacrifice [*piaculum,* sin offering] is slain; and where the image has been buried no Roman magistrate may lawfully ascend [i.e., upon the tumulus].

But if he chooses to devote himself, as Decius did, but does not die, he cannot rightly offer sacrifice either for himself or for the people, whether it is with a sacrificial victim or something else that he wishes to offer. The one who devotes himself may dedicate his arms to Vulcan or to any other god he chooses [as a rule, the enemies' weapons were dedicated to Vulcan]. The spear on which the consul had stood and prayed must not be allowed to fall into enemy hands. If this happens, expiation must be made to Mars, with swine, sheep, and bull [*Marti suovetaurilibus piaculum fieri*]. These details, though the memory of both divine and human customs has now been wiped out by the preference shown to new and foreign ways rather than to the ancient and ancestral, I have thought it worth while to relate in the very words which were fashioned and handed down [from the days of old].

THE VER SACRUM

Livy, *History of Rome*, XXII. 9. 7–10. 10. In 217 B.C. Hannibal was moving down the Italian peninsula from the north, crushing all opposition and ravaging the whole country. Checked momentarily at Spoletium, sixty miles from Rome, he rested his troops for a time and then resumed the invasion. Gnaeus Servilius, one of the consuls, had won a skirmish with the Gauls only to learn of the total destruction of his colleague's army. In this crisis, Fabius was again made dictator. See text and English translation of the whole passage by B. O. Foster in LCL (1929).

Quintus Fabius Maximus, now dictator once more, convened the Senate on the day he took office. Beginning with matters of religion, he convinced the Fathers that the consul Gaius Flaminius had erred more through his neglect of the ceremonies and the auspices than through recklessness and ignorance, and that they ought to consult the gods themselves as to what way [*quaeque piacula*] their anger might be appeased. He prevailed upon them to do what is not usually done except when terrible prodigies have been reported—they ordered the decemvirs to consult the Sibylline books. When the decemvirs had inspected the books of fate they reported to the Fathers that the vow made to Mars on account of this war had not been properly [*rite*] performed, and must be performed again from the beginning and on an ampler scale; that Great Games must be vowed to Jupiter, and sanctuaries [*aedes*] to Venus Erycina and to Mens; and that a supplication and a *lectisternium* must be held, and a Sacred Spring [*ver sacrum*] must be vowed, if they should have been victorious [by then] and the state remained as it had been before the war began. The Senate, seeing that Fabius would be busy with the conduct of the war, directed the praetor Marcus Aemilius, as the pontifical college had recommended, to see that all these directives were promptly carried out.

(10) When the Senate had adopted these resolutions, the praetor consulted the college and Lucius Cornelius Lentulus,

the Pontifex Maximus, urged that, first of all, the people must
be consulted about the Sacred Spring; for without the consent
of the people it was impossible to vow it. The question was
put to them in these words: "Do you will and order that these
things be done as follows? If the republic of the Roman people,
the Quirites, is preserved during the next five years—as I would
wish it to be preserved—in these wars, viz., the war of the
Roman people with the Carthaginians and the wars with the
Gauls on this side of the Alps, then let the Roman people, the
Quirites, offer up as a fixed [ratum] sacrifice to Jupiter what
the spring shall have produced in swine, sheep, goats, and
cattle—i.e., those which shall not have been consecrated to
some other deity [quaeque profana erunt]—beginning with the
day which the Senate and the people shall have designated
[i.e., the period from March 1 to April 30]. Whoever offers a
sacrifice, let him do so at whatever time and by whatever rite
[lege] he chooses; whatever the rite, let it be accounted as correctly done. If the animal which he ought to sacrifice dies, let
it be deemed unconsecrate [profanum] and let no guilt [scelus]
attach to him; if anyone injures it or kills it unawares, let it
not be a sin; if anyone steals it, let no guilt attach to the
people nor to the one from whom it shall have been stolen; if
he sacrifices unwittingly on a black day [atro die], let the sacrifice be deemed to have been correctly done; whether by night
or by day, whether a slave or a freeman offer the sacrifice, let
it be deemed to have been correctly done; if a sacrifice is
offered before the day set by the Senate and the people, let the
people be absolved therefrom and free from obligation."

For the same cause Great Games were vowed, to cost
333,333 1/3 bronze asses [it is not certain whether the as was
in 217 B.C. the equivalent of one, four, or sixteen ounces of
copper], in addition to a sacrifice to Jupiter of three hundred
oxen and of white oxen and other customary victims to many
other gods. When the vows had been duly [rite] pronounced,
a supplication was ordered; it was performed not only by the
urban population, with their wives and children, but also by
such country people as, having something of their own at

stake, were beginning to feel concern for the public welfare. Next a *lectisternium* was celebrated during three days under the supervision of the decemvirs who had charge of sacrifices. Six couches were laid out in the open: one for Jupiter and Juno, another for Neptune and Minerva, a third for Mars and Venus, and a fourth for Apollo and Diana, a fifth for Vulcan and Vesta, a sixth for Mercury and Ceres. Then the sanctuaries were vowed—the one to Venus Erycina by Quintus Fabius Maximus the dictator, because the books of fate had ordered that he who held the greatest authority in the city should make the vow; the temple of Mens was vowed by the praetor Titus Otacilius.

[The vow described above was not fulfilled until twenty-two years later (195 B.C.; Livy, XXXIII. 44. 1–3), and on account of a flaw had to be repeated the following year.]

A *ver sacrum* had been observed the preceding year, Marcus Porcius and Lucius Valerius being consuls. But since the pontifex Publius Licinius informed first the pontifical college and then, at the bidding of the college, the Senate, that it had not been properly performed, the Senate decided, upon the advice of the pontifices, that it should be repeated, and that the Great Games, which had likewise been vowed, should be held with the usual expenditure [for entertainment]; the *ver sacrum* should include the cattle born between the 1st of March and the 30th of April in the year of the consuls Publius Cornelius and Tiberius Sempronius.

THE LUPERCALIA

Dionysius of Halicarnassus, *Roman Antiquities,* I. 80. 1. This ancient festival, celebrated on February 15, began with the sacrifice of a goat and a dog at the Lupercal, a cave below the western corner of the Palatine Mount; then youths clad only in girdles made from the skins of the sacrificed animals ran about the borders of the Palatine striking all whom they met with strips of the goat skin. Women so struck were thought to be rendered fertile. The whole rite resembled the "beating of the bounds" for purposes of purification, a feature which Ovid stressed in his interpretation. See J. G. Frazer, Commentary on Ovid, *Fasti*, II. 19–36, 267–452; W. W. Fowler, *Roman Festivals* (1899) 310–321; G. Wissowa, RKR, 209 f.; A. K. Michels, "The Topography and Interpretation of the Lupercalia," in *Transactions of the American Philological Association*, LXXXIV (1953), 35–59, with bibliography.

As Aelius Tubero, who was a great man and very careful in gathering historical information, says, the people of Numitor [the grandfather of Romulus and Remus] knew in advance that the youths were to celebrate the Lupercalia in honor of Pan, i.e., the Arcadian sacrifice instituted by Evander, and so they set an ambush for that moment in the sacred festival [*hierourgia*] when, following the sacrifice, some of the youths living round about the Palatine must circle it on the run, starting from the [cave] of "Lycaeus" [Lupercus], naked except for their loins being girt with the skins of the animals just sacrificed. This was a traditional kind of cleansing [*katharmon*] of the villagers, and is still performed at the present day [i.e., late first century B.C.].

Ovid, *Fasti*, II. 19–37.

[February is the month for purification.] The Roman fathers called the means of purification [*piamina*] by the name of *februa* [expiatory rites]; even now there are plenty of proofs that this was the meaning of the word. The pontifices asked the king [the *rex sacrorum*] and the flamen [the *flamen dialis*] for wool, which of old was called *februa*. When houses are swept clean, the toasted spelt and salt which the lictor takes as the means of cleansing are also called *februa*. The same word is used for the branch, cut from a pure tree, which wreathes the sacred brows of the priests. I myself have seen the flaminica [the flamen's wife] begging for *februa*: she was given a sprig of pine. In brief, anything by which our bodies are cleansed [*piantur*] went by this name among our unshorn ancestors. So the month gets its name from this word, because the Luperci purify [*lustrant*] the whole ground with strips of skin, which are the instruments of cleansing; or else (perhaps) it is because the season is a holy one after the peace offerings have been made at the graves [*placatis . . . sepulcris*] and the days devoted to the dead are over. For our ancestors believed that every sin and every source of evil could be removed by rites of cleansing [*Omne nefas omnemque mali purgamina causam / Credebant nostri tollere posse senes:* this statement is one of the keys to the understanding of ancient religion]. Greece set us an example . . . . [In lines 267–452 Ovid gives a series of poetic, legendary, or wholly fanciful explanations of the details of the rite.]

THE FLAMEN DIALIS AND HIS WIFE

Aulus Gellius, *Attic Nights,* X. 15. See also W. W. Fowler, *Religious Experience of the Roman People* (1911), ch. 2; H. J. Rose, *The Roman Questions of Plutarch* (1924), pp. 109–112; G. Wissowa, RKR, 506 ff.

A great many ceremonies are imposed upon the Flamen Dialis [the priest of Jupiter], and also many restraints [*castus multiplices,* taboos], about which we read in the books *On the Public Priesthoods* and also in Book I of Fabius Pictor's work. Among them I recall the following: it is forbidden [*religio est*] the Flamen Dialis to ride a horse; it is likewise forbidden him to view the "classes arrayed" outside the pomerium [the sacred boundary of Rome], i.e., armed and in battle order; hence only rarely is the Flamen Dialis made a consul, since [the conduct of] wars is entrusted to the consuls; it is likewise unlawful [*fas numquam est*] for him ever to take an oath by Jupiter [*jurare dialem*]; it is likewise unlawful for him to wear a ring, unless it is cut through and empty [i.e., without a jewel?]. It is also unlawful to carry out fire from the *flaminia,* i.e., the Flamen Dialis' dwelling, except for a sacral purpose; if a prisoner in chains enters the house he must be released and the chains must be carried up through the *impluvium* [the opening in the roof above the *atrium* or living room] onto the roof tiles and dropped down from there into the street. He must have no knot in his head gear or in his girdle or in any other part of his attire. If anyone is being led away to be flogged and falls at his feet as a suppliant, it is unlawful [*piaculum est*] to flog him that day. The hair of the [Flamen] Dialis is not to be cut, except by a free man. It is customary [*mos est*] for the Flamen neither to touch nor even to name a female goat, or raw [?] meat, ivy, or beans.

He must not walk under a trellis for vines. The feet of the bed on which he lies must have a thin coating of clay, and he must not be away from this bed for three successive nights, nor is it lawful for anyone else to sleep in this bed. At the foot of his bed there must be a box containing a little pile of sacrificial cakes. The nail trimmings and hair of the Dialis must be buried in the ground beneath a healthy tree. Every day is a holy day [*feriatus est*] for the Dialis. He must not go outdoors [*sub divo*] without a head-covering—this is now allowed indoors, but only recently by decree of the pontiffs, as Masurius Sabinus has stated; it is also said that some of the other ceremonies have been remitted and canceled.

It is not lawful for him to touch bread made of fermented meal [i.e., with yeast]. His underwear ["inner tunic"] he does not take off except in covered places, lest he appear nude under the open sky, which is the same as under the eye of Jove. No one else outranks him in the seating at a banquet except the *Rex sacrificulus*. If he loses his wife, he must resign his office. His marriage cannot be dissolved [*dirimi ius non est*] except by death. He never enters a burying ground, he never touches a corpse. He is, however, permitted [*non est religio*] to attend a funeral.

Almost the same ceremonial rules belong to the Flaminica Dialis [i.e., his wife]. They say that she observes certain other and different ones, for example that she wears a dyed gown, and that she has a twig from a fruitful tree tucked in her veil [which was worn over her head at a sacrifice], and that it is forbidden [*religiosum est*] for her to ascend more than three rungs of a ladder (except what the Greeks call "ladders" [steps?]), and even that when she goes to the Argei [when twenty-four puppets were thrown into the Tiber] she must neither comb her head nor arrange her hair.

I have added here the words of the praetor from the perpetual edict concerning the Flamen Dialis and the Priestess of Vesta: "Throughout my whole jurisdiction I will not compel the Priestess of Vesta or the Flamen Dialis to take an oath." And the words of Marcus Varro in Book II of his *Antiquities of Divine Things* are these: "He alone wears a white cap [or mitre, *galerum*], either because he is the greatest [of the priests] or because the victims offered to Jupiter must be white."

PRODIGIES AND THEIR EXPIATION

Livy, *History of Rome*, XXII. 1. 8–20. 217 B.C.—the terrible year of Hannibal's invasion. See also the account of portents, rites, and dances on a much earlier occasion in Dionysius of Halicarnassus, *Roman Antiquities*, VII. 67–73.

Men's fears were increased by the prodigies reported simultaneously from many places. In Sicily the javelins of several soldiers had taken fire; in Sardinia, as a horseman was making the rounds of the night watch, the same thing had happened to the staff which he held in his hand; many fires had blazed up on the shore; two shields had sweated blood; some soldiers had been struck by lightning; the sun's orb had been seen to grow smaller; at Praeneste flaming stones had fallen from the sky; at Arpi light shields had appeared in the sky and the sun [had seemed to be] fighting with the moon; at Capena two moons had risen in the daytime; the waters of Caere had flowed mixed with blood, and bloodstains had appeared even in the water that trickled from the spring of Hercules; at Antium, where some men were reaping, bloody heads of grain had fallen into their basket; at Falerii the sky had seemed to be cleft asunder as with a great crack, through which a bright light had shone; the [divining] lots had shrunk and one had fallen out of its own accord, on which was written, "Mavors [Mars] brandishes his spear"; in Rome, at about the same time, the statue of Mars on the Appian Way and the images of the wolves had sweated; at Capua there had been the spectacle of the sky on fire and the moon falling down during a shower of rain. Later on less important prodigies were also given credence, as that some people's goats had grown wool and that a hen had turned into a cock and a cock into a hen.

When the consul had laid these reports before the Senate, just as they had come to him, and had introduced in the Curia the men who had reported them, he consulted the Fathers regarding proper religious procedure [de religione]. It was voted that these prodigies should be expiated [prodigia . . . procurarentur], in part with larger victims, in part with sucklings, and that a supplication should be held for three days at all the couches of the gods; as for the rest, when the decemvirs should have examined the [Sibylline] books, those rites were to be observed which should be set forth from the sacred verses as most pleasing to the gods. Being thus directed by the decemvirs, they decreed that the first gift should be made to Jupiter, a golden thunderbolt weighing fifty pounds; that Juno and Minerva should be given gifts of silver; that Juno Regina on the Aventine and Juno Sospita at Lanuvium should receive a sacrifice of larger victims; that the matrons, each contributing as much as she could afford, should collect a sum of money and carry it as a gift to Juno Regina on the Aventine and [there] celebrate a lectisternium; and that even the freedwomen also should contribute money, in proportion to their abilities, for an offering to Feronia.

All this having been done, the decemvirs sacrified the greater victims in the market place at Ardea. Finally (it was now December) victims were offered at the temple of Saturn in Rome, and a lectisternium was ordered—this time senators strewed the couches—and a public feast, and throughout the City, for a day and night, "Saturnalia" was shouted, and the people were ordered to keep that day as a festival and to observe it ever thereafter.

A MEAL FOR JUPITER BEFORE THE SOWING

Cato, *On Agriculture*, 132. Marcus Porcius Cato, the "Censor," was a soldier and farmer of the old Italian type, very conservative and opposed to Greek ideas and "modern" luxury. His work on agriculture, written about 160 B.C., was intended to be a practical handbook, especially for farmers in central Italy, and is full of archaic and traditional rites, customs, and religious views. See text and translation by W. D. Hooper and H. B. Ash in LCL (1934).

The offering is to be made in this way: Offer to Jupiter Dapalis a cup of wine of whatever size you wish. Observe the day as a holiday [*feria*] for the oxen, their drivers, and those who make the offering. When you make the offering, say as follows: "Jupiter Dapalis, since it is due and proper [*oportet*] that a cup of wine be offered thee, in my house, among my family, for thy sacred feast; for that reason, be thou honored by this feast that is offered thee." Wash your hands, and then take the wine and say: "Jupiter Dapalis, be thou honored by this feast that is offered thee, and be thou honored by the wine that is placed before thee." If you wish, make an offering to Vesta. The feast of Jupiter consists of roasted meat and an urn of wine. Present it to Jupiter religiously, in the proper form [*Jovi caste profanato sua contagione*]. After the offering is made, plant millet, panic grass, garlic, and lentils.

THE HARVEST SACRIFICE

Cato, *On Agriculture*, 134. The offering of a pig as a "preliminary" was perhaps originally intended to placate the *Di Manes*, offended by the disturbance of the soil or by some accidental or unintentional wrong committed during the sowing, growth, or maturing of the grain. Eventually it was understood to refer solely to the harvest. See G. Wissowa, RKR, pp. 193 f., and quotations (under *praecidaneus*) in Lewis and Short, *Latin Dictionary*.

Before the harvest the sacrifice of the *porca praecidanea* must be offered in this manner: Offer a sow as *porca praecidanea* to Ceres before you harvest spelt, wheat, barley, beans, and rape seed. Offer a prayer, with incense and wine, to Janus, Jupiter, and Juno, before offering the sow. Offer a pile of cakes [*strues*] to Janus, saying, "Father Janus, in offering these cakes to thee, I humbly pray that thou wilt be propitious and merciful to me and my children, my house and my household." Then make an offering of cake [*fertum*] to Jupiter with these words: "In offering thee this cake, O Jupiter, I humbly pray that thou, pleased with this offering, wilt be propitious and merciful to me and my children, my house and my household." Then present the wine to Janus, saying: "Father Janus, as I have prayed humbly in offering thee the cakes, so mayest thou in the same way be honored by this wine now placed before thee." Then pray to Jupiter thus: "Jupiter, mayest thou be honored in accepting this cake; mayest thou be honored in accepting the wine placed before thee." Then sacrifice the *porca praecidanea*. When the entrails have been removed, make an offering of cakes to Janus, and pray in the same way as you have prayed before. Offer a cake to Jupiter, praying just as before. In the same way offer wine to Janus and offer wine to Jupiter, in the same way as before in offering the pile of cakes, and in the consecration of the cake [*fertum*]. Afterward offer the entrails and wine to Ceres.

EXPIATION ON CLEARING A GROVE

Cato, *On Agriculture*, 139 f. As in ancient Greek religion, the cutting of trees in a grove, usually sacred to a god or *numen*, was accompanied by an expiatory rite.

The thinning of a grove [*lucum conlucare*] in Roman fashion must be done as follows: A pig is to be sacrificed [i.e., as a piaculum] with the following prayer: "Whether thou art a god or a goddess to whom this grove is sacred, as it is thy right to receive a pig as a sacrifice for the thinning of this sacred grove, therefore and for this reason, whether I or someone at my command offer it, let it be rightly [recte] done. To this end, therefore, in offering this pig to thee I humbly pray that thou wilt be propitious and merciful to me, to my house and household, and to my children. Mayest thou be honored in accepting this pig which I offer thee for this purpose."

If you wish to till the ground, offer another sacrifice in the same way, saying in addition, "for the sake of doing this work." As long as the work continues, this ritual must be performed somewhere on the land every day. If you skip a day, or if either public or household feast days intervene, this second offering must [still] be made.

EXPIATION FOR THE FIELD BORDERS

Cato, *An Agriculture*, 141. Compare the ritual of the Ambarvalia. Cf. G. Wissowa, RKR, p. 143.

The lustration of the fields must be done as follows: Order the *suovetaurilia* [the sacrificial pig, lamb, and calf] to be led around, and say, "That with help of the gods success may crown our labors, I bid you, Manius [i.e., whoever has charge of the ritual], to take care to purify my farm, my fields, my land, with this *suovetaurilia*, in whatever part you think best for them to be either led or carried around." First offer a prayer, with wine, to Janus and Jupiter, and then say: "Father Mars, I pray and beseech thee that thou wilt be propitious and merciful to me, my house, and our household; for this reason I have ordered a *suovetaurilia* to be led around my fields, my land, my farm; that thou mayest keep away, ward off, and remove sickness, both seen and unseen, barrenness and destruction, ruin [of crops] and intemperate weather; and that thou mayest permit my harvests, my grain, my vineyards, and my bushes to flourish and to bring forth abundantly; protect my shepherds and my flocks, and grant good health and strength to me, my house, and my household. For this purpose, and in order to purify my farm, my land, my fields, and for purifying and making expiation, as I have said, be honored to accept the offering of these suckling victims. Father Mars, for this same reason be pleased to accept the offering of these sucklings." Also make a heap [*struem*] of the cakes with a knife and place the oblation cake [*fertum*] beside it, and then offer [them]. When you sacrifice the pig, the lamb, and the calf, you must say: "For this purpose be honored to accept the offering of these victims" [*suovetaurilibus;* the next six words do not make sense in this context: "it is forbidden to name Mars, or the lamb or the calf"] . . . If favorable omens are not obtained in response to all this, say as follows: "Father Mars, if nothing is pleasing to thee in this offering of sucklings, let these victims make atonement." If there is doubt about one or two, use these words: "Father Mars, since thou art not pleased by the offering of this pig, I make atonement with this pig" [i.e., let the sacrifice be a *piaculum,* since it has not been accepted as a gift-offering].

ANCIENT ROMAN MAGICAL FORMULAS

Cato, *On Agriculture,* 160. At the end of his book Cato gives a number of home remedies. He was a great believer in the efficacy of cabbage. But dislocations and fractures required more powerful treatment; hence the resort to magic. Compare the Greek formulas given in F. C. Grant, HR, pp. 45–48.

Every kind of dislocation can be cured by the following charm: Take a green stick four or five feet long and split it down the middle, and let two men hold it to the hips. Begin to chant: *"Motas uaeta daries dardares astataries dissunapiter,"* and continue until they meet. Brandish a knife over them. When the ends meet so that one touches the other, take hold of them with your hand and cut to right and left. If the pieces are bound to the dislocation or the fracture, it will be healed. Nevertheless say the chant every day over the dislocation, or else the following: *"Huat haut haut istasis tarsis ardannabou dannaustra."*

Varro, *On Agriculture,* I. 2. 27. The quotation is from an agricultural treatise of the time of Sulla. Cf. R. Heim, *Incantamenta magica graeca latina (Jahrbücher für classische Philologie,* Suppl., 1893, No. 55).

I have heard Tarquenna say that when a man's feet begin hurting he can cure them by thinking of you [or, that Tarquenna—perhaps a mythical hero—said . . . thinking of me]. [Therefore say:]
"I remember you; heal my feet. Let the earth take hold of my illness; let soundness remain in my feet." One should recite this three times nine times [= 27], touching the earth, and spitting on it. Do it fasting.

Marcus (or Marcellus?) Medicus, XV. 11 (Nedermann, p. 113, 25; K. Latte, RR, p. 19). Marcus was a Christian, of unknown date; see M. Schanz, *Geschichte der Römischen Literatur,* IV. 2, 1126.

Be fasting when you recite [the following]. Touch the affected part of the body with three fingers, the thumb, the middle, and the ring finger, with the other two extended outwards. Then say: "Go away, whether begun today or begun earlier, whether created today or created earlier. This sickness, this disease, this pain, this swelling, this redness, this goiter, this tonsil [growth?], this abscess, this inflammation [swelling], this [infected] gland, and these little [infected] glands I call out, I take out, I declare out [and gone] by this magic, from these limbs and bones."

SUPERNATURAL VOICES

Cicero, *On Divination*, I. 101. Cicero's arguments *for* divination, in Bk. I, are chiefly from Greek sources, e.g., Posidonius. Those *against*, in Bk. II, are from Carneades. The following passage is Cicero's own, from the legends and histories of Rome. See text and translation by W. A. Falconer in LCL (1922). See also Edwyn Bevan, *Sibyls and Seers* (1929), p. 101.

Fauns have often been heard speaking in battles, and in times of disturbance voices speaking the truth are said to have come forth from the unseen [*ex occulto*]. Of many examples of this I will cite only two, but these most important ones. A little before the City was captured [by the Gauls], a voice was heard coming from the grove of Vesta, which slopes down from the Palatine hill and the New Road, ordering that the walls and gates be repaired; unless this was done in time, Rome would be taken. The warning having been disregarded at the time, while it was still possible to heed it, atonement was made [*expiatum est*] after the great catastrophe had occurred; an altar to Aius Loquens ["the speaker"], which we have seen enclosed by a hedge, was dedicated across from the spot. Again, many writers have reported that when the earthquake happened, a voice came out of the temple of Juno on the Citadel, ordering the sacrifice of a pregnant sow as a means of averting it [*procuratio fieret*]. For this reason Juno was called "Moneta" ["the Juno of Warning"]. Are we to spurn, then, the warnings sent by the gods, which our ancestors so highly regarded?

THE NUMINOSITY OF THE PALATINE

Virgil, *Aeneid*, VIII. 280–369. See W. W. Fowler, *Aeneas at the Site of Rome* (1918). In Bk. VIII of the Aeneid, Virgil describes the Trojans' arrival at the Tiber, where in a dream Aeneas is welcomed by the river god (lines 26–65), arises and offers a prayer to the god and the Laurentine Nymphs who preside over rivers (66–80). He is confronted with a portent, a gleaming white sow with her milk-white brood, and sacrifices them to Juno. As a result the Tiber is calm all night long and their two chosen vessels slip swiftly and silently up the stream. The next day at noon they espy, in the distance, the walls and citadel and the rooftops of Arcadian Evander's humble city—destined in future ages to become mighty Rome (81–101). The Arcadian king is that very day offering sacrifice to Hercules and the other gods in a grove before the city; he welcomes the Trojans and invites them to share in the sacrifice (102–174). During the feast that follows, Evander tells Aeneas the story of Hercules' visit and his slaughter of the fire-breathing monster Cacus in the cave on the Aventine, the mighty deed which the annual sacrifice now commemorates —and still continued to commemorate, in Virgil's own day, under the supervision of two families, the Potitii and the Pinarii (175–279). Virgil's reconstruction of the primitive worship follows in lines 280–305.

Meanwhile the evening star draws nearer, down the slope of heaven, and now the priests go forth in procession, Potitius at their head, girt with skins after their fashion, and bearing flaming torches. They renew the banquet, and bring the welcome gift of a second repast, and heap the altars with loaded platters. Then the Salii come and sing around the lighted altar fires, their brows bound with poplar twigs, the one a chorus of young men, the other of old, and extol in song the praises of Hercules and his great deeds: how first he strangled in his grip the twin serpents, the monsters sent by his stepmother [Juno]; how he likewise shattered in war the two famous cities, Troy and Oechalia; how under King Eurystheus [of Mycenae] he bore a thousand hard toils by decree of cruel Juno. "Thy hand, Unconquered One, slays the cloud-born creatures with double shape [centaurs], Hylaeus and Pholus, and the monster of Crete, and the huge lion beneath the Nemean Rock. Before thee the Stygian pools tremble; before thee trembles the door-keeper of Hades, lying on half-gnawed bones in his bloody cave; to thee no shape is terrible, not even Typhoeus himself, uprearing his lofty arms; nor wast thou bereft of thy senses when the snake of Lerna [the hydra] enfolded thee with its thronging heads. Hail, thou offspring of Jove, added glory to the gods! Graciously visit us, and these thy rites, with favoring foot." Such are their hymns of praise;

and they crown them all with the tale of the cavern of Cacus, and of the fire-breathing monster himself. All the woodland rings with the sound, and from the hills it re-echoes.

[All this is by way of introduction to the description of the Palatine Mount in primitive times—the hill which was in the time of Virgil, and for many centuries before and after, the very heart of Rome, the sacred citadel of gods and kings, and was now, once more, under Augustus, the center of Roman religion.]

Thence, as soon as the sacred rites were completed, they all return to the city. The aged king walked with Aeneas and his son at his side for companions on his way, and lightened the journey with varied talk. Aeneas marvels as he turns his eyes lightly here and there, charmed with the scene, and gladly inquires and learns at one spot after another the memorials of the men of old. Then King Evander, founder of the Roman citadel, replies:

"In these woodlands once dwelt the Fauns and Nymphs sprung from the soil, and a race of men born from tree trunks and solid oak; who had neither law nor worship [neque mos neque cultus], nor did they know how to yoke oxen or lay up stores [of food] or preserve their gains, but were nourished by the forest boughs and the savage fare of the hunter. First from ethereal Olympus came Saturn, fleeing the weapons of Jove, an exile from his lost realm. He gathered together the unruly race scattered on the mountain heights, and gave them laws; and he chose Latium for the name of their country, since within these borders he had found a safe hiding place. Under his reign were the so-called golden ages, since he ruled the nations in perfect peace and quiet; but gradually there crept in a worse and darker time, with the madness of war and the lust of gain. Then came the Ausonian hosts and the peoples of Sicania, and many a time the land of Saturn laid aside her name. Then kings arose, and fierce Thybris with his giant bulk, from whose name we of Italy have now called our river the Tiber; the true ancient name, Albula, has disappeared.

Myself, an outcast from my fatherland, and following on to the utmost limits of the sea—omnipotent Fortune and inevitable Fate have settled me in this place. It was my mother, the nymph Carmentis, whose warnings and the god Apollo whose counsel drove me hither."

Scarcely had he said this when, going forward, he points out the altar and the Carmental Gate, as the Romans call it in age-old honor of the nymph Carmentis, the soothsaying prophetess who first foretold the coming greatness of the descendants of Aeneas and the glory of Pallanteum [Evander's city, i.e., Rome]. Next he points out the vast grove where shrewd Romulus re-established his place of refuge and, in a cool hollow of the rock, the Lupercal [a grotto on the Palatine] dedicated to Lycean Pan in the manner of the Parrhasia [in Arcadia]. He also shows him the sacred woods of Argiletum, and calls the spot to witness as he tells of the slaying of his guest Argus. From here he leads him to the Tarpeian house and the Capitol, golden now, but once covered with forest thickets. Even then the dread sanctity [religio] of the place held the terrified rustics in awe; even then they shuddered before the wood and the rock. "This grove," he cries, "this hill with its leafy crown is the dwelling of a god—though which god it is we do not know; our Arcadians believe that here they have looked upon Jove himself, when often he shook out the darkening aegis in his hand and gathered the storm clouds. You see, moreover, these two towns with their broken walls, relics and monuments of the men of old. For this fortress was built by Father Janus, the other by Saturn; the name of this was Janiculum, and of the other Saturnia."

With such talk they drew near the house of poor Evander, and saw scattered here and there the lowing herds on the Roman Forum and down the beautiful Carinae. When they had reached his dwelling he said, "This threshold Alcides the Conqueror [Hercules] stooped to cross, this palace [regia] received him. Do not be afraid, my guest, to despise riches; fashion yourself likewise to be worthy of deity; and come in, not disdainful of our poverty." So speaking, he led great

Aeneas under the low roof of his humble home, and laid him
on a couch of strewn leaves and a Libyan bearskin. Then
night swept down and folded the earth in her dusky wings.

ROME IS PROTECTED BY THE GODS

Livy, *History of Rome,* V. 50–52. Rome had scarcely won its great
victory, in 390 B.C., after nine years of war, over the rival Etruscan
city of Veii, ten miles to the north, when the Gauls who had been
plundering Etruria arrived on the scene, won the battle of the Allia,
and sacked Rome. Livy tells the story in Bk. V, chs. 34–55.

[Lured by the wealth and the fertile soil of Italy, the land-
hungry, over-populous Gauls had swept across the Alps and
founded a city, Mediolanum—now Milan. Other bands had
followed the first, and pressed on beyond the earlier invaders,
until finally the Senones pressed on, by a leap-frog movement,
and swarmed about Clusium and eventually Rome. The Senate
now sent ambassadors to protest and warn the Gauls, but the
embassy "acting more like Gauls themselves than Romans"
had insulted the invaders—who asked only for surplus land to
till (ch. 36) —and provoked them to attack. Fortune blinded
the eyes of the Romans to the calamity which was overtaking
them: the very tribunes whose rash conduct had provoked the
war were still in command; they minimized the growing
danger; and they went into battle without taking the auspices
or studying the sacrificial omens (37. 1), and were totally defeated, almost without a blow. When news of the disaster of
the Allia reached Rome, the men of military age and the senators withdrew, with their wives and children, to the Capitol
and the Citadel (the latter at the north of the Capitoline
Mount). Here it was proposed to defend "the gods, the men,
and the name of Rome" (39. 10). Meanwhile, the flamen and
the priestesses of Vesta were to remove the sacred objects (*sacra
publica*) far from contact with bloodshed and the danger of
fire, and to continue their cultus until there were none left to
carry it on. For "if the Citadel and the Capitol, where the gods
lived, and the Senate, the center of public counsel, and the
youth who were of military age, survived the impending ruin
of the city, they could bear to let the others die—the old men
left in the city, who were soon to die anyway." Faced with the
necessity of choosing which of the *sacra publica* to leave behind (40. 7), since they were unable to remove them all, the

flamen of Quirinus and the Vestal virgins decided to bury them in jars at the shrine beside the flamen's house, "where now it is forbidden to spit"; the rest were taken across the Sublician Bridge to the Janiculum. As they climbed the hill a plebeian named Lucius Albinius caught sight of them, as he was removing his family in a wagon along with the rest of the fleeing multitude. His piety is evident from the story Livy tells (39. 10): "Even then [under circumstances like these], he observed the distinction between things divine and human, and thinking it a sacrilege for the public priestesses to go afoot, bearing the sacred objects of the Roman people, while his family were seen riding in a cart, he ordered his wife and children to get down, seated the Virgins with their sacred objects in the vehicle, and took them to Caere, their destination."

[It was during this siege (46) that one of the Fabii slipped down from the Capitol and returned home to the Quirinal Mount to perform the annual sacrifice offered by his family. Bearing the sacred objects (vessels and implements), he passed through the enemy lines, offered the sacrifice and returned unharmed, the Gauls being either "overwhelmed by his marvelous audacity or moved by religious feeling"—something for which that race is quite remarkable.

[Meanwhile the old men, seated in full attire in their houses down in the city, had been murdered (41. 9 f.), since one of them had resisted a Gaul who ventured to stroke his long beard—one of the most famous incidents in Roman history. Meanwhile also the geese, sacred to Juno, had warned the defenders of the Citadel of a night attack (47)—another famous incident. And meanwhile, likewise, a message was sent to Camillus, in exile at Ardea, begging him to return and take command of the beleaguered Citadel. Returning, he rallied the Roman forces and routed the Gauls—"for by this time Fortune had turned about and the power of the gods and human wisdom were both engaged in aiding Rome" (49. 5).

[As soon as the Gauls were driven out, Camillus faced an almost equally serious problem: the proposal of the tribunes and the plebs to abandon their ruined city and remove to the recently conquered but still intact Veii (50).]

His first act, since he was a most diligent observer of religion, was to present to the Senate all matters relating to the immortal gods, and to obtain a *senatus consultum* [decreeing] that all shrines which had been in the enemy's possession should be restored, their boundaries marked, and [their fabric] expiated [*restituerentur, terminarentur, expiarenturque*], the proper rites of expiation to be ascertained from the [Sibylline] books by the Duumvirs; that a treaty of hospitality should be established with the people of Caere, who had admitted the sacred objects [*sacra*] of the Roman people and their priests, so that by their kindness the worship of the immortal gods had not been interrupted; that Capitoline games should be instituted, since Jupiter Optimus Maximus had protected both his own sacred dwelling and also the citadel of the Roman people in time of great danger; and that Marcus Furius the dictator should appoint a College for this purpose made up of men living on the Capitol and the Citadel. It was also decided to expiate the [supernatural] Voice which had been heard by night before the Gallic War [32. 6] foretelling the calamity, but which had been disregarded; a temple to Aius Locutius was ordered to be built in the Nova Via [which ran along the north slope of the Palatine where the Voice had been heard; 52. 11]. The gold which had been taken from the Gauls and that collected from the other temples during the invasion and placed in the shrine [*cella*] of Jove, since no one could remember exactly where it belonged, was all declared sacred and ordered to be deposited under the throne [*sella*] of Jove. Even earlier, the scrupulosity [*religio*] of the citizens in this matter had been manifested, for when the gold in the public treasury proved insufficient to make up the indemnity demanded by the Gauls, they accepted what the women-folk gathered together, rather than lay hands on the sacred gold. For this act a vote of thanks was given the matrons, and they were granted the privilege of a solemn eulogy at their funerals, equally with the men.

After these matters had been settled—matters relating to the gods and wholly within the competence of the Senate—Camillus, at the request of the tribunes, who were strongly urging the plebs to leave their ruins and migrate to Veii, which was all ready for them, went up to the Assembly, accompanied by the whole Senate, and made an address.

[The magnificent speech which Livy places on the lips of Camillus follows in chs. 51–54. In it he opposed the plan to remove to Veii, for it seemed the height of folly, having just won back the city and site of Rome, now to abandon them. Though the Gauls were in possession of the city, "the Capitol and the Citadel were still held by the gods and the men of Rome; and shall victory now lead to the abandonment of its fruits? Had Rome no religious rites whatever, handed down by tradition from the foundation of the City, it would now be necessary to establish them here—so evident is the divine purpose with regard to Rome!" The events of the past few years— which he next reviews, show clearly the concern of the gods in the welfare of the City, and also the unceasing devotion of the people and their representatives to the gods. "Even when deserted by gods and by men, we nevertheless unceasingly continued our worship of the gods: therefore they have given us back our native land once more, together with the victory, and the restoration of our ancient military renown." He then continues:]

"When you consider the momentous consequences for human affairs of worshiping or of neglecting the gods, do you not begin to realize, O Quirites, that, although we are scarcely clear of the shipwreck due to our former guilt and disaster, we are moving on toward another grave sin? We have a City which was founded with due observance of the auspices and of augury; there is no corner of it which is not filled with religion and the gods; for our annual sacrifices, the fixed days are no more securely established than are the exact places where they are to be performed. Are you planning, O Quirites, to forsake all these gods, both public and private [i.e., those of the state and those of the family]? How does your behavior compare with that of the distinguished youth, Gaius Fabius, during the recent siege, whose deed the enemy observed with no less admiration than you yourselves, when he slipped down from the Citadel amid the darts of the Gauls and offered the annual sacrifice of the Fabian clan on the Quirinal Hill? Would you permit no interruption, not even in war, of the family rites, and then desert the state cultus [the *publica sacra*] and the Roman gods in time of peace? Would you have the

pontiffs and the flamens less careful in observance of the public ceremonies [*publicarum religionum*] than a private individual has been of the religious solemnities of his clan? Possibly
someone may say that we shall either continue these observances at Veii, or else send our priests hither [from Veii to
Rome] to observe them; but neither course can be followed
with proper safeguards to [i.e., without violation of] the sacred
ceremonies. For, without listing all the various kinds of rites
and all the different gods, is it possible on the Feasts of Jupiter
[Epulum Jovis, Sept. 13] to spread the couch anywhere else
than on the Capitol? Why should I speak of Vesta's undying
fires, or the image [*signum*, i.e., of Pallas, the Palladium
brought to Italy from Troy by Aeneas] which is preserved in
her temple as our guarantee of empire? What of your sacred
shields [which fell from heaven], O Mars Gradivus and Quirinus our Father? All these you would leave behind in unconse-
crated territory [*in profano*]—sacred objects coeval with the
founding of the City, and some of them even more ancient
than that?

"And see what a difference there is between us and our ancestors! They handed down to us certain sacred rites which were
to be observed on the Alban Mount and in Lavinium. But if
we had scruples about transferring sacred rites from enemy
cities to ourselves here in Rome, can we without sacrilege
[*sine piaculo*] now transfer them further to Veii, an enemy
city? Recall, if you will, how often sacrifices are repeated [i.e.,
have to be begun all over again] because some detail of the
ancestral ritual has been omitted, either by negligence or by
accident. What was it, not long ago, after the portent of the
Alban Lake, that brought about the salvation of the republic,
then in the midst of the war with Veii, if it was not a restoration of sacred rites and auspices? Even more than that, like
men who call to mind the ancient religious fervor, we not only
transferred foreign deities [*peregrinos deos*] to Rome but also
established new ones. Queen Juno was recently transported
from Veii and housed on the Aventine: how memorable was
that day, both for the noble zeal of the matrons and for the

immense crowd that gathered! We have now ordered a temple to be built for Aius Locutius because of the heavenly Voice, which was heard in the Nova Via. We have added Capitoline Games to the other annual festivals, and by authority of the Senate we have created a new College for their supervision. Which of these things did we need to undertake, if we were about to abandon Rome along with the Gauls, or if we were remaining in the Capitol, through so many months of the siege, not because we chose to do so but only through fear of the enemy?

"We are talking about sacred rites and temples; but what about the priests? Has it not dawned upon you what a sacrilege you are about to commit? The Vestals certainly have only their one habitation, from which nothing ever forced them to remove except the capture of the City; and for the Flamen Dialis to remain for a single night outside the City is a sin. Will you make these priests Veientines instead of Romans? And shall thy Virgins forsake thee, O Vesta, and shall the Flamen, as he lives away [from Rome] night after night, bring all this guilt upon himself and upon the Republic? What about the other affairs, most of which, after taking the proper auspices, we transact inside the pomerium? To what state of oblivion and neglect are we about to hand them over? The comitia curiata which deals with military affairs; the comitia centuriata, where you choose the consuls and the military tribunes; where can their auspices be held, except in the customary places? Shall we transfer them to Veii? Or must the people, for the sake of the comitia, assemble at great inconvenience here in the City, deserted by both gods and men?"

[The speech goes on (53-54) to refute the argument that everything in Rome is now polluted beyond the possibility of expiation, and has been left a devastation and ruin, whereas Veii is undamaged, by showing that this is a mere pretext, since the proposal to move thither had been made after the capture of Veii but before the arrival of the Gauls. The folly of this proposal was clear: What if a fire ravaged Veii? Would the Romans move again? What if enemy people moved into vacant Rome, and took over the Roman deities? The site of Rome, in the very heart of Italy, is both too valuable and too important to be abandoned. Thus considerations of religion, national pride, and political intelligence demand that the Romans remain where they are, and rebuild their ruined homes. The peroration is extremely fine:]

"Your courage you can take with you and go elsewhere, but the fortune of this place [*fortuna loci*] surely cannot be transferred elsewhere! Here is the Capitol, where once a human head was discovered and men were told then the place should someday be the head of the whole world and center of an empire. Here while the Capitol was being cleared [for occupation or for sacral uses] by augural rites, [the gods] Juventas and Terminus, to the great joy of your ancestors, would not consent to be moved. Here are the fires of Vesta, here are the shields sent down from heaven, here all the gods are propitious, if you remain."

(55) It is said that this speech of Camillus moved them, especially what he said about religion; but the doubtful question was really settled by a voice [*vox*] that was uttered at just the right time. While the Senate was considering the matter a little later in the Curia Hostilia, some cohorts of soldiers returning from guard duty happened to be crossing the Forum and as they passed the Comitia the centurion called out, "Sign bearers, set up your ensigns; here is the best place to stay." Hearing this sentence and accepting it, the Senators came out of the Curia and shouted it, the plebs gathering about and expressing their approval . . . .

AN ANCIENT ROMAN CALENDAR

From the *Fasti Praenestini*, preserved in the National Museum at Rome. The annotations and later additions, in smaller letters, are omitted. Incomplete as it is (note the lacunae in marking the days, as F, C, N, or NP), differing as it does from other ancient examples, and crediting April with thirty days (formerly twenty-nine), the structure of this calendar is undoubtedly very ancient. The later annotations and additions only show the growth of the calendar through successive generations. See other examples in G. Wissowa, RKR, Appendix I; H. Dessau, ILS, 8744–45; W. W. Fowler, *Roman Festivals*, pp. 21–32; RC, I, § 9; E. H. Warmington, ROL, pp. 450–465; F. Richter, *Lateinische Sacralinschriften* (Kleine Texte 68, Bonn, 1911), nos. 5–9. See also A. K. Michels, "The 'Calendar of Numa' and the Pre-Julian Calendar," in *Proceedings of the American Philological Association*, LXXX (1949), 320–346; W. W. Fowler, "Calendar (Roman)" in ERE. See Introduction, above, p. xii.

(March)					(April)		
D	K.	MART.	NP	C	K.	APR.	F
E	vi	F		D	iiii		F
F	v	C		E	iii		C
G	iiii	C		F	PR		C
H	iii	C		G			NON. N
A	PR	NP		H	vii		NP
B		NON		A			
C	viii	F		B			
D		C		C			
E		C		D			
F				E			N
G				F	PR		N
H				G			EID
A				H	xiix		N
B				A	xvii		FORD
C				B	xvi		N
D				C	xv		N
E				D	xiiii		N
F	xiiii	QVINQ N		E	xiii		CER
G	xiii			F	xii		N
H	xii			G	xi		PAL
A	xi			H	x		N
B	x	TVBIL NP		A	viiii		VIN F
C	viiii	Q.R.C.	F	B	viii		C
D	viii	C		C	vii		ROB NP
E	vii			D	vi		F
F				E	v		C
G				F	iiii		NP
H				G	iii		C
A		C		H	PR		C
B	PR	C					
	XXXI				XXX		

II. FOREIGN INFLUENCES

The crises which led to the admission of foreign cults and
deities were chiefly the Etruscan domination during the
period of the kings, and the Punic Wars, when Rome became desperate and turned to the Sibylline oracles for guidance, prepared to adopt any powerful rite that promised to
stave off destruction. But the "necessary evil" of such foreign
importations was severely limited under the Republic. Alien
gods were not, at first, allowed within the *pomerium* or
sacred boundary of the City, and Romans were forbidden to
participate in their rites. That resident aliens were present
in numbers sufficient to support such foreign cults indicates
the size of the City and its heterogeneous population at the
time. The later attitude of toleration and even of encouragement is illustrated by the great Bacchic inscription in the
Metropolitan Museum in New York, from the second
century of the Christian era, which lists hundreds of members of the cult in one household. For the history of this
period see: G. Wissowa, RKR, §§ 7–11, 38–53; W. W.
Fowler, RERP, chs. 10–15; N. Turchi, RRA, Pt. II. 2. On
the *pomerium,* see N. Lewis and M. Reinhold, RC, I, § 6.
See also F. Altheim, *Griechische Götter im alten Rom*
(RGVV, XXII. 1, 1930).

CYBELE IS WELCOMED TO ROME

Livy, *History of Rome,* XXIX. 14. The mood of the public which
made possible this extraordinary step has been intimated by Livy in
many passages earlier than the following one—e.g., in Bk. XXV. 1. 6–8.
"The longer the war dragged on [i.e., the Second Punic War; it was
now 213 B.C., soon after the terrible disaster at Cannae] and the ups
and downs of the conflict changed the hearts of men as much as it
did their fortunes, various superstitious cults, mainly of foreign
origin [*tanta religio, et ea magna ex parte externa*], swept into
the City to such a degree that either the gods or men were suddenly
changed. Not only in secret now and within private walls were the
Roman rites abandoned; but even in public, in the Forum and on
the Capitol, there was a crowd of women who no longer followed

the ancestral customs either in sacrifices or in prayers. Petty priest-
lings and prophets had also captured the minds of the men." We
are thus prepared for the account of the arrival of Cybele in Bk.
XXIX. This took place in 204 B.C. See W. W. Fowler, *Religious Experience of the Roman People*, ch. 14. See text and translation by
F. G. Moore in LCL (1949).

Although Africa had not been openly decreed to be a province—since the senators kept the matter secret, I believe, for
fear the Carthaginians might know about it in advance—nevertheless the city was stirred by the hope that the war might be
waged that year in Africa, and that accordingly the end of the
Punic War was at hand. This had led to the filling of men's
minds with superstitious fears, and so they were prone both to
report and to believe in prodigies. Thus more and more of
them were circulated, e.g., that two suns had been seen, and
that at night there had been daylight for a while; at Setia a
meteor had been seen shooting from east to west; at Tarracina
a city gate had been struck by lightning [lit., touched from
heaven], at Anagnia a gate and also many places in the wall;
while in the temple of Juno Sospita at Lanuvium a noise was
heard, with a horrible crash. To expiate these there was one
day of prayer, and on account of a shower of stones nine days
of rites [*novendiale sacrum*] were observed.

In addition they deliberated on the reception of the Idaean
Mother [the Mother of the Gods], regarding whom not only
Marcus Valerius, one of the legates who arrived in advance of
the others, reported that she would soon be in Italy, but also
there was recent news that she had already reached Tarracina.
It was no light matter that engaged the attention of the Senate
—the question was, who was the best man in the city. It was
certain that every man would have preferred a victory in this
contest to any high command or other honor, whether conferred by vote of the Fathers or that of the people. Publius
Scipio, son of the Gnaeus who had fallen in Spain, was the
young man, not yet old enough to be a quaestor, whom they
judged to be the best of good men among all the citizens. . . .
Publius Cornelius was ordered to go to Ostia with all the ma-

trons to meet the goddess, himself to receive her from the ship, carry her to land and turn her over to the matrons to carry. When the ship reached the mouth of the Tiber river, just as he had been ordered he sailed out into open water in a ship and received the goddess from her priests and carried her to land. The foremost matrons in the city—among whom the name of one, Claudia Quinta, is most conspicuous—now received her. Claudia's reputation, previously in doubt, according to tradition, has made her modesty all the more celebrated by posterity as a result of this devout ministration. The matrons passed the goddess from hand to hand, in unbroken succession one after another, while the whole city poured out to meet her. Incense burners had been placed in front of the doors along the way, and, on lighting their incense, people prayed that she might enter the city of Rome willingly and propitiously. They carried the goddess to the Temple of Victory, which is on the Palatine; it was the day before the Ides of April, and this was a festival. The people crowded the Palatine, bearing gifts for the goddess. There was a *lectisternium* [banquet of the gods], and also games called the Megalesia.

THE SUPPRESSION OF THE BACCHANALIA

Livy, *History of Rome*, XXXIX. 16. 6–9. The account of the trial of the *bacchantes* (chs. 8–19) formed part of the story of the investigation of secret conspiracies. The suppression of this particular cult was no doubt inspired, at least in part, by fear of any secret cult or religious association which was spreading among the lowest class of the population, including the slaves. Such a movement might easily become political or social and lead to revolt. The attitude here taken was characteristic of Roman conservatism and suspicion of foreign religions (*externa superstitio*) down to the last days of the conflict with Christianity. See R. M. Grant, *The Sword and the Cross* (1955). Cf. N. Lewis and M. Reinhold, RC, 1, § 176. The consul Spurius Postumius Albinus is speaking. As he concludes his speech (15–16), he appeals to the strongest motive for the suppression of foreign cults —one which is age-old, primitive, and perennial:

Nothing is more deceptive in outward appearance than a false religion. Where the majesty of the gods is set out as cover for a crime, a fear steals into one's mind lest in punishing human misbehavior we may do violence to some matter of divine law which has got mixed up with it. From this scruple [*hac religione*] innumerable decisions of the pontiffs, decrees of the Senate, and finally responses of the haruspices have set you free. How often, in the days of our fathers and our grandfathers, has it been the task turned over to the magistrates to forbid the introduction of foreign cults, to exclude quack sacrificers and fortunetellers from the Forum, the Circus, and the City, to search out and burn books of prophecies, and to abolish every system of sacrifice except that which conforms to the Roman way. For the wisest men, in all laws divine and human, were convinced that nothing was so effective in destroying religion as where sacrifices were offered not by native but by foreign rites.

THE SENATE DECREE CONCERNING THE BACCHANALIA

CIL, I. 2. 581. H. Dessau, ILS, 18. E. Diehl, *Altlateinische Inschriften* (3d ed., 1930), No. 262; J. E. Sandys, *Latin Epigraphy* (2d ed., 1927), pp. 257 f.; E. H. Warmington, ROL, pp. 254–259 (text and translation with notes). Cf. N. Lewis and M. Reinhold, RC, I, pp. 472 f.; W. W. Fowler, RERP, pp. 344–349; F. Cumont, RO, pp. 196 ff.; R. Pettazzoni, "State Religion and Individual Religion in the Religious History of Italy," in *Essays on the History of Religions* (Eng. tr. by H. J. Rose, 1954), ch. 18; N. Turchi, RRA, pp. 208 ff.; T. Frank, "The Bacchanalian Cult of 186 B.C.," in *Classical Quarterly,* XXI (1927), 128 ff. The inscription, now in Vienna, is dated 186 B.C. and sets forth the letter addressed by the Roman consuls to the people of the Ager Teuranus, among the Bruttii, in which they quote the *senatus consultum* regarding the Bacchanalian orgies.

The consuls Quintus Marcius son of Lucius and Spurius Postumius son of Lucius consulted the Senate on the 7th October in the temple of Bellona. The record was kept by Marcus Claudius son of Marcus, Lucius Valerius son of Publius, Quintus Minucius son of Gaius.

With regard to the Bacchanalian celebrations, it was decided to inform the allies as follows: "No one of them is to maintain a shrine of Bacchus [or, observe the Bacchanalia]. If anyone affirms that he is under obligation to do so, he must appear before the Praetor of the City of Rome, and after a hearing our Senate shall render a decision in the case, not less than a hundred senators being present when the matter is being considered. No Roman citizen, or member of the Latin League, or of any allied state, is permitted to attend a meeting of the Bacchae, without first appearing before the Praetor of the City and obtaining from him, by decree of the Senate, in the presence of not less than a hundred senators, permission to participate. (Adopted.)

"No man is to become a priest. No man or woman may become head of the organization [magister]; they are not permitted to maintain a common fund; no one, either man or woman, is to be made an official, or is to allow himself to be nominated for such an office, either as master or submaster. Nor may anyone, henceforth, bind himself by any oath, vow, pledge, or promise, nor enter into any mutual agreement. No one is permitted to conduct a secret celebration of the rites. Neither in public places nor in private, nor beyond the city limits, may anyone betake himself for this purpose without first appearing before the Praetor of the City and obtaining from him by decree of the Senate, in the presence of not less than a hundred senators, permission to participate. (Adopted.)

"Not more than a total of five men [persons] are permitted to hold a celebration of the rite; among them may not be more than two men and three women, and then only by permission of the Praetor of the City and of the Senate under the conditions named above."

These orders shall be proclaimed at an assembly on not less than three market days, and in order that you may know this decree of the Senate, they decreed as follows: "If any persons act contrary to the above-written regulations, they shall be liable to capital punishment." Also "let this be inscribed upon a bronze tablet," according to the decree of the Senate, "and placed where it can most easily be read. The Bacchanalian shrines which now exist [i.e., if there are any] shall—unless they contain sacred objects—be dismantled, as is stated above, within ten days of the receipt of this order." IN THE AGER TEURANUS [in Southern Italy, where the inscription was found].

THE GREAT BACCHIC INSCRIPTION AT TUSCULUM

This inscription, now in the Metropolitan Museum in New York, was published by A. Vogliano and F. Cumont, "La grande inscrizione bacchica del Metropolitan Museum," *American Journal of Archeology*, XXXVII (1933), 215 ff. See M. P. Nilsson, "En Marge de la Grande Inscription Bacchique de Metropolitan Museum," *Studi e Materiali*, X (1934), 1 ff., reprinted in his *Opuscula Selecta* (1952), II, 524–541; *Geschichte der Griechischen Religion*, II (1950), 343 ff.; "New Evidence for the Dionysiac Mysteries," *Eranos*, LIII (1955), 28–40; "Dionysos Liknites," *Bulletin de la Société des Lettres* (Lund, 1950), No. 1, "The Bacchic Mysteries of the Roman Age," *Harvard Theological Review*, XLVI (1953), 177 ff. See also F. Cumont, RO, pp. 195–204, appendix on the Bacchic mysteries at Rome; H. Jeanmaire, *Dionysos: Histoire du Culte de Bacchus* (1951), pp. 470–472.

Bacchanalia was the Latin name for the Dionysiac *orgia*, since Dionysus was identified with the Italian god Bacchus. The first trace of the cult in Italy is an inscription at Cumae, from the first half of the fifth century B.C., forbidding the burial of any but its members in the cemetery of the association: "It is not lawful to bury anyone here unless he has been initiated in the Bacchic rites" (F. Cumont, RO, p. 197). The rites probably reached Rome from Magna Graecia, i.e., southern Italy, perhaps from Tarentum after its capture by Fabius in 208 B.C. Certainly the cult was viewed as a political conspiracy and not as a mere band of religious enthusiasts, and this can be more easily explained if the members were captives sold as slaves in Campania and Latium and even farther north. The Senate suppressed the cult with extreme cruelty; of its members, numbering 7000, many were executed. But suppressed cults usually revived, and Julius Caesar reintroduced the rites, probably from Alexandria, after which they became popular, especially among the growing segment of the Italian population which came from the East.

Dionysus had long been identified with Father Liber, an old vegetation god with a consort Libera and a cult center on or near the Aventine, the chief foreign quarter of ancient Rome. Sarcophagi decorated with Dionysiac motifs and the wall paintings in Rome and Campania, especially the famous scene depicted in the Villa Item at Pompeii (see A. Maiuri, *La Villa dei Misteri*, or his *Pompeii* [1951]; the interpretation is still contested), show the influence of Bacchic symbolism and perhaps of the cult and its beliefs, which included the hope of a blessed hereafter for all its initiates.

The great Bacchic inscription at the Metropolitan Museum, dating presumably from *ca.* A.D. 165, was found at Tusculum, a few miles south of Rome. It originally listed several hundred (at least 316) members of the cult, presumably living at Tusculum where Pompeia Agripinilla and her opulent husband, returning early in the second century of the Christian era from Asia Minor, brought with them a large entourage of servants who were devotees of Dionysus. The inscription, in Greek, is chiefly of interest for the wide range of titles of officers—or officiants—in the cult, and (presumably) in its religious processions. Unlike the early Bacchic cult, which apparently had no hierarchy, the cultus now has a long list of officiants and ministers.

[To] Agripinilla the mystae whose names appear below [erected this statue]: Macrinus, the hero [*hērōs*], Kathēgilla the torch-bearer [*dadouchos*], priests [7 names], priestesses [2 names], hierophant Agathopous, god-bearers [*theophoroi, 2*], assistant and tirer of Silenus [*hypourgos* and *seilēnokosmos, 1*], chest-bearers [*kistaphoroi,* 3 women], chief herdsmen [*archiboukoloi,* 3], holy herdsmen [*boukoloi hieroi,* 7], leaders of bacchants [*archibassaroi,* 2; *bassaroi* were Thracian bacchants], acolytes [*amphithaleis,* 2], bearers of the winnowing fan [*liknaphoroi,* 3 women], bearer of the sacred phallos [*phallophoros,* 1 woman], fire-bearers [*purphoroi,* 2], secretary [(?) *hieromnēmōn,* 1], youth leaders [*archineaniskoi,* 1], women leaders of bacchants [*archibassarai,* 4], herdsmen [*boukoloi,* 11], initiates [*apo katazōseōs,* i.e., girded, or with their sacred robes girdled, 89 men and women], bacchant initiates [*bakchoi apo katazōseōs,* 15], female bacchant initiates [*bakchai apo*

katazōseōs, 3], holy bacchants [*hieroi bakchoi,* over 100 names]
. . . [a lacuna follows, where once perhaps were listed the
women *bakchai*], guardians of the sacred cave [*anthrophylakes,*
2], female bacchants [*bakchai,* 44 names of women], novices
[*seigētai,* who must "keep silence," 23 men and women]. [The
significance of many of these titles and functions and of many
of the offices named is unknown. Similar titles occur in other
Dionysiac inscriptions, e.g., at Athens, Pergamum, Ephesus,
Magnesia, and elsewhere in the East, from which, obviously,
the cult had been brought to Italy.]

III. PHILOSOPHY AND RELIGION

The ancient Roman was not a natural-born philosopher, and took slowly and reluctantly to the study—which was imported into Italy from the East, i.e., from Greece, in the second and first centuries B.C., though a minimal influence from Magna Graecia, i.e., Sicily and Southern Italy, had long been observable. Varro's attitude toward the religion of the philosophers is well known: St. Augustine's quotations enable us to recognize his threefold classification and his contrast of the civic cult, which he preferred, with both the religion of the philosophers and that of the poets. Cicero, a diligent student of philosophy, was trying, in the middle of the first century B.C., to introduce his fellow countrymen to such studies—though he himself maintained an attitude of reserve, "suspense of judgment," and criticism toward all the schools of philosophy. Never, in the history of Roman religion, was there such a union of philosophy and religion as took place in the Greek world, as in the thought of Pindar, Aeschylus, or Plato. No such union was possible, for Roman religion was essentially a cultus, not a body of ideas or beliefs, and its invariable test of the value of any rite or practice was pragmatic: Does it work? Does it produce results? Is it useful to the state? Thus there was never a purely Roman philosophy nor a purely Roman philosophy of religion.

For Roman religion in relation to philosophy see: E. V. Arnold, *Roman Stoicism* (1911); C. Bailey, "The Advent of Philosophy," in CAH, Vol. VIII (1930), pp. 454–465, with bibliography, pp. 773 f.; E. Bevan, *Stoics and Sceptics* (1913); W. W. Fowler, RERP, chs. 16–17, *Roman Ideas of Deity* (1914); R. M. Grant, *Miracle and Natural Law in Graeco-Roman and Early Christian Thought* (1952); F. C. Grant, HR, pp. 71–104 (on criticism of traditional religion in the Hellenistic age); R. D. Hicks, *Stoic and Epicurean* (1910); R. Philippson, "Cicero—Philosophische Schriften," in Pauly-Wissowa-Kroll, PW, cols. 1104–92; E. Zeller, *Philosophie der Griechen* (4th ed., 1876 ff., latest ed., 1920 ff.; several volumes have been translated: see esp. *Stoics, Epi-*

cureans, and Sceptics, 1870), *Geschichte der Griechischen Philosophie (Grundriss* of the large Zeller, 13th ed., by W. Nestle, 1938; also an English translation, 1931). See also N. Lewis and M. Reinhold, RC, II, § 65; W. Windelband, *Lehrbuch der Geschichte der Philosophie* (11th ed., 1924), Pt. II, esp. p. 136; *Geschichte der Abendländischen Philosophie im Altertum* (4th ed., 1923); *Friedrich Ueberwegs Grundriss der Geschichte der Philosophie des Altertums* (11th ed., by Karl Praechter, 1920), esp. §§ 54a–77. On Cicero's philosophical writings, see also O. Weissenfels, *Auswahl aus Ciceros Philosophischen Schriften,* Hilfsheft (2d ed.) ed. by P. Wessner (3d ed., 1915); R. Harder, *Die Einbürgerung der Philosophie in Rom (Die Antike,* V, 1929).

VARRO'S ACCOUNT OF ROMAN RELIGION

The fullest contemporary account of ancient Roman religion was probably the lost work of Marcus Terentius Varro, *Antiquities Human and Divine (Antiquitatum humanarum et divinarum libri XLI),* written by that learned scholar in 47 B.C. Fortunately for the historian of religion, the numerous quotations which St. Augustine made in his *City of God* enable us to reconstruct much of it, at least in general outline and point of view, even though Augustine's intention was only to ridicule and demolish Varro's exposition—or rather the religion he described.

The *City of God* is a long work, in twenty-two books, occasioned by the criticisms levelled against Christians as a result of the sack of Rome by Alaric in A.D. 410. It is the Christians who have been winning away their adherents from the ancient gods, interfering with the age-old public rites of worship upon which the commonwealth relied for its continuance and prosperity, and provoking the ancient deities with their stubborn and unpatriotic loyalty to Christ. Augustine's work is a counterattack upon the old pagan religion. The criticism of polytheism fills the first five books, and shows that the pagan gods have not protected Rome in the past—a survey of Roman history and religion proves this—and hence the Christians cannot be blamed for the fall of the City, as if the desertion of the pagan altars had led to the abandonment of the Romans by their ancient deities. Bks. VI and VII take up in detail the "civil" theology as it had been set forth by Varro, and show its contradictions and absurdities and the inability of the pagan gods to confer immortality. Bk. VIII surveys Greek philosophy from the pre-Socratics to "Hermes," to the same effect. Begun in 413 and completed in 426, it provided the

Christian Church with a vast outline of a philosophy of history, in which the sacred and the secular, the religious and the political aspects of human life were studied in their mutual relations—the City of God *versus* the City of this World. Augustine's polemical, rhetorical, often prolix style is interesting—an example of the highest literary achievement of later classicism. Ever since its first appearance the *City of God* has been one of the most influential books in European literature.

Varro's *Antiquities* was divided, like its subject, into two main parts. The first twenty-five books dealt with human antiquities, the last sixteen with divine. The arrangement of material was simple: Varro posed, and tried to answer, these questions in each case he dealt with: Who? Where? When? What? The sixteen books on divine antiquities began with an introductory book (26), followed by five main divisions: priests (27–29), temples (30–32), festivals and games (33–35), sacred objects and rites (36–38), the gods (39–41).

There is a translation of St. Augustine's *City of God* in the Library of the Fathers (1888), and a more recent one by Pierre de Labriolle, *La Cité de Dieu* (1941; 2 vols., but incomplete). There are many editions of the Latin text, beginning with that of Erasmus (1528–29). I have used the Teubner text edited by B. Dombart (1877). See the reconstruction of Varro, Bks. I, XIV, XV, XVI, by R. Agahd, in Fleckeisen's *Neue Jahrbücher für Philologie,* Supplement to Vol. XXIV (1898). On *a diis electa,* see Nock's article, "A Chapter in the Religious History of the Third Century," *Harvard Theological Review,* XXIII (1930), 250–274.

[We begin with Bk. VI, ch. 1, of the *City of God*. After recapitulating the argument of the first five books, Augustine proceeds to take up the point that it is impossible that the gods, who cannot provide temporal goods, should be thought to be able to confer eternal life.] We must now, as the plan of this work requires, refute and instruct those who maintain that it is necessary to worship the gods of the nations, which the Christian religion destroys, not on account of this life but on account of that which is to follow death. Let me begin my disputation with the truthful oracle of the holy psalm, "Blessed is the man whose hope is the Lord God, and who has no regard for vanities and lying follies" [Ps. 40:5 = 39:5, in the Old Latin translation]. Nevertheless, among these "vanities" and "lying follies" it is the philosophers who are to be

listened to with far more toleration, those who have repudi-
ated the opinions and errors of the nations; for the nations
have set up images to the gods, and have either made up or
have accepted many false and unworthy fictions concerning
the immortal gods, as they call them; and after believing them
have mingled them with their worship and their sacred rites.

With these men who, though not freely disclosing their convictions, do nevertheless by veiled allusions in their discourses
testify to their disapproval of these errors, it may not be inappropriate to discuss the following question: Whether, for
the sake of the life to come, we ought to worship the one God
who made all creatures, spiritual and corporeal, or those many
gods who, as some even of the noblest and most excellent of
these same philosophers maintain [e.g., Plato, *Timaeus*, § 40],
were created by that one God and placed by him in their respective spheres on high.

But who will assent when it is affirmed and contended that
those gods, certain of whom I have mentioned in my fourth
book [see chs. 11 and 21], to each of whom is allotted the care
of little things, are able to bestow eternal life on whom they
will? Will those most skillful and acute men, who glory in
having explained for the benefit of mankind how each god is
to be worshiped, and what is to be asked from each—for fear
lest, by a most disgraceful absurdity, of the kind a mime exploits for the sake of merriment, water [not wine] should be
sought from Liber, or wine from the Nymphs [Lat. *a Lymphis*]
—will these men really advise the devotee who supplicates the
immortal gods and has asked wine from the Nymphs, and has
received the response, "We have only water; ask for wine from
Liber," that he may rightly say to them, "If ye have no wine,
at least give me eternal life"? What is more ridiculous than
this absurdity? Will not these Nymphs, laughing loudly—since
they are easily made to laugh—and supposing they do not attempt to deceive, like the demons, will they not answer the
suppliant, "O man, do you think that we have life [*vitam*] in
our power, when as you have heard, we do not even control

the vine [*vitem*]?" [The rest of the chapter amplifies and re-inforces this point.]

(2) Who has investigated these things more carefully than Marcus Varro? Who has made more learned discoveries? Who has studied them with closer attention? Who has drawn sharper distinctions? Who has written about them more dili-gently and more fully? His style is not pleasing, but his learn-ing and his thought are so ample that in all that erudition which we call "secular" but which the world calls "liberal" he will teach the student of facts quite as thoroughly as Cicero delights the student of words.

Even Tully [Cicero] himself bears this testimony to him, for in his *Academics* he states that the disputation contained in that work had been carried on with Marcus Varro, "with a man who is unquestionably the keenest of all men, and with-out any question the most learned." He does not call him "the most eloquent" or "the most fluent," for in truth he was quite deficient in these qualities; but he says, "of all men the keen-est." And in those same books—that is, in the *Academics*—where he maintains that everything is to be doubted, he adds of him, "without any doubt (!) the most learned." In fact, he was so certain about this matter that he laid aside the doubt which he was accustomed to apply to everything, as if, when about to dispute in favor of the doubt of the Academics, he had, with respect to this one thing, forgotten that he was an Academic. But in the first book [I. 3. 9], when he extols the literary work of the same Varro, he says, "We were wandering about like strangers in our own city until your books led us home and enabled us to recognize who we were and where we lived. You have made clear to us the age of our country, its various periods [i.e., in the *Antiquities*]; the laws about sacred things and the priesthoods; the traditional disciplines, both domestic and public; and the lore about sacred regions and places; in brief you have explained to us the names, the classes, the offices, the causes of all things divine and human."

This man, then, with such distinguished and excellent ac-

quirements, and, as Terentianus [Maurus] briefly says of him
in a most elegant verse, "Varro, a man so learned on every
subject," who read so much that we wonder when he had any
time to write, who wrote so much that we scarcely believe anyone can have read it all—this man, I say, so great in talent, so
great in learning, had he been an opponent and a destroyer of
the "divine things" about which he wrote, and had he said
that they belonged to superstition rather than to religion,
would not, perhaps, have written so many things which are
ridiculous, contemptible, detestable. But he worshiped these
gods, and commended their worship; in this same work he says
that he fears lest they should perish, not by the invasion of
enemies but by the negligence of the citizens; and he adds that
he wishes to deliver them from this disaster, and preserve them
in the memory of the good by means of such books—a service
more useful than that by which Metellus is said to have rescued the sacred things of Vesta from the flames and Aeneas to
have rescued the penates from the burning of Troy. But when
he hands on to the centuries to come traditions which deserve
the reprobation of both the wise and the foolish, and can only
be viewed as inimical to true religion, what must we think of
him, if not that he is an acute and learned author, but one
who was not set free by the Holy Spirit, and was borne down
by the customs and laws of the City. At least, he could not
keep silence about those things which interested him—under
the guise of commending religion.

(3) Varro wrote forty-one books of *Antiquities*. He divided
his subject into "things human" and "things divine." Twenty-
five books he devoted to "human" things, sixteen to "divine,"
following a plan by which he gave six books to each of the four
main divisions of "human things." He considered one after another the questions: who perform, where they perform, when
they perform, what they perform. Thus in the first six books
he discussed men; in the second six, places; in the third six,
times; in the fourth and last six, things. Four times six, however, make only twenty-four. But he placed at the head of

them a separate book, which formed an introduction to the whole subject.

In the series on "divine things," he preserved the same order, dealing with the cultus offered the gods. For this cultus is performed by men, in certain places, at certain times, [and with certain forms]. These four things which I have mentioned he set forth in twelve books, allowing three to each division. Thus he wrote the first three about persons, the next three about places, the third about times, and the fourth three about sacred rites, showing who should perform them, where, when, and what they should perform, subtly drawing the distinctions.

But since it was also necessary to say, especially because it was expected, *to whom* they should perform sacred rites, he wrote about the gods themselves in the last three books; and so these five times three made up the fifteen books. But there are in all, as we have said, sixteen. For here also he placed at the beginning of the series one distinct book, as an introduction to all that followed. After this introductory book he proceeded to subdivide the first three under the same fivefold plan which he followed in dealing with men: the first concerns the pontiffs, the second concerns the augurs, the third concerns the Quindecemvirs [i.e., the fifteen men who presided over sacred ceremonies]. The second group of three relates to places, one dealing with small chapels, the second with temples, and the third with sacred places. The next three relate to times, that is, to festivals: one deals with holidays, another with games in the circus, and the third with the theater. The fourth triad, relating to sacrifices [i.e., sacred rites], deals first with consecrations, then with private sacrifices, finally with public sacrifices. In the three remaining books, the gods themselves to whom all this cultus has been offered follow as in a procession. The first book deals with the "certain" gods [*di certi*], the second with the "uncertain" [*di incerti*], the third and last with the chief and "select" gods [*di selecti*].

(4) [It is impossible to hope for eternal life from such gods,

who are not "good demons" but wicked spirits.] Varro himself
testifies that he wrote first about "human" things, then about
"divine," because cities existed first, and afterwards these
divine institutions were established by them. But the true religion was not instituted by any earthly state; instead, it itself
established the celestial City. And it is inspired and taught by
the true God, the giver of eternal life to His true worshipers.

The following is the reason which Varro gives when he confesses that he had written first concerning "human" things, and
afterwards of "divine," inasmuch as the "divine" things were
instituted by men: "Just as the painter exists prior to the
painted tablet, and the mason prior to the building, so cities
exist before the things which are instituted by cities." But he
says that he would have written first about the gods, and then
about men, if he had been writing on the subject of the entire
nature of the gods—as if he were really writing only about
some portion and not the whole of the nature of the gods; or
as if, indeed, some portion, but not the whole of the nature
of the gods, ought not to be placed before that of men! How,
then, does it come that in those three final books, where he
carefully explains the "certain," "uncertain," and "select"
gods, he seems not to pass by any portion of the nature of the
gods? . . .

(5) Now what are we to say of his next proposition, viz.,
that there are three kinds of "theology," that is, of rational
explanation of the gods? Of these, one is called "mythical,"
another "physical," and the third "civil." If Latin usage permitted, we might call the first kind "fabular," but we call it
"fabulous," for "mythical" is derived from the Greek *mythos*,
a fable. The second we call "natural," since usage now allows
it. The third Varro himself has given a Latin name, calling it
"civil."

Then he goes on to say, "They call that theology mythical
which the poets chiefly use; physical, that which the philosophers use; civil, that of the people. As to the first of these, it
contains many fictions, contrary to the dignity and the nature
of the immortals. Here we find that one god has been born

from the head, another from the thigh, another from drops of blood; we find that gods have stolen, committed adultery, been slaves to men; in brief, here are attributed to the gods all such evils as may befall, not merely men, but the most contemptible of men." He certainly, wherever he could, wherever he dared, wherever he thought he could do it with impunity, has set forth, without the least obscurity or ambiguity, how great an injury has been done to the nature of the gods by these lying fables; for he was speaking, not about "natural" theology, nor about "civil," but about the "fabulous" theology, which he assumed he could freely criticize.

Let us see, now, what he says about the second kind. "The second kind, as I have shown," he says, "is that concerning which the philosophers have left many books, in which they treat such questions as these: what gods there are, where they live, of what kind and character they are, at what time they were born or if they have existed from eternity; whether their nature is that of fire, as Heraclitus believes; or of number, as Pythagoras holds; or of atoms, as Epicurus says; and other such things, which men's ears can more easily hear inside the walls of a school than outside in the Forum." He finds nothing to criticize in this kind of theology, which they call physical and which belongs to philosophers, except that he has related their controversies which have given rise to a multitude of dissenting sects. Nevertheless, he has removed this kind from the Forum, that is, from the populace, and has shut it up in schools. But that first kind, which is the most false and pernicious, he has not removed from the cities. Oh, what religious ears the people must have, and among them even the Romans! They are not able to endure what the philosophers argue about the gods; but the songs of poets and the plays of actors, which contradict the dignity and the nature of the immortals and ascribe to them such things as may befall not merely men but the most contemptible of men, they not only bear but listen to with pleasure. And not only this—they even consider that these things please the gods, and serve to appease them.

But someone may say, Let us distinguish these two kinds of

theology, the "mythical" and the "physical"—i.e., the fabulous and the natural—from the "civil" kind about which we are now speaking. Varro himself has distinguished them: let us now see how he explains the civil theology. I realize, of course, why it is necessary to set off the fabulous, since it is false, base, unworthy. But to try to distinguish the natural from the civil, what else is this but a confession that even the civil is false? For if it is natural, what is wrong with it and why should it be excluded? And if the civil is not natural, what right has it ever to be admitted? This is probably the reason why Varro wrote first about human things and afterwards about divine; for in divine things he did not follow nature [or the nature of the gods?], but the institutions of men.

Let us now take a look at the civil theology. "The third kind," he says, "is that which in cities the citizens, and especially the priests, ought to know and to practice. For it teaches what gods are to be publicly worshiped, and what sacred rites and sacrifices each is to receive" [or "each person is to offer"]. Let us now listen carefully to what follows: "The first theology," he says, "is especially appropriate to the theater, the second to the world, the third to the city." Who does not see to which of them he gives the palm? Certainly to the second, which he said above is that of the philosophers. For he testifies that this one belongs to the world, and nothing, according to the philosophers, is better than the world [a Stoic doctrine; cf. Cicero, *De Natura Deorum*, II. 18]. But as for the other two theologies, the first and the third, those of the theater and of the city, has he separated them or joined them? For although the cities are in the world, we cannot see how it follows that whatever belongs to the city belongs also to the world. For it is perfectly possible that as a result of false opinions the city may believe in and worship what has no real existence either in the world or outside it. But the theater, where is it but in the city? Who else has instituted the theater, if not the city? For what purpose was it instituted, if not for scenic plays? And to what do scenic plays belong, if not to those "divine things" about which these books of Varro's were written with such great ability?

[Ch. 6 deals with the "mythical" and the "civil" kinds of religion. Augustine repeats some of the arguments of Greek philosophers in criticism of the traditional cults and the fancies of the poets, and insists again that eternal life cannot be obtained through devotion to the popular deities.]

When we say these things, it may possibly seem to someone who is quite ignorant of these matters that it is only in the songs of the poets and in plays acted on the stage that episodes unworthy of the divine majesty, ridiculous and detestable, are celebrated; whereas those sacred rites, which not actors on the stage but the priests perform, are pure and free from everything that is improper. Had this been so, no one would ever have thought that these theatrical abominations should be celebrated in honor of the gods, nor would the gods themselves ever have ordered them to be performed for them. But if men are not ashamed to perform such things as these in the theaters, it is because similar things are carried on in the temples.

In short, when this famous author attempted to distinguish the civil theology from the fabulous and natural, and to represent it as a third and distinct kind, he wished it to be thought of as tempered by both rather than separated from either of them. For he says, in effect, that what the poets write is something less than what the people ought to follow, and that what the philosophers say is much more than it is expedient for the people to look into. "These two theologies," he says, "are in complete disagreement; yet in such a way that not a few things derived from both have been taken over to form the civil theology. Accordingly, in our treatment of them, we shall indicate what each has in common with the other, and what each shares with the civil—though its major connection ought to be with the theology of the philosophers." Thus the civil theology is not wholly unconnected with that of the poets.

Nevertheless, in another place, speaking of the genealogies of the gods, Varro says that the people are more inclined toward the poets than toward the "physicians" [the "physical" theologians]. In this passage he tells us what ought to be done, in the other, what really took place. He says that the "physicians" wrote for the sake of utility, the poets for the sake of amusement. And hence the things written by the poets ought not to be followed by the people, such as the crimes of the gods; nevertheless, they amuse both the people and the gods. Is it for the sake of amusement, did he say, that the poets write, and not for that of utility? Nevertheless, they write such things as the gods request, and the people perform!

(7) It is true that the theology which is called "fabulous," i.e., theatrical, scenic, and full of all baseness and unseemliness, is incorporated in the civil theology, and so that theology which as a whole is judged worthy of reprobation and rejection becomes a part of the one which is pronounced worthy to be cultivated and practiced. It is no heterogeneous part, as I have tried to show, or one alien to the totality of the whole body, and hence only attached to or suspended from it, but a part wholly congruous with it, and therefore most harmoniously fitted into the rest, as a member of the same body.

For what else do these statues of the gods portray but their form, age, sex, and equipment? If the poets describe Jupiter with a beard and Mercury as beardless, have not the priests done the same? Is the Priapus of the priests less obscene than the Priapus of the players of mimes? Is he set up to receive the adoration of worshipers, in some sacred place, in any different form from that in which he moves about on the stage amid the roars of laughter? Is not Saturn old and Apollo young, not only as represented by actors, but also by their images in the temples? Why are Forculus, who presides over doors, and Limentinus, who presides over thresholds, male gods, while Cardea, who stands between them and presides over hinges, is feminine? Are there not details to be found in the books [by Varro] on "divine things" which serious poets have deemed unworthy of their verse? Does the Diana of the theater carry arms, while the Diana of the city is simply a young woman? Is Apollo on the stage a lyrist, while the Delphic Apollo is unfamiliar with this art?

But these things are fairly decent compared with the more shameful. What idea of Jupiter himself was in the mind of those who placed his wet nurse in the Capitol? Did they not support the view of Euhemerus, who, not with the garrulity of a fable-teller but with the diligence of a historian, maintained that all these gods had once been mortal men? And those who prepared the Epulones, as parasites at the table of Jupiter [at the feast of *Epulum Jovis*]—what else were they trying to do but mimic sacred rites [or to turn sacred rites into comedies]? For if any mime had said that parasites of Jupiter were present at his table, he would certainly have been thought to be trying to provoke a laugh. But it was Varro who said it, not when he was mocking the gods, but when he was trying to encourage respect for them. His books on "divine" things, not on "human," testify that he wrote this; and not where he was dealing with the scenic games, but where he was explaining the [sacred] rules of the Capitol. In a word, he is embarrassed, and acknowledges that, as they fashioned the gods in human form, so they believed them to be delighted with human pleasures.

Furthermore, the malicious spirits are not so slothful in their own business as not to confirm these noxious opinions in the minds of men by making sport of their intelligence. From this source comes that story about the sacristan of Hercules. Having nothing to do, he took to playing dice as a pastime, throwing them alternately with the one hand for Hercules and with the other for himself, on condition that if he won, he should from the funds of the temple provide himself a supper and hire a mistress; but if Hercules won, he would, at his own expense, provide the same entertainment for Hercules. Then, when he had been beaten by himself, as though by Hercules, he provided the god Hercules with the supper he owed him, including the courtesan Larentina. But she, having fallen asleep in the temple, dreamed that Hercules had visited her, and had told her that she would receive her payment from the first youth she should meet after leaving the temple, and that she was to consider this as paid to her by Hercules. She went away, and the first young man she met was the fabulously wealthy Tarutius, who kept her a long time as his mistress, and when he died left her as his heir. She thus obtained a vast fortune, and in order not to appear ungrateful for the present from the god, did what she thought would be most acceptable to the heavenly powers, and in her turn made the Roman people her heir. She then disappeared, but her will was found, and it was for this meritorious service, they say, that she deserves divine honors.

Now if all this had been made up by the poets or acted by the mime, one would surely say that it belonged to the theology called "fabulous" and that it ought to be separated from the dignity of the "civil" theology. But when these shameful stories are related by so great an author and assigned, not to the poets, but to the people; not to the mime, but to the "sacred" things; not to the theaters, but to the temples—that is, not to the "fabulous," but to the "civil" theology, then it is not in vain that the comedians represent in the theater such great baseness in the gods; but surely it is in vain that the priests attempt, by rites which are called sacred, to adorn the gods with a nobility of character which does not exist.

Juno has her sacred rites, which are celebrated in her beloved island of Samos, where she was given in marriage to Jupiter. Ceres has her sacred rites, in which Proserpine is sought for after being carried off by Pluto. Venus has her sacred rites, in which her beloved Adonis is lamented, a most beautiful youth who was killed by a boar's tusk. The Mother of the Gods has her sacred rites, in which the sweet youth Attis, beloved by her but also castrated by her through her woman's jealousy, is mourned by men who themselves have suffered the same misfortune, who are called the Galli. Since, then, these rites are more hideous than any scenic obscenity, why do they go to the trouble of trying to separate, if possible, the fabulous tales of the poets about the gods, as belonging to the theater, from the civil theology which they wish to assign to the city—as if they were separating what is decent and honest from what is unworthy and defiled? We ought rather to thank the comedians who have spared the eyes of men and not disclosed by displaying in the theater all the things which are hidden behind the walls of the temples.

What good can be thought of those sacred rites which are concealed in darkness, when those which are brought out into the light are so detestable? And certainly they themselves [the actors?] have seen what goes on in secret through the agency of mutilated and effeminate men. Yet they have not been able in the least to conceal these unhappy men themselves—so hideously vile, enervated, corrupt. Let our adversaries persuade whom they can that anything holy is performed by such men, who, it cannot be denied, are included among the regular personnel of their cults and are familiar with their sacred rites. What they transact we cannot know; but we know by whom it is transacted. On the other hand, we know what things are transacted on the stage where never, not even in a chorus of harlots [e.g., at the *Floralia?*], has one of these mutilated creatures or a pervert been allowed to appear, but where, nevertheless, the scenes are performed by vile and infamous characters; and in fact they ought not to be acted by men of good character. [If this is true of the stage,] what, then, are those sacred rites for the performance of which devout piety has selected such ministers as not even the obscenity of the stage can tolerate?

[Ch. 8 deals with the "physical" interpretation of the pagan cults and myths, i.e., with the view that they symbolize the processes of nature—a popular view in the Hellenistic-Roman age, especially among the Stoics.] For many have interpreted even these things in a similar way, so that even that myth which is the most monstrous and most horrible of all, Saturn devouring his own children, has been interpreted by some to mean that *length of time,* which is signified by the very name of Saturn, consumes whatever it begets; or rather, following the opinion of Varro, Saturn has some connection with *seeds,* which fall back into the earth from whence they have come. Others interpret it in other ways, and so with all the other myths. . . .

(9) What shall we say of the various offices of the gods, so meanly [*viliter*] and so minutely portioned out that each must be supplicated according to his special function? We have already said a good deal on this subject [especially in Bk. IV], though by no means all that could be said. Are these views not more consistent with the buffoonery of the mimics than with the majesty of God?

If anyone should engage two nurses for his child, one of whom was to give him nothing but food, the other nothing but drink—as they picture two goddesses thus occupied, Educa and Potina—he would certainly be thought a fool who was putting on a mime in his own house. They derive the name Liber from "liberation," because, thanks to him, males, during sexual intercourse, are "liberated" by the emission of semen. They also say that Libera, whom they identify with Venus, exercises the same function in the case of women, who they say also emit seed. And they also say that it is on this account that the parts of the male and of the female are placed in the temple, that of the male being offered to Liber, that of the female to Libera. Beyond these things they add those women who are assigned to Liber, and the wine for exciting desire. So it is that the Bacchanalia are celebrated with the utmost insanity —regarding which Varro himself admits that such things could not be done by the bacchants unless their minds were disturbed and delirious. These orgies, however, afterwards displeased a saner Senate, and it ordered them suppressed. Here then, at length, they perhaps perceived how much power unclean spirits, when held to be gods, can exercise over the minds of men. One thing is certain, these performances were not permitted in the theaters; for there they play, not rave, though to have gods who are pleased with such plays is very much like raving.

But what kind of a distinction is that which he makes between the religious man and the superstitious man, saying that the gods are *feared* by the superstitious man, but are *reverenced* as parents by the religious man, and by no means feared as enemies; and that their goodness is such that they will sooner spare the impious than injure the innocent? And yet he tells us that three gods are assigned as guardians to a woman after she has been delivered, lest the god Silvanus come in by night and annoy her; and that in order to show the presence of these protectors, three men go round the house during the night, and first strike the threshold with a hatchet, next with a pestle, and the third time sweep it with a broom, in order that, these three symbols of agriculture having been exhibited, the god Silvanus may be prevented from entering—since trees are not cut down or pruned without a hatchet, nor is grain ground without a pestle, or corn heaped up without a broom. From these three things three gods have been named: Intercidona, from the cut of the hatchet; Pilumnus, from the pestle; Deverra, from the broom. And so these are the guardian gods who protect the recently delivered woman from the violence of the god Silvanus! And so also the guardianship of good deities would not succeed against the malice of a mischievous god unless they were three to one, and opposed him with the emblems of cultivation—for, being an inhabitant of the woods, he is a rough, horrible, uncultivated deity. Is this the innocence of the gods? Is this their concord? Are these the health-giving deities of the cities, more ridiculous than the acts which rouse laughter in the theaters?

When man and woman are united, it is the god Jugatinus who presides. Well, let this be put up with. But the married woman must be brought home; enter the god Domiducus. She must be installed in the house, and here is the god Domitius. She must remain with her husband, and so the goddess Manturna is introduced. Why should we explore further? Let us have pity for human modesty! Let the lust of flesh and blood take care of the rest, the secret of shame being preserved. Why must the nuptial chamber be filled with a crowd of divinities, when even the bridal party has departed? Moreover, if it is thus filled, it is not that the thought of their presence will increase the respect for chastity, but that by their help the woman, by nature the weaker sex, and trembling with the novelty of her situation, may without difficulty surrender her virginity. For here are the goddess Virginensis, and the godfather Subigus, and the goddess-mother Prema, and the goddess Pertunda, and Venus, and Priapus. What does all this mean? If it was absolutely necessary that the man, engaged in this task, should be aided by the gods, would not some one god or goddess have sufficed? Would not Venus alone have sufficed, especially when it is said that she derives her name from the fact that without force (*vis*) a woman does not cease being a virgin? If there is any shame left in men, though it is not in the deities . . . ?

Let them go on, and let them try with every subtlety to distinguish the civil theology from the fabulous, the cities from the theaters, the temples from the stages, the sacred rites of the pontiffs from the songs of the poets, as one distinguishes decency from impurity, truth from lies, grave matters from frivolous, serious from ridiculous, things desirable from things to be rejected! We understand what they are doing. They know that the "theatrical" and "fabulous" theology depends upon the civil, and is reflected in the songs of the poets as in a mirror; not daring to condemn that theology whose contents have been exposed to view, they more freely attack and condemn the reflection of it, so that intelligent readers come to detest both the image and the original. But the gods themselves, viewing themselves in the same mirror, are so taken with it that one can thus see more clearly both who and what they are.

This is why the gods have compelled their worshipers, with terrible commands, to dedicate to them the infamies of the "fabulous" theology, to give them a place among their solemn rites, and reckon them among "divine things"; and thus they have shown themselves not only the more clearly to be most impure spirits, but they have also made that despicable and reprobate theatrical theology a part and a member of the chosen and approved theology of the city; so that, although the whole of it is shameful and false, and is peopled with imaginary gods, one part of it is to be found in the books of the priests, the other in the songs of the poets.

Whether or not there may be still other parts is another question. For the present, confining myself to the division proposed by Varro, I think I have sufficiently shown that the theology of the city and that of the theater belong to one and the same civil theology. And since both are equally disgraceful, absurd, shameful, and false, far be it from truly religious men to hope for eternal life from either the one or the other.

Finally, even Varro himself, in his enumeration and naming of the gods, begins at the moment of a man's conception, and starts with Janus; he then carries on the series of deities concerned with the details of human life to the moment when the decrepit old man dies, and he closes it with the goddess Naenia, who is sung at the funerals of the aged. After that, he passes in review the other gods, whose province is not man himself but the things he uses, such as food, clothing, and whatever is necessary for this life. In each case he explains what is the special office of the appropriate god, and for what he ought to be supplicated. But in all this scrupulous and far-reaching inquiry, he has neither pointed out nor named any god from whom eternal life is to be sought—the one purpose for which we are Christians.

Who, then, is so stupid as not to perceive that this man [Varro], by setting forth and explaining so carefully the "civil" theology, and by showing its likeness to the "fabulous" theology, so shameful and so disgraceful, and also by openly teaching that the latter is only a part of the former, was trying to find a lodging in the minds of men for none but the "natural" theology, that of the philosophers? The subtlety by which he censures the fabulous, while not daring to criticize the civil, succeeds in showing its reprehensible character by the simple process of exhibiting it. Both being thus rejected

by the judgment of the intelligence, it is the natural alone
that remains. And this, in due time, we shall discuss in more
detail, with the help of God.

[Augustine's promise is kept in Bk. VII where, following
Varro, he deals with the "chosen" gods (*electi*) or leading deities. These are twelve male gods—Janus, Jupiter, Saturn, Genius, Mercury, Apollo, Mars, Vulcan, Neptune, the Sun, Orcus,
Liber—and eight female—Tellus, Ceres, Juno, the Moon,
Diana, Minerva, Venus, Vesta. He discusses the theory that
they are symbols of supernatural realities, and continues his
polemic, showing that even on the "physical" theory none of
the gods either is able or undertakes to confer eternal life,
which is the essence of the Christian revelation. Quoting
Varro at numerous points and examining the "theological"
views regarding the various gods, one after another, he criticizes the whole theory of "chosen" deities—the choice is entirely irrational, and the reasons for it cannot be made out,
while the worshipers often maltreat their own "chosen" gods.
He also criticizes the indistinctness of their attributes, and
their claim to prerogatives which belong to other gods or to
all alike; the theory that the gods are identical with the heavenly bodies named for them; the Euhemerist theory which
made them out to be deified men—a view which Augustine
seems inclined to accept; and the efforts of Varro to defend
the theory of the *electi*. He ends Bk. VII with a discussion of
other cults than those of the Roman gods, viz., Attis and the
Great Mother, and considers the role of demons. After summarizing this book, in ch. 33, he adds an appendix in two
chapters on the discovery of the Books of Numa, as a confirmation of the views already reached. Many of these subjects
are discussed still further in later parts of *The City of God*.
It is obvious how little is left of Varro's work, and how difficult it is to reconstruct it; but this is all we have.]

THE NATURE OF THE GODS

Cicero, *The Nature of the Gods*, Bks. I–III. This was one of the
most important works in the history of ancient religious thought and
in the philosophy of religion. It marked a summation and turning
point in the perennial discussion, for Cicero recognized the difficul-

ties which educated men faced in his own time, viz., the decline of confidence in the traditional gods and in divine providence, i.e., the divine rule of the world, and at the same time a half-conscious longing for a rational and defensible belief in divine purpose. The book appeared at a point in history which marked a parting in the ways. It just preceded the Augustan restoration of the old cults, and—by a slightly longer period—the westward tide of the oriental religions. There were those for whom the solution of the problem lay in a mystical awareness of deity or an objective divine revelation; there were others for whom the frustration of their religious longings meant the renunciation of all hope of finding out the truth about these matters. Cicero stood at the last line of defense of the old religion; if this position were to be lost—as it was eventually—there was nothing to hold back the sweeping invasion of Eastern cults, astrology, magic, and theurgy. Cicero's own contribution to the scene was neither confidence nor personal conviction but merely hard-headed, rational objectivity in the presentation of rival views. If we grasp the significance of the setting of this dialogue, its bearing upon contemporary thought in the middle of the first century B.C. will become apparent at once.

Cicero's positive contribution to the discussion is his Academic "suspense of judgment." This kept him from siding with either the Stoics or the Epicureans, or even with the founder of his own school, Plato. His philosophical skepticism was checked only by his respect for the traditional—and politically indispensable—religion of Rome. He is an objective reporter and critic, though his account of the theistic views set forth in Greek philosophy, i.e., by successive philosophers, is extremely journalistic: see his accounts of Plato and Aristotle! Nevertheless, he gives the popular criticisms and the arguments of the schools in his day—or rather in his youth, when he studied philosophy at Rhodes. Many readers suspect that he followed a student's outline for much of his material. Nor was he the only writer of a book on "the nature of the gods"—the other works have perished. Yet he cleared the way, and he opened the debate which has continued down through the Middle Ages and beyond, almost to modern times. In fact, the formulation he gave to the problems is still important for the present-day philosophy of religion. The early Christian apologists made great use of this dialogue in their criticism of paganism; Minucius Felix took it as his model, and Lactantius preserved several passages which enable us to fill in some of the missing sections. Indeed, the dialogue was preserved to posterity by its inclusion in the medieval corpus of Lactantius' philosophical writings, from which the manuscripts of the Carolingian period were derived.

The book was written in the summer of 45 B.C., and was published soon after his other philosophical works, the *Tusculan Disputations* and the *Academics;* it was followed by one *On Fate* (of which only fragments survive) and one *On Divination. The Nature of the Gods* was never entirely finished; there are also several serious lacunae in the text (see below). Cicero's philosophical writing had a twofold object: to provide solace for his own mind after his forced retirement from public life and especially after the death of his beloved daughter Tullia, and to acquaint his fellow citizens with the best of Greek thought translated and interpreted in their own Latin tongue. His method was that of the popularizer; he used summaries and anthologies and histories as well as the works of the earlier philosophers (see his *Letters to Atticus,* XIII. 8, June, 45 B.C., asking him to send "Brutus' epitome of the works of Caelius"; other references in H. Rackham's edition of *The Nature of the Gods* in LCL, p. xiii).

The arrangement of the dialogue is simple. Gaius Aurelius Cotta and his friends have gathered at his villa during the Latin Festival in the summer of the year 76 B.C. They are Gaius Velleius, the leading Roman expert in Epicureanism, Quintus Lucilius Balbus, the eminent Stoic, and Gaius Cotta, the host, an acute and eminent exponent of the New Academy. Cicero is present, an Academic and an eclectic, but appearing here chiefly as the reporter of the discussion. Following an introduction which states the importance and difficulty of the subject, Velleius sets forth the main principles of Epicurean teaching on the existence and nature of the gods (§§ 18–56). This consists of an attack on the theology of Plato and the Stoics, followed by a refutation of the theology of all the other schools from Thales of Miletus down. Here Cicero gives us a brief conspectus of the various schools as seen from the Epicurean point of view. The remainder of Bk. I is the reply made by Cotta the Academic, who completely demolishes Epicurean theology and shows that philosophy to be wholly destructive of religion (§§ 57–124). Bk. II sets forth in detail the positive teachings of the Stoic theology as expounded by Balbus under four main headings: (1) the existence of the gods, proved by many arguments (§§ 4–44); (2) their nature (§§ 45–72); (3) their providential government of the world (§§ 73–153); and (4) their providential care for man (§§ 154–168). As contrasted with the Epicurean critique in Bk. I, the great positive affirmations of Stoic "natural theology," which were destined to influence all later European religious thought, are written out with loving care and deep enthusiasm, even though Cicero, as an Academic, can never bring himself wholly to accept them.

Bk. III contains Cotta's criticism, from the Academic point of view, of Balbus' exposition of Stoicism, following the same four headings, but concluding with a note of regret that the Academic position is not in turn to be refuted. Obviously, Cicero's head is with the Academy but his heart with the Stoa. Following a dramatic introduction, the division of Bk. III is as follows: (1) §§ 7–19, with a serious lacuna between 13 and 14; (2) §§ 20–64, with a possible dislocation of §§ 43–52 and 53–60, which some editors reverse; but there is something missing from the text, especially at the beginning of § 61; (3) § 65, all that is left of what must have been a fairly long division in the book; some passages may be recovered from quotations made by Lactantius; (4) §§ 66–95. Since our oldest manuscripts of the work are from the ninth century, and all go back to one archetype with all its errors, transpositions, and omissions, it is clear that conjectural emendation must sometimes be resorted to, at least as a tentative solution of our difficulties, until, by some lucky discovery, a few far earlier manuscripts turn up. See the Commentary in three volumes by J. B. Mayor (1885); text and translation in LCL by H. Rackham (1930); text and French translation in Classiques Garnier by Charles Appuhn; and the exhaustive and most valuable Commentary by A. S. Pease (1955 ff.).

BOOK ONE

As you, Brutus, are well aware, there are many things in philosophy which have not yet been satisfactorily explained, particularly that most obscure and most difficult question concerning the nature of the gods, which is so extremely important both for a knowledge of the human mind [or soul] and also for the regulation of religion. Concerning this the opinions of even the most learned men are so various and so divergent as to lend strong support to the inference that the source and origin of philosophy is ignorance; and that the Academic philosophers have been wise in "withholding assent" to beliefs that are uncertain: for what is more unbecoming in a wise man than rash judgment! And what is more rash or more unbecoming the gravity and constancy of a philosopher than either to maintain an opinion that is false, or to defend without any hesitation what has not been thoroughly examined and understood?

(2) As for the question now before us, the majority of thinkers have affirmed—what is most probable, and what we are all led by nature to suppose—namely, that the gods exist. But

Protagoras doubted whether there were any, while Diagoras of Melos and Theodorus of Cyrene held that there are none whatsoever. Moreover, those who have affirmed that there are gods have expressed such a variety of views, and with such great disagreement, that it would be wearisome to list their opinions. There are many different views about the outward form of the gods, and about their location and dwelling places, and about their way of life; these are subjects about which the philosophers debate most earnestly. But the main point of the debate, viz., whether the gods are wholly idle and inactive, being unconcerned with the care and administration of the world, or whether, on the contrary, all things were both created and constituted by them from the beginning, and are controlled and kept in motion by them throughout infinite time—this is the most hotly disputed point of all. And until this question is decided, mankind must of necessity continue to wander in the greatest uncertainty, and remain ignorant of the most important things of all.

(3) For there both are and have been some philosophers who have held that the gods exercise not the least control over human affairs. But if their view is the true one, how can piety, sanctity, or religion exist?—for these are the tribute which is to be offered to the power of the gods, in purity and holiness, on the sole ground that they take some notice of it, and that some benefit has been conferred upon the human race by the immortal gods. But if, on the contrary, the gods have neither the power nor the will to help us; if they pay no attention whatsoever to us, and take no notice of our actions; and if there is no way in which they can possibly influence the life of men—then what reason is there for offering them either worship, honors, or prayers? But piety, like the other virtues, cannot exist in empty show or pretense; and if piety goes, both sanctity and religion will also disappear: and when these have gone, disturbance of life and great confusion must follow. (4) In fact, if piety toward the gods disappears, I am not sure that good faith as well, and the unity of human society, and

even justice, that most excellent of all the virtues, will not likewise disappear.

There are, however, other philosophers, men of very great eminence and nobility, who believe that the whole world is ruled and governed by the will and wisdom of the gods; and not only this, but they likewise conceive that the gods consult and provide for the preservation of mankind. For they think that the fruits and other products of the earth, and the seasons and the variety in the weather and the change in climates by which whatever the soil produces is brought to maturity and ripened, are contributed by the immortal gods to the human race. They cite many other things, which will be related in the following books, which are of such a nature as almost to make us believe the immortal gods created them for the use of men. Against these opinions Carneades has argued at such great length that his words should arouse in men who are not too slothful a desire to search for the truth. (5) There is no subject upon which both the learned and the unlearned differ so greatly as this; and since their views are so diverse, and so diametrically opposed, it is clear that, while perhaps none of them may be true, it is absolutely impossible that more than one should be true. [Cf. the conclusion of the *Academics*, II. 147.]

Now in a case like this, I may be able to pacify well-meaning critics and to confute invidious fault-finders, so as to lead the latter to repent of their unreasonable censures, and the former to be glad to learn; for those who admonish one in a friendly spirit should be instructed, those who attack one like enemies should be repelled. [Mayor shifts this sentence to follow the next paragraph.]

(6) I observe that the number of books which I have recently published has occasioned a good deal of talk, somewhat varied in its tone and temper; some people have wondered what is the reason why I have applied myself so suddenly to the study of philosophy, others have wished to know what positive views I can hold on such subjects. Still others, I no-

tice, wonder at my choice of a philosophy which seems to them to blot out the light and flood the world with the darkness of night; and they wonder why I should have turned to defend a school that has long been deserted and forsaken. [Cf. *Academics*, II. 65–71.]

But it is a mistake to assume that my devotion to philosophical studies is something recent or suddenly begun. I have applied myself to them from early youth, devoting to them no small amount of time and attention; and I have been in the habit of philosophizing the more diligently when I seemed least to be thinking about it—witness my orations, which are filled with quotations from philosophers, and also my intimacy with those learned men who have always frequented my house, chiefly Diodotus, Philo, Antiochus, and Posidonius, who were my teachers. (7) Further, if all the teachings of philosophy have reference to the conduct of life, I think I may say that, both publicly and privately, I have consistently practiced such principles as are established by reason and sound teaching. And if anyone should ask what has induced me at this late date to write upon these subjects, nothing is more easily explained. For when I discovered myself languishing in idleness, and public affairs reduced to such a state that it was inevitable the commonwealth would be governed by the counsel and foresight of one man, I thought it my duty, in the interest of the nation, to instruct my countrymen in philosophy; for it seemed to me that it would contribute to the honor and glory of our City to have such important and brilliant ideas set forth in the Latin tongue. (8) I am the less repentant of my undertaking, now that I can plainly see how many of my readers have been moved not only to study but to write on the subject. There have been a good many Romans, thoroughly familiar with the learning of the Greeks, but unable to communicate to their countrymen what they had learned for the reason that it seemed impossible to express in Latin what they had received from the Greeks. On this point I think we have now progressed so far that even in adequacy of diction the Greeks do not outdo us.

(9) Still another inducement to these studies was the depression of spirit which resulted from the hard and crushing blow which Fortune dealt me [the death of his daughter Tullia in 45 B.C.]. If I had been able to find any better remedy, I would not have sought relief in this particular way; but I could not find it in any other way than by not only devoting myself to the reading of books but also making an examination of the whole range of philosophy. And the best way to grasp the subject as a whole and in all its branches is to set forth all of its questions in writing. For there is really a remarkable continuity and sequence of things, so that each [part of a system] is seen to be connected with the rest, and all of them are linked together and united.

(10) Now those who desire to know my own private opinion on these various subjects have more curiosity than is necessary. For in philosophic discussions it is not so much authority as the force of argument that should be looked for. In fact, the authority of the teacher is often a handicap to those who desire to learn; for they cease to use their own judgment, and accept as a reason what they receive from their chosen teacher. Nor could I ever approve the custom attributed to the Pythagoreans, who, whenever they affirmed anything in disputation and were asked by their opponents why it should be so, used to reply, "He himself has said it" [*Ipse dixit*]—"he himself" being Pythagoras. So powerful was an opinion which was already decided that authority prevailed even without the support of reason.

(11) Again, those who wonder at my being a follower of this particular system [the Academic] will find a sufficient answer in the four books of my *Academica*. But I deny that I have undertaken the defense of a school that is neglected and forsaken. For the opinions of men do not die with them, though they may perhaps suffer from the lack of the author's own expositions. Take the example of this very principle of philosophy, viz., of disputing every statement and refusing to make any private judgment: the method was begun by Socrates, revived by Arcesilas, confirmed by Carneades, and has flourished

vigorously down to the present age—though I am told that it is now almost wholly abandoned in Greece itself, a situation which I do not ascribe to any fault in the Academy but to the dullness of the human mind. If it is a difficult task to master all the doctrines of any one system of philosophy, how much more difficult is it to comprehend those of them all! Yet this is necessarily the task confronting those who set out to discover the truth by arguing both for and against all the various schools. (12) In an undertaking as vast and as difficult as this, I do not claim to have achieved success; but I do claim to have made the attempt.

It is, of course, impossible that those who adopt this method of pursuing philosophy should abandon all standards or principles to be followed. I have dealt more fully with this matter in another place. [In the *Tusculan Disputations* or the *Academics?*] But as some readers are too slow in apprehension, and some too dull, they seem to need frequent explanations. For it is not correct to say that we do not believe anything whatever to be true; but we say that all true sensations are so combined with false ones, which clearly resemble them, that there is no absolute mark or sign to guide our judgment and justify our assent. From this follows the maxim that many things are probable which, though not evident to the senses, are still so distinct and clear that a wise man can use them for his guides in life. [Yet see *Academics,* II. 46.]

(13) Now, in order to free myself from the charge of narrowness, I propose to set forth the teachings of various philosophers concerning *the nature of the Gods*. By considering them all, it may be judged which of them are to be considered true. And if it happens that all agree, or that some one philosopher can be found who has discovered what is really true [cf. § 5], then at long last I will give up the Academy as hypercritical. Thus I can cry out, in the words of [Statius in his] *Young Comrades,*

Ye gods, and all ye people, young and old, I call upon you,
I beg you, pray you, ask you,
I entreat you and implore you, one and all!

Yet it is not on some trifling matter, as when the person in the play complains,

> In this city has been found a most flagrant iniquity—
> A courtesan who will take no money from her lover!

(14) Instead, our summons is to attend the court session, try the case, and render a verdict as to what views ought to be held regarding religion, piety, sanctity, ceremonies; about fidelity and oaths; about temples, shrines, and solemn sacrifices; and even about the auspices, over which I myself preside [as augur, 53 B.C.]; for all these subjects are related to the present question, viz., the nature of the immortal gods. Certainly the wide divergence of views found among the most learned men on a subject of such importance must create doubts even in the minds of those who imagine they possess positive knowledge about it.

(15) This is something which has often impressed me at other times, but it did so more especially once during a careful and searching discussion about the immortal gods that was held at the home of my friend Gaius Cotta. It was during the Latin Festival [probably in early summer], when at his invitation and request I paid him a visit. I found him sitting in an alcove, engaged in a discussion with Gaius Velleius the senator, who was then looked upon by the Epicureans as their ablest representative among our countrymen. Quintus Lucilius Balbus also was there, so great an expert in the doctrine of the Stoics that he was thought to be equal to the most eminent Greek expounders of that system.

As soon as Cotta saw me he said, "You have come just at the right time!—for I am having an argument with Velleius on a very important subject, one in which, considering the nature of your studies, you will surely be interested."

(16) "Indeed," I replied, "I too think I have come at the right moment, as you say; for here you are—the three leaders of the three chief schools of philosophy meeting together! If Marcus Piso [the Peripatetic] were only present, no really important school of philosophy would fail to be represented."

"But," answered Cotta, "if Antiochus' book, which he recently sent to our friend Balbus, is correct, you have no need to regret the absence of your friend Piso. For Antiochus holds that the Stoics do not really differ in substance from the Peripatetics, but only in words. I should like to know what you think of that book, Balbus."

"What I think?" he replied. "I am surprised that Antiochus, a man of the sharpest intellect, should not have seen what a vast difference there is between the Stoics, who distinguish what is honest from what is expedient, not only in name but in essential nature, and the Peripatetics, who combine the honest with the expedient in such a way that they differ only in quantity and degree, not in kind. This is not some slight difference in words, but a great difference between the things themselves! (17) However, we can discuss this subject some other time. Now, if you please, let us go back to the one we had already begun."

"By all means," said Cotta. "But to let our guest, who has just arrived" (here he looked at me), "know what we are talking about, I will explain that we were discussing the nature of the gods, a subject which seemed to me—and always seems—extremely obscure; and so I was asking Velleius to give us the views of Epicurus. And so," he continued, "if you don't mind, Velleius, please resume what you began telling us."

"Very well, I will do so," said he, "though our guest will be no ally on my side, I fear, but on yours; for both of you," he added with a smile, "were taught by the same Philo to know nothing as certain."

"What we have learned," I replied, "Cotta will show; but please do not think I have come as an ally of his, but only as a listener, one with an impartial and unbiased mind, and not under obligation to defend any particular principle, whether I like it or not."

(18) At this Velleius began, with the confidence which is characteristic of his school, afraid of nothing so much as of seeming to have any doubts on any subject. One might have thought he had just come down from the council of the gods,

and from Epicurus' intermundane spaces! "You are not going to hear," said he, "any doctrines of the futile and fictitious kind—as about that artisan and builder of the world, the God of Plato's *Timaeus;* nor that old fortune-telling grandam, the *Pronoia* of the Stoics, which in Latin we may call Providence; nor about that spherical, burning, rotary deity, the World, possessing a mind and senses of its own: all these are the prodigies and monstrosities, not of articulate philosophers, but of dreamers!

(19) "For with what eyes of the mind was your Plato able to recognize that factory of such enormous operation, in which he makes out the world to be constructed and erected by God? What skill, what tools, what bars, what machines, what workmen were employed on so vast a work? How could the air, fire, water, and earth obey and carry out the will of the architect? From whence arose those five regular solids [pyramid, cube, octahedron, dodecahedron, eicosihedron, the forms of the basic particles of fire, earth, air, ether, and water], of which all the rest were composed, so aptly designed to impress the mind and produce sensations? It would be tedious to go through them all, as they are of such a sort that they look more like things desired [i.e., dreamed or thought up] than discovered [i.e., through scientific research]. (20) But what is most remarkable is that he gives us a world which not only has been created—one might almost say has been built by hand —but which he says is to be eternal. Can you suppose anyone to have the least skill in natural philosophy if he is capable of thinking that anything which has had a beginning will be everlasting? For what possible combination of things is incapable of separation again? Or what is there that has had a beginning but will never have an end?

"As for your [Stoic] Providence, Lucilius, if it is the same as Plato's God, then I ask you the same questions I have just asked [Cotta]: Who were the assistants, what were the engines, what was the plan of the whole work, and how was it carried out? If, however, it is not the same, then why did she [Pronoia] make the world mortal, and not everlasting as Plato's God did?

(21) "But I would ask this question of you both: Why did these world-builders start all of a sudden, after lying dormant for countless ages? For we cannot assume that, although there was no world, there were therefore no ages. (I do not mean such ages as are measured by a certain number of days and nights in their annual courses; for I acknowledge that these could not exist apart from the revolution of the universe; but there was a certain eternity from the infinite past, not measured by any divisions of seasons but to be thought of in terms of space—for it is simply inconceivable that there was never a time when time did not exist!) (22) What I therefore desire to know, Balbus, is why this Providence of yours was idle for such an immense space of time? Was she escaping hard work? But that could scarcely appeal to the deity; nor could there be any toil, since all nature, the sky [air], fire, earth, and sea [water], obey the divine will. Moreover, what was it that inspired the deity to act like an aedile and decorate the world with signs and luminaries? If it was in order to adorn his own dwelling, then he must previously have been living for an infinite time in darkness as in a dismal hovel! And are we to imagine that therefore he was delighted with all this variety with which we see heaven and earth adorned? How could these things possibly please a god? If they did, how could he have gone without them for so long?

(23) "Or, as you commonly assert, were these things designed by God for the sake of men? Was it for the wise? If so, then this great effort was undertaken for the sake of a very few! Or was it for the sake of fools? First of all, there was no reason why God should do anything to benefit the wicked; and further, what good did he accomplish?—since all fools are, without any doubt, the most miserable of men, primarily because they *are* fools. (For what can we name more miserable than folly?) And, moreover, there are many inconveniences in life which the wise can learn to treat lightly by thinking more about the advantages they enjoy, but which fools can neither avoid when they see them coming nor endure when they arrive.

"On the other hand, those who affirm the world itself to be an animate, intelligent being have by no means discovered the nature of the mind, nor are they able to conceive in what form that essence can exist. Of this I shall say more later; (24) at present, I only express my surprise at the stupidity of those who hold that a being who is both animate and immortal, and also blessed, should be spherical in shape, simply because Plato says that this is the most beautiful form. For my part, I think either a cylinder, a cube, a cone, or a pyramid is more beautiful. Further, what mode of existence do they attribute to their spherical deity? Why, it is spinning, with a swiftness beyond anything one can conceive! But what opportunity this affords for a steadfast mind or for a life of blessedness, I fail to see.

"Furthermore, how can a condition which is painful to the human body, if even the smallest part of it is affected, be thought painless to the deity? For the earth itself, since it is a part of the world, is therefore also a part of the deity. Yet we see vast tracts of land which are barren and uninhabitable; some, because they are scorched by their nearness to the sun; others, because they are frost-bound and snow-covered, because of the sun's great distance from them. Therefore, if the world is God and these are parts of the world, it must be said that some of the deity's limbs are scorched, others frozen.

(25) "So much, Lucilius, for the doctrines of your [Stoic] school. To see what the other schools are like, I will trace their history from the earliest beginnings. Thales of Miletus, who was the first to inquire into such subjects, said that water is the first principle of things; and that God was the mind which had formed all things out of water—assuming that gods can exist without sensation. But if the mind can exist without a body, why did he join a mind to water?

"It was Anaximander's belief that the gods [are not eternal but] are born, rising and falling at great intervals of time; and that there are innumerable worlds [stars?]. But how can we conceive of a god who is not eternal?

(26) "Anaximenes, after him, taught that the air is God; and that it has a beginning, and is immeasurable, infinite, and

always in motion. As if air, which has no form whatsoever, could possibly be a god!—especially when it is proper for the deity not only to have some form or other, but the most beautiful form. Or as if whatever has had a beginning must not be subject to mortality!

"Anaxagoras, who derived his views from Anaximenes, was the first to affirm that the orderly system and arrangement of the universe is designed and perfected by the power and reason of an infinite mind. However, he failed to see that in the infinite there can be no continuous motion or union with the senses, nor can there be any sensation whatsoever where the nature itself is incapable of receiving any such impulse. Further, if he viewed this mind as a kind of living creature, then it must have some internal principle of vitality to justify its description as 'living.' But mind itself is that inner principle [lit., what can be more internal than the mind?]. Mind therefore must be clothed with an external body! (27) But this he will not admit. Yet the idea of a mind, bare and simple, without anything attached to it by which it can receive sensations, wholly escapes our powers of understanding.

"Alcmaeon of Croton, who attributed divinity to the sun, the moon, and the other heavenly bodies, and also to the mind, did not realize that he was ascribing immortality to things that are mortal.

"Pythagoras, who supposed the universe to be penetrated and permeated by one soul, from which our souls are taken, did not consider that the deity himself must, in consequence, be maimed and torn by the rending of human souls from it; nor that when the human mind is miserable (as is often the case) then that part of the deity must likewise be miserable; which simply cannot be! (28) Again, how can the human mind be ignorant of anything if it is a god? Besides, how could this deity, if it is nothing but soul, be mixed with, or infused into, the world?

"Next, Xenophanes, who [also] credited the universe with mind, held that, since it [the universe or mind?] is infinite, it is therefore God. But his view of mind is as reprehensible as that of the others, while on the subject of infinity it must be even more vehemently rejected, since the infinite can have no sensation or contact with anything outside itself.

"Parmenides formed a picture of something round like a crown (he called it *Stephanē*), a continuous ring of blazing lights encircling the heavens; this he named God. But no one would suspect this to possess either divine form, or sensation. He also got off many other absurdities, as when he deified war, discord, lust, and other passions of the same kind, things which are destroyed by disease, or sleep, or forgetfulness, or age. He also deified the stars; but this view having been already criticized in another philosopher [§ 27], it may be omitted here.

(29) "Empedocles likewise, who erred in many things, is most grossly mistaken in his view of the gods. He assigns divinity to the four 'natures' [elements] from which he thinks all things have been made; yet it is obvious that they both have a beginning and pass into extinction, and also that they are wholly lacking in sensation.

"Protagoras denied that he had any clear ideas about the nature of the gods, whether they exist or not, or what they are like.

"And what shall I say of Democritus? At one time he identifies as gods their roving 'images,' at another the substance from which these 'images' are projected, and at still another human knowledge and intelligence [which perceives the images]—in what a tangled maze of error he himself was wandering! And because nothing ever continues in the same condition, he denies that anything can be everlasting; does he not thereby so completely rule out the deity that it is impossible even to form any conception of him?

"And what about Diogenes of Apollonia, who looks upon the air as a deity? But how can air have any sensations? Or what divine form can it possess?

(30) "It would be tedious to describe the inconsistencies of Plato. In the *Timaeus* [28c] he denies the possibility of naming the father of the universe; and in his books of *Laws* [VII.

821] he does not approve any inquiry whatsoever into the nature of the deity. Again, he asserts that God is completely incorporeal (*asōmatos,* as the Greeks say, i.e., 'without a body'), something which it is certainly impossible to conceive, for an incorporeal god would necessarily be incapable of sensation and would also lack prudence and be incapable of pleasure, all of which are essential to our conception of the gods. In both the *Timaeus* and the *Laws* he states that the world, the heavens, the stars, the earth, and souls are divine, in addition to those gods in whom we believe by tradition from our ancestors. But these views, when taken separately, are clearly false; and when taken together, are violently opposed to one another.

(31) "Xenophon likewise committed almost the same mistakes, but in fewer words. In those sayings which he has related of Socrates [in the *Memorabilia*], he represents him as denying the propriety of inquiry into the form of the deity; but at the same time he makes him assert that the sun and the soul are deities, and represents him as speaking at one time of a single God and at another time of several. These are errors of almost the same kind as those which we quoted from Plato.

(32) "Antisthenes also, in his book called *The Natural Philosopher,* says that while there are many gods according to popular belief, there is by nature only one—a view which robs the gods of their power and also of their nature. Similarly Speusippus, following his uncle Plato and saying that a certain power governs all things, and that it is alive, virtually tries to root out of our minds all knowledge of the gods.

(33) "Aristotle, in Book III of his *Philosophy* [now lost], has many confused ideas, in this [not ?] disagreeing with his master Plato. At one time he attributes all divinity to the intellect, at another he asserts that the world itself is a god. Presently he sets some other being to preside over the world, and assigns to it the capacity to regulate and sustain the world's motion by means of certain revolutions, forward or backward. Then he asserts that the celestial heat [the ether, in the highest sphere] is God—not reflecting that the heavens are a part of

the world, which in another place he had described as God. How can that divine consciousness which he ascribes to the heavens be preserved along with such rapid motion? And where, moreover, do the great multitude of the gods dwell, if heaven itself is a deity? Further, when he says that God is without a body he deprives him of both sensation and wisdom. Besides, how can the world move [itself] if it lacks a body? Or how, if it is in perpetual self-motion, can it enjoy tranquillity and bliss?

(34) "Xenocrates, his fellow pupil, does not appear much wiser on this subject; for in his work *On the Nature of the Gods* no divine form is described, though he says there are eight of them. Five are the moving planets; the sixth consists of all the fixed stars which, though dispersed, are so many separate members of a single deity; the seventh is the sun, the eighth the moon. But in what sense it is possible for them to be happy, it is impossible to conceive.

"From the same school of Plato, Heraclides of Pontus stuffed his books with childish fables. Sometimes he thinks the world divine, at other times the mind. He also attributes divinity to the wandering stars [the planets], he deprives the deity of sensation, and makes his form mutable; and again, in the same work, he views earth and heaven as gods.

(35) "The inconsistency of Theophrastus is equally unbearable. At one time he attributes a divine prerogative to the mind, at another to the heavens, at another to the stars and constellations.

"Nor is his disciple Strato, who is called the Naturalist, worthy of a hearing; for he thinks that the divine power is entirely diffused throughout nature, which contains in itself the causes of birth, growth, and decline; but that it is entirely lacking in sensation and form.

(36) "Zeno—to come at last to your school, Balbus—thinks that the law of nature is divine, and that it has the power to order us to do what is right, and to restrain us from the opposite. But how this law can be an animate being I cannot conceive; but that is certainly what we expect a god to be! The

same person says, in another place, that the ether is God; but can we possibly conceive that God is a being insensible, one who never draws near to us in our prayers, our petitions, our vows? And in other books he sets forth the view that there is a kind of rational essence [*ratio,* Gk. *logos*] pervading all nature, and endowed with divine power. He also attributes the same power to the stars, then to the years, to the months, and to the seasons. In his interpretation of Hesiod's *Theogony,* i.e., 'The Origins of the Gods,' he entirely does away with the customary and accepted ideas of the gods; for he excludes even Jupiter, Juno, and Vesta, and every one having a personal name, from among them, and holds that these are only names which have been assigned by a kind of poetic allusion to mute, inanimate things.

(37) "His disciple Aristo held equally erroneous views. He thought it impossible to conceive the form of the deity, and refused to allow the gods sensation; in fact, he was entirely uncertain whether God is a living being or not.

"Cleanthes, who was a student of Zeno's at the same time as Aristo, at one time says that the world itself is God; at another, he bestows the title on the mind and soul of universal nature; then again he asserts that the most remote, the highest, the all-surrounding, the all-enclosing and embracing fire, which is called the ether, is most certainly the deity. In those books which he wrote against pleasure [i.e., against Hedonism], in which he seems to be out of his mind, he imagines the gods to have a certain form and shape; then he ascribes all divinity to the stars; finally, he pronounces that nothing can be more divine than reason. Thus the God whom we know mentally and try to match with a [speculative] idea, as if tracing a footprint, has simply and completely vanished!

(38) "Persaeus, another pupil of Zeno, says that those who have made some discovery advantageous to human life have been esteemed as gods; and that the things which are useful and healthful have themselves received divine names—he does not say that it was the gods who invented them, but that the

things themselves are divine. What could be more absurd than to ascribe divine honors to things sordid and deformed? Or to rank among the gods men who are dead and gone, whose entire cultus could be nothing but lamentation?

(39) "Chrysippus, who is looked upon as the most skillful interpreter of the dreams of the Stoics, has mustered a great crowd of unknown deities—so completely unknown that we are not able to form any conjectural idea about them, even though our mind seems capable enough of framing some image or other of its thoughts. For he says that the divine power resides in reason, and in the soul and mind of universal nature; that the world itself is God, and that its universally diffused soul [the world-soul], or the guiding principle of this soul, which acts through mind and reason, or the common, universal, all-embracing nature of things, or the power of Fate and the Necessity which controls future events, or that celestial fire which I have called the ether, or those elements which naturally flow from it, and pervade all things, such as water, earth, and air, the sun, moon, and stars, and the total unity of things which embraces the whole universe—and even those men who have achieved immortality [—all these are divine].

(40) "He also maintains that the god men call Jupiter is the ether, that Neptune is the air which surrounds [*manaret*] the sea, and that the goddess called Ceres is the earth. In the same way he deals with the names of the other gods. He also says that Jupiter is the universal and eternal power of law, which is our guide in life and our teacher of duty—but at the same time he calls it Necessity or Fate, and the everlasting truth [or certainty] of coming events—none of which is of such a nature as to imply any inherent divine power. (41) These are the doctrines set forth in Book I of his *Nature of the Gods*. In Book II he tries to reconcile the myths of Orpheus, Musaeus, Hesiod, and Homer with the views he has advanced about the immortal gods in Book I, in order to make it appear that even the most ancient poets, who never dreamed of such things, were really Stoics. Diogenes the Babylonian was his fol-

lower, and in the book which he wrote, entitled *Minerva*, he
rationalized the myth of Jupiter's parturition, and the birth of
that virgin goddess, as an allegory of nature's processes.

(42) "Thus far I have been expounding the dreams of madmen rather than the considered judgments of philosophers.
They are almost as absurd as the effusions of the poets, which
are all the more harmful because of the beauty of their style.
For the poets have represented the gods as inflamed with anger
and mad with lust; they have pictured to us their wars and
battles, their combats and their wounds; their hatreds, dissen-
sions, and quarrels; their births and their deaths; their complaints and their lamentations; their unrestrained indulgence
in every kind of intemperance; their adulteries; their prison
chains; their amorous adventures with human beings, and the
birth of mortals from immortal parents. (43) Along with these
delusions of the poets we may class the portents of the Magi
and of the Egyptians, which belong to the same type of insanity, and also the wild notions of the populace, which are completely inconsistent and are derived from total ignorance of
the truth.

"Now anyone who considers the rashness and absurdity of
these views ought to venerate Epicurus, and rank him among
those divine beings who are the subject of this inquiry. For
(*a*) he alone recognized, first, that the gods exist, since *nature
itself has left an impression* of the idea [of God] upon the
mind of every human being. For what nation or what race of
men is there which does not, even without any instruction,
possess a natural idea [lit., "a kind of anticipation," i.e., pre-
conception] of the gods? Epicurus calls this a *prolēpsis,* i.e., a
kind of antecedent conception or mental picture of a thing,
without which nothing can be understood, investigated, or
discussed. The logical force and usefulness of this argument
we learn from that volume of the divine Epicurus, *Concerning
Rules and Judgment* [i.e., *Logic,* or *The Critique of Judgment*].

(44) "Thus you see that the foundation of this inquiry has
been carefully laid. For it is not something established by au-

thority, either by custom or by law, but [something] which rests upon the firm and unanimous conviction of all mankind, viz., that it is necessary to assume the existence of the gods. For we possess an implanted, or rather an innate, knowledge of them and a belief in which all men by nature agree must of necessity be true. Therefore it must be acknowledged that the gods exist. And since this inference is accepted by almost all men, not only among the philosophers but also among the unlearned, we must also recognize it to be a fact that we really do possess an 'anticipation' or, as I said before, a 'preconception' of the gods. (For we have to use new terms for new ideas, as Epicurus himself did when he used the word *prolēpsis* in a sense never used before.) (45) We therefore possess such a 'preconception' [or "prior notion"] of the gods that we assume (b) that they are *blessed and immortal*. For nature, in providing us with the idea of gods, also enforced upon our minds the belief that they are eternal and blessed [i.e., this belongs to the very concept of a god]. If so, what Epicurus has declared in his famous saying is true: 'That which is blessed and eternal cannot itself know trouble, nor can it cause trouble to another, nor can it feel either resentment or favor [or personal affection], since all such things belong only to the weak.' [Cf. Diogenes Laertius, X. 139 for the Greek text.]

"If we were seeking only to worship the gods in piety, and to be freed from superstition, what has been said so far would be enough. For the exalted nature of the gods would receive men's pious adoration, since it is both eternal and supremely blessed (for whatever excels has a right to veneration); moreover, all fear of the power and anger of the gods would be banished (for it must be understood that anger and favor alike are inconsistent with the nature of a blessed and immortal being); once these apprehensions are removed, no dread of the powers above remains hanging over us. But the mind tries to go beyond this, and to confirm the view by discovering the form, the mode of life, and the mental activity of the deity.

(46) "As for *the divine form*, (c) we are guided partly by nature and partly by reason. From nature all mankind in

every race receives the [inborn] notion that the gods possess none but a human shape. For under what other form do they ever appear to anyone, either waking or sleeping? But even without relying solely upon our primary notions, reason itself makes the same declaration. (47) For it is proper to conceive that the nature which is the most exalted, whether because of its beatitude or its eternity, should also be the most beautiful; and what arrangement of limbs, what cast of features, what shape or aspect can be more beautiful than the human form? You Stoics, Lucilius (unlike my friend Cotta, who sometimes says one thing and sometimes another), when you describe the divine art and skill are always pointing to the human body, how everything about it is not only designed for use but also for beauty. (48) Therefore, since the human figure excels that of all other living beings, and since God is a living being, he must surely possess that form which is the most beautiful of all. And since the gods, it is agreed, are supremely happy, and since one cannot be happy without virtue, and since virtue cannot exist without reason, and since reason is found only in the human form, it follows that the gods must possess human form. (49) Yet that form is not corporeal, but something like a body; it does not contain blood, but something like blood.

"These discoveries are in themselves too acute and were too subtly expressed by Epicurus for the ordinary person to grasp; but I am relying on your intelligence and understanding, and I shall be somewhat briefer than the subject deserves. Epicurus, then, who not only sees with his mind things occult and almost hidden but handles them with ease, teaches first of all that the power and nature of the gods is not perceived by the senses, but by the mind. They are not to be considered as having any solidity or specific number, like those things which because of their firmness he calls *steremnia*. Instead, it is by means of 'images,' which we recognize by their similarity and constant succession—for an endless series of identical images are given off by innumerable atoms and flow toward the gods [they also flow from the gods: cf. § 114]—that our mind is centered intently and steadily and with the greatest pleasure upon them, and so arrives at an understanding of the nature which is both blessed and eternal.

(50) "Another principle of supreme importance is the power of infinity, one which deserves the most careful and diligent study. The nature of infinity is such that in the universe as a whole everything has its exact counterpart, to which it corresponds. This is called by Epicurus the principle of *isonomia,* that is, of equal distribution. From this he inferred that, since there is a specific number of mortals, there must also be no less a number of immortals; and if those that perish are innumerable, then those that survive must also be of infinite number. . . .

"But you Stoics, Balbus, are also forever asking us about (d) the *mode of life of the gods,* and how they pass their time. (51) Their life is such that nothing more blessed, or better provided with all good things, can possibly be conceived. A god does nothing. He is not burdened with any occupation, nor does he engage in any kind of work. He rejoices in his own wisdom and virtue. He knows for a certainty that he will always enjoy pleasures which are as complete as they are eternal. (52) Such a god may properly be called blessed; but your [Stoic] god is a most laborious one! For let us suppose that the world itself is God: what could be a less restful state than, with never the tiniest moment's intermission, to whirl about the celestial axis with unbelievable speed? But nothing can be blessed if it lacks peace and quiet. Or let us suppose the deity resides inside the world, governing and directing it like a pilot, controlling the courses of the stars, the changes of the seasons, and all the vicissitudes and sequences of things [in nature], keeping his eye on earth and sea in order to safeguard the interests and the lives of men—would you not say he was heavily burdened with toil and trouble? (53) For our part, we assume a blessed life to consist in tranquillity of mind and complete freedom from obligation. The one who taught us everything else also taught is that *the world was made by nature;* that there was no need for a factory in which to build it;

and that, though you insist that such a work can be done only by divine skill, it is so easy a task that nature has already made, is now making, and will continue to make worlds innumerable. You, on the other hand, do not see how nature is able to produce all this without the aid of some intelligence, and so, like the tragic poets, you are forced—since you cannot wind up your argument in any other way—to have recourse to a god, (54) whose assistance you would not require if you would only view the vast and boundless extent of space which stretches off in all directions, where the mind, projecting and propelling itself, travels onward far and wide without finding any end, any point at which to stop. [Cf. Lucretius, *De rerum natura*, I. 958–1113. This is the answer to the third question at the end of § 45; divine intelligence is not needed.] In this immensity of breadth, length, and height, an infinite quantity of innumerable atoms are fluttering about, which, notwithstanding their separation in empty space, meet and cohere, and continue clinging to one another; it is by this union that the forms and figures of things arise, which, in your opinion, could not be created except by the use of bellows and anvils! Thus you have placed on our necks an eternal master, whom we must fear by day and night. For who would not fear a deity who foresees, and considers, and takes notice of everything; one who thinks everything is his affair—an inquisitive busybody of a god?

(55) "The first consequence of your teaching is the doctrine of fatal necessity, or *heimarmenē,* as you call it, the belief that whatever happens is a consequence of some eternal truth [combined] with an endless chain of causation. But what is the value of a philosophy which, like illiterate old women, attributes everything that happens to fate? The next consequence is your doctrine of *mantikē,* which in Latin is called *divinatio,* divination, which, if we chose to listen to you, would plunge us into such superstition that we should soon all be devoting ourselves to augurs, oracle-mongers, prophets and seers. (56) But Epicurus having set us free from these terrors and having restored our liberty, we have no dread of

those beings whom we understand to be entirely free from all trouble themselves and do not seek to cause it for others. Meanwhile, with piety and devotion we worship nature, transcendent and supreme.

"But I am afraid my zeal for this doctrine has made me somewhat too prolix. However, it was difficult to leave so great and important a subject unfinished, though it was not my intention to speak but to listen."

[In the remainder of Bk. I, Cotta demolishes the Epicurean argument, point by point. After a polite introduction, in which he says that his reply will be critical rather than constructive, he insists (61–64) that the argument from universal consent is weak and inadequate; that (65–75) the atomic theory (i.e., in the Epicurean form) is unscientific and inconsistent with divine immortality; that the doctrine of the "swerve" of the falling atoms is absurd, as also (76–104) is the theory of corporeal gods; that the theory of *isonomia* would equally apply to men (105–110a), while the notion that idle gods are happy (110b–114) is ridiculous; finally (115–124), that the whole Epicurean system is totally opposed to religion. We give herewith the last two of these main points in Cotta's argument.]

"Now let us inquire into the divine happiness. It is certain that without virtue there can be no happiness; but virtue consists in action, and your god does nothing; therefore he is lacking in virtue, and consequently cannot be happy. (111) What sort of life, then, does he lead? 'He has a constant succession,' you say, 'of good things without any admixture of bad.' What are those 'good things'? Sensual pleasures, I suppose, i.e., those pertaining to the body; for your school recognizes no delights of the mind which do not arise from the body and return to it. I do not suppose, Velleius, that you are like some of the Epicureans, who are ashamed of those expressions of Epicurus in which he testifies that he cannot understand any good that is wholly separate [i.e., different in kind] from the pleasures of luxury and wantonness—pleasures which, without a blush, he proceeds to name. (112) What food, then, or what drink, what variety of music or flowers, what kind of pleasures of touch, what odors will you present to the gods in order to fill them with pleasure? The poets, indeed, provide them with banquets of nectar and ambrosia, with Hebe or Ganymede to attend them as cupbearer; but what is it, Epicurus [or, Epicurean], that you do for them? For I do not see either where your deity is to procure these things, or how he is going to use them. It seems, then, that man is by nature better equipped for enjoying happiness than the gods are, since man enjoys a wider variety of pleasures.

(113) "But you [say that you] look on all these pleasures as superficial which merely 'tickle' the senses—the word is Epicurus'. When are we going to stop joking! Even our friend Philo [the founder of the New Academy, and Cicero's teacher] could not put up with the Epicurean pretense of renouncing soft and delicious delights; for with his excellent memory he could repeat many utterances of Epicurus in the very words in which they were written. He could also quote many, even more shameless, from Metrodorus, who was Epicurus' colleague in philosophy. Metrodorus blamed his brother Timocrates because he doubted that everything belonging to happiness was to be measured by the belly—this was no isolated remark but one which he often repeated. I see that you nod in agreement with what I say, for you know the passages, and if you were to deny it I would produce the books!

"But I am not now arguing with you for testing all things by the standard of pleasure; that is another question. What I am now trying to prove is that your gods are incapable of pleasure, and that therefore, according to your view, they cannot be blessed.

(114) " 'But they are free from pain,' you say. Is that enough to meet the requirement of that abundance of 'good things' which belongs in the life of blessedness? 'God,' they say, 'is constantly meditating upon his own blessedness,' for he has nothing else to occupy his mind. But consider this a little, and picture to yourself a deity thinking nothing else throughout eternity but 'How happy I am! How well everything is going with me!' And yet I cannot see how this happy god can escape

the fear of being destroyed, since, without any intermission, he is forever being attacked and bombarded by a constant stream of atoms, while from his own person images are forever streaming away. Your god is therefore neither happy nor eternal!

(115) " 'But,' you say, 'Epicurus, it seems, wrote books about holiness and piety toward the gods.' But what kind of language does he use in these books? You might think you were listening to Coruncanius or Scaevola, the high priests, not to the man who destroyed the very foundations of religion and overthrew the temples and altars of the immortal gods—not with hands, like Xerxes, but with arguments. What reason have you for saying that men ought to worship the gods, if the gods not only do not take care of men but have no care for anything whatsoever, and in fact do nothing at all?

(116) " 'But,' you say, 'they are so glorious and transcendent in nature that the wise man is drawn by their very excellence to adore them.' Can there be any glory or excellence in a nature which does nothing but rejoice in its own happiness, and neither will do, nor does, nor ever has done anything at all? Besides, how can you owe an obligation of piety to a being from whom you receive nothing? Or how can you be indebted to one who has done you no favor? For piety is simply justice toward the gods; but what rights have they if men have nothing in common with God? And holiness is the knowledge of how we ought to worship them; but I do not understand why they should be worshiped, if we neither receive any good from them nor expect to receive it. (117) On the other hand, why should we worship them out of admiration for the divine nature, if we cannot see anything excellent in it?

"As for that freedom from superstition, of which your school is in the habit of boasting, it is easy enough to be free from it when you have taken away from the gods all their power! Unless, indeed, you suppose that Diagoras or Theodorus, who absolutely denied the existence of the gods, was capable of being superstitious. For my part, I do not suppose that even Protagoras could be, who only doubted whether there were gods or not. For the doctrines of all these philosophers not only abolish superstition, which arises from a baseless fear of the gods, but also religion, which consists in the pious worship of the gods. (118) Or what do you think of those who have asserted that the whole idea of the immortal gods was the invention of clever men, acting in the interest of the state, so that those whom reason could not control might be led to follow their duty by means of religion? Does not such a view take away the very foundations of religion? Or what religion was left to men by Prodicus of Ceos, who said that everything beneficial to human life should be numbered among the gods? (119) Or those who teach that brave, famous, or powerful men have become gods after death, and that it is really these we are accustomed to worship, to offer prayers and adoration to—are not such teachers wholly lacking in religious feeling? Euhemerus, whom our friend Ennius translated and followed more closely than other authors, has been the chief advocate of this doctrine. Yet it was Euhemerus who described the death and burial of gods; is he then to be thought to have supported religion, or rather to have completely undermined it? I shall say nothing of that sacred and august sanctuary at Eleusis

> Where folk from earth's remotest shores become
>   initiates,

nor Samothrace or Lemnos

> Where secret mysteries are celebrated in the depths of
>   night,
> Guarded by thick forest mazes—

for if these mysteries were properly explained, in reasonable terms, they would throw more light on the processes of nature [i.e., vegetation] than on the gods.

(120) "Even that great man Democritus, from whose fountains Epicurus watered his little garden, seems to me to waver considerably when he deals with the nature of the gods. For at one time he supposes that the universe contains images endowed with divinity; at another he says that the same universe contains the elements [or principles] of mind, and that these are gods; again, he attributes divinity to animate images

which exert either a wholesome or a harmful influence over us; finally, he speaks of certain images so huge that they enclose the whole external universe. All these opinions are more worthy of Democritus' native city [Abdera, whose people were thought stupid] than of Democritus himself; (121) for who can conceive in his mind any images of this sort? Who can admire them? Who can think them worthy of worship or religious veneration?

"But Epicurus, when he robs the gods both of the power and the will to do good, was really uprooting all religion from the hearts of men. For though he says the divine nature is the highest and best of all natures, he at the same time denies that there exists in God any quality of benevolence; in so doing he destroys what is the most essential attribute of the best and supremely transcendent being. For what can be better or more exalted than goodness and beneficence? Take from God this quality and you deprive him of all care, love, or affection for any other being, human or divine. And from this it follows that the gods not only have no concern for men but do not care in the least for one another.

"How much sounder is the doctrine of the Stoics, whom you censure! They hold that the wise are friends to the wise, though unknown to each other, for since nothing is more lovable than virtue, the one who possesses it will be loved by us, wherever he lives. (122) On the other hand, what evils follow, when you make kindness and benevolence a sign of weakness! For, not to mention the power and the nature of the gods, do you suppose that even men would not be either kind or generous unless they were weak? Is there no natural charity among good men? The very sound of the word 'love' [amor], from which the word 'friendship' [amicitia] is derived, is dear to men. But if friendship is to be based on its advantage to us, and not to the one whom we love, it will not be friendship at all, but a commercial arrangement valued for its profit. Pastures, fields, herds of cattle are valued in this way, i.e., by the profit we derive from them; but love and friendship expect nothing in return. How much more so is that of the gods, who lack nothing themselves, yet not only love one another but also watch over the interests of men. If this were not so, why should we reverence or pray to the gods? Why should the priests preside over sacrifices, or augurs over the auspices? What would we have to ask of the gods, and why would we make vows to them?

" 'But Epicurus,' as you say 'has written a book concerning holiness.' (123) The man was making fun of us!—though he was not so much facetious as lax and careless in writing. For how can there be any such thing as holiness if the gods have no interest in human affairs? Worse yet, how can an animate being exist and not be interested in anything whatsoever?

"It is therefore truer to say, as our good friend Posidonius maintained in Book V of his work *On the Nature of the Gods,* that Epicurus really believed there were no gods at all, and that he said what he did about the immortal gods only to escape popular execration. He could not have been so foolish as to imagine that the deity has only the external features of a feeble mortal but not any real solid substance, possessing all the limbs of a man but without the least power to use them, a thin, transparent being, showing neither kindness nor beneficence to anyone, caring for nothing whatsoever and doing nothing whatsoever! In the first place, such a being cannot possibly exist; and Epicurus recognized this, for, though he retains the gods verbally, he destroys them in fact. (124) And in the second place, even if God exists but is really of such a nature that he feels no benevolence, no love for mankind, goodbye to him! I do not even say the 'God be gracious' with which we end our prayers—why should I? For he cannot be gracious to anyone, since, as you are saying, all kindness and benevolence are signs of weakness!"

BOOK TWO

When Cotta had finished speaking, Velleius replied. "I certainly was rash to undertake to argue with a member of the Academics who is also an orator! I should not have feared an

Academic who lacked eloquence, nor an orator however eloquent who lacked training in that philosophy; for I am never disturbed by an empty flow of words, nor by the most subtle reasoning if it is delivered in a dry style. But you, Cotta, excel in both [philosophy and oratory]. All you lacked was a public assembly and a jury! However, enough of this for the present. Let us now hear what Lucilius has to say, if he is willing."

(2) "I would much rather," said Balbus, "hear Cotta continue his discourse and present the true gods with the same eloquence which he used in destroying the false. For on the subject of the immortal gods a philosopher, a pontiff, and a Cotta ought not to hold the vague and wandering doctrines of the Academy but firm and definite ones, like those of our school. Epicurus already has been more than sufficiently refuted; I would like to hear what you yourself think, Cotta."

"Have you forgotten," replied Cotta, "what I said at the beginning [I. 57, 60], that it is easier for me, especially on subjects like this, to tell what I do *not* think than tell what I *do?* (3) Even if I did feel certain on any one point, I would prefer now to hear you speak in your turn, since I have already said so much myself."

"Very well," replied Balbus, "I will yield, and I will be as brief as possible; for since you have refuted the errors of Epicurus, I have no excuse for a long discourse. Generally speaking, our school divides the whole subject of the immortal gods into four parts: first they prove that gods exist; next they explain their nature; then they show that the universe is ruled by them; and finally that they [the gods] are concerned with human affairs. But in our present discussion let us limit ourselves to the first two of these; the third and fourth, being much bigger questions, I think we should postpone until another time."

"By no means," replied Cotta; "we have time enough right now, and we are discussing a subject which ought to take precedence even over serious business."

(4) "The first point, then," said Lucilius, "does not seem to require any argument to prove it. For, when we look up at the

heavens and contemplate the celestial bodies, what can be so plain and obvious as the existence of a supreme divine intelligence, by whom all these things are ruled? If it were not so, how could Ennius say, with the approval of every reader,

> Look up to the shining heaven above,
> Which all men everywhere invoke as Jove.
> [Frag. 351.]

Indeed, it is Jupiter, the ruler of the universe, who governs all things with his nod and, as Ennius also says, is

> the Father of gods and men,

an omnipresent and omnipotent god. And if anyone doubts this, I really do not see why he should not also doubt the existence of the sun. (5) For in what way is the latter more evident than the former? For if we did not possess in our minds a firmly held concept of God, it would be impossible to explain either the stability or the permanence of belief in him—belief which only grows stronger with succeeding ages and grows more deeply rooted as the generations pass. Other opinions, being false and groundless, have already faded away with the lapse of time. Who now believes that Hippocentaurs or Chimeras ever existed? Or where can an old woman be found stupid enough to fear those monsters of the lower world which mankind once believed in? For time destroys the figments of the imagination, but confirms the judgments of nature.

"It is for this reason that both among us and among other nations the worship of the gods and respect for religion grows steadily stronger and deeper. (6) Nor is this the result of chance or accident; instead, it is due to the fact that the gods frequently manifest their power by their bodily presence. For example, in the Latin War when the dictator Aulus Postumius attacked Octavius Mamilius of Tusculum at Lake Regillus, [the gods] Castor and Pollux were seen mounted and fighting among our troops; more recently these same sons of Tyndareus brought the news of the defeat of Perses. For as Publius Vatinius, the grandfather of the young man who now bears that name, was returning by night to Rome from Reate, where

he was governor, two young men on white horses appeared to
him and told him that King Perses had that day been taken
prisoner. This news he carried to the Senate, but he was immediately thrown into prison for spreading an unfounded
rumor on a matter concerning the safety of the state. But when
a dispatch arrived from [Aemilius] Paulus, confirming the
exact date, he was recompensed by the Senate with a grant of
land and immunity from military service. It is also recorded
that when the Locrians defeated the people of Crotona, in the
great battle on the banks of the river Sagra, news of the victory was reported the same day at the Olympic Games. Moreover, the voices of the Fauns have often been heard, and the
visible forms of divine beings have often appeared, so that
everyone who was not feeble-minded or lacking in piety has
been compelled to admit the real presence of the gods.

(7) "Moreover, what do prophecies and premonitions of
future events mean, unless they are proof that the future can
be foretold, pointed out, portended, or predicted to men?
Hence we have the very words—omens, signs, portents, prodigies [there is a play on words in the Latin]. Even though we
may view as fabulous the stories about [the five famous ancient
Greek seers] Mopsus, Tiresias, Amphiaraus, Calchas, and Hele-
nus—who certainly would never have been described as augurs,
even in legend, unless their art had amounted to something—
do not the examples from our own history compel us to acknowledge the power of the gods? Does the rash act of Publius
Claudius during the First Punic War leave us unmoved?
When the [sacred] chickens were let out of their cage and
would not eat, he ordered them thrown into the water, saying,
in a jest that mocked the gods, 'If they won't eat, *let them
drink!*' But this smart bit of ridicule was followed by the loss
of his fleet; it brought him many tears, and to the Roman
people a great disaster. Furthermore, did not his colleague
Junius, in the same war, lose his fleet in a storm after disre-
garding the auspices? As a consequence of these disasters,
Claudius was tried and condemned by the people, and Junius
killed himself. (8) Caelius relates that Gaius Flaminius, having

neglected religion [i.e., the prescribed rites], fell in the battle at the Trasimene Lake, with great injury to the Republic. These examples of calamity enable us to recognize that Rome owes her greatness to those commanders who were scrupulous in religious observances. And if we wish to compare ourselves with other peoples, we find that, although in other things we may be only their equals or even their inferiors, in religion, i.e., in the worship of the gods, we are by far their superiors.

(9) "Can we disregard the augural staff of Attus Navius with which he marked off the regions of the vineyard to find his pig? I should be willing to disregard it, if it were not that King Hostilius fought great wars guided by his auguries. But now, by the negligence of our nobility, the augural discipline has been forgotten, the truth of the auspices is despised, and only the outward form is observed. As a result, the most important affairs of state, even the wars on which the public safety depends, are conducted without any auspices. There is no taking of omens when crossing rivers. No attention is paid when lights flash from the points of the soldiers' javelins. No auspices attend the calling up of men to military service—and therefore no wills are drawn up at the time, since our generals now begin their wars only after they have laid down their augural authority. (10) Among our ancestors religion had such influence that some of the commanders, with faces veiled and using the prescribed religious formulas, dedicated themselves to death on behalf of their country. I could cite many of the Sibylline prophecies and many of the responses of the haruspices in confirmation of these facts, which no one ought to question.

"For example, when Publius Scipio and Gaius Figulus were consuls, the discipline both of our augurs and of the Etruscan haruspices was vindicated by concrete facts. For when Tiberius Gracchus, who was consul for the second time, was proceeding with a fresh election [of his successors], the first rogator of the assembly, while reporting the persons elected, suddenly fell dead. Nevertheless, Gracchus went ahead with the elections. Sensing the fact that the people felt religious scruples about proceeding further, he brought the matter before the Senate. But the Senate only referred the matter 'to the proper officials.' Soothsayers [*haruspices*] were brought in, who replied that the rogator of the elections was out of order. (11) Whereupon Gracchus, so I have heard my father say, replied angrily, 'What is that? Am I not in order, in putting these names to the vote—I who am consul and augur and favored by the auspices? Are you Tuscans, you barbarians, claiming to exercise authority over the Roman auspices, and to give decisions as to the legality of our assemblies?' And so he then commanded them to withdraw; but not long afterwards he wrote from his province to the College of Augurs, acknowledging that while reading the sacred books he recalled that he had illegally chosen a place for his augural tent in the gardens of Scipio, and had afterwards crossed the pomerium [in entering the city] to hold a meeting of the Senate but on returning across the same pomerium had forgotten to take the auspices; the consuls, therefore, had not been properly elected. The College of Augurs laid the case before the Senate, and the Senate decreed that the consuls must resign their office, which they did. What more striking examples can we ask for? The wisest of men, and perhaps I may say the most distinguished, chose to make public confession of his fault, which he might have concealed, rather than permit the Republic to suffer from the least stain of impiety; and the consuls chose to resign the highest office in the state, rather than hold it for a moment in violation of religion.

(12) "How great is the authority of the augurs! And is not the art of the soothsayers divine? And must not anyone who considers these and innumerable other instances of the same kind be compelled to admit the existence of the gods? For (*a*) if there are persons who act as interpreters, (*b*) those for whom they interpret must certainly exist; now (*c*) there are interpreters of the gods; therefore (*d*) we must confess that the gods exist. But it may perhaps be said that not all predictions come true. We might as well conclude that there is no art of medicine, seeing that not all sick persons recover. The gods

show us signs of future events; if men occasionally have been mistaken in their interpretation, it is not the nature of the gods but the conjectures of men that are at fault. All nations agree that there are gods; this is an innate belief, engraved, as it were, in the minds of all men. (13) *What* they are, is a matter of opinion; *that* they are, no one denies.

"Cleanthes, one of our [Stoic] teachers, explained how the idea of the gods is implanted in the minds of men, in four ways. The *first* is what I just now mentioned, viz., the foreknowledge of future events. The *second* is the great advantages we derive from the temperature of the air, the fertility of the earth, and the vast abundance of other benefits. (14) The *third* cause is the terror with which the mind is affected by thunder and lightning, by tempests and storms, snow, hail, floods, pestilences, earthquakes often accompanied by subterranean noises, showers of stones, and rain like drops of blood; by caving-in and sudden openings of the earth; by monstrous births of men and beasts [*praeter naturam . . . portentis,* unnatural phenomena viewed as portents]; by the appearance of celestial figures, by those stars which the Greeks call 'comets' and we call 'long haired stars,' the appearance of which, in the recent Octavian War [87 B.C.], were harbingers of great disasters; by the doubling of the sun, which, as I have heard my father say, happened during the consulship of Tuditanus and Aquilius, the year [129 B.C.] in which the light of another sun, Publius Africanus, was extinguished. All these things have terrified mankind and have convinced them of the existence of some celestial and divine power. (15) The *fourth* and strongest cause of belief is the harmonious motion and revolution of the heavens, the distinction, variety, beauty, and order of the sun, moon, and all the stars, the mere sight of which itself is enough to convince us they are not the results of chance. When one enters a house, a gymnasium, or a forum, and observes the exact order and arrangement of everything, and the science involved in it, he cannot imagine that these things happened without a cause, but must assume that there is someone in control who can compel obedience. How much the more must the vast motions and changing phases [of the heavenly bodies] with their many great bodies and diverse orders, none of which has ever played false during the immense and infinite past, compel one to infer that these vast motions of the universe are governed by some Mind."

[Chrysippus is next quoted to show that this mind is more than human, i.e., is divine; that the ether, the purest of elements, is the appropriate home of the gods; that reason, the noblest element in man, must be derived from the noblest element in the universe; and that "reason and wisdom must necessarily belong to the nature (*necesse est haec inesse*) of the being whom we conceive to be supreme"—arguments destined to exercise great influence in medieval philosophy and theology. The truth of all this is further supported by the sympathy or harmony—like musical harmony—which pervades the universe, maintained as it is by one divine, all-pervading spirit. Next in the exposition of early Stoic teaching, Zeno's concise syllogisms are quoted to prove that the world is rational, and therefore divine. Cleanthes' argument is also given, that the functions of heat and light show that a vital force pervades the universe, the fiery, rational, ruling element found in all things, without which the world would long since have perished. This vital force possesses wisdom, is perfectly rational, and holds all things in its embrace; it is the principle called *logos* by the Stoics, though Cicero does not use the term. Spontaneous motion, as Plato ("practically the god of the philosophers") has said, resides in the soul; hence the motions of the universe, derived from its heat, prove that its heat is soul; therefore the world is animate, a living universe (i.e., divine: the distinction seems lost, for the moment, between a divine being who is in control of the universe and one identical with it, in the sense of Stoic pantheism). Further, since the world is superior to its component elements, one of which is mind, the universe itself must possess intelligence—otherwise man, who is rational, would be superior to the universe of which he is a part. Still another argument is derived from the scale of existence: the "ladder of being" points upward from vegetable, animal, and human existence to its "climax," the deity supreme above all. The vegetable kingdom possesses the quality of nurture and growth, the animals possess sensation and motion, man is endowed with reason, but there is a still higher level of being in the universe.]

(34b) "The fourth and highest level is that of beings which are by nature wise and good, who from the beginning of their existence possess the innate qualities of right reason and consistency, which must be considered something superior to man and deserving to be attributed to God, that is to say to the world, in which it is necessary that this perfect and absolute reason should inhere. (35) Nor is it possible to deny to any organic structure a goal of completion and perfection. Thus in vines and cattle we see that nature, if not prevented by some [contrary] force, proceeds by her own proper path to her destined goal; also that in painting, architecture, and the other arts, there is a point of absolute perfection; so likewise in nature as a whole it is even more necessary that there should be a movement toward completion and perfection. Many external accidents may block the path of other natures and impede their progress to perfection, but nothing can hinder universal nature, since she herself contains and controls all natures. There must exist, therefore, this fourth and highest level, which no external power can assail. (36) Since this is the level upon which the nature of the universe depends, and since it is superior to all things and cannot be frustrated by any, it necessarily follows that the world is an intelligent, even a wise, being.

"But what can be more unreasonable than to question [lit., not to call best] the perfection of that nature which embraces all things; or, while calling it perfect, to deny that it must first be living, then rational and intelligent, finally wise? Without these qualities how could it be 'the best'? If it were like vegetables, or even like animals, there would be no more reason for thinking it best than worst. Or if it were possessed of reason, but had not exercised wisdom from the beginning, the world would be in a worse condition than mankind; for a man may grow wise, but the world, if through an eternity of past ages it has lacked wisdom, obviously can never acquire it, and hence will be inferior to man. But as that is absurd, the world must be supposed to have been wise from the beginning, and divine [lit., god].

(37) "In fact, nothing exists that is not defective except the universe, which is well equipped, complete, and perfect in all its parts and details. For, as Chrysippus neatly put it, as the shield-case is made for the shield, and the scabbard for the sword, so all things, except the universe, were made for the sake of something else. Thus the crops and fruits which the earth produces were made for the sake of animals, and animals for the sake of man; for example, the horse for riding, the ox for plowing, the dog for hunting and keeping watch. But man himself was born to contemplate and imitate the world, being by no means perfect but a kind of 'particle of perfection.' (38) The world, on the other hand, since it embraces all things and nothing exists that is not contained within it, is entirely perfect. What can it lack, then, since it is perfect? Nothing is better than intelligence and reason; therefore the world cannot possibly lack them.

"The same Chrysippus also teaches, by the use of illustrations, that every kind of thing becomes better when it arrives at maturity and perfection, as a horse is better than a colt, a dog than a puppy, and a man than a boy; similarly, whatever is best in the whole universe must be possessed by some complete and perfect being. (39) But nothing is more perfect than the world itself, and nothing is better than virtue. Virtue, therefore, is an essential attribute of the world. Human nature is not perfect; nevertheless virtue is produced in it; how much the more readily, then, will the world produce it? Therefore the world [has virtue,] is wise, and consequently is a god.

"The divinity of the world being now clearly recognized, we must ascribe the same divinity to the stars, which are formed from the most mobile and purest part of the ether, without any admixture of other matter, being fiery hot and wholly translucent; so that they may truly be said to possess life, sensation, and intelligence. (40) Cleanthes thinks that it may be proved by the evidence of two of our senses, viz., touch and sight, that the stars are entirely composed of fire; for the heat and brilliance of the sun far exceed any other fire, since it illumines the whole length and breadth of the universe; and the touch of its rays is so powerful that they not only warm, but often even burn—neither of which could it do if it were not made of fire. 'Therefore,' he says, 'since the sun is made of fire, and is nourished by the vapors of the ocean (for no fire can continue without some kind of sustenance), it must be either like that fire which we use for warmth or for preparing our food, or like that which is contained in the bodies of animals. (41) But this fire, which the needs of daily life require, is destructive and consumes everything, and it disturbs and dissipates whatever it invades. On the other hand, bodily heat is living and salutary; it preserves, nourishes, causes growth, and sustains all things, and bestows sensation.' Therefore, he concludes, there can be no doubt which of these fires the sun resembles, since it causes all things to flourish and increase in their respective kinds. Now since the fire of the sun is like those contained in the bodies of living beings, the sun itself must likewise be alive; and so must the other stars also, which originate in that celestial fire which we call the ether or heaven.

(42) "Since, then, some animals are born on the earth, some in the water, and some in the air, Aristotle thinks it absurd to assume that no animate beings are formed in that part of the universe which is the most capable of producing them. But the stars are located in the ethereal space; as this is the most subtle element, continually in motion and vigorous, it follows of necessity that every animate being which is produced in this element must be endowed with the keenest sense and the swiftest motion. Since stars come into existence in the ether, it is a natural inference that they possess sensation and intelligence. From this it follows that they are to be included among the gods.

"For it may be observed that the inhabitants of countries with pure and clear air have a quicker apprehension and a keener understanding than those who live in a thick, foggy climate. (43) Moreover, it is thought that a man's customary diet has some effect on mental acumen; therefore it is probable that the stars possess unusual intelligence, since they occupy the ethereal part of the universe, and are nourished by the vapors of the earth and the sea, which are rarefied by their long passage upward. Further, the invariable order and regularity of the stars clearly demonstrates their consciousness and intelligence. For no regular or harmonious motion is possible without forethought, in which there is no trace of either rashness, inconsistency, or accident. And this order and everlasting regularity of the stars points neither to any natural process, since it is fully rational, nor to chance, since chance loves variety and hates constancy. It follows, therefore, that the stars move spontaneously, guided by their own intelligence and divinity.

(44) "Aristotle also deserves high commendation for his view that all motion is the result either of nature, some external force, or personal will. Now the sun, the moon, and all the stars are in motion; but things which are moved by nature are either carried downward by their weight or upward by their lightness—neither of which could be true of the stars, because they move in a regular circle and orbit. Nor can it be said that some superior force causes them to move in a manner contrary to nature. For what superior force can there be? It follows, therefore, that their motion must be voluntary.

"Anyone who recognizes the truth of this would display not only great ignorance but great impiety if he were to deny the existence of the gods. Nor does it matter much whether a man denies their existence or deprives them of all providential care [of the universe] and activity; for whatever is wholly inactive seems to me not to exist at all. Their existence, therefore, seems to be so clear that I can scarcely think anyone who denies it to be in his right mind."

[The speaker, Balbus, now takes up Part II of the subject, the Divine Nature, and continues with the astronomical considerations already advanced. The gods, like the stars and the universe, must possess a perfect form, viz., the spherical; likewise the divine motion must be rotary, like the stars and their spheres—even sun, moon, and planets display this perfect type of motion. He sums up, and proceeds:]

(54) "This regularity in the planets, this exact agreement through all eternity despite the variety of their courses, is incomprehensible apart from mind, reason, and purpose. And since we observe these qualities in the planets, we must also include them among the gods.

"Those which are called the fixed stars indicate the same intelligence and foresight. Their daily revolution is regular and constant. They are not carried along by the ether, nor are they attached to the firmament, as most people say who are ignorant of natural philosophy. For the ether is not of such a nature as by its own power to whirl along the combinations of the stars, for being thin, transparent, and suffused with an equal heat, it does not seem capable of containing them. (55) The fixed stars, therefore, have their own sphere, separate and unattached to the ether. Their perpetual courses, and their marvelous and incredible regularity, so clearly manifest divine power and intelligence in them that anyone who cannot perceive that they themselves possess divine power must be incapable of understanding anything whatever.

(56) "In the heavens, therefore, there is nothing fortuitous, accidental, inconstant, or futile; all is order, accuracy, reason, and regularity. Whatever lacks these qualities and is false, spurious, and full of error has its proper place around the earth beneath the moon, the lowest of all the heavenly bodies, and on the earth's surface. Anyone, therefore, who believes that this admirable order and incredible regularity of the heavenly bodies, which preserves and safeguards all things, is lacking in intelligence, must himself be viewed as lacking a mind.

(57) "I believe, therefore, that I shall not go wrong if in conducting this disputation I set out from the principles of Zeno, that prince of investigators. Zeno defines nature as 'a creative fire [*ignis artificiosus,* Gk. *pur technikon*], proceeding in a regular way to generation.' For he thinks that the special function of art is to create and beget, and that whatever is wrought by the hands of our craftsmen is much more skillfully done by nature—that is, by this 'creative fire,' which is the

master of all other arts. Following this reasoning, every specific nature is [artistically] creative, operating in agreement with its own method, which has been marked out for it to follow; (58) while the nature of the universe, which embraces and controls all things, is said by Zeno to be not only creative, but actually a creator [*artifex,* craftsman], ever thinking in advance and providing for the use and occasion of everything. And just as every specific nature owes its rise and growth to its own proper seed, so the nature of the universe enjoys all those motions of the will, those affections and desires (which the Greeks call *hormae*), leading to the appropriate actions, as they do with us who are moved by feeling and sensation. Such then is the mind of the universe, which may be rightly termed prudence or providence (in Greek *pronoia*), since its chief concern and occupation is, first, to provide the world with what is needed for its permanence; then to see that it lacks nothing; above all, to provide that it may be adorned with perfect beauty and decoration.

(59) "Thus far we have been speaking about the universe as a whole, and about the stars; from which it appears that there is an almost infinite number of gods, always in action yet without either toil or fatigue. For they have no veins, nerves, or bones. Nor is their food and drink such as to cause their humors to grow either too gross or too subtle. Nor are their bodies such as to lead them to fear falling or blows, or to dread diseases resulting from weariness of the limbs—which anxiety led Epicurus to invent his sketchy, do-nothing gods. (60) But our gods are of the most beautiful form, and are assembled in the purest region of the heavens, and so control and rule their courses that they appear to have agreed to preserve and care for all things.

"Besides these, there are many other deities, who, because of the great benefits derived from them, have with good reason been recognized and named both by the wisest of the Greeks and also by our ancestors. For they believed that whatever was of great utility to mankind must result from divine benevolence, and so the name of the deity was applied to that which the deity produced [or gave: *datum,* or *donatum;* MS *natum*], as when grain was called Ceres, or wine Liber, so that Terence could write,

> Without Ceres and Liber, Venus grows cold.

(61) In other cases, some quality which possesses an exceptional power is itself called a god: such as Faith [*Fides*] and Mind [*Mens*], which have recently received dedications on the Capitol by Marcus Aemilius Scaurus; Faith had already been deified by Aulus Atilius Calatinus. You can see the temple of Virtue and that of Honor, restored by Marcus Marcellus, but erected not many years before, during the Ligurian War, by Quintus Fabius Maximus [233 B.C.]. Need I mention those dedicated to Wealth [*Ops*], Safety [*Salus*], Concord, Liberty, and Victory, all of which have been called gods because their power is so great as to imply a divine control? In the same class belong the names of Desire [*Cupido*], Pleasure [*Voluptas*], and the Lubentine [willing] Venus, which have been deified even though they were things vicious and unnatural (though Velleius thinks differently), since the power of these vices is often so overwhelming. (62) Those are gods who are constituted such by the magnitude of the benefits which they produce, and so also are those whose names, just mentioned, express their various powers.

"The life of mankind and common custom have also, by fame and universal consent, exalted to heaven those men who have rendered important services to the public. Thus Hercules, Castor and Pollux, Aesculapius, and Liber became gods. (I mean Liber the son of Semele, not the one whom our ancestors consecrated as Liber, with such pomp and solemnity, along with Ceres and Libera—the significance of which may be learned from the mysteries; but because we call our own children *liberi,* so the offspring of Ceres were called Liber and Libera—a usage which survives in Libera, but not in Liber.) And so likewise Romulus—who is thought to be the same as Quirinus—became a god. Since their souls survive and enjoy immortality, they are rightly esteemed to be gods, for they are both supremely good and also immortal.

(63) "There is another theory, too, one based on natural philosophy, which has contributed greatly to the number of the gods, namely, by way of the custom of representing them in human form and thus supplying the poets with myths but also filling human life with all kinds of superstition. Zeno dealt with this subject, and it was afterward discussed at greater length by Cleanthes and Chrysippus. For example, ancient Greece was of the opinion that Caelus [Uranus] was castrated by his son Saturn, and that Saturn was chained by his son Jove [Zeus]. (64) In these impious fables a really not inelegant scientific theory is contained. For they signified that the celestial, or most exalted, ethereal element—that is, the fiery element, the one which by itself produces all things—lacks that part of the body which is necessary for union with another in the act of procreation. By Saturn they meant that being which maintains the course and revolution of the times and seasons; which god bears this very name in Greek, for he is called *Kronos,* which is the same as *Chronos,* a period. But [in Latin] he is called Saturn, because he is filled (*saturaretur*) with years; the myth relates that he was in the habit of swallowing his sons, because time, ever insatiable, devours the ages and the years that are past. But to restrain him from his immoderate course, Jove has chained him with the bonds of the stars. Jupiter himself (i.e., *juvans pater*) signifies a 'helping father,' whom by a change in case we call Jove (from *juvare,* to help). The poets call him 'the father of gods and men,' but our ancestors named him 'the best and greatest' [*optimus maximus*], placing the title 'best' (i.e., most beneficent) ahead of 'greatest,' since beneficence is greater, and certainly more lovable, than the possession of great wealth. (65) He is the one to whom Ennius referred in the lines already quoted [§ 4],

Look up to the shining heaven above,
Which all men everywhere invoke as Jove,
[Frag. 351]

which states it more plainly than this other passage of the same poet,

> Whate'er the power that gives me light,
> On him I lay my curse.
> [Frag. 388]

Our augurs also mean the same thing when they say, 'If Jove lightens, or thunders,' meaning 'if the sky lightens or thunders.' Euripides, among many great passages, has this brief one:

> You see the boundless ether spread above
> The earth, which lies beneath, within its soft embrace:
> This you must believe is Jove, supreme among gods.
> [Frag. 836]

(66) "According to the Stoics, the air which lies between the sea and the sky is deified under the name of Juno [Hera], and is called the sister and wife of Jove, because it resembles the ether, and is closely connected with it. They have made it feminine, and assigned it to Juno, because there is nothing softer. But I believe it is called Juno from *juvare*, to help.

"To complete the three separate realms, recognized by the myths, there still remained water and earth. Accordingly, the dominion of the sea was assigned to Neptune, Jove's brother, as he is called, whose name, Neptunus, was derived from *nare*, to swim, the first letters being a little changed, and the rest modified like Portunus [the harbor god], from *portus* [port]. The whole sovereignty and substance of the earth was dedicated to Father Dis (i.e., Dives, the rich one, or in Greek *Ploutōn* [Pluto, the rich one]), because all things return to the earth, and all arise from it. They say that he married Proserpina (a Greek name, she is identical with the goddess called *Persephonē* in Greek), by which the poets mean the seed of grain and describe her as hidden away [like stored or sown grain] and sought for by her mother. (67) The mother is called Ceres, which is the same as Geres, from *gero*, because she 'bears' the crops—the first letter of the word being accidentally changed in the same way by the Greeks, who also called her *Dēmētēr*, which is the same as *Gē Mētēr* [Mother Earth].

Again, the one who 'overthrows the great' is called Mavors [*qui magna verteret;* Mars]; while Minerva is so called either because she diminishes [*minueret*] or menaces [*minaretur*].

"And as the beginning and the ending of every action are of the greatest importance, they held that their sacrifices began with Janus [i.e., in the sacrificial formulae]. His name is derived from *ire* [to go], hence passageways are called *jani,* and the outside doors of ordinary houses *januae.* Again, the name of Vesta comes from the Greeks—it is the same as their *Hestia.* Her jurisdiction includes altars and hearths, and so all prayers and sacrifices conclude with the name of this goddess, since she is the keeper of innermost things. (68) The Di Penates or household gods have a function somewhat closely related to this, and are so called either from *penus,* which means a store of any kind of human food, or because they reside *penitus,* i.e., in the inmost part of the house, and so they are also called *penetrales* by the poets. Apollo, which is also a Greek name, is identified with the sun (*Sol*) and Diana with the moon (*Luna*). He is named *Sol* the sun either because he is 'alone' (*solus*) in his supremacy over all other heavenly bodies, or because when he rises he obscures all the stars, and so appears 'alone.' Luna, the moon, is so called from *lucere,* to shine; it is the same as Lucina; and as among the Greeks women in childbirth invoke Diana *Lucifera* [the light-bringer], so here our women invoke Juno *Lucina.* She is likewise called Diana *Omnivaga* [the far wanderer], not from her hunting, but because she is included among the seven planets that seem to 'wander' [*vagari*]. (69) She is called Diana because she makes a kind of 'day' of the night; and she presides over childbirth because the birth takes place sometimes after seven or more usually after nine courses of the moon; which, because they cover *mensa spatia* ('measured spaces') are called *menses,* months. This led the historian Timaeus to make one of his many clever statements. Having said that the same night in which Alexander was born the temple of Diana at Ephesus was burned down, he added that this was not in the least surprising since Diana was absent from home, assisting Olympias [Alexander's mother] at the birth. The goddess who 'comes' [*veniret*] on every occasion we name Venus; her name is not derived from *Venustas* [beauty], but [contrariwise] *venustas* is derived from her name.

(70) "Do you not see, therefore, how from a sound and useful explanation of nature has arisen this imaginary pantheon of deities? This is what has produced the false beliefs, confused errors, and silly superstitions. For we know how the gods look, how old they are, their wearing apparel and ornaments, their ancestry, marriages, relatives—in fact, everything about them is forced into conformity with human weakness. They are represented as moved by passion: we hear of their lust, their grief, their anger; according to the myths they even have wars and battles—not only, as in Homer, when two different armies are engaged and they take opposite sides, but they have fought battles of their own, as against the Titans and Giants. These stories, which are repeated and believed, are utterly stupid, full of the utmost folly and nonsense.

(71) "But, while we reject these myths with contempt, we nevertheless recognize that a god is concerned with each part of nature—Ceres the land, Neptune the sea, other parts, other gods. They can be known, both who they are and what they are, and also by what names they are customarily called; these are the gods whom it is our duty to revere and to worship. The best, the purest, the holiest and most pious worship of the gods is to reverence them always with a pure, sincere, uncorrupted mind and tongue.

"Not only the philosophers but likewise our ancestors distinguished religion from superstition. (72) Those who prayed and offered sacrifices all day long that their children might outlive them [*ut . . . superstites essent*] were called 'superstitious,' a word which later took on a wider meaning. But those who carefully studied and, we might say, retraced [*retractarent et . . . relegerent*] everything that related to the worship of the gods, were called 'religious' (*religiosi*), from *relegere*, 'to read again,' as elegant comes from *eligere*, 'to choose'; diligent from *diligere*, 'to care for'; intelligent, from *intellegere*, 'to understand'; for all these words are components of *legere*, 'to pick out,' just as we also find it in *religio*. Thus the words 'super-stitious' and 'religious' came to be terms of reproach and of commendation, respectively. I think I have now sufficiently demonstrated both that the gods exist, and also what is their nature.

(73) "It is now my task to prove that all things are gov-erned by their providence. This is certainly a vast subject, and one which is hotly debated by your school, Cotta—and they will be my chief opponents. As for you and your friends, Vel-leius, you hardly know enough about it to discuss the subject —you never read any writings but your own [i.e., the Epi-curean], and are so taken with them that you presume to pass judgment on all the other schools of philosophy without hear-ing their case. For example, you told us yesterday that the Stoics drag in *Pronoia* [Providence] like a dried-up old gypsy fortuneteller—for you assume that they view providence as a kind of goddess who rules and governs the whole universe. (74) But 'providence' is an abbreviated expression. If you say, 'The Athenian State is governed by the Council,' you are omit-ting the words 'of the Areopagus': so likewise when we say the world is governed by providence, we imply the missing words 'of the gods'—the full statement would be, 'The world is governed by the providence of the gods.' So you and your crowd might as well save your wit and not waste it in making fun of us! By Hercules, if you listen to me, don't try it: humor doesn't fit your style; you lack the gift; you simply don't know how to crack a joke! I am not speaking of you personally; you yourself have the fine manners of your family, and the pol-ished urbanity of a Roman. But it does apply to the rest of your tribe, and especially your founder [Epicurus], who was an artless, uneducated person who went about insulting every-one but without any keenness, authority, or charm.

(75) "And so I say the world and all its parts were set in orderly arrangement at the beginning and always have been ruled by divine providence—a teaching which our school is ac-customed to divide into three sections. The first is based on the principle that the gods exist: if this is granted then it must

follow that the world is governed by their wisdom. The second teaches that all things are subject to a conscious Nature, by whom the whole is brought about in the most beautiful way: if this is granted then it follows that all things were derived from animate first causes [or 'principles']. The third is based on the wonder we feel in the presence of the natural universe, both celestial and terrestrial.

(76) "To begin, then, one must either deny the existence of the gods—as Democritus did when he called them 'apparitions' and Epicurus 'images'—or else (as anyone must do who admits their existence) grant that they are active, indeed superlatively active, which means the government of the universe, since nothing is more supreme than this. Hence the world is ruled by the wisdom of the gods. If this is not so, there certainly must be something or other which is more powerful than God, either inanimate nature or necessity, hastening on with superior power to create these sublimely beautiful things that we behold. (77) In this case, it is not the nature of the gods which is supreme in power and excellence, since it also is subject to some kind of nature or necessity which rules sky, sea, and land. But the truth is, nothing is superior to God. Necessarily, therefore, the world is ruled by God. And therefore, also, God is not obedient to or subjected to any kind [or part] of nature—instead, he himself rules all nature.

"Hence, if we grant that the gods are intelligent, we must also grant their providence—a providence exercised in matters of the greatest importance. But are the gods ignorant as to what things are of the greatest importance, and how these are to be controlled and handled? Or do they lack the power to sustain and manipulate things so great? But ignorance is alien to the divine nature, while weakness and inability to handle the task is most inappropriate to the divine majesty. From this it follows that, as we maintain, the world is governed by the providence of the gods.

(78) "Moreover, if the gods exist (assuming as we must that they do) it follows of necessity that they are living beings, and not only living but also rational and bound together in some

kind of civil community or society, ruling the one world as a united commonwealth or a city. (79) It also follows that they possess the same kind of rationality that we do, and the same standard of truth, and the same law commanding what is right and condemning what is wrong. And from this we recognize that wisdom and intelligence have been derived by mankind from the gods. That is why our ancestors deified Mind, Faith, Virtue, and Concord, and publicly dedicated shrines to them. How then can we deny them a place with the gods, if we reverence their majestic, sacred images? And if we find men possessing mind, faith, virtue, and concord, wherever have these [qualities] come into the world from unless they have flowed down from above [i.e., from the gods]? Further, since we possess wisdom, reason, and prudence, it must follow that the gods also possess them in greater measure; and not only possess them but also use them in affairs of the greatest importance and value. (80) But there is nothing more important or more valuable than the universe; it follows, therefore, of necessity, that the universe is ruled by the wisdom and providence of the gods. Finally, since we have already proved the deity of those beings whose immense power and splendor we can see—I mean the sun and moon and planets and the fixed stars and the sky and the world itself and the power of all things that are therein, throughout the world, with their great usefulness and advantage to the human race—it follows that all things are ruled by divine intelligence and providence. This now concludes the first part of my subject.

(81) "My next task is to prove that all things are under the control of nature, and are managed by her in the most beautiful way. But first let me explain briefly what the term 'nature' means, so that our doctrine may be the more easily understood. Some persons think that nature is a kind of nonrational force causing the necessary motions in physical bodies; others that it is a rational and orderly power, acting by method, openly declaring the means chosen for every end and what that end is, and possessing such skill as no art, no human hand, no craftsman can imitate or equal. For a seed, they say,

has such power that, tiny as it is, if it falls into the substance that will conceive and enfold it, and finds there the material which will nourish it and make it grow, it shapes and produces the various living creatures after their kind, some fed only through their roots, others able to move about, endowed with sensation and appetite and capable of reproducing their own species.

(82) "There are some, however, who apply the word nature to all existence—as Epicurus does, who classifies everything as either 'bodies' [atoms], the 'void,' or their attributes. But when *we* say that nature sustains and governs the world, we do not mean to imply that the world is like a clod of earth or a piece of stone or anything of that sort, having no principle of coherence, but rather that it is like a tree or an animal, whose appearance owes nothing to chance, but to order and even something like art.

(83) "But if it is by nature's art that plants live and grow, then no doubt the earth itself must be sustained by the same power; for, when impregnated with seeds, she brings forth from herself every kind of vegetable, and, embracing their roots, she nourishes them and causes them to grow; she herself, in turn, receives her nourishment from the upper and outer elements. Her exhalations, in turn, nourish the air, the ether, and all the heavenly bodies. If nature thus supports and invigorates the earth, the same principle must be at work in the rest of the world, since plants are rooted in the earth, animals live by breathing air, and the air shares with us in the acts of seeing, hearing, and uttering sounds—without the air none of these would be possible. It even moves with us; for wherever we go, however we move, it seems to give way to make room for us.

(84) "Furthermore, those things which tend downward, i.e., toward the center of the earth, and those which rise from the center upward [i.e., to the surface], and also those which rotate about the center, constitute the one and continuous nature of the world. Moreover, since there are four kinds of matter, the

continuance of nature is maintained by their constant changes. Thus water comes from earth, air from water, and ether from air; reversing this order, air is derived from fire, water from air, and earth, the lowest of the four elements, from water, of which all beings are formed. Thus by their continual motions upward and downward, backward and forward, the various parts of the universe are held together. (85) And this system, in the beautiful form in which we now see it, necessarily must be either everlasting or at least of very long duration, for an almost infinite length of time. Whichever it is, the universe must in consequence be governed by nature. Take the art of navigating a fleet or of marshaling an army, or, to return to the processes of nature, take the reproductive process of vines or trees, or the shape and harmony of limbs of animals—which of these shows such evidence of skill as appears in the world itself? Therefore we must either say that nothing is ruled by a conscious nature, or else admit that the whole world is governed by it. (86) Indeed, since the world contains all other natures, and also their seeds, how can we deny that it is itself governed by nature? That would be like saying that the teeth and the beard of a man are the work of nature, though the man himself is not. And this would ignore the principle that things which of themselves produce other things are superior to the things produced. Now it is the universe, we may say, that sows, plants, begets, trains, nourishes and sustains whatever nature governs as members and parts of itself. But if the parts of the universe are governed by nature, then the universe itself must also be governed by nature. In nature's administration there is nothing that could possibly be criticized; from the existing elements nature has produced the best possible result. (87) Let anyone show how it could have been better! But no one can ever do that, and anyone who tries to improve upon nature will either make it worse or will be longing for the impossible.

"But if all the parts of the universe are so constituted that nothing could have been better for use or more beautiful in form, let us consider whether this is the result of chance, or whether the parts of the world are in such a state that they could not possibly cohere unless controlled by wisdom and divine providence. If, therefore, the things produced by nature are superior to those produced by art, and if art produces nothing without reason, it follows that nature too must possess reason. How consistent is it if, when you see a statue or a picture, you recognize it as a work of art; or if when you see from a distance a ship under full sail, you judge that it is navigated by reason and skill; or if when you see a sundial or a water clock, you recognize that it tells the hours by art and not by chance—you nevertheless imagine the universe, which contains all these arts and their inventors, to be lacking in reason and purpose?

(88) "But suppose someone carried off to Scythia or Britain that sphere [i.e., orrery] which was recently built by our friend Posidonius to show by its revolutions the daily and nightly course of the sun, the moon, and the five wandering stars [planets], would anyone in those barbarous lands doubt that this sphere had been perfected by the use of reason?

"Yet these thinkers have doubts about the universe, from which all things arise and exist, whether it is the result of chance or of some kind of necessity rather than the work of reason and divine mind. According to them, Archimedes was more skillful in making a model to show the motions of the celestial globe than nature was in causing them, though the original in its many parts is so vastly superior in its craftsmanship to the copy. (89) The shepherd in Accius [i.e., in his play *Medea*], who had never before seen a ship, when from a mountaintop he saw far off the divine new vessel of the Argonauts, was at first surprised and alarmed and said as follows:

'So vast a bulk, it glides
Out of the deep with whistling roar of the wind;
Waves roll before it, great whirlpools surge beside,
And falling forward the ocean's foam breaks in spume!
As if the bursting storm cloud fell apart
Or a rock flew skyward with the hurricane

Or a whirling waterspout rose from the clashing waves—
Unless the sea now threatens to assault the land,
Or Triton with his trident opens up the deep sea caves
And hurls aloft their rocky roofs into the sky.'

"At first, he wonders what this unknown thing may be; but when he sees the young sailors and hears their songs, he adds,

'Like playful dolphins, cleaving the sea with their
    snouts,'

and so on, line after line—

'It brings to my ears and hearing such a song
As once I heard the god Silvanus sing.'

(90) "Just as at first sight the shepherd thinks he sees something inanimate and unfeeling, but afterward, judging by clearer signs, he begins to suspect the true nature of that of which he had hitherto been in doubt, so the philosophers, though perplexed by their first sight of the universe, ought afterward, when they had observed its regular, uniform motions and all its phenomena governed by established order and immutable system, to have inferred that there is in it some Being who not only inhabits this divine, celestial dwelling, but is also its ruler and governor, the architect, so to speak, of this mighty fabric."

[The remainder of this third division of the subject emphasizes the wonderful harmony and mutual adaptation of the physical universe, something which cannot be the result of an accidental concourse of atoms. As Aristotle said, it is really our too great familiarity with the marvels of nature that blinds us to their meaning—or as Emerson once paraphrased the argument, if the stars appeared once in a thousand years their effect on mankind would be far different than it is now. Sections 98–153 review in detail the wonders of nature, with many fine quotations from the poets, and expound the theory that the world is held together by centripetal force—we now call it gravitation—and dies and is regenerated through vast cycles of time. (The influence of astronomy upon Stoic thinking is obvious.) In all this mutual adaptation of the universe for the purpose of its own preservation and for man's survival and convenience, we may recognize the hand of Providence: we may see it even in man's physical structure and in his intellectual capacity. The argument concludes with § 153, after which the fourth main division begins with § 154.]

(153) "Moreover, has not man's reason penetrated even the heavens? We alone of all living creatures have observed the courses of the stars, their rising and setting, and have marked the bounds of day, month, and year, and have foreseen the eclipses of the sun and moon, and foretold them for all time to come, marking their extent, duration, and date. Thus, by contemplating the heavenly bodies, the mind acquires a knowledge of the gods—a knowledge which produces piety, with which is joined justice and all the other virtues; and from this comes a life of happiness, in no way inferior to that of the gods except that it lacks immortality, which really is not indispensable to a happy life. Having now explained all these things, I think that I have sufficiently demonstrated the superiority of man to all other living creatures; and this ought to make it clear that neither the form and arrangement of man's body, nor the power of his mind and understanding, could possibly be produced by chance.

(154) "I must now prove, by way of conclusion, that everything in the world which is used by men was made purposely for man's use.

"First of all, the universe itself was made for the sake of gods and men, and everything therein was prepared and provided for our enjoyment. For the universe is as it were the common dwelling of gods and men, or the city belonging to both; for they are the only beings that make use of reason, they alone live by justice and law. As, therefore, it must be presumed the cities of Athens and Sparta were built for the [use of the] Athenians and Lacedaemonians, and as everything contained in these cities is rightly said to belong to those two peoples, so everything contained in the universe may be said to belong to the gods and to men.

(155) "In the next place, though the revolutions of the sun, moon, and all the stars contribute to the coherence of the uni-

verse, they may nevertheless also be considered as objects designed for the contemplation of men. There is no sight of which it is less possible to become tired, none more beautiful, none that displays more wisdom and skill. For by measuring their courses we learn when the different seasons will arrive, with their variations and changes; and if these are known only to men, it must be inferred that they were created for the sake of men.

(156) "Does the earth bring forth its fruits, of grain and various kinds of vegetables, in such excessive abundance and variety, for the use of wild beasts or for the use of men? What can we say of the abundant and exhilarating fruit of the vine and of the olive tree, which are totally useless to the beasts? They know nothing about sowing or cultivating, or reaping and gathering in the fruits of the earth in due season, or about laying them up and preserving them. Man alone has the care and enjoys the advantage of these things. (157) And so, just as the lyre and the flute were made for those who are able to play on them, so we must agree that the products of the earth, of which I have spoken, were designed for those only who make use of them; and even though some of the beasts may carry off and rob us of a small part, it does not follow that the earth produced them for their sakes too. Men do not store up corn for mice and ants, but for their wives, their children, and their families; the animals, therefore, as I have already said, share them only by stealth, while their masters freely and openly enjoy them.

(158) "It must be admitted, then, that all this abundance of nature has been provided for the sake of men—unless perchance this great plenty and variety of fruit, which delight not only with their taste but also with their smell and appearance, lead us to suspect that nature never intended them for men alone? [i.e., but also for the gods, as in ancient tales]. The animals, far from being partakers of this blessing, were themselves obviously made for the use of man. Of what use would sheep be except for their wool, which is carded and woven into human apparel?—for they are, in fact, incapable of pro-

ducing anything themselves, or even of obtaining food and sustenance, without man's care and attention. Or consider the fidelity of a dog, his affectionate fawning on his master, his antagonism to strangers, his incredible keenness of scent in discovering a trail, and his eagerness in hunting—what do these qualities suggest but that he was created for the use of men? (159) Why do I need to mention oxen? Their very backs show that they were not meant to carry burdens, but their necks were born for the yoke and their strong, broad shoulders were designed to draw the plow. In the Golden Age, so the poets say, no violence was ever offered them, so indispensable were they in breaking up the clods and tilling the fallow soil.

> But then the Iron Age began; men dared
> To forge the deadly blade
> And feasted on the tame domestic ox.
>   [Aratus, *Phaenomena*, 129 ff.]

So useful was the service rendered by oxen that to eat their flesh was viewed as a crime.

"It would take a long time to recount the utility of mules and asses, which undoubtedly were provided for human use. (160) What is the pig good for except to eat?—whose life, Chrysippus says, was given it in lieu of salt to keep it from putrefying; and, as it is a proper food for man, nature has made no animal more prolific. Why should I mention the swarming multitudes of edible fish? Or of birds, which are so delicious to our taste that our [Stoic] Providence seems to be an Epicurean! But they also could not even be caught except by man's cleverness and skill. Though there are some birds, we think—the 'birds of flight' and 'birds of utterance,' as our augurs call them—which were born for the purposes of augury.

(161) "The large wild animals, moreover, we take by hunting, partly for food, partly to exercise ourselves [in the hunt] in an imitation of martial discipline; also to [seize for] use those which we can tame and train, such as elephants; or to extract from their bodies remedies for wounds and diseases, as we also do from certain roots and herbs, the value of which we have learned from long use and experience. Let your mind's

eye sweep the whole earth and all the seas, and you will behold immense fertile plains and mountains thickly clad with forests, the pasturage of herds, and ships sailing over the deep with incredible speed; (162) nor is it only on the surface of the earth, but also in its dark depths many useful things lie hidden which, having been made for man, can be discovered only by men.

"Another proof that the providence of the gods is concerned with human affairs, and in my opinion the strongest proof of all, is divination, though it is one which both of you, perhaps, will seize upon and attack—you, Cotta, because Carneades used to enjoy inveighing against the Stoics, and you, Velleius, because there is nothing Epicurus ridicules so much as the prediction of future events. Divination is practiced in many places, for many purposes, on many occasions, often in private but more especially in public concerns. (163) Many things are discerned by the haruspices, many things are foreseen by the augurs, many are declared by oracles, many by prophecies, many by dreams, many by prodigies. By such knowledge it often happens that many things turn up for men's enjoyment and use, and that many dangers are avoided. This ability, therefore, to foresee the future—whether it be a power, an art, or a natural gift—has certainly been granted to men, and to men only, by the immortal gods.

"If these proofs, taken separately, fail to move you, nevertheless when they are all combined, they must certainly do so.

(164) "Furthermore, the care and providence of the gods is not only for the human race as a whole but for individual men. We may thus gradually bring down this universality to smaller and smaller groups, until finally you reach single individuals. For if the reasons which I have already given prove that the gods take care of all men everywhere, in every land and on every shore however remote from our continent, they must also take care of those who dwell on the same lands with us, from the rising of the sun to its setting; (165) and if they care for those who inhabit this vast island, so to speak, which we call the round earth, they must also care for those who in-

habit various parts of this island, Europe, Asia, and Africa; and therefore they also favor the various parts of these parts, such as Rome, Athens, Sparta, and Rhodes; and they also love individual men in these cities, quite apart from the whole populace, men like Curius, Fabricius, Coruncanius in the war with Pyrrhus; in the First Punic War, Calatinus, Duellius, Metellus, Lutatius; in the Second, Maximus, Marcellus, Africanus; after these, Paulus, Gracchus, Cato; and in our fathers' time, Scipio and Laelius; and many besides—both our own country and Greece have produced many illustrious men, who cannot be thought to have been what they were without the help of God. (166) This is why the poets, Homer especially, were led to attach their chief heroes—Ulysses, Diomede, Agamemnon, Achilles—to certain deities as companions in their adventures and dangers. Moreover, as I have already stated, the gods have frequently appeared in person, thus showing their concern for both cities and individual men. This is also apparent from the indications of coming events which are portended to men, sometimes sleeping, sometimes when awake. We are likewise forewarned by many signs and by the entrails of [sacrificial] victims, and by many other means which by long continued usage have been so carefully observed that the art of divination has resulted.

(167) "There was never, therefore, any great man without some measure of divine inspiration. It is no disproof of this if a storm should damage someone's fields or vineyards, or if an accident should rob him of something of value, and we should infer from this that God hates or neglects him. 'The gods take care of great matters, and neglect the small.' But to great men everything always turns out prosperously—as has perhaps been sufficiently elaborated by us [Stoics] as also by Socrates, that prince of philosophy, in our discourses on the abundant wealth which virtue provides.

(168) "This is about everything that has come into my mind which I thought appropriate to say on the nature of the gods. And you, Cotta, if you listen to me, will defend the same cause. Remember that you are both a leading citizen and a pontiff.

And since your school is free to argue on both sides, take mine, and devote to it that power of eloquence which you have acquired by your rhetorical exercises and which the Academy has fostered. For it is a wicked and impious custom to argue against the gods, whether it is done seriously or only in pretense."

BOOK THREE

[Bk. III opens with the Academic criticism of the Stoic theology. Cotta is the speaker once more; his attitude is typically Roman, conservative and reserved, as well as typically Academic, i.e., skeptical and critical. He admits the force of Balbus' exposition, but is himself content with the ancestral religion of Rome. The four main divisions of the subject, as outlined by Balbus, are now followed. (1) The divine *existence* can be assumed—but if belief in the gods is both logically necessary and in fact universal, argument may only awaken doubts. The sight of the heavens does not always move men to faith, and common ideas are not innate but really very unreliable. Stories of apparitions are mere legend. Divination is not only not true, but if true would be useless, and would not prove the existence of gods. (2) The divine *nature* is not a philosophical conclusion, as the philosophers are in disagreement and their arguments are invalid. Carneades has proved conclusively that all living things are mortal, and therefore even the gods are not immortal. The Stoic deification of the stars, of grain and wine (i.e., following their allegorism), and of departed great men (Euhemerism) is wholly irrational, while their deified abstractions are absurd. (3) On the providential government of the universe only one paragraph survives from this section (see p. 81). Presumably Cotta also refuted this view. (4) On the providential care for man, Cotta insists that the gift of reason has been a misfortune; only a virtuous use of reason is advantageous, and that depends upon the individual. "Providence" ought to have foreseen this, and withheld the gift! The long tale of human misfortunes also proves the absence of any divine *Pronoia,* and this is the sum of the matter. He then continues:]

(79) "But at this point we may bring our discussion to an end. For if, by the general consensus of all philosophers, folly is a greater evil than all the evils of fortune and of the body

when balanced against it, and if wisdom, on the other hand, is achieved by no one, then we are all in the very depths of misfortune—we, of whom the gods have taken the greatest care. For just as there is no difference between saying that no one *is* healthy and saying that no one *can be* healthy, so I fail to see any difference whether you say that no one *is* wise or that no one *can be* wise.

"However, we need say nothing more on a point that is already perfectly clear. Telamon dismisses the whole subject, viz., that the gods pay no attention to man, in a single line [of Ennius' play]:

> If they cared [for us], the good would prosper
> and the evil suffer:
> But this does not happen.
> [Frag. 330]

Indeed, the gods should have made all men good, if they were really concerned over the welfare of the human race; (80) or at the very least they should certainly have taken care of the good. But why, then, were the two Scipios, the bravest and best of men, defeated in Spain by the Carthaginians? Why did Maximus have to bury his son, a consul? Why was Hannibal permitted to kill Marcellus? Why was Paulus overwhelmed at Cannae? Why was Regulus handed over to be tortured by the Carthaginians? Why was not Africanus protected by his own walls? [He was murdered in bed by an unknown assassin.] But these instances and many others belong to the past; let us look at more recent ones. Why is my uncle, Publius Rutilius, a man of unsullied character and of the greatest learning, now in exile? Why was my colleague Drusus murdered in his own house? Why was that model of temperance and prudence, Quintus Scaevola, the Pontifex Maximus, assassinated in the very presence of the statue of Vesta? And before that, why were so many of the foremost citizens put to death by Cinna? Why was that most treacherous man of all, Gaius Marius, given the power to order the death of that noblest of men, Quintus Catulus? (81) The day would be too short if I set out to make a list of the good men who have been overwhelmed by adversity, or, equally, the wicked who have prospered. Why did Marius die comfortably at home, an old man, and a consul for the seventh time? Why did that utterly cruel man Cinna rule for so long? 'But,' you say, 'he was punished.' It would have been far better had he been prevented from murdering all those eminent men, rather than himself eventually punished. That savage barbarian Quintus Varius was put to death with the most painful torments and penalties; but if this was his punishment for stabbing Drusus and poisoning Metellus, it would have been far better to have kept them alive than to punish Varius for his crimes. Dionysius was a despot for thirty-eight years over the wealthiest and happiest of cities [Syracuse]; (82) and before his time, for how many years did Pisistratus prosper in the very flower of Greece [Athens]! 'But,' you say, 'Phalaris and Apollodorus—surely they were punished!' Yes, but not until they had tortured and murdered a great many persons. Brigands, too—many of them are often punished; but surely we cannot say that the captives they have cruelly murdered are fewer in number than the brigands who are executed! Further, we are told that Anaxarchus, the follower of Democritus, was slaughtered by the tyrant of Cyprus, and that Zeno of Elea was tortured to death. Why should I mention Socrates, of whose death I can never read, in Plato [in the *Phaedo*], without weeping? Do you not see, then, that the judgment of the gods, supposing they pay any attention to human affairs, has obliterated all distinctions? [I.e., between good and evil, or between the upright and the wicked. Cf. § 84 *ad fin.*]

(83) "Diogenes the Cynic used to say that Harpalus, a bandit in those days who was looked upon as a happy man, was the standing witness against the gods, since he lived and prospered for so long. Dionysius, whom I have just mentioned, after plundering the temple of Proserpine at Locri, was sailing back to Syracuse, and as he held his course with a strong following wind, smiled and said, 'Do you see, my friends, what a fine voyage the immortal gods provide those who commit sacrilege?' He was a very clever fellow, and he caught hold of the

truth so thoroughly and so clearly that he persevered in this view. When his fleet touched the coast of the Peloponnese and he arrived at the temple of Olympian Zeus, he stripped off the immensely heavy gold mantle of the god which the tyrant Gelo had devoted to Jove out of the spoils taken from the Carthaginians; and he actually joked about it, saying that a golden mantle was much too heavy for summer and too cold for winter and tossing him a woolen mantle, which was good for any time of year.

"He also ordered the removal of the gold beard of Aesculapius at Epidaurus, saying it was not proper for the son to wear a beard when his father [Apollo] in all his temples appeared without one. (84) He even ordered the silver tables removed from the shrines, since in accordance with ancient Greek custom they were inscribed, 'The property of the good gods'; for he said he wished to benefit by their goodness. Moreover, he did not hesitate to remove the little gold images of Victory, and the gold cups and crowns which were held in the outstretched hands of the statues, saying that he did not *take* them but only *accepted* them since it was ridiculous to pray for good things and then refuse to take them when they were held out to you! It is also said that he offered in the markets the spoils of the temples I have mentioned, and sold them at auction; then, when he had got his money, he issued a proclamation that anyone possessing any article taken from a holy place must restore it, before a certain day, to the shrine to which it belonged. And so along with impiety to the gods he combined injustice to men. Well, this Dionysius was never struck dead by a thunderbolt from Olympian Jupiter, nor did Aesculapius let him die with some lingering and painful disease. He died in his bed, and was laid out upon a noble pyre, and the power he had seized by wickedness was passed on by inheritance to his son, as if it were perfectly just and legitimate.

(85) "I hesitate to expound this subject [further], since it seems to authorize crime. And this would be the correct inference, if it were not for the heavy weight of conscience,

whether innocent or guilty, which operates without regard for divine sanction. Take this away, and everything tumbles into ruin. For just as a household or a state seems to be without any rational discipline or order if there are no rewards for good conduct and penalties for bad, so there can be no such thing as a divine government of the world if there is in it no distinction between good men and bad.

(86) " 'But,' it may be urged, 'the gods pay no attention to little matters [cf. II. 167], and are not concerned with the tiny farms and poor vines of individual persons, so that any small damage done by blight or hail can scarcely have come to Jupiter's attention. In kingdoms the rulers do not look after every last detail of affairs.' This is your argument. As if it were Publius Rutilius' estate at Formiae about which I was complaining [§ 80], and not his total loss of safety! But this is a way mortals have: their external commodities ["the good things of life"], vineyards, grain fields, olive groves, abundant harvests of fruit and grain—in short, all the comforts and prosperity which enrich their life—these, they say, are derived from the gods; but no one ever looked upon virtue as the gift of a god! (87) And no doubt with good reason, since our virtue entitles us to receive praise from others, and in virtue we have a right to take pride, which we could not do if it came as a gift from God and not from ourselves. On the other hand, when we gain new honors, or are blessed with some increase in our property, or when we receive any other of the good things that come by fortune or luckily escape any of the evils, we then return thanks to the gods, and do not assume that any praise is due to ourselves. But who ever thanked the gods that he was a good man? No, but we thank them that we are rich, honored, safe and sound. That is why men describe Jupiter as Best and Greatest [*Optimus et Maximus*], not that he makes us just, temperate, or wise, but because he keeps us safe, secure, opulent, rich! (88) No one ever vowed a tenth [of the spoils of war or of discovered treasure] to Hercules in order to be made wise! It is true, there is a tale that Pythagoras sacrificed an ox to the Muses every time he made some new discovery in geom-

etry; but I do not believe it, since he refused to sacrifice to
Apollo even at Delos, lest he should defile the altar with blood.
But to return to my point. It is agreed by all mankind that
good fortune must be asked of the gods, but wisdom must be
obtained by oneself. Let us consecrate as many temples as we
will to Mind, to Virtue, and to Faith, yet we must acknowledge that they are things which belong within ourselves. In
regard to safety, wealth, and victory, these are gifts we must
implore the gods to give us. Hence it follows, as Diogenes used
to say [cf. § 83], that the prosperity and success of the wicked
completely disprove the power and sovereignty of the gods.

(89) " 'But good men sometimes end their lives happily.'
Yes, and so we seize their examples and without the least show
of reason attribute their success to the gods. Diagoras, who was
called the Atheist, once visited Samothrace, where one of his
friends showed him several pictures of people who had survived very dangerous storms. 'You assume,' he said, 'that the
gods pay no attention to human affairs. Do you not recognize
from all these painted tablets how many persons through their
vows to the gods have escaped the violence of tempests and
reached port in safety?' 'Sure enough,' replied Diagoras, 'but
there are no pictures of those who were shipwrecked and lost
at sea.' On another voyage he himself ran into a storm, and
the sailors, alarmed and terrified, told him they justly deserved their misfortune for admitting him on board their ship.
But he pointed out to them several other ships laboring
through the storm and asked if they thought these ships also
had a Diagoras on board. And so with regard to good or bad
fortune, it makes not the slightest difference what you are or
how you have lived.

(90) " 'The gods, like kings, do not pay attention to everything,' it is said [cf. § 86]. But what is the parallel here? If
kings knowingly overlook anything [for which they are re-
sponsible], they are very guilty; but a god cannot plead ignorance as an excuse. Yet what an extraordinary defense you
make for his case when you say that even if a wicked man escapes his punishment by dying, the penalty is inflicted on his

children, his children's children, and all his posterity. What
a marvelous example of divine justice! Would any city tolerate
the proposal of a law like that, which sentenced a son or a
grandson for the crime committed by a father or a grandfather?

> When will the feud of the Tantalidae end?
> What punishment for Myrtilus's murder
> Will ever satisfy the lust for vengeance?
> [Attius, *Thyestes*]

(91) Whether the poets have corrupted the Stoics, or the Stoics
have authorized the poets, I cannot readily say—certainly both
of them relate monstrous, revolting tales. The person lashed
by the poem of Hipponax or wounded by the verses of Archi-
lochus did not receive a wound from a god, nor one that was
self-inflicted. Nor do we try to trace out a divine penalty when
we see Aegisthus and Paris sunk in licentiousness, for we can
almost hear their guilt crying out [for punishment]. Nor do I
attribute the recovery of many persons from illness to Aesculapius, but rather to Hippocrates; and I cannot allow that
Sparta received her rule of life from Apollo rather than from
Lycurgus. It was really Critolaus who overthrew Corinth,
Hasdrubal who conquered Carthage; these two generals put
out the two 'bright eyes of the seashore,' not some angry god
who, as you maintain, cannot possibly be angry. (92) But at
least some god could have come to the rescue of those brilliant, magnificent cities and preserved them! For, as you yourselves are always saying, there is nothing a god cannot do, and
that without the least exertion. As a man's limbs are moved
without opposition merely by his own mind and volition, so it
is possible for anything to be made, moved about, or changed
by the will of the gods. This view you hold, not as a relic of
superstition or an old wives' tale, but as a sound, scientific
principle. For matter, you say, of which and in which all
things consist, is entirely flexible and changeable, so that there
is nothing which cannot be formed or altered instantaneously;
[you also say] that the shaping and controlling power in the
universe is divine providence; and therefore providence can,

wherever it moves, perform whatever it will. From this it follows that providence either does not know the extent of its own power, or has no interest in human affairs, or is incapable of judging what is the best thing to do.

(93) " 'Providence,' you say, 'does not concern itself with individual men' [cf. II. 164]. No wonder!—since it does not care for cities. Not even for cities? No, nor for whole nations or peoples. If, therefore, it even despises whole nations, what wonder is there if it scorns the whole human race? But how can you assert that the gods do not concern themselves with all the petty circumstances of life, and at the same time hold that specific, individual dreams are distributed to men by the immortal gods! I take up this question with you because your school believes in the truth of dreams. And do you also maintain that men ought to obligate themselves with vows? But vows are taken by individuals; hence it appears that the divine mind listens even to private matters, and can you not see, accordingly, that it is not so heavily engrossed [with public affairs] as you supposed? Assume that it is busily engaged in moving the heavens and looking after the earth and controlling the seas: why does it permit so many gods to be idle and do nothing? Why is not the management of human affairs handed over to some of those idle deities, which you, Balbus, described as innumerable?

"This is about what I have to say concerning the nature of the gods; not with a desire to destroy [the idea], but merely to let you see how obscure a subject it is, and how difficult to explain" [cf. I. 1].

(94) When he had said this, Cotta ceased speaking. But Lucilius replied, "You have been very severe in your attack upon divine providence, that doctrine established by the Stoics with the greatest piety and wisdom! But as it is growing late, please set another day for our answer to your views. For it is my duty to challenge you in defense of our altars and hearths, the temples and shrines of the gods, nay, even the walls of the City, which you pontiffs declare to be sacred—for you surround the City with religion [ceremonies] even more carefully than

you do with walls. This is something which, as long as I am able to breathe, I think it utterly wrong for me to abandon."

(95) To which Cotta replied, "I really wish that you would refute me, Balbus! What I have set forth was intended not to decide this debate, but to discuss it; and I am sure that you can easily defeat me."

"No doubt of that," said Velleius, "when he even believes that our dreams are sent from Jupiter, which, unsubstantial as they are, still have more weight than a Stoic discourse on the nature of the gods!"

Here the conversation ended and we parted, Velleius believing that Cotta's arguments were the soundest, while to me it seemed that those of Balbus came closer to the semblance of truth.

THE DREAM OF SCIPIO

Cicero, *On the Republic,* VI. 9–26. This treatise on the principles of government was written probably in 54 B.C. The dialogue is assumed to have been spoken during the Latin holidays in 129 B.C., in the garden of Scipio Africanus the Younger. The work was in six books, spread over three days, and the Dream of Scipio is the conclusion of the whole treatise, emphasizing the eternal rewards awaiting heroic self-denial and conspicuous service to the state. The *Republic* was once one of Cicero's most popular writings. From as late as the fifth or sixth century there survives an uncial manuscript which was later used as a palimpsest for a copy of St. Augustine's *Commentary on the Psalms.* After this the treatise disappeared completely, and only the Dream was copied and handed on, independently. About A.D. 400 Macrobius had written a commentary on the Dream, and this helped to preserve it. But in 1820 Cardinal Angelo Mai discovered the palimpsest in the Vatican Library, recognized and identified it, and so recovered about a fourth to a third of the original work, chiefly fragments of Bks. I–III. See the text and translation in LCL by C. W. Keyes (1928); the annotated translation by J. A. Kleist (1915); and Wm. H. Stahl, *Macrobius: Commentary on the Dream of Scipio* (1952).

[Scipio is speaking:] "When I went to Africa on the staff of the consul Manius Manilius with the rank, as you know, of military tribune of the Fourth Legion [i.e., in 149 B.C., at the beginning of the Third Punic War], my strongest desire was to meet King Masinissa, who for very good reason was a devoted friend of our family. When I entered the king's presence, that grand old man threw his arms around me and wept freely. After a little time he looked up to heaven and said, 'I give thee thanks, O Sun supreme, and you also, ye other heavenly beings, that before I depart this life I see within my kingdom and under my roof Publius Cornelius Scipio, the very sound of whose name refreshes me—so little can I forget that noble and invincible man!' [I.e., Scipio Africanus the Elder, Scipio's grandfather.]

"I then questioned him about his kingdom, while he in turn inquired about our Republic; thus we spent the whole day in conversation. (10) After we had been entertained with royal hospitality, we continued our conversation until late in the night, the old king talking of nothing but Africanus, and recalling not only his every deed but also all his words. At last we parted for the night, and as I was tired from my journey, and also had sat up late, I fell at once into a much sounder sleep than usual. Then the following dream came to me, suggested no doubt by the subject of our conversation. For it often happens that our thoughts and words affect us during sleep somewhat in the way that Ennius records with reference to [the vision of] Homer, about whom, as you know, he was constantly thinking and speaking during his waking hours. In my case, Africanus appeared to me in the form with which I was familiar from his bust, rather than from my personal recollection. When I recognized him, I trembled with terror, but he said, 'Courage, Scipio; do not be afraid, but remember carefully what I am about to tell you.

(11) " 'Can you see that city yonder, which I forced to obey the Roman people, but which is now renewing its old hostility and cannot be at rest?' (He was pointing to Carthage, from a high starlit place, bathed in light.) 'That city,' he continued, 'you, now scarcely more than a common soldier, have come to lay siege to; but within two years, you, a consul, will lay it

level with the ground. The surname [Africanus] to which you are now only an heir will then be your own through personal achievement. After destroying Carthage you will celebrate a triumph; then you will be censor, and will go on embassies to Egypt, Syria, Asia, and Greece. Finally, though absent from Rome, you will be elected consul for a second time and by the destruction of Numantia you will bring a great war to a close. However, after your triumphal entry into the Capitol you will find the Republic disturbed as the result of the schemes of my grandson [Tiberius Gracchus]. (12) At that critical moment, Africanus, you must show forth in the service of your fatherland the light of your spirit, your abilities, your wise counsel.

" 'Nevertheless, at that time, I see, two paths of destiny will confront you. For when your age has reached eight times seven solar circuits [i.e., 8×7 years], and when in the course of nature these two numbers—each of which is perfect, though for different reasons—have combined to produce the sum [$= 56$] so big with fate for you, then the whole State will turn to you and to your name alone. The Senate, all good citizens, the allies, the Latin peoples, will all look to you. You will be the only one who can save the nation. In a word, it will be your duty as dictator to restore order to the commonwealth—provided you escape the wicked hands of your kinsmen [the Gracchi].' "

(At this Laelius cried aloud, and the others uttered deep groans. But Scipio smiled gently and said: "Shh! I beg you, do not wake me from sleep, but listen for a little while and hear the rest.")

(13) " 'However, Africanus, in order to encourage you in your endeavors to safeguard the State, consider this: all those who have preserved, aided, or extended their fatherland have a special place assigned to them in heaven where they may enjoy an eternal life of happiness. For nothing done on earth more greatly pleases the supreme deity who rules the entire universe than assemblies or communities of men bound together by justice, which are called states. Their rulers and preservers go forth from here, and hither they return.'

(14) "By this time I was thoroughly terrified, not so much

fearing death as the treachery of my own kin. Nevertheless, I [went on and] inquired of Africanus whether he himself was still alive, and also whether my father Paulus was, and also the others whom we think of as having ceased to be.

" 'Of course they are alive,' he replied: 'They have taken their flight from the bonds of the body as from a prison. Your so-called life [on earth] is really death. Do you not see your father Paulus coming to meet you?'

"At the sight of my father I broke down and cried. But he embraced me and kissed me and told me not to weep. (15) As soon as I had controlled my grief and could speak, I began: 'Why, O best and saintliest of fathers, since here [only] is life worthy of the name, as I have just heard from Africanus, why must I live a dying life on earth? Why may I not hasten to join you here?'

" 'No indeed,' he replied. 'Unless that God whose temple is the whole visible universe releases you from the prison of the body, you cannot gain entrance here. For men were given life for the purpose of cultivating that globe, called Earth, which you see at the center of this temple. Each has been given a soul, [a spark] from those eternal fires which you call stars and planets, which are globular and rotund and are animated by divine intelligences, and which with marvelous velocity revolve in their established orbits. Like all god-fearing men, therefore, Publius, you must leave the soul in the custody of the body, and must not quit the life on Earth unless you are summoned by the one who gave it to you; otherwise you will be seen to shirk the duty assigned by God to man.

(16) " 'But, Scipio, like your grandfather here, like myself, who was your father, cultivate justice and the sense of duty [*pietas*], which are of great importance in relation to parents and kindred but even more in relation to one's country. Such a life [spent in the service of one's country] is a highway to the skies, to the fellowship of those who have completed their earthly lives and have been released from the body and now dwell in that place which you see yonder' (it was the circle of

dazzling brilliance which blazed among the stars), 'which you, using a term borrowed from the Greeks, call the Milky Way.'

"Looking about from this high vantage point, everything appeared to me to be marvelous and beautiful. There were stars which we never see from the Earth, and the dimensions of all of them were greater than we have ever suspected. The smallest among them was the one which, being farthest from Heaven and nearest the Earth, shone with a borrowed light [the Moon]. The size of the stars, however, far exceeded that of the Earth. Indeed, the latter seemed so small that I was humiliated with our empire, which is only a point where we touch the surface of the globe.

(17) "As I gazed still more intently at the Earth, Africanus said: 'How long, I wonder, will your mind continue to be fastened to the soil? Do you not see what a temple you have entered? Here are the nine circles, or rather spheres, by which all things are held together. One of these, the outermost, is Heaven, which contains within it all the rest, and is itself the supreme deity, embracing all, enclosing all. Within it are fastened those [spheres] that revolve, the everlasting courses of the stars. Beneath it are seven spheres revolving the other way, in the direction opposite to that of Heaven. One sphere is occupied by that star which on earth they call Saturn. Next comes that of the bright light called Jupiter, bringing prosperity and health to mankind. Then there is one which you call Mars, of reddish hue and horrifying to the lands of men. Farther down, nearly midway between Heaven and Earth, is the region ruled by the Sun, who is the leader, prince, and governor of the other lights, the mind of the universe and its guiding principle, of such magnitude that he illumines and fills all things with his light. He is followed by two companions, so to speak, Venus and Mercury, in their courses. In the lowest sphere revolves the Moon, lighted up by the rays of the Sun. But below the Moon there is nothing but what is mortal and doomed to decay, except souls which are given by the gods to the human race. Above the Moon all things are

eternal. The Earth, which is the ninth and central sphere, does not rotate, being at the lowest point of all; toward it all things are drawn by reason of their weight.'

(18) "When I had recovered from my astonishment over this great panorama, and had come to myself, I asked: 'Tell me, what is this loud, sweet harmony that fills my ears?'

"He replied, 'This music is produced by the impulse and motion of these spheres themselves. The unequal intervals between them are arranged according to a strict proportion, and so the high notes blend agreeably with the low, and thus various sweet harmonies are produced. Such immense revolutions cannot, of course, be so swiftly carried out in silence, and it is only natural that one extreme should produce deep tones and the other high ones. Accordingly, this highest sphere of Heaven, which bears the stars, and whose revolution is swifter, produces a high shrill sound, whereas the lowest sphere, that of the Moon, rotates with the deepest sound. The Earth, of course, the ninth sphere, remains fixed and immovable in the center of the universe. But the other eight spheres, two of which move with the same speed, produce seven different sounds—a number, by the way, which is the key to almost everything. Skillful men reproducing this celestial music on stringed instruments have thus opened the way for their own return to this heavenly region, as other men of outstanding genius have done by spending their lives on Earth in the study of things divine.

(19) " 'Men's ears, being always filled with this music, have grown deaf to it. For it is a fact that none of your senses is so dull as that of hearing. Thus in the neighborhood of Catadupa, where the Nile comes rushing down [in a cataract] from high mountains, the people that live there have lost their sense of hearing as a result of the deafening noise. But this mighty music of the spheres, produced by the swift speed with which the whole universe spins round, is so overwhelming that no human ear can sense it, any more than you can look straight at the sun, whose rays would overpower the keenness of your sight.'

"While I marveled at this explanation, I still kept turning my eyes back in the direction of the Earth. (20) Then Africanus went on: 'I see that you are still looking in the direction of the home and dwelling place of man! If the Earth appears small to you, as it really is, then keep your gaze fixed upon these heavenly things, and disregard the human and earthly. For how can you achieve fame merely from the lips of men, or how can you gain real glory? You see that the Earth is inhabited only sparsely and in limited areas, and that vast stretches of wilderness lie between these scattered patches, as we may call them, which are inhabited. Moreover, the inhabitants of the Earth are so widely separated that no communication is possible between the different groups. Some live in a different zone [i.e., northern or southern] from you, others live under different meridians, while still others are at your antipodes. Surely, you cannot expect any glory from them!

(21) " 'The Earth, you will further notice, is girdled about with something like belts. Two of these zones, which are in entirely opposite parts of the Earth and which at either end lie directly under the celestial poles, are buried, as you see, under ice and snow; while the middle zone, which is also the widest, scorches under the heat of the Sun. There remain only two zones that are habitable; of these the southern, whose inhabitants set their footsteps in an opposite direction to yours, is cut off from all communication with your zone; the other zone, the northern, which you inhabit—see how small a territory belongs to you [i.e., the Romans]. In fact, the whole region inhabited by you is only a small island, narrow from south to north, though wider from west to east, and surrounded by that sea which on Earth you call the Atlantic, the Great Sea, or Ocean—but you can see how small it is in spite of its great name!

(22) " 'Now, do you suppose that from these lands that are known and settled, your name or that of any of us could ever cross over this Caucasus which you see, or swim across yonder Ganges? Who among the dwellers in the rest of the Orient or Occident, or in the farther North or South, will ever hear of

your name? Leave these out of account, and you will certainly realize what a limited area it is over which your glory is so eager to spread!

" 'Moreover, those who actually do speak of us—how long will they keep on doing so? (23) And even if the generations to come were willing to transmit to their descendants the fame of each and every one of us as they had received it from their sires, still we can acquire no glory for any length of time, much less for ever, because of the floods and conflagrations of the earth, which necessarily recur at stated times.

" 'Besides, what does it really matter if you are going to be talked about by generations who are still unborn, when you have not been mentioned by those who lived before you? (24) Yet the men of the past were not fewer in numbers and they were certainly better men. Furthermore, at the very best not one of those who do hear our names can for even the space of a year retain the memory of us.

" 'People ordinarily measure the length of a year by the complete revolution of the sun, that is, of a single star. But when all the stars have returned to their starting points and have restored, after long periods, the original configuration of the entire heavens, then that can truly be called a revolving year [i.e., the "great year" of Plato]. I hardly venture to say how many generations of men are contained within it. As once upon a time the Sun appeared to men to suffer total eclipse when the soul of Romulus entered this region, so, when the Sun undergoes another eclipse in the same part of the heavens and on the same date, then you may assume that all the stars and constellations will have returned to their original positions and that a [great] year has elapsed. But you may be sure that thus far not a twentieth part has yet elapsed.

(25) " 'Consequently, if you despair of ever returning to this place, which is the reward of great and eminent men, how slight, I ask, must be your fame on Earth if it endures for only a fraction of a single year? Therefore, look up on high and contemplate this, your eternal home and dwelling place, and pay no attention to the foolish talk of the vulgar herd nor

set your hope on human reward for your great deeds. Virtue herself, by her own charms, ought to lead you on to true glory. What others say of you is their own concern—they will see to it, and whatever it is they will talk anyway. But all their talk is limited to those narrow regions which you now look upon, nor will any man's fame last forever, since what men say dies with them and is extinguished in the silence of posterity.'

(26) "When he had finished speaking, I replied, 'Yes, dear Africanus, though from my boyhood up I have walked in my father's footsteps and in yours, and have never lacked in honor, still if such a pathway to Heaven lies open to those who have served their country faithfully, I am determined to redouble my efforts, spurred by the prospect of so splendid a reward.'

" 'Yes, you must use your best efforts,' he replied, 'and be sure that it is not *you* who are mortal, but only your body; nor is it *you* whom your outward form represents. Your spirit is your true self, not that bodily form which can be pointed to with the finger. Know yourself, therefore, to be a god—if indeed a god is a being that lives, feels, remembers, and foresees, that rules, governs, and moves the body over which it is set, just as the supreme God above us rules this world. And just as that eternal God moves the universe, which is partly mortal, so an eternal spirit moves the fragile body.

(27) " *'That which is always in motion is eternal.* But, on the other hand, that which imparts motion to something else, but is itself set in motion by some external force, must cease to exist when its motion ceases. Consequently, that alone never ceases to move which moves by its own inherent power, since it never abandons itself. Nay, it is itself the source and first cause of motion for all other things that move. But this first cause has no beginning, since all things spring from the first cause, while it itself cannot originate from any other: that would not be a first cause which derived its origin from something else. And since it never has had a beginning, it can never come to an end. For if a first cause were once extinct, it could never begin again from anything else, nor could it bring any-

thing else into existence, since everything has to originate from a first cause. Hence it follows that motion begins with that which is moved by itself. But this can neither be born nor die: otherwise, the whole structure of the heavens would fall and all nature would perish and never revive, since it possesses no power from which to derive the first impulse to motion.

(28) " 'Since it is evident, then, that that is eternal which moves of itself, who can deny that this is the nature of the spirit? For whatever is moved by an external force is lifeless; whereas whatever is animate moves by its own inner power, for that is the proper nature of the soul and its power. And as spirit is the only force that moves itself, it surely has never had a beginning and is also eternal.

(29) " 'Exercise it, therefore, in the noblest pursuits! The best occupations concern the welfare of your country. A spirit exercised and trained in such patriotic activities will fly the more swiftly to this its true home and habitation. Its flight will be even swifter if, while yet an inmate of the body, it looks without and by contemplation of the world outside frees itself as much as possible from the body. The souls of those who are given to sensual pleasures, and are, so to speak, its slaves, who follow their desires in a life devoted to pleasure, and violate the laws of gods and men—such souls, after leaving their bodies, still fly about close to the earth, and do not return to this place until after many centuries of torment.'

"Africanus departed, and I awoke from sleep."

IV. RELIGION UNDER THE IMPERIAL REPUBLIC

During the long period from the expulsion of the kings (traditional date, 509 B.C.) to the end of the Republic (27 B.C.), the "primitive" or prehistoric religion of Rome continued to be practiced, and amalgamated with itself the various cults of conquered or allied peoples. The process known as "syncretism" was as characteristic of Italy during these centuries as it was of the East after its conquest by Alexander (see F. C. Grant, HR, pp. xiii–xx). The attitude of foreign peoples toward Rome prepared for the later development of emperor worship; but in Italy itself, at least in the countryside, the ancient agricultural rites continued to be observed, as the poets testify, without these extraneous political additions. In the City, and in the larger centers, there was a decline in religious belief and practice during the last two centuries of the Republic.

For this period see: G. Wissowa, RKR, §§ 12–14; N. Lewis and M. Reinhold, RC, I, §§ 175–184; J. Marquardt, *Römische Staatsverwaltung*, Vol. III, *Das Sakralwesen* (2d ed., by G. Wissowa, 1885). See also titles listed on pp. 3 f.; add T. Mommsen, *History of Rome* (Eng. tr., 1894), Bk. I, ch. 12, IV. 12, V. 12.

ROMAN LAW, CUSTOM, AND RELIGION

Polybius, *Histories*, VI. 56. Polybius (203–120 B.C.) was a Greek historian of Rome, a great admirer of the Roman character, and a believer in the divine destiny of the Roman state. Bk. VI is devoted to a consideration of the Roman constitution, and toward the end Polybius credits the upstanding character of the ancient Roman to his religious convictions. See text and translation by W. R. Paton in LCL (1923).

Again the laws and customs relating to the gaining of wealth are better among the Romans than among the Carthaginians. At Carthage nothing that results in gain is looked upon as disgraceful; at Rome nothing is more shameful than to accept bribes or seek a profit by improper means. For strong as is their approval of money-making by proper means, so also is their scorn of greed for improper gains. A proof of this is the fact that at Carthage candidates obtain public offices by openly presenting gifts, whereas at Rome the penalty for this is death. Therefore, as the rewards of merit are opposed in the two cases, it is natural that the means taken to obtain them should also be unlike.

But in my opinion the difference by which the Roman commonwealth is most definitely superior is in their religion. I believe that the very thing which among other nations is criticized, I mean an excessive religious scrupulosity [*deisidaimonia*], holds together the Roman state. These things are handled with such pomp, and are carried over into their public and private life to such a degree, that nothing could exceed it. This is something which will surprise many readers. It is my opinion, at least, that they have done this in the interest of the common people. If it had been possible to found a commonwealth composed solely of wise men, such a course, perhaps, would not have been necessary; but as the masses are always fickle, full of lawless desires, unreasoning passion, and violent anger, they must be held in check by invisible terrors and by pomps and vanities of this kind. For this reason the ancients seem to me not to have acted rashly or by hazard when they introduced among the people notions about the gods and beliefs about the terrors of hell; but that, on the contrary, people today are very rash and stupid to ban such beliefs. Not to mention other things, one result is that among the Greeks even members of the government, if they are entrusted with no more than one talent [about $1100], though they have ten clerks checking it and as many seals and twice as many witnesses, cannot keep their faith; whereas among the Romans those who as magistrates and legates are handling vast sums of money maintain their honesty through the good faith which they have sworn to keep. Whereas elsewhere it is something

rare to find a man who keeps his hands off public money and
has a clean record, among the Romans it is something rare to
find a man who has been caught in such a practice.

THE PRAYER OF SCIPIO AFRICANUS

Livy, *History of Rome,* XXIX. 27. 1–4. As the great expedition
was about to sail from Sicily to attack Carthage, in 204 B.C., Scipio
Africanus offered the following prayer for a successful voyage.

At dawn Scipio on his flagship offered a prayer, after the
herald had ordered silence. "Ye gods and goddesses, who inhabit the seas and the lands, I supplicate and beseech you that
whatever has been done under my command, or is being done,
or will later be done, may turn out to my advantage and to
the advantage of the people and the commons of Rome, the
allies, and the Latins who by land or sea or on rivers follow
me, [accepting] the leadership, the authority, and the auspices
of the Roman people; that you will support them and aid
them with your help; that you will grant that, preserved in
safety and victorious over the enemy, arrayed in booty and
laden with spoils, you will bring them back with me in triumph to our homes; that you will grant us the power to take
revenge upon our enemies and foes; and that you will grant to
me and the Roman people the power to enforce upon the
Carthaginians what they have planned to do against our city,
as an example of [divine] punishment."

CULTUS OF THE ROMAN PEOPLE AND THE
GODDESS ROMA

Th. Wiegand (ed.), *Milet: Ergebnisse der Ausgrabungen,* Vol. I,
Pt. 7 (1924), No. 203 (pp. 290 ff.). *Ca.* 130 B.C. The cultus of the City
of Rome (*Roma*) began before that of the emperor. It began in the
same area, viz., in the East, and chiefly in the Province of Asia. The
date of the following inscription is three years after "Asia" became a

Roman province. As Th. Wiegand noted, the inscription provided a whole new festival calendar for the year. The "perfect victim" is presumably a full-grown sheep or other animal (a sheep if not otherwise specified): see Dittenberger, *Sylloge* 2, 625. 15 and note; 3, 1039. 11 and note.

For good luck! Whoever purchases the priesthood of the Roman people and of Roma must at once nominate to the officials of the treasury and the King Archons, in writing, a man at least twenty years of age [to be the priest]. The person thus named holds the office for three years and eight months from the month Metageitnion under the Stephanephoria of Kratinos; or, if he appoints in place of himself one who is already a priest, it shall be from the time he received priestly consecration of Zeus Telesiourgos. From the treasury he shall receive every year on the 1st of Taureon 600 drachmas, and in consideration therefor he shall offer to the Roman people and to Roma, on the 1st of Taureon, a perfect victim [a full-grown sheep]. So likewise the gymnasiarchs, on the 11th of the same month, upon taking their office, together with the ephebes of the gymnasium that year, shall offer a perfect victim. So also the gymnasiarchs who are going out of office, with their own ephebes, let them offer a perfect victim. Let both of them render the prescribed dues [of honor] to the priest. . . .
[Military games are provided for in what follows.]
These other contests [*athlēmata*] are to be attended to with great zeal, corresponding to the piety of the community toward the deity and its gratitude [*eucharistia*] to Rome. The gymnasiarchs of the youths are to share with the priest in the arrangement and overseeing of the games, in order that they may be as magnificent as possible. On the 28th of the same month he [the priest] shall organize a torch race in the Youths' Wrestling School, along with other appropriate contests. The arrangement and overseeing of this shall be shared with him by the athletic instructors of the youth. The dedication of the prize weapons offered in the Romaia shall follow, for the present, in the Youths' Gymnasium, but when the temple of Roma is finished, in the Romaion.

The priest shall also, on the first of every month, sacrifice a perfect victim to the Roman people and to Roma, and for this sacrifice the treasury officials shall give him 10 drachmas. On the 7th of Thargelion the Aisymnēte shall offer to the Roman people and to Roma a full-grown ox, and give to the priest the prescribed [portion of honor]; so also on the 12th of Metageitnion, likewise giving the portion of honor to the priest. If the god buys the Aisymnētia, the Proshetairoi of the god are to bring, on each of the two days, a perfect victim, and give the prescribed portion of honor to the priest. On the 18th of Boedromion, the fifty officials are to offer a full-grown swine, and give to the priest the prescribed [portion of honor]. . . .

RELIGION AND AGRICULTURE

Marcus Terentius Varro, *On Farm Management (Rerum Rusticarum Libri Tres),* I. 1. Varro lived 116–27 B.C. and wrote works on philology, religious antiquities, agriculture, biography, and even an encyclopedia of the liberal arts. His purpose in the present work was to arouse an interest in country life, a theme also stressed by Horace and Virgil. The dedication to his wife, given here, shows the close relation between religion and agriculture, as it had existed for centuries in ancient Italy. See the annotated translation in *Roman Farm Management: the Treatises of Cato and Varro, done into English, with notes of modern instances, by a Virginia Farmer* (1913); also the text and translation by W. D. Hooper and H. B. Ash in LCL (1934).

If I had the leisure, Fundania, this book would be far worthier of you; but I write as best I can, conscious always of the necessity for haste. For if, as the saying goes, all life is but a bubble, then all the more fragile is that of an old man; and my eightieth year reminds me to pack up my bundle and get ready for the long journey.

You have bought a farm and you wish to increase its fertility by good cultivation, and so you ask me what I would do with it if it were mine. Not only while I am still alive will I try to advise you about this, but I will make my advice available to you even after I am dead. For as it befell the Sibyl to be of service not only while she was alive, but even to the latest generations of men after her death—for even now, after all these years, we still turn to her books for guidance in the interpretation of strange portents—so may not I, while I am still alive, bequeath my counsel to my nearest and dearest? I will then write three books for you, to which you may turn for guidance in all those things which must be done in the management of a farm.

And since, as men say, the gods aid those who propitiate them, I will begin my book by invoking divine approval—not, like Homer and Ennius, that of the Muses, nor even that of the great Twelve Gods of the City, whose golden images stand in the Forum, six male and as many female—but from a solemn council of those twelve who are the special deities of husbandmen.

First I call upon Father Jupiter and Mother Earth, who fertilize all the processes of agriculture both in the air and in the soil, and hence are called the great "parents." Secondly I invoke the Sun and the Moon, by whom the seasons for sowing and reaping are marked off. Thirdly I invoke Ceres and Bacchus, because the fruits which they mature are those most necessary for life [grain and wine] and by their aid the land yields food and drink. Fourthly I invoke Robigus and Flora, by whose influence the blight is kept from crop and tree and in due season they bear fruit—for this reason the annual festival of the Robigalia is celebrated in honor of Robigus and the Floralia in honor of Flora. Next I supplicate Minerva, who protects the olive, and Venus, the goddess of the garden, who accordingly is worshiped at the rural wine festivals. Lastly, I adjure Lympha, the goddess of fountains, and Bonus Eventus, the god of good fortune, since without water all vegetation is starved and stunted, and without due order and good luck all tillage is in vain.

And so having paid my duty to the gods, I proceed to recount some conversations about agriculture in which I have recently taken part. [The rest of the chapter names the sources, over fifty in number, on agricultural science, chiefly by Greeks; however, says Varro, it was Mago the Carthaginian who was the most learned of all earlier writers on the subject.]

RURAL RELIGION

Tibullus, I. 1. 7–40. Albius Tibullus (d. 19 B.C.) was a Roman elegiac poet of the late Republican and early Imperial age. His style was described by Quintilian as "terse and elegant." His personal life is almost unknown. His poems were evidently gathered together by his friends, and later were published by an editor, probably in the time of Claudius. He was a lover of country life, as the two following selections show. His farm lay somewhere east of Rome, in the hills between Praeneste and Tibur. See text and translation by J. P. Postgate in LCL (1913); also the edition by K. F. Smith (1913).

When the full time arrives, let me plant tender vines and tall apple trees with my own skillful hands, as a true countryman. Nor may Hope betray me, but ever grant me heaps of grain and rich new wine to fill my vat! For I bow in reverence wherever I come upon a wreath of flowers lying on an abandoned stump in the fields or an old stone beside a crossway, and of whatever fruit the new year brings I present the first as an offering to the rural deity. Golden haired Ceres, let my farm produce the spiked crown to hang before thy temple doors! And in the fruitful garden let red Priapus be appointed guardian, to scare away the birds with his cruel sickle.

You too, O Lares, who keep watch over an estate once rich but now poor, accept your gifts. Once a slain heifer was the peace offering for unnumbered cattle; now a lamb is sacrifice for the impoverished farm. A lamb shall fall for you, and round it the country lads will shout: "Hail! Send us good crops and wine!" [Io, messes et bona vina date!]

As for me, let me be content to live with a little, no longer given always to distant journeys. But when the Dog Star [Sirius] rises, let me escape the heat beneath some shady tree on the bank of a flowing stream; let me not be ashamed to pick up the two-bladed mattock now and then, or prick the lazy oxen with the goad, or bring home in my arms some tiny lamb or goat deserted by its mother. [These eight lines may belong between vs. 6 and 7.]

But you, thieves and wolves, have mercy on my poor flock; instead, seize your prey from vast herds! Here is all I have with which to make yearly lustration for my herdsman, and to sprinkle milk over gentle Pales. Be with me, O gods [adsitis, divi]! Do not spurn gifts that come from a humble table and on plain earthenware. Such were the cups which the old-time farmer made for himself, modeling them out of soft clay.

THE FESTIVAL OF THE AMBARVALIA

Tibullus, II. 1. 1–26. The officiant begins:

"Let all present keep silence! [Quisquis adest faveat!] We are about to purify [i.e., to lustrate, which means both purify and go around] the crops and the fields, following the rite handed down from our earliest ancestors. Come to us, Bacchus, with the cluster of sweet grapes hanging from thy horns! And Ceres, bind thy temples with the ears of grain!

"On this holy day, let the soil, let the plowman rest. Hang up the plowshare, and let hard labor cease. Loosen the straps of the yokes; now beside the full manger let the oxen stand with garlands round their heads. Let all things await the service of the god. Let no spinner dare lift her hand to work with wool. You also I order to stand far off—keep away from the altar, all those to whom the goddess of Love granted pleasure last night! Only the chaste can placate the heavenly powers [casta placent superis]! Come in clean apparel and with clean hands to draw water from the spring." (See how the consecrated [sacer] lamb advances to the shining altar, and behind it the procession in white with olive twigs binding their hair!)

"Gods of our fathers, we cleanse the fields, we also cleanse the farmers. Outside our boundaries, may you drive away all evils. Let our sown fields not mock the harvest with deceitful grass. Let our slow-footed lambs not fear the swift-running wolves. Then the plump farmer, confident of his lush fields, will heap great logs upon the blazing hearth; while a troop of young home-born slaves, fair images of the lusty yeoman, will play about in front of the fire and build themselves cabins out of sticks.—My prayers will be heard! Do you not see by the favorable entrails how the markings declare that the gods will be gracious?"

RUSTIC PIETY

Horace, *Odes*, III. 13, 22, and 23. The gentle, antique piety of these odes expresses the ancient rustic devotion to the *numina* or local powers, though of course the poet idealizes it. The Bandusian spring was probably on his Sabine farm, a few miles northeast of Rome. See E. C. Wickham, *The Works of Horace* (3d ed., 1896), I, 232.

(13) O spring of Bandusia, clearer than crystal, you deserve [offerings of] sweet wine and flowers, and tomorrow you shall be given a young goat whose brow, swollen with budding horns, betokens both love and struggle! Instead, this offspring of the lusty herd shall stain your cool waters with his own red blood.

You, the hot season of the flaming Dog Star never touches; your welcome coolness you offer the bulls weary with drawing the plow, and likewise the wandering flock. You, too, shall be named among fountains renowned when I sing of the red oak which grows above the grotto where your babbling waters leap forth!

The gods love piety more than lavish gifts. The piety here described is the good old-fashioned kind, that of the Sabine country housewife and mother.

(23) If you raise your upturned palms toward heaven, O Phidyle, good country housewife, at each new moon, and if with incense and the first fruits of this year's grain and a

greedy sow you placate the Lares, then your loaded vine will not feel the pestilent South Wind, nor will the standing grain be touched by rust, nor the tender young of the flock by the sickness of fruit-bearing autumn.

True, the chosen victim that is now grazing among the oaks and ilexes on snowy Mount Algidus, or growing fat on the grassy Alban hills, will stain with its bloody neck the axes of the priests [i.e., in the public sacrifices]; but you, instead, have no need to beseech the gods with much slaughter of sheep—if only you crown their little images with rosemary and sprigs of myrtle. When innocent hands have touched the altar, though there is no sumptuous sacrifice to flatter [the gods], they soothe the estranged Penates with their offering of the sacred ground barley and crackling salt.

The dedication of a pine tree to Diana. This also was no doubt on Horace's Sabine farm. Diana was *triformis:* Luna in heaven, Diana on earth, Hecate in Hades.

(22) O Virgin Goddess, guardian of the hills and groves, thou who, thrice invoked, dost hear the cry of young mothers in their travail and dost rescue them from death—goddess threefold in nature: thine be the pine tree that rears itself above my country dwelling, so that gladly as each happy year comes round I may offer to it the blood of a young boar just beginning its slanting thrusts!

ANNUAL FUNERAL RITES

Virgil, *Aeneid,* V. 42–103. The description of the rites at the tomb of Anchises (near Segesta in western Sicily) given by Virgil in Bk. V of the *Aeneid* is indubitably accurate. Though adapted to the purpose of the poem, the ritual must be correct: otherwise Virgil would have spoiled his own effect. Even some of the sacred language of the rite is probably preserved (e.g., in line 71). Compare the funeral rite for Misenus in Bk. VI. 212–235. See G. Showerman, "Death and Disposal of the Dead (Roman)," in ERE.

Next day, as soon as early dawn had driven away the stars in the East, Aeneas calls together his comrades from along the beach, and from a little hill he addresses them: "Great sons of Dardanus, born of the noble blood of gods, the year with its round of months is now complete since we laid in the earth the dust, which was all that remained, of my divine father, and consecrated our altars of grief. And now, if I am not mistaken, the day is at hand which I will ever keep—for such, O gods, was your will—as a day of grief, a day of honor. If I were spending it in exile on the Gaetulian quicksands [in Morocco], or hemmed in on the Argolic sea, or in the town of Mycenae, even so I would fulfill the yearly vows and the solemn ordinances of the festival, and pile the altars with their appropriate gifts. But now we are here, beside the very dust and ashes of my father (certainly not, as I believe, without divine purpose and will), having been borne hither to the friendly haven [of Trapani]. Come now, and let us all celebrate the sacrifice with joy; let us pray for winds, and that he [Anchises, now a hero-god] may grant me to pay him these rites year after year in an established city and in a consecrated temple. Acestes, who is by birth a Trojan, gives two head of oxen to each of our ships; so then invite to the feast both your own ancestral gods of the household and also those whom our host Acestes worships. Moreover, when the ninth dawn uplifts her gracious light upon men and her rays unveil the world, I will ordain contests for my Trojans; first, for swift ships; then for those who excel in the foot race and for those who, confident in their strength, come forward as champions with the javelin or light arrows, or venture to take on opponents with gloves of rawhide; let all be here, and look forward to the merited prize and palm of victory. Now let all be silent, and wreathe your temples with leafy twigs."

So he spoke and shrouded his own brows with his mother's myrtle. So did Helymus, and so did Acestes ripe in years, and also the boy Ascanius, the rest of the young men following. Then from the assembly he advances to the funeral mound, amid the throng of many thousands that crowd about him.

Here he pours on the ground, in due libation, two goblets of unmixed wine, two of fresh milk, two of consecrated blood, and scatters dark red blossoms, saying thus: "Hail, holy father, once again! Hail, ashes of the one I rescued, but in vain! Hail, soul and shade of my sire! It was not permitted [me] to share with thee the search for the bounds of Italy and its destined fields, nor Ausonian Tiber—whatever that may be." Thus had he spoken, when from beneath the shrine a serpent slid out with seven huge coils and seven smoothly arching rolls, quietly circling the grave and gliding from altar to altar; its back was checked with blue spots and its scales were ablaze with the sheen of dappled gold, as in the clouds the rainbow darts out a thousand changing hues athwart the sun. Aeneas stood in awe at the sight. At last, winding its long train among the bowls and polished cups, and tasting the feast, and then leaving the altars where it had fed, it crept harmlessly back beneath the tomb. Aeneas now renews even more devoutly the rites he had begun for his father. Uncertain whether to think it the Genius of the place [*genius loci*] or his father's attendant spirit [*famulus parentis*], he slays, as is proper, two sheep, two swine, and two dark-backed steers, pouring, meanwhile, bowls of wine, and calling upon the shade of great Anchises and the ghost released from Acheron. Meanwhile his comrades joyfully bring gifts, each from his own store; they heap the altars, and slay steers in sacrifice. Others arrange the cauldrons in order, and, lying on the grass, place live coals under the spits and roast the flesh.

[Then follows (lines 104–603) the account of the traditional ancestral games, the "contests held in honor of the holy ancestor."]

V. THE AUGUSTAN RESTORATION

The motives of Augustus in "restoring" the Republic and its ancient worships have been variously interpreted, sometimes as purely selfish ambition, sometimes as completely altruistic and patriotic. The truth probably included both motives—as those who stood closest to him were the first to intimate. Any man, king or president or dictator, who identifies himself with the state, and its welfare with his own, is likely to think in such terms. If he is a high-minded, noble, patriotic person, the result will be good—as it was, on the whole, in the case of Augustus. Certainly his "restoration" marked the end of two centuries of ceaseless bloodshed, conquest, and destruction, of wars at home and abroad, and laid the foundations for the long era of the "Roman peace" which culminated in the era of the Antonines. As some of the early Church Fathers insisted, the creation of the Roman Empire was a universal blessing to mankind, and should be looked upon as an act of God. The religion of this period is best reflected in the poetry of Virgil.

See G. Wissowa, RKR, §§ 15, 54 f.; W. W. Fowler, RERP, chs. 18–19; N. Lewis and M. Reinhold, RC, II, §§ 2, 3, 13–17; F. C. Grant, HR, pp. 63–69 (on divine honors paid to kings in the Hellenistic age); M. P. Nilsson, GGR, II, 366–376 (on the Caesar cult); N. Turchi, RRA, Pt. II. 3. See also M. P. Charlesworth, "Some Observations on Ruler-Cult, Especially at Rome," in *Harvard Theological Review*, XXVIII (1935), 5–44. On the place of the army in Roman religion, see A. von Domaszewski, *Die Religion des römischen Heeres* (1895).

THE ACHIEVEMENTS OF THE DIVINE AUGUSTUS

CIL, III (2), 769–799 (1873), ed. by Th. Mommsen; also separately 1865 and 1883; text and translation in E. G. Hardy (ed.), *Monumentum Ancyranum* (1923); also F. W. Shipley in LCL (1924) and J. E. Sandys in *Latin Epigraphy* (1927), pp. 258–276. The complete text was published by Mommsen in 1883. See introduction and bibliography in Shipley's edition, pp. 341–343. On the story of the recovery of the inscription, see introduction to Hardy's or Shipley's edition. The monument at Ankara was a copy of the original at Rome, where a magnificent reproduction was set up not many years ago.

A copy of the acts of the deified Augustus, by which he subjected the whole world to the sovereignty of the Roman people, and the amounts which he expended upon the Republic and the people of Rome, as engraved upon the two bronze pillars which have been set up at Rome.

At the age of nineteen, I raised an army at my own initiative and my own expense and thus restored the liberty of the Republic which had been oppressed by the tyranny of a faction . . . . Those who murdered my father [Julius Caesar] I drove into exile, punishing them by due legal process, and afterward when they attacked the Republic I twice defeated them in battle. I waged wars, on sea and land, both civil and foreign, in various parts of the world, and when I had conquered I spared those citizens who sued for mercy. The foreign nations which could safely be pardoned I chose to save rather than destroy . . . . For my successful operations by sea and land, led either by myself or by my officers under my direction [lit., auspices], the Senate decreed, on fifty-five occasions, that thanksgiving should be offered the immortal gods. The days on which these thanksgivings were offered by decree of the Senate totaled 890. In my triumphs nine kings or children of kings were led before my chariot. As I write these words I have been consul for thirteen times [the thirteenth was 2 B.C.] and in the thirty-seventh year of my tribunician power [A.D. 14]. [I have also been] *princeps senatus* for forty years; [and] I have been *pontifex maximus, augur,* a member of the *quindecimviri sacris faciundis,* of the *septemviri epulonum,* an Arval brother, a *sodalis Titius,* and a fetial priest . . . . The Senate decreed that every fifth year vows were to be taken for my health by the consuls and the priests. In fulfilment of these vows, games have been frequently held during my lifetime, sometimes by the four leading colleges of priests, sometimes by the consuls. In addition, the whole body of the citizens, either privately or by municipalities, offered continual sacrifices for my health at all the couches of the gods. By decree of the Senate my name was included in the Salian hymn [i.e., along with names of the gods], and it was ordained by law that my person should be forever sacred, and that I should hold the tribunician power as long as I lived. I declined to be made *pontifex maximus* in succession to a still-living colleague, though the people offered me the honor of that priesthood which my father had held. Some years later I accepted the sacred office, when at last he [Lepidus] was dead who had taken advantage of a public disturbance to seize the office for himself; such a multitude gathered from all of Italy for my election . . . as was never before recorded to have visited Rome. In honor of my Return, the Senate consecrated an altar to Fortuna Redux [the Fortune who Leads Back] at the Porta Capena, near the temple of Honor and Virtue, and ordered the pontiffs and the Vestal Virgins to offer a yearly sacrifice on the anniversary of my return from Syria; . . . this day was named, after my cognomen, the Augustalia . . . . When I returned from Spain and Gaul, . . . the Senate voted to honor my return by the consecration of an altar to Pax Augusta; on this altar the magistrates, priests, and Vestal Virgins were ordered to offer an annual sacrifice. Janus Quirinus, [the gate] which our ancestors ordered closed whenever there was peace with victory throughout the whole realm of the Roman people, on land and sea, and which before my birth had been closed only twice since the foundation of the City, the Senate has ordered closed three times while I have been *princeps*.

I built the curia and the Chalcidicum adjoining it, the temple of Apollo on the Palatine, with its porticoes, the temple of the divine Julius, the Lupercal, the portico at the Circus Flaminius, which I allowed to be called the Octavia in honor of the builder [Octavius, 168 B.C.] of an earlier portico on this site, the state box at the Circus Maximus, the temples on the Capitoline Mount in honor of Jupiter Feretrius and Jupiter Tonans, the temple of Quirinus [on the Quirinal Mount], the temples of Minerva, of Juno Regina, and of Jupiter Libertas on the Aventine, the temple of the Lares at the highest spot on the Sacra Via, the temple of Di Penates on the Velia, and the temple of Youth and the temple of the Great Mother on the Palatine. The Capitolium [the great temple to Jupiter Optimus Maximus, overlooking the Forum, burned and rebuilt in the first century B.C.] and the theater of Pompey I rebuilt, both at very great expense, without adding any inscription giving my own name . . . . As Master of the College of Quindecimvirs, together with my colleague Marcus Agrippa, I conducted the Secular Games in the consulship of Gaius Furnius and Marcus Silanus [June 1–3, 17 B.C.; see the inscription translated below]. In my thirteenth consulship I gave for the first time the Games of Mars [in 2 B.C., when the temple of Mars Ultor was dedicated]; since that time the consuls, by decree of the Senate, have held the games in co-operation with me . . . . After my victory [at Actium, 31 B.C.] I restored to the temples in all the cities of the Province of Asia the ornaments which my antagonist [Antony] had appropriated to his own use when he plundered the temples. Silver statues of me, afoot, on horse, and in chariot, were erected throughout the City, in number about 80; these I removed [by my own orders], and from the money derived from them [they were melted up] I placed in the temple of Apollo golden offerings in my own name and in the name of all who had honored me with statues . . . . Among my officers were 170 priests . . . . I compelled the Parthians to restore to me the standards of three Roman armies [in 20 B.C.], and to sue as suppliants for the friendship of the Roman people. These standards I deposited in the inner shrine which is in the temple of Mars Ultor.

[From the summary at the end, perhaps added by some local magistrate in Ancyra when the inscription was set up:] He restored the Capitol and the sacred buildings, 82 in all [in addition to the new temples named above].

DIVINE HONORS IN THE EAST

Dittenberger, OGIS, II. 458; P. Wendland, HRK, p. 409, no. 8; F. H. von Gaertringen, *Inschriften von Priene* (1906), No. 105. This decree of the Provincial Assembly *(Koinon)* of Asia is dated 9 B.C. It sets forth the usual reasons for the worship of the emperor, viz., the benefits of the Roman peace. At the proposal of the proconsul, Paulus Fabius Maximus, the new year is to begin with the emperor's birthday, the ninth day before the Kalends of October (September 23). We have fragments of the decree, including even a Latin translation, from Priene, Apamaeia, Eumeneia, and Dorylaeum. Lines 1–29 give the letter of the proconsul, lines 30–77 the decree of the Assembly. The Greek of the inscription is especially interesting for its use of terms also found in early Christian literature.

[It is difficult to say] whether the birthday of the most divine Caesar has brought more of joy or of benefit; it would be right for us to consider him equal to the Beginning [*archē*] of all things, if not indeed by nature, certainly in usefulness; for when everything was falling [into disorder] and tending toward dissolution, he restored it once more and gave to the whole world a new aspect; it might have wished for death, had not Caesar been born, the common good fortune of all. One may therefore rightly view as the Beginning of life and of vitality what has given to the misery of being born an end and a limit. Since for either public and [*sic*] private advantage no one can begin [an undertaking] on any luckier day than this, which has brought good fortune to all; and since, moreover, the beginning of public office in the cities of [the Province of] Asia falls about this time, evidently a mark of divine intention in order to show honor to Augustus; and since, moreover, it is most difficult to make any equivalent return for his extraordinary acts of beneficence, unless we conceive some new kind of thanksgiving; and since all men will more gladly celebrate the birthday since there already exists an occasion for it in the inauguration of new officials: it is my wish that all the cities unanimously adopt the birthday of divine Caesar as the new beginning of the year, and that on it they shall all enter at the "beginning," i.e., nine days before the Kalends of October. [Then follows the decree of the Provincial Assembly of the Province of Asia:]

Decree of the Hellenes in Asia upon motion of the High Priest Apollonios, son of Menophilos, from Azanoi:

Whereas the Providence [*Pronoia*] which has regulated our whole existence, and which has shown such care and liberality, has brought our life to the climax of perfection in giving to us [the emperor] Augustus, whom it [Providence] filled with virtue for the welfare of men, and who, being sent to us and our descendants as a Savior [*Sōtēr*], has put an end to war and has set all things in order; and [whereas,] having become manifest [*phaneis*], Caesar has fulfilled all the hopes of earlier times . . . , not only in surpassing all the benefactors [*euergetai*] who preceded him but also in leaving to his successors no hope of surpassing him; and whereas, finally, the birthday of the god [Augustus] has been for the whole world the beginning of good news [*euaggelion*] concerning him [therefore, let a new era begin from his birth, and let his birthday mark the beginning of the new year].

Another inscription, somewhat more literary, was found at Halicarnassus (*British Museum Inscriptions*, 894). It is dated sometime after 2 B.C. when Augustus received the title, "Father of the Fatherland." See P. Wendland, HRK, p. 410, no. 9.

Since the eternal and deathless nature of the universe has perfected its immense benefits to mankind in granting us as a supreme benefit, for our happiness and welfare, Caesar Augustus, Father of his own Fatherland, divine Rome, Zeus Paternal, and Savior of the whole human race, in whom Providence has not only fulfilled but even surpassed the prayers of all men: land and sea are at peace, cities flourish under the reign of law, in mutual harmony and prosperity; each is at the very acme of fortune and abounding in wealth; all mankind is filled with glad hopes for the future, and with contentment over the present; [it is fitting to honor the god] with public games and with statues, with sacrifices and with hymns.

Still another, from A.D. 48 (Dittenberger, *Sylloge²*, 347, ³ 760) shows the rhetorical grandiloquence still in use. The inscription is in stone, from Ephesus. Note that the Roman legend ascribed the descent of the Julii from Mars and Venus, whose Greek names are given.

The Council and people [of the Ephesians and the other Hellenic] cities which dwell in Asia and the nations [acknowledge] Gaius Julius the son of Gaius Caesar [as] high priest and autocrat and consul for the second time, the God Manifest born of Ares and Aphrodite, and the common Savior of human life.

Compare also the inscription at Myra in Lycia, under a statue of Augustus. It is given in E. Petersen, *Reisen in Lykien*, II, 43, and is quoted by U. von Wilamowitz in *Der Glaube der Hellenen*, II, 429 n.

The god Augustus, Son of God, Caesar, Autocrat [*Autokra-tōr*, i.e., absolute ruler] of land and sea, the Benefactor and Savior of the whole cosmos, the people of Myra [acknowledge, or, have set up this statue].

Compare with this an earlier Athenian inscription with a marble base. Dittenberger, *Sylloge²*, 346,³ 759; P. Wendland, HRK, p. 408.

The people [acknowledge] Gaius Julius Caesar as high priest and dictator, their own Savior [*Sōtēr*] and Benefactor [*Euergetēs*].

Even more fulsome were Augustus' official Egyptian titles, as conferred upon him by the priests. See the passage in P. Wendland, HRK, p. 410, no. 10; quoting Mommsen, *Römische Geschichte*, V, 565 n. Some of the titles were as old as the Pharaohs. Cf. Hans Lietzmann, *Der Weltheiland*, pp. 51 ff.

The beautiful Youth, dear by his lovableness, the Prince of Princes, chosen by Ptah and Nun the Father of the gods, King of Upper Egypt and King of Lower Egypt, Lord of the two lands, Autocrat, Son of the Sun [the Sun God], Lord of the diadems, Caesar, Ever-living, beloved of Ptah and Isis.

An interesting papyrus from the Thebaid, edited by Kornemann in *Klio*, VII. 278 ff; P. Wendland, HRK, p. 411, no. 14. In it Apollo the Sun God announces Trajan's ascent to heaven and proclaims his successor Hadrian. He was "consecrated" the end of August or the beginning of September, A.D. 117. The festival to which the people are here invited probably took place the following October.

Riding up [the sky] in the chariot drawn by white horses, now Trajan's, I come to you, O people—the not unknown god Phoebus—proclaiming the new hero Hadrian, to whom everyone is a slave because of [his] virtue and the fortune of his father. Rejoicing, therefore, and offering sacrifice, let us light the hearths, with laughter and drinking [wine] from the fountain, cheering the souls of the youth with ointments—all of which have been provided by the piety of the governor toward his [new] master [Hadrian].

THE SAECULAR CELEBRATION

CIL, VI. 32. 323; H. Dessau, ILS, 5050. In the *Res Gestae Divi Augusti* (the *Monumentum Ancyranum*), Augustus states (ch. 22) that he celebrated the Saecular Games in the year 17 B.C. "on behalf of the College of the Quindecimviri, as its Master." The occasion was the renewal of the *imperium*, i.e., imperial authority, which in 27 B.C. he had been persuaded to accept for ten years. The directions for the celebration were found in the Sibylline Books—the story and the oracle itself are both given by Zosimus, a fifth-century Greek historian. The inscription which records the events of the celebration was found in 1890; its fragments had been built into a medieval wall near the Tiber, on the edge of the ancient Campus Martius where the nightly celebration (as well as the daytime games, presumably) had been held. The series of sacrifices offered by the Emperor or by Agrippa were as follows:

June 1–3, A.U.C. 736 [= 17 B.C.]

1. On the three successive *nights*, "in the Campus Martius beside the Tiber,"
   a. A sacrifice to the Moirae [Fates] of ewe-lambs and goats,
   b. An offering to the Ilithyiae of cakes,
   c. A sacrifice to Terra Mater.
2. On the three successive *days*,
   a. A sacrifice to Jupiter Optimus Maximus on the Capitoline Mount of two oxen [*boves mares*],
   b. A sacrifice to Juno, also on the Capitoline, of two cows [*boves feminae*],
   c. An offering to Apollo and Diana, on the Palatine, of cakes [as above to the Ilithyiae].
3. On the last day the hymn (*carmen*) written by Quintus Horatius Flaccus was sung by the chorus of 27 boys and 27 girls, presumably first on the Palatine, following the final sacrifice, and then on the Capitol (*eodemque modo in Capitolio*).

THE ORACLE

Zosimus, *On the Decline of Rome*, II. 6. This Greek writer lived under Theodosius II and died *ca.* A.D. 425. The Greek text of the following passage is given in E. C. Wickham, *The Works of Horace*, (3d ed., 1896), I, 340–342. Note the antique style of the poem, which I have tried to reproduce in the translation.

When now the longest time has run its course that man
May live, and years a century and ten have closed
Their circuit, then think, O Roman, if perchance you
    forget,
And recall all this: To the eternal gods thou shalt
Make offering in the valley where the Tiber flows,
At its narrowest course, when night descends
And the sun is hiding its light. To the dread Moirae,
Cause of existence, bring there sheep and goats,
And to the dark Eileithyiae sacrifice with ancient rite
And reconcile the grave helpers-on of birth.
To Earth bring then a black sow, big with young,
And let white bulls be led to Zeus's altar—

But by day, not night, for to the heavenly gods
'Tis proper to sacrifice by day; and thus do thou.
To Hera's temple bring a white cow;
To Phoebus Apollo, who is also called the Sun,
Belongs the same offering as to the Eileithyiae.
In the god's temple sing a Latin song;
Let youths and maidens sing it, each in separate choirs,
Whose parents are still living, their family stem abloom.
Let the matrons daily bow the knee
Humbly in adoration before Hera's altar.
Let offerings for atonement be portioned out to all,
Both to men and women, but chiefly to the women.
From his own house let everyone bring a gift
From his own store, what is right and good to offer
To the gods below and to the gods above, to offer
As expiation. Let all lie together in a heap
Until the sacrifice to the gods below be completed.
Gifts shalt thou give to all who pray,
To the men as to the women, for a remembrance.
Day and night, without cease, let the folk keep festival
Sitting clad in rich garments, and let gay jest
And laughter mingle with earnest, as is meet.
   This shalt thou fix steadfast in mind,
And so shall all Italy and the Latin land
Forever bow before thy scepter's might.

THE INSCRIPTION

   CIL, VI. 32. 323. H. Dessau, ILS, 5050. The title, *Acta Sacrorum
Saecularium Celebratorum A.U.C. 736, d. Jun. 1–3,* has been supplied by modern editors. The first eighty-nine lines are omitted by
Dessau, as far too fragmentary for reconstruction. They dealt with
details of the preparations for the celebration.

During the following night [from 31 May to 1 June] Caesar
Augustus sacrificed to the Moirae in the Tiber valley nine
female sheep, which were wholly burnt, in accordance with
the Greek rite, and in accordance with the same rite nine
female goats; and he prayed as follows:

"O Moirae, as it is written prescribed for you in those
books, that on our behalf and for the benefit of the Roman

people, the Quirites, an offering shall be made of nine sheep and nine goats; to you, I pray and ask that ye will increase the realm and power of the Roman people, the Quirites, both in war [abroad] and at home; that ye will ever guard the Latin name, and grant safety, continual victory, and power to the Roman people, the Quirites; send good fortune to the Roman people, the Quirites; maintain the welfare of the armies of the Roman people, the Quirites, and the state of the Roman people, the Quirites; that you may be gracious and favorable to the Roman people, the Quirites, to the College of the Fifteen, to me, my house, my servants, and accept this offering of nine full-grown sheep and nine goats. For this reason you are being honored with this offering of these goats. Be favorable and gracious to the Roman people, the Quirites, to the College of the Fifteen, to me, my house, my servants."

After the conclusion of the sacrifice, games were held by night on a stage without any space or seats for spectators; while 110 wives of freemen, chosen by the College of Fifteen, presented a *sellisternium* and provided two seats for Juno and Diana.

On the first of June Caesar Augustus offered a full-grown bull to Jupiter Optimus Maximus on the Capitol, and M. Agrippa offered a second one there also. They prayed as follows:

"O Jupiter Optimus Maximus, as it is prescribed for thee in those books, that on our behalf and for the benefit of the Roman people, the Quirites, an offering shall be made to thee of this fine bull; to thee I pray and ask . . ." [as above].

These ministered as assistants with the sacred vessels [? *ad atallam;* the word is otherwise unknown] Caesar, Agrippa, Scaevola, Sentius, Lollius, Asinius Gallus, Rebilus.

Thereupon Latin dramas were presented in the wooden theater that had been erected in the valley beside the Tiber, and the wives of the freemen likewise presented a *sellisternium,* and the nightly games also continued without interruption. The following proclamation was made:

"Since, in accordance with a good custom, of whose observance there are many examples—since the proper occasion has often arisen for general rejoicing—it has been decided to shorten the time of mourning for the wives of freemen; and [since] the restoration and careful observance of this custom at the present time, together with a solemn celebration and games, is appropriate as an honor to the gods and as furthering their worship; we therefore look upon it as our duty to grant permission to [free] women [thus] to shorten their period of mourning."

That night, Caesar Augustus presented to Ilithyia a sacrifice of nine flat cakes, nine pastry cakes, nine cupcakes, and prayed as follows:

"O Ilithyia, as it is prescribed for thee in those books, that on our behalf and for the benefit of the Roman people, the Quirites, an offering shall be made to thee of nine flat cakes, nine pastry cakes, nine cupcakes; to thee I pray and ask . . . [as above]."

On the 2nd of June Caesar Augustus sacrificed a cow to Juno Regina on the Capitol, while M. Agrippa offered a second one, and prayed as follows:

"O Juno Regina, as it is prescribed for thee in those books, that on our behalf and for the benefit of the Roman people, the Quirites, an offering shall be made to thee with this fine cow; to thee I pray and ask . . . [as above]."

Then he said . . . 110 married wives of freemen, chosen for this [office] . . . the following words:

"O Juno Regina, for the benefit of the Roman people, the Quirites, . . . we, the married wives of freemen, beseech thee upon [our] knees that thou . . . wilt increase the power of the Roman people, the Quirites, both in war [abroad] and at home; that thou wilt ever guard the Latin name, and grant safety, continual victory, and power to the Roman people, the Quirites, and to the armies of the Roman people, the Quirites; and maintain the welfare of the state of the Roman people, the Quirites; be favorable and gracious to the Roman people, the Quirites, to the Fifteen, to us. . . . So we pray and beseech thee [we] 110 wives of freemen of the Roman people, the Quirites, upon [our] knees."

These ministered as assistants with the sacred vessels [?]: Agrippa. . . .

Games were held as on the preceding day.

At night Caesar Augustus sacrificed to Mother Earth, beside the Tiber, a pregnant sow, and prayed as follows: [the same form of prayer as above].

The wives of freemen presented a *sellisternium* as on the day before.

On the 3d of June, Caesar Augustus and M. Agrippa offered a sacrifice to Apollo and Diana, on the Palatine, of nine flat cakes, nine pastry cakes, nine cupcakes, and prayed as follows:

"O Apollo, as it is prescribed for thee in those books, that on our behalf and for the benefit of the Roman people, the Quirites, a sacrifice shall be offered to thee of nine flat cakes, nine pastry cakes, nine cupcakes; to thee I pray and ask . . . [as above].

"O Apollo, as I have recited a good prayer to thee, after offering the pastry cakes, that so by these things thou mightest also be honored through the offering of these flat cakes, be favorable and gracious."

Likewise with the cupcakes.

With the same words for Diana.

After the completion of the sacrifice, a hymn was sung by twenty-seven chosen youths, whose parents were both still living, and also by the same number of maidens. This was on the Capitol. The hymn was composed by Q. Horatius Flaccus.

As [members of] the Fifteen were present: Caesar, M. Agrippa, Q. Lepidus, Potitus Messalla, C. Stolo, C. Scaevola, C. Sosius, C. Norbanus, M. Cocceius, M. Lollius, C. Sentius, M. Strigo, L. Arruntius, C. Asinius, M. Marcellus, D. Laelius, Q. Tubero, C. Rebilus, Messala Messallinus.

After the ending of the dramatic performances, about [. . . o'clock], at the same place where the sacrifice was offered the night before, a grandstand and a stage were erected, the goal posts were set up, and the four-horse [chariot race] was started; Potitus Messalla gave the signal to the acrobatic riders.

Proclamation by the Fifteen: "With [these] ritual games we conclude the seven-day celebration in honor of the [Saecular] Festival, on the 5th of June in the wooden theater beside the Tiber, at 8 a.m. . . ."

THE *CARMEN SAECULARE* OF HORACE

Horace's *Carmen Saeculare* or *Saecular Hymn* is referred to in the inscription recording the celebration. It was sung on the last day of the festival, by a chorus of 27 (= 3 × 9) boys and 27 girls whose parents were still living—a detail which emphasizes the symbolic character of the rite, perhaps also its real efficacy. Horace himself conducted the chorus; in *Epistles* II. 1. 126–129 he is still thinking of the great occasion. The music was probably in one part. The tune is unknown. The meter is sapphic, and very difficult. The following four lines may convey something of its form:

> Phoebus, and thou queen of the forest, Dian,
> Splendor of heaven, O ye twain adored
> Ever, for ever: what we pray for now grant,
>   This holy season.

But the meter is really inimitable in English—its effect in Latin, as in Greek, is far different. Note the importance of the precise epithets used: Diana is identified with Ilithyia, who aids in birth; *Lucina* is the one who brings light or brings into the light; *Genitalis* describes the one who causes to grow or brings to birth. See "The Carmen Saeculare of Horace and its First Performance" in W. W. Fowler, *Roman Essays* (1920), pp. 111–126.

Phoebus, and Diana, queen of the woodlands, bright glory of the heavens, ye who are ever worshiped and ever to be worshiped, grant what we now pray for in this holy season, at which the Sibylline verses command chosen maidens and unsullied youths to chant a hymn to the gods who have favored the Seven Hills.

Kind Sun, who in thy radiant chariot dost bring in the day and then hide it, who art born another and yet the same, may it never be possible for thee to behold another city greater than Rome!

O Ilithyia, whose office it is gently to bring to birth in due time, watch over our mothers, whatever the name by which thou art pleased to be invoked, whether it be "Lucina" or "Genitalis." O Goddess, rear [i.e., both protect and increase] our youth, and prosper with abundant offspring the decrees of the Fathers [the Senate] concerning marriage and the marriage law; so that the fixed circuit of eleven decades may ever bring again music and games for three bright days and as many thronged and happy nights!

Ye also, O Fates, who have truly foretold what has been once for all decreed and serves as the boundary mark for the unchanging order of events, join good fortune to come with that which has gone before!

Fertile in fruits and in herds, may the earth crown Ceres with her spiky coronet [of grain stalks]; and may Jove's health-bringing showers and winds nourish the coming harvest.

And thou, Apollo, gentle and placid, lay aside thy darts, and hear thy sons making their supplication! And thou also, O Luna, crescent-crowned queen of the stars, give ear to thy daughters!

If Rome be your creation, if from Ilium came the troops that seized the Etruscan shore, the remnant which had been commanded to change their Lares and their homes by a fortunate [i.e., divinely guided] course—those for whom holy Aeneas, survivor of his family, escaping unconquered from the flames of Troy, built a highway for the free, and was destined to give more than had been left behind: [then,] O gods, grant that our youth may be teachable and learn the ways of virtue, and that our old people may enjoy peace and tranquillity; and to the descendants of Romulus grant wealth and offspring and every glory!

And what the glorious son of Anchises and Venus [i.e., Augustus] asks of you, with a sacrifice of white steers, that grant to him, victorious over the warring, but generous to the defeated! Even now the Mede [the Parthian] fears his arms, powerful by land and sea, and the Alban axes [symbols of his authority]; already the Scythians and the Indians, recently scornful, are asking for terms. Even now Faith and Peace and Honor and ancient Shame and neglected Virtue are venturing to return, and blessed Abundance with her full horn [the cornucopia] manifests herself.

May Phoebus the Prophet, adorned with his flashing bow, who is beloved by the nine Muses, and who by his healing art restores the weary body—may he, if he looks with favor upon the altars on the Palatine Mount, continue Rome's wealth and Latium's prosperity, to new periods and ages ever better!

May Diana, who reigns on the Aventine Mount and on Mount Algidus, attend to the prayers of the Quindecimvirs, and turn her kindly ears to the prayers of children [i.e., the chorus]!

Homeward now we go, with good hope and confident that this is the will of Jove and of all the gods—we the chorus who have been taught to sing the praises of Phoebus and Diana.

THE *FERIALE CUMANUM*

CIL, X. 8375. H. Dessau, ILS, 108. The festival calendar of an Italian temple of Augustus. Its date is between A.D. 4 and 14. Three fragments are found in the Naples Museum. (See ch. 1, above, for the old pre-Julian calendar.) Note that the year now begins in August.

19 August	On this day Caesar entered upon his first Consulship. Prayer:
3 Sept.	On this day the army of Lepidus went over [yielded] to Caesar. Prayer:
23 Sept.	Birthday of Caesar. To him a sacrificial animal is brought. Prayer:
7 Oct.	Birthday of Drusus Caesar. Prayer to Vesta.
18 Oct.	On this day Caesar assumed the toga virilis. Prayer to Hope and Youth.
16 Nov.	Birthday of Tiberius Caesar. Prayer to Vesta.
15 Dec.	On this day the altar of the Fortune who Leads Back was dedicated, who brought home

	Caesar Augustus from the Provinces overseas. Prayer to the Fortune who Leads Back.
7 Jan.	On this day Caesar was first accompanied by a guard of Lictors. Prayer to the Everlasting Jupiter.
15 Jan.	On this day Caesar was named Augustus. Prayer to Augustus.
30 Jan.	On this day the Altar of Peace was dedicated. Prayer to the Dominion [*Imperio*] of Caesar Augustus, the Protector of the Roman citizens and of the whole world.
6 March	On this day Caesar was made Pontifex Maximus. Prayer to Vesta and the State Gods of the Roman people.
14 April	On this day Caesar won his first victory. Prayer to Victoria Augusta.
15 April	On this day Caesar was first hailed as Imperator. Prayer to the Felicity of his Reign [*Felicitati imperi*].
12 May	On this day the temple of Mars was dedicated. Prayer to the Toils of Mars.
24 May	Birthday of Germanicus Caesar. Prayer to Vesta.
12 July	Birthday of the god Julius. Prayer to Jupiter, Mars the Avenger, and Venus the Ancestress. . . .
....	.... Prayer to Jupiter.

For a still later calendar, the *Feriale Duranum* (i.e., that of a Roman auxiliary cohort at Dura-Europos on the Euphrates, *ca.* A.D. 225–227), see A. D. Nock, "The Roman Army and the Roman Religious Year," *Harvard Theological Review*, XLV (1952), pp. 187–252.

VIRGIL'S VISION OF THE FUTURE

Virgil, *Eclogues*, IV. 4 ff. This "messianic" eclogue was written in 40 B.C. and voices the hopes for a new age of peace and prosperity which now centered in the growing power of Caesar Augustus. Some of the language seems to echo the Old Testament, and it is not impossible that Virgil knew the Hebrew prophets through the Greek translation of the Old Testament, the Septuagint. There is a large literature of criticism and interpretation; among the more important works may be mentioned: J. Carcopino, *Virgile et le mystère de la IVe Eglogue* (1943); J. Conington, *The Works of Virgil with a Commentary* (4th ed., 1881); T. L. Papillon, *Virgil with an Introduction and Notes* (1882); A. Sidgwick, *P. Vergili Maronis Opera with Introduction and English Notes* (1894); J. B. Mayor, W. W. Fowler, R. S. Conway, *Virgil's Messianic Eclogue* (1907); Ed. Norden, *Die Geburt des Kindes* (1924); H. Jeanmaire, *Le Messianisme de Virgile* (1930) and *La Sibylle et le Retour de l'Age d'Or* (1939); H. J. Rose, *Eclogues of Virgil* (1942); T. F. Royds, *Virgil and Isaiah* (1918).

Now has come the last age of the prophetic song of Cumae. The great cycle of the centuries is born anew. The Virgin [Justice] returns, and the reign of Saturn comes again. Now a new generation is descending from heaven. And do thou, O chaste Lucina, smile graciously upon the birth of that boy by whom the iron race shall come to an end and the golden race rise up throughout the world; for now thine own Apollo is king.

In thy consulship, in thine, O Pollio, this glorious age shall begin, and the mighty months begin their march. Under thy rule whatever traces of our guilt remain shall vanish, and free the earth from its perpetual alarm. He shall live the life of the gods, he shall see gods mingling with [ancient?] heroes, he shall himself be seen by them, and shall rule the world to which his father's virtues have brought peace.

For thee, O child, the earth, untilled, shall first bring forth everywhere, as gifts for thy childhood, foxglove and wandering ivy tendrils, and marsh lilies mingled with smiling acanthus. Untended, the she-goats shall bring home their udders swollen with milk; no huge lions shall alarm the herds; unasked, thy cradle shall break forth with caressing blossoms. The snake too shall die, and likewise the deceitful poison-plant shall die, and scented Assyrian spice shall grow wild.

As soon as thou art able to read the praises of the heroes

and the deeds of thy father, and to know what virtue is, slowly the plain shall grow yellow with the soft cornspike, the purpling grape shall hang from the wild briar, and tough oaks shall drip with sweet honey.

Even so, some traces of ancient sin shall still survive, to bid men venture upon the sea in ships, to gird towns with walls, and cleave the earth with furrows. Then a second Tiphys shall appear, and a second Argo shall carry chosen heroes. New wars shall arise, and another great Achilles shall be sent to Troy.

Later on, when the strengthening years have made thee a man, even the trader shall quit the sea, and ships of pine shall no longer exchange their merchandise. Every land shall bear every fruit; the soil shall no longer suffer the mattock, nor the vine the pruning hook. The sturdy plowman shall now loose his oxen from the yoke. Wool shall no longer learn to counterfeit various hues, but the ram in the meadows shall himself dye his own fleece, now a softly glowing sea-purple, now a saffron yellow; a natural scarlet shall clothe the lambs in their pasture.

"O ages like these, run on," cried the Fates to their spindles, voicing in harmony the steadfast decree of Destiny.

Enter upon thy high honors, dear offspring of the gods, the destined father of an earthly Jupiter, for the hour is close at hand! See how the world bows beneath her rounded dome, see the wide lands and the far-flung sea and the unfathomable depth of the sky! See how all things rejoice in the age to come!

Ah, may the last days of my long life still continue, and sufficient breath to tell thy deeds! Not Thracian Orpheus, nor Linus, shall surpass me in song, though one have his mother, the other his father to aid him—Orpheus Calliope, and Linus beautiful Apollo. Even if Pan were to contend with me, and all Arcady were to be the judge, even Pan would acknowledge himself defeated.

Begin, O baby boy, to recognize thy mother with a smile, thy mother to whom ten months have brought much weariness. Begin, O baby boy! For one who has never smiled on his parents is not honored by a god at his table or by a goddess on her couch.

PAST GUILT AND PRESENT SIN

Horace, *Odes*, III. 6. The awareness of sin reflected here and in Virgil's *Fourth Eclogue*—not to mention the cults which stressed guilt or pollution—reflect the background of Augustus' restoration of religion. Horace does not say that all Romans are like this, but that such women existed in Roman society (impossible in an earlier age?) shows the depths to which the nation has fallen. The guilt is chiefly the consequence of the Civil Wars. Horace writes almost like an Old Testament prophet (cf. Isaiah 1).

Your fathers' sins, O Roman, you, though not guiltless of them, must expiate, until you restore the temples and the ruined shrines of the gods and their statues blackened with smoke. It is by making yourself subject to the gods that you rule; with them everything begins—also assign to them the outcome! Neglected, they have sent woes unnumbered upon weeping Hesperia. Already Monaeses and the troops of Pacorus [the Parthians] have twice thrown back our attacks, which we had launched without taking the auspices; they now smile with glee to have added our spoils to their tawdry necklaces. Torn with sedition, the City has barely escaped destruction at the hands of the Dacian and the Aethiopian [Cleopatra], the one terrifying with his fleet, the other more skilful with the flying arrow. Full of sin, our age has defiled first the marriage bed, our offspring, and our homes; springing from such a source, the stream of disaster has overflowed both people and nation. The young maiden is eager to learn Ionian dances, and soon acquires coquettish arts; even in childhood she devises unchaste affairs. Soon she is looking for young lovers, even at her husband's table, and does not even choose out those on whom she will speedily bestow illicit joys when the lights are low. When invited, she openly, and not without her husband's knowledge, gets up and goes, whether it is some peddler who calls for her or the master of some Spanish ship, lavish buyer of infamy!

Not from such parents were born the youths who reddened the sea with Punic blood, and cut down Pyrrhus, and Antiochus the Great, and that nightmare Hannibal. Instead, they were the manly breed of peasant soldiers, skillful in turning the clods with Sabine hoes and at their stern mother's command bringing in cut firewood, when the sun had stretched out the mountain shadows and taken off the yoke from the weary oxen, bringing the welcome hour of rest when his chariot had gone.

What ruin does time not threaten! Our parents' age, which was worse than our grandparents', has brought forth us, who are even less worthy and are about to bear offspring still more depraved!

VIRGIL'S VISION OF THE OTHER WORLD

Virgil, *Aeneid*, VI. Virgil's *Aeneid* is primarily a work of art, not a book of religion. But so essential was religion to the Roman view of life, and to the mind of Virgil himself, and especially to the purpose of his great epic, that almost every page throws light upon our subject. This is especially true of Bk. VI, recounting Aeneas' visit to the underworld, a parallel to the Nekyia in Homer's *Odyssey* (Bk. XI). One might undertake to isolate the "religious" element in this book; but as a work of art it must be studied as a whole, and as a whole it has more to tell than could be told by any series of selections. The patriotic-religious motive is apparent throughout: and this is anything but jingoism, and reflects the noble idealism which inspired Augustus and the men about him in their determination to build, after two centuries of foreign and civil war, a new order of justice and peace (see especially lines 847–853). The philosophic motive is here—Virgil's type of eclecticism, including the Stoic doctrine of the world-soul, the Platonic ideas, the Orphic-Pythagorean belief in the pre-existence of the soul and in reincarnation, and even surviving traces of his early Epicureanism (see lines 703–751). Mythology is here in abundance, a combination of Homeric tradition, parallel and later Greek developments, fresh creations of the Hellenistic age, and native Italian legend. Archeology is here, some of it fanciful; though there are scholars who believe that remains of a Minoan foundation at Cumae still existed in Virgil's day—relic of the age of the great "sea kings" of Crete. The national history is stressed—a common feature in most ancient religions (see the Pentateuch, the historical books, and the Psalms in the Old Testament), and one which differentiates it from modern: our national history is usually secular, at least when we get beyond the landing of the Pilgrims. Recent and contemporary history is reflected here, including the tragic death of the young Marcellus (lines 860–886), no afterthought, but the climax of the whole long historical passage, and so moving in its depth of feeling that it is said his mother Octavia fainted when the lines were read to her.

The arrangement is simple and straightforward, and the book is a unified whole. First is described the landing at Cumae and the visit to the shrine of Apollo and Diana (lines 1–41), then the Sibyl's greeting and prophecy (42–97). Aeneas now descends to Hades to see his father Anchises (98–294), after duly performing the funeral rites for Misenus (156–235). Aeneas and the Sibyl cross the river Acheron (295–416); Cerberus is pacified and they enter Hades (417–425); they visit (a) the neutral region of infants, suicides, the unjustly condemned, and warriors fallen in battle (426–547), (b) Tartarus, the region of punishment for crimes done on earth (548–627), and finally (c) Elysium, the realm of the heroic dead, where Anchises explains the doctrine of the *anima mundi* and that of the transmigration of souls (628–751)—the noble souls who are to be famous in Roman history are already awaiting their birth above, chief among them the young Marcellus (752–893). At last Aeneas returns to the upper world through the ivory gate (894–900).

It is obvious that Virgil's other world is much more specific and detailed than Homer's. But his view is not a systematic theological one: it is a melange of poetic fancies. He gathered together the leading views of his time, and the result had an enormous influence upon later religious thought, even Christian, as Dante testifies. The student should read the whole *Aeneid*. H. R. Fairclough's text and translation in LCL (2 vols., 1916, 1918) is unsurpassed. See also the standard commentaries: J. Conington (1883); T. L. Papillon (1882); A. Sidgwick (1894), and the exhaustive work of Eduard Norden on Bk. VI (1903); W. Y. Sellar, *Roman Poets of the Augustan Age: Virgil* (3d ed., 1897); T. R. Glover, *Virgil* (1904); C. Bailey, *Religion in Virgil* (1935). On Virgil's later influence, see D. Comparetti, *Vergil in the Middle Ages* (1895); J. W. Mackail, *Virgil and His Meaning to the World Today* (1939; with bibliography). See also M. P. Nilsson, GGR, II, 520–535.

Thus Aeneas spoke, with tears, and gave the reins to his fleet, and at last glided up the shore of Euboean Cumae. They turn the prows toward the sea and with the firm grip of the anchors' teeth hold the ships fast; the curving hulls fringe the beach. Swiftly the band of young men leap out like a stream of sparks upon the Hesperian shore. Some go looking for the seeds of flame hidden in veins of flint; some plunder the woods, the shelter of wild beasts, and point out the streams as they discover them. But pious Aeneas seeks out the hilltop which Apollo protects and the vast cave nearby, the secret dwelling of the dread Sibyl into whom the Delian seer [Apollo] inbreathes a mighty mind and soul and uncovers the future. Presently they enter the grove of Trivia [Hecate or Diana] and pass under the golden roof.

(14) Daedalus, they say, when he fled the Minoan kingdom, ventured to entrust himself to the sky, flying on swift wings, and on his unfamiliar route drifted up toward the cold North and at last stood lightly poised above the heights of Chalcidice [i.e., the Aegean colony at Cumae]. Here first, when safely restored to earth, he consecrated to you, O Phoebus, his oary plumage and erected a huge temple. On its doors is [portrayed] the death of Androgeos; then the people of Cecrops [the Athenians], compelled, pay over their yearly tribute of seven children—there stands the urn, the lots having just been drawn. On the opposite side, rising out of the sea, the Gnosian land [Crete] faces this one; here is shown the bull's cruel love, Pasiphae's secret mating, and the monstrous two-natured offspring of this union, the Minotaur, monument of a passion so vile; here too is that house of toil and of inextricable wandering [the Cretan labyrinth]—but Daedalus, out of pity for the great love of the princess, himself unwound the tangled maze of the palace, guiding blind steps with a thread. You too, O Icarus, would have had large share in the tale had grief allowed; twice he attempted to picture in the gold your fall [from the sky], twice his paternal hands drooped helpless.

Eagerly would their eyes have studied it all had not Achates now returned from his mission, bringing with him the priestess of Phoebus and Trivia, Deiphobe the daughter of Glaucus, who addressed the king: "Not idle gazing like this is expected of you at present! Far better now would it be to offer a sacrifice—seven bullocks from the unyoked herd, with an equal number of selected ewes." After speaking thus to Aeneas—and they do not delay to carry out her sacred command—the priestess invites the Teucrians to enter the lofty temple.

(42) Hewn in the side of the Euboean rock is a vast cavern with a hundred wide mouths opening into it, a hundred gateways from which rush out an equal number of voices, the [oracular] responses of the Sibyl. They had now reached the threshold when the virgin cried out, "It is time to inquire of the oracles—look, the god, the god!" As she said this before the doors, suddenly neither her countenance nor her color remained the same, nor did her hair remain combed; her bosom panted and her heart swelled in wild fury, she looked taller, and her voice no longer seemed human, as she felt inspired by the power of the god now close at hand. "Are you hesitating with your vows and prayers, Trojan Aeneas? Are you delaying? For not until [they are offered] will the great mouths of the house open up." She spoke, and was silent. A cold shudder ran through the Teucrians' very bones, and their king poured out his prayers from the depths of his heart:

(56) "O Phoebus [Apollo], you have ever pitied the heavy woes of Troy. It was you who guided the Dardan shaft and hand of Paris against the body of Aeacus' son [Achilles]. Under your guidance I entered so many seas and visited such vast countries, the remote lands of the Massylian people and the fields bordering the Syrtes. Now at last we have caught the fleeting shores of Italy; grant that Troy's fortune may follow us only thus far [and no farther]; ye too, O all ye gods and goddesses to whom Troy and the great glory of Dardania were an offense, may ye now rightly spare the race of Pergamus. And you, most holy prophetess, who foreknow the future, grant—I do not ask a realm not promised by my fates—that the Teucrians may settle in Latium, with their wandering gods and the storm-driven powers [numina] of Troy. Then to Phoe-

bus and Trivia will I erect a temple of solid marble, and establish festival days in the name of Phoebus. For you also there awaits a noble shrine [*penetralia*] in our kingdom; for here I will place your oracles and secret utterances addressed to my people [the Sibylline books], and I will consecrate chosen men, O gracious lady, [to have charge of them]. Only do not trust your verses to leaves, lest they fly about scattered by the winds: chant them yourself, I pray." Thus he ended his prayer.

(77) But the prophetess, not yet submitting, raved wildly [*bacchatur*] in the cavern, to shake off, if possible, the mighty god from her breast; but he only wore out the more her raving mouth, subduing her untamed heart, and molded her by his pressure. And now the hundred vast mouths of the house have opened of their own accord, and through the air they bring the prophet's response: "O ye who have at last finished the great dangers of the sea—yet still graver ones await you by land —into the realm of Lavinium the Dardanians shall come (drive this anxiety from your heart!); yet they shall not rejoice that they have come. Wars, savage wars, I foresee, and the Tiber foaming with streams of blood. You shall not lack [here also] a Simois, or a Xanthus, or a Dorian camp. Even now another Achilles [Turnus] has been born in Latium, he likewise the son of a goddess. Nor shall Juno fail to follow up the Teucrians, while you, a suppliant in your great need—what peoples of Italy and what cities will you not implore [for help]! Once more, the cause of all this evil for the Teucrians is an alien bride [Lavinia], once more a foreign marriage. But you, see that you do not yield to misfortune, but advance boldly to face it, even more boldly than your Fortune permits you! Your first safe pathway, little as you guess it, will lie open from a Greek city" [i.e., Evander's Pallanteum, later the site of Rome].

(98) With such words the Cumaean Sibyl chants from the inmost sanctuary the awful enigmas, and shouts from the cavern, enfolding truths in obscurity; for so Apollo shakes out the reins as she rages on and presses the spur beneath her breast. As soon as the frenzy was over and her raving lips were

silent, the hero Aeneas spoke· "For me, O virgin, no kind of
toil arises which is either strange or unexpected; all this I
have foreseen and considered in my mind. Only this one thing
I ask: since here, it is said, is that gateway of the King of the
Lower World and the gloomy marsh from Acheron's overflow,
let me go down to the sight and presence of my dear father.
Teach me the way, and open the sacred portals! For it was he
whom I rescued, in the midst of flames and a thousand spears
flung after us, and bore on these shoulders out of the midst of
the enemy. It was he who was my fellow on the way, enduring
with me all the seas and the dangers of the deep and of the
skies—weak as he was, far beyond the strength and lot of old
age. More than that, he pleaded with me and gave command
that I should come to you as a suppliant and approach your
threshold. Pity us both, I pray you, gentle lady—pity both son
and sire; for you are all-powerful, and it is not for nothing
that Hecate has appointed you guardian of the groves of Avernus. If Orpheus could summon his wife's shade, relying upon
his Thracian harp and its melodious strings; if Pollux, by an
alternate death, could redeem his brother [Castor] and thus go
and return this way an equal number of times—not to mention great Theseus, or Alcides [Hercules]—I too am a descendant of Jove most high!"

(124) With such words he was pleading and clasping the
altars, when the prophetess thus began to speak: "O sprung
from the blood of gods, son of the Trojan Anchises, the descent to Avernus [Hades] is easy: night and day the gate of
gloomy Dis stands open; but to recall your steps and pass on
into the upper air, this is a task, this is toil! [Only] a few have
succeeded, sons of gods, whom kind Jupiter has loved, or
whose own virtue has raised them up to heaven. All around it
lies deep forest, and [the river] Cocytus encloses it with its
smooth black coils. Yet if such love possesses your mind, and
such deep desire, as twice to swim across the Stygian lake, twice
to look upon dark Tartarus—if it is your pleasure to plunge
into the insane task, then learn what first must be accomplished. Hidden in a shady tree is a bough whose leaves and

pliant stem are all of gold, held sacred to the nether Juno
[Proserpine]; it is wrapped in the depths of the woodland and
shut in by dim, dusky vales. Only to him who first has plucked
from the tree this golden-tressed fruitage is it given to descend
to the hidden places of the earth: for beautiful Proserpine has
ordained that it must be borne to her as her proper gift. When
the first [branch] is torn away, another takes its place, also of
gold, and the spray leafs out with the same ore again. Search
for it then, with eyes looking upward, and, when it is found,
seize it with your hand; for easily and of itself it will follow
you, if the Fates are calling you; otherwise no force can compel it, nor can hard steel cut it away.

(149) "However, a friend of yours is lying a lifeless corpse—
alas, you do not know it!—and is defiling all the fleet with
death, while you are here seeking our counsel and lingering at
our threshold. First lay him in his resting place and hide him
in the tomb. Lead black cattle; let these first be your expiation. Then at last you shall behold the Stygian groves and the
realms untrodden by the living." She spoke, and her closed
lips were silent.

(156) Aeneas leaves the cavern and goes forth with lowered
eyes and sad countenance, revolving in his mind the dark issues. At his side goes faithful Achates, and plants his footsteps
with an equal burden of care. Much talk they wove back and
forth between them: Who was the dead comrade referred to
by the prophetess? Whose body awaited burial? And even as
they came, they see on the dry beach Misenus, cut off by un-
timely death—Misenus the son of Aeolus, excelled by none in
stirring men with the bugle and kindling the god of battle
with his trumpet note. He had been the companion of mighty
Hector; at Hector's side he waged battle, renowned alike for
bugle and for spear; but after victorious Achilles had robbed
Hector of life, the valiant hero had joined the company of
Dardanian Aeneas, following no inferior leader. Yet there
came a day when he was making his hollow shell echo across
the seas—ah fool!—and was calling the gods to rival his blast;
jealous Triton (if the tale is worthy of belief) sunk him in

foaming waves among the rocks.—So all gathered round him lamenting with loud cries, the foremost good Aeneas. Still weeping, without delay they carry out the Sibyl's command, and toil at piling trees for his altar of burial, and heap it up toward the sky. They enter the ancient forest, the deep coverts of wild beasts; pitch-pines fall flat, the ilex rings to the stroke of the ax, logs of ash and of oak are split apart with wedges; from the hills they roll down huge mountain-ashes.

(183) Aeneas likewise is first in this work, and cheers on his crew and equips himself with their tools. But alone within his sad heart he ponders it all, and facing the endless forest, he thus happened to pray: "If only now that bough of gold might show itself to us on a tree in this deep wood! For everything the prophetess said of you, Misenus, was, alas! all too true." Scarcely has he said this when twin doves chanced to come flying down from the sky and alighted on the green grass before him. At once the great hero recognized them as his mother's birds, and prayed with joy: "Oh, be my guides, if any way there be, and through the air lead the way into that grove where the rich bough casts its shadow on the fertile ground! And thou, O Goddess Mother, fail me not in my dark hour!" So speaking he stood still and marked what signs they brought, and which way they continued their course. As they fed they flew on a little at a time, as far as keen eyes could follow and keep them in view; then, when they had come to the jaws of pestilent Avernus, they rose swiftly, and, gliding down through the liquid air, chose their seat and alighted side by side on the tree through whose green boughs glistened the sheen of gold. As in chill midwinter the woodland is wont to blossom afresh with the strange leafage of mistletoe, sown on an alien tree and wreathing the smooth stems with its yellow print, so on the shadowy ilex appeared that leafy gold, so its foil rustled in the gentle breeze. At once Aeneas seizes it and eagerly breaks off the stem, and carries it beneath the Sibyl's roof.

(212) Meanwhile on the beach the Teucrians were lamenting for Misenus, and paying the last rites to the thankless dust. First they build a vast pyre of pitchy pine and cloven oak. Its

sides they entwine with dark leaves and place funereal cy-
presses before it, and adorn it above with shining armor. Some
heat water in caldrons bubbling over the flames, and wash and
anoint the cold body. As they do it they moan. Then, their
weeping done, they lay his limbs on a cushion, and spread
over it purple clothing for the customary pall. Some lift up
the heavy bier, a sad service, and, following ancestral custom,
with averted faces they apply the torch below. Gifts of frank-
incense, food, bowls of flowing olive oil are piled upon the
fire. After the embers fell in and the flame died away, they
washed with wine the remnant of the thirsty dust, and Cory-
naeus gathered the bones and placed them within an urn of
brass. Three times he encircled his comrades with fresh water,
and purified them with light spray sprinkled from a fruitful
olive bough, and spoke the words of farewell. Then good
Aeneas heaps over him a massive mounded tomb, [sur-
mounted] with his own armor, his oar, and his trumpet; it lies
beneath a lofty mountain, which now is called Misenum after
him, and thus keeps his name immortal from age to age.

(236) When this had been done, he hastens to fulfill the
Sibyl's command. A deep cave yawned vast and wide, with a
floor of sharp stones, sheltered by a dark lake and the gloom of
the forest. Over it no flying creature could safely wing its way,
such a vapor poured from its black jaws and rose into the over-
arching sky. (Hence the Greeks called it Avernus [Aornos], the
"birdless.") Here the priestess first led up four black-backed
bullocks and poured wine upon their foreheads; then, plucking the topmost hairs from between their horns, she lays them
on the sacred fire for the first-offering, calling loudly on
Hecate, mistress of both heaven and hell. Others laid knives to
their throats, and caught the warm blood in bowls. Aeneas
himself killed with the sword a black-fleeced lamb to [Night]
the mother of the Eumenides and her mighty sister [Terra],
and to thee a barren heifer, O Proserpine. Then he uprears
nocturnal altars to the Stygian king [Pluto], and lays whole
carcasses of bulls upon the flames, pouring fat oil over the
blazing entrails. And lo! about the first rays of sunrise the

ground moaned underfoot, and the wooded ridges began to tremble, and through the gloom dogs seemed to howl as the goddess [Hecate] drew near. "Go away! Go away! all who are unsanctified!" cries the prophetess. "Leave every part of the grove! And you, rush on ahead and unsheathe your sword— now you need your courage, Aeneas, now your stout heart." This much she said, and plunged in fury into the open cave; he with unflinching steps keeps pace with his advancing guide.

(264) O ye gods who hold dominion over spirits! Ye silent shades! And thou Chaos, thou Phlegethon, and ye wide sound-less realms of night! Grant that it be lawful for me to tell what I have heard; grant me by your grace to unfold things hid deep and dark within the earth!

(268) On they went alone in the darkness, beneath the dusky night, through the empty halls of Dis and his vacant realm, even as one makes his way in the forest beneath the jealous light of an inconstant moon, when Jupiter has shrouded the sky in shadow and black Night has blotted out the world's colors. Right in front of the doorway, even in the entrance of the jaws of Orcus [hell], Grief and avenging Cares have made their bed; there pale Diseases dwell and sad Old Age, and Fear, and evil-counseling Famine, and shameful Want, shapes terrible to see; and Death and Toil, and next to them Sleep, Death's brother, and the soul's Guilty Joys, and at the oppo-site threshold death-dealing War, and the Furies [the Eumen-ides] in their iron cells, and crazy Discord with bloodstained fillets entwined in her snaky locks.

(282) In the midst a vast, shadowy elm spreads its boughs and ancient arms, where, they say, false Dreams dwell in clus-ters, clinging beneath every leaf. Many monstrous creatures be-sides, in the shapes of wild beasts, are stabled at the gates— centaurs and double-shaped Scyllas, and the hundredfold Briareus, and the beast of Lerna [the hydra] hissing horribly, and the Chimera armed with flame, Gorgons and Harpies, and the form of the triple-bodied shade [Geryon]. Here in a surge of terror Aeneas quickly grasps his sword, and turns its naked

edge against them as they approach; and had not his wise companion reminded him that their lives were thin and bodiless, as they flitted about in an empty semblance of form, he would have rushed upon them and vainly lashed through the phantoms with his steel.

(295) From here a road leads to Tartarus and the waves of Acheron. Here a turbulent whirlpool seethes with thick mud and disgorges into Cocytus all its load of sand. Charon, the grim ferryman, guards these streams and rivers, ragged and awful, his chin covered with untrimmed masses of grey hair, his eyes like flames of fire, and his filthy mantle hanging from a knot on his shoulder. Alone he plies the pole and trims the sails, and in his rust-colored boat transports the dead; stricken now in years, but a god's old age is vigorous and fresh. Hither rush the whole throng, and pour streaming to the banks—mothers and men and bodies of high-souled heroes, dead and done with life, boys and unwedded girls, and sons laid on the pyre before their parents' eyes; thick as the leaves that drop fluttering down in the forest with autumn's earliest frost; thick as the birds that swarm landward from the seething deep, when the yearly chill drives them overseas and sends them to sunny lands. They stood pleading to be the first to be carried across, and stretched out their appealing hands to the farther shore. But the grim boatman takes now some and now others, still others he pushes back far from the strand. Moved and astonished at the tumult, Aeneas spoke, "Tell me, O maiden, what means this crowding to the river? What are the spirits seeking? Or by what rule do some leave the banks, while others with sweeping oars cross over the leaden gray ford?"

(321) To him the aged priestess made brief reply. "Son of Anchises, true offspring of the gods, you see the deep pools of Cocytus and the Stygian marsh, by whose power the gods fear to swear falsely. This crowd which you see are all helpless and unburied; Charon is the ferryman; those whom the waves bear across have found a tomb. Nor is it permitted to cross these awful banks and hoarse-throated streams until their

bones have found a resting-place. A hundred years they wander here and there, flitting about the shore; then at last they gain entrance, and revisit the pools so longed for."

(331) Anchises' son stood still, pondering deeply and pitying in his heart their cruel lot. There he discerns, sad and unhonored in death, Leucaspis and Orontes, captain of the Lycian fleet, whom, as they sailed together from Troy over the windy seas, the southerly gale overwhelmed—ships and men alike were swept down.

(337) Lo, Palinurus the helmsman passed by, who of late, while he was watching the stars on their Libyan voyage, had fallen from the stern and been hurled into the waves. As soon as he recognized the melancholy form in that deep gloom, Aeneas addressed him. "What god, O Palinurus, tore you from us and plunged you into the depth of the sea? Come, tell us. For in this one response Apollo—never before found false!—deceived me when he prophesied that you would cross the sea safely and arrive on the Ausonian shore. Lo, is this his faithful promise?"

(347) But he replied: "Neither did the tripod of Phoebus deceive you, my captain, son of Anchises, nor did any god plunge me into the sea. For by chance the tiller to which I clung as my appointed charge, steering our course, was jerked away; as I fell I seized it and dragged it with me. By the rough seas, I swear it was not for myself I feared so much as for your ship, lest, the rudder being lost and its pilot dragged away, it might be overcome by the rising waves. Three stormy nights in the water the violent southwind drove me over the endless seas; by the faint light of the fourth dawn I caught sight of Italy, as I rose on the crest of a wave. Little by little I swam shoreward; already I was clinging there safely, when, weighed down as I was with my dripping clothes, I caught with bent fingers at the jagged mountain cliffs, but the barbarous people attacked me with weapons, ignorantly deeming me a prize. Now the wave holds me, and the winds toss me on the shore. By heaven's sweet light and air I beg you, by your father, by Iulus your rising hope, rescue me from these woes, uncon-

quered one! Either cast earth over me as quickly as you can, and seek out once more the haven of Velia; or else, if there is any such way, if your Goddess Mother shows you one—for it is not without divine favor, I am sure, that you venture to cross these vast streams and ford the Stygian pool—then lend a hand to one in misery, and take me with you across the waves, so that at least in death I may find a quiet resting place!"

(372) Thus he ended, and the prophetess thus began: "Whence comes, O Palinurus, this fierce longing of yours? Are you, without burial, to behold the Stygian waters and the awful river [Cocytus] of the Furies, and draw near the bank unbidden? Cease to hope that heaven's decrees may be turned aside by prayer! But keep my words in your memory, for comfort in your sad hard lot. Far and wide the neighboring cities will be driven by celestial portents to appease your dust; they shall build a tomb, and at the tomb pay solemn offerings, and for evermore the place shall bear the name of Palinurus" [Cap Palinuro]. The words took away his cares, and for a while grief was driven from his sorrowing heart; he rejoices over the place that bears his name.

(384) So they continue the journey already begun, and approach the river. Already, even from the Stygian wave, the boatman catches sight of them as they advance through the silent woods and turn their feet toward the bank, and turns on them with these words of rebuke: "Whoever you are who approach our river bearing arms, tell us why you come, and do not advance a step further! This is the land of Shadows, of Sleep, and drowsy Night; it is not permitted to living bodies to cross in the Stygian ferryboat. And in truth I had no joy in taking Alcides [Heracles] on his journey across the lake, nor Theseus and Pirithous, though they were sons of gods and invincible in valor. The one tried to drag in chains, even on his throne, the warder of Tartarus, and carried him off trembling; the others tried to carry away our queen from the bridal chamber of Dis."

(398) To this the Amphyrsian prophetess made brief reply: "No such trickery is here. Do not be troubled. Our weapons

offer no violence. The huge gatekeeper may go on barking forever from his cavern and frighten the bloodless ghosts. Proserpine may preserve her chastity within her uncle's gates. Aeneas of Troy, renowned both for piety and arms, is descending to meet his father in the deep shades of Erebus. If the sight of such filial piety fails to stir you, at least this bough" (she uncovers the bough hidden in her dress) "you must recognize." At this his heaving breast loses its anger, and he says nothing more; but marveling at the awful gift, the fated wand seen after so long a time, he turns in his bluish bark and nears the shore. Then the other souls that sat on the long benches he routs out and clears the gangways, and takes on board huge Aeneas. Under the weight the galley groaned in every seam, and streams of marsh-water poured in fast. At last both prophetess and hero are landed unharmed on the ugly mire and the gray sedge.

(417) These regions ring with the triple-throated baying of vast Cerberus, his huge form crouching in the opposite cavern. To him the prophetess, seeing the serpents already bristling around his necks, throws a cake made drowsy with honey and drugged meal. Opening his three ravenous throats, he catches it, and his immense frame relaxes and sinks to the ground, sprawling hugely all over his den. The warder overcome, Aeneas gains entrance, and quickly passes beyond the bank of that stream whence none return.

(426) At once are heard loud wailing voices, the souls of infants crying, who were taken from sweet life at its very doorway, and torn from the breast; a black day cut them off and plunged them in bitter death. Close by are those who had been put to death on false charges. Yet their dwellings were not assigned without lot, or without a judge; for Minos presides and shakes the urn; he summons a court of the silent ones, and looks into [men's] lives and misdeeds. The next region is occupied by those sad souls who, though innocent, took their own lives, and, hating the day, flung away their lives. How gladly, now, in the upper air would they endure their poverty and hard toil! But Fate prevails; the gloomy

marsh with its hateful waves confines them, and Styx encircles them with her ninefold barrier.

(440) Not far from here are seen stretching away on every side the Fields of Mourning; that is the name they are given. Here those whom pitiless love has wasted in cruel decay hide themselves among the untrodden paths, shrouded in thickets of myrtle; even in death their pangs do not cease. In this region he sees Phaedra and Procris, and sad Eriphyle, pointing out the wounds given her by her merciless son, and Evadne and Pasiphae; Laodamia goes with them, and she who was once Caeneus, a youth, but now a woman, turned back once more by Fate into her former shape. Among them is Dido the Phoenician, her death-wound still fresh, wandering in the vast forest. As soon as he stood beside her, the Trojan hero recognized the dim form through the darkness, even as one sees or thinks he sees the moon at the month's beginning, peering through the clouds. He shed tears, and spoke to her in words of tender love:

"Unhappy Dido! was the tale true that reached me?—that you were no more, and had met your doom with the sword? Was I, alas, the cause of your death? By the stars above I swear, by the heavenly powers, and by whatever is sacred beneath the earth, I left your shores unwillingly, O queen. But it was the gods' decrees, which even now compel me to pass through these shadows, through these rough lands and the depths of night, which imperiously drove me forth; nor could I believe that my departure would bring you pain so great. Stay your footsteps, and withdraw not from our gaze! From whom do you flee? The last word Fate allows me to say to you is this."

(467) With such words and with flowing tears Aeneas soothed the anger of the burning, fierce-eyed spirit. She turned away, her gaze fixed on the ground, and was no more changed in countenance by the speech he tried to make than if she were made of hard flint or Marpesian rock. At length she tore herself away and, still angry, fled into the shadowy grove, where Sychaeus, her husband of long age, shares her sorrows and

answers her with equal love. Nevertheless, Aeneas, dismayed at her cruel doom, follows her from afar with pitying tears.

(477) From thence he followed the appointed path. And now they trod those farthest fields where the renowned in war dwell apart by themselves. [Here Aeneas meets the heroes who fell in the defense of Troy—their enemies, the Greek heroes, try to flee, as once before they had fled from Aeneas in battle. Deiphobus, the son of Priam, who married Helen after the death of Paris, now describes how he fell through Helen's trickery. Aeneas has already erected a cenotaph to him on the shore of the Troad, "calling thrice upon thy spirit"; hence Deiphobus has been able to enter this realm of the departed. In turn the hero inquires of Aeneas how he has fared since leaving the conquered city.]

(535) During such exchange of talk, Dawn in her rosy chariot had already crossed midheaven on her skyey journey, and thus they might easily have used up all the allotted time; but in brief words the Sibyl admonished her companion: "Night falls, Aeneas; we waste the hours in weeping. Here is the place where the road divides; there to the right as it goes below the walls of great Dis is our pathway to Elysium; but the way to the left wreaks vengeance on the wicked and sends them to unrelenting Tartarus." But Deiphobus replied, "Do not be angry, great priestess, I will go my way, I will retake my place and return into the darkness. Go, our glory, go! and be yours a happier fate!" This much he said, and with this last word turned away his steps.

(548) Suddenly Aeneas looks back, and sees beneath the cliff on the left hand a wide city, girt with a triple wall and encircled by a swift river of boiling flame, Tartarean Phlegethon, rolling along its thundering rocks. In front is the gate, huge, with pillars of solid adamant, which no might of men, nor even the sons of heaven, can overthrow in war; there stands the iron tower, soaring to the sky, where Tisiphone [one of the three Furies] sits girt in blood-stained pall and keeps sleepless watch at the portal night and day. From within were heard moans and the sound of lashes, the clank of iron and the

dragging of chains. Aeneas stopped, rooted to the spot by terror at the din. "Tell me, O maiden, what forms of crime are these? With what punishment are they afflicted? Why all this turmoil rising to the skies?"

(562) Then the prophetess thus began to speak: "Illustrious Teucrian chieftain, no pure soul is permitted to cross this accursed threshold; but when Hecate set me to rule the groves of Avernus, she herself taught me the penalties of the gods, and guided me through all. Gnosian Rhadamanthus here maintains his iron rule; he chastises, and listens to tales of crime, and compels confession, whenever in the world above someone vainly rejoices in secret guilt and puts off until the hour of death the expiation of his crimes. Straightway avenging Tisiphone, girt with her lash, leaps upon the guilty to scourge them, and, brandishing the fierce snakes in her left hand, summons her band of sisters." (Then at last the sacred gates open wide, grating on their jarring hinges.) "Can you see what sentry is sitting in the doorway? Or what shape guards the threshold? [Tisiphone.] Within, even more grim, sits the monstrous Hydra with her fifty black, yawning throats. Then Tartarus itself drops sheer, stretching down into the gloom twice as far as in the world above one looks upward to Olympus and the heavenly sky. Here the ancient sons of Earth, the Titan crew, hurled down by the thunderbolt, lie wallowing in the abyss. Here also I saw the twin sons of Aloeus, immense giants in frame, who with their own hands tore down high heaven and expelled Jove from the realm above. I also saw Salmoneus, paying the cruel penalty for mocking Jove's flames and the thunders of Olympus. Drawn by four horses and brandishing a torch, he rode in triumph among the Greeks and through his city in the middle of Elis, and claimed for himself the worship due the gods. Madman! to mimic the storm clouds and the inimitable thunderbolt with brass and the tramp of his horn-hoofed steeds! But the omnipotent Father hurled his shaft through thick clouds (no mere firebrand his, nor the smoky glare of pine torches!) and plunged him headlong with a terrible whirlwind. There also might

Tityos be seen, fosterling of Earth the mother of all. His body stretches over nine full acres, and a monstrous vulture with crooked beak eats away his undying liver and vital organs, fruitful of suffering, and probes deep within the breast that gives it food and lodging; nor is any rest given to the tissues that always grow again. Why tell of the Lapithae, of Ixion and Pirithous, over whom a black rock hangs, just slipping and as if about to fall? High festival couches gleam with golden frames, and before them is spread a feast with royal luxury; but lying close by, the eldest of the Furies keeps their hands from touching the tables, and springs up with torch aloft and with thunderous roars.

(608) "Here are those who hated their brothers, while they lived, or struck down a parent, or entangled a client by fraud; or who brooded in solitude over treasure they had gained and shared none of it with their kin—this was the largest group of all; and those who were killed for adultery, and those who took up unholy arms [i.e., against their country] and feared not to break their plighted loyalty to their leaders. Imprisoned, they await their doom. Do not seek to learn what doom [is theirs], or what form of crime or what fortune has overwhelmed them. Some roll a huge stone, or hang stretched out on spokes of wheels; unhappy Theseus sits, and shall sit forever, and Phlegyas, the most miserable, gives counsel to all and with a loud voice bears witness through the gloom: *Take warning! learn to do justice, and do not slight the gods!* This man sold his country for gold, and handed her over to a tyrant; he made and unmade the laws for a price. This one invaded his daughter's chamber and a forbidden marriage. All dared some monstrous crime, and achieved what they attempted. Not if I had a hundred tongues, a hundred mouths, and a voice of iron, could I sum up the forms of crime or name over all the punishments."

(628) So spoke the aged priestess of Phoebus [Apollo], then added, "But come now, hasten on your way and complete your task; let us move on faster; I can see the walls forged in the Cyclopean furnaces, and in front the arched gateway where

they bid us lay the appointed gifts." She ended, and, advancing side by side along the shadowy ways, they soon cross the intervening space and approach the gates. Aeneas gains the entrance, sprinkles his body with fresh water, and lays the bough on the opposite threshold.

(637) This at last fully done, and the task of the goddess completed, they came to a land of joy, the green pastures and blessed dwellings within the Fortunate Groves. Here an ampler air clothes the meadows with rosy light, and they know [i.e., have] their own sun, and stars of their own. Some exercise their limbs in wrestling on the grass, or contend in games, or wrestle on the yellow sand. Some dance with beating footfall and sing songs; with them is the Thracian priest [Orpheus] in sweeping robe, making music to their measures with the seven distinct notes, plucking them now with his fingers, now with his ivory quill. Here is Teucer's ancient line, a family of noble mien, great-souled heroes born in happier years, Ilus and Assaracus, and Dardanus, the founder of Troy. From afar he marvels at their shadowy armor and chariots; their lances stand fixed in the ground, and their unyoked horses graze freely over the plain. The same delight in chariot and arms which was theirs in life, the same care in pasturing their sleek horses, follows them now when hidden beneath the earth. Lo! others he beholds on the right and the left, feasting in the meadow and singing in a chorus the joyful paean [a hymn to Apollo] within a fragrant laurel grove whence flows the river Eridanus [Po] and rolls upward in its fullness through the wood.

(660) Here is the band of those who received wounds in fighting for their country; and those who in their lifetime were chaste priests, and devout poets who sang worthily of Apollo; and those who made life richer by the arts which they invented; and those who by their service have earned a remembrance among others—all these have their brows bound with snowy fillets. As they circled round, the Sibyl spoke to them, to Musaeus before them all; for he is the center of all this multitude, and stands out head and shoulders among them as they

gaze up to him: "Tell me, happy souls, and you, the best of poets, what region belongs to Anchises? Where does he live? It is for his sake that we have come, and have sailed across the great rivers of Erebus."

(672) And to her the hero thus briefly replied: "No one has a specified dwelling here; we live in the shady woodlands; on soft banks and in meadows beside fresh streams we have our habitation. But you, if this be your heart's desire, climb this ridge, and then I will start you on an easy path." He spoke, and led the way before them, and pointed down toward the shining fields. After that they left the mountain heights.

(679) But deep in a green valley father Anchises was earnestly considering the imprisoned souls who were destined for the light above, and, as it chanced, reviewing his beloved children and the tale of his descendants, their fates and their fortunes, their works and ways. When he saw Aeneas coming to meet him across the meadow, he stretched forth both his hands eagerly, while tears rolled down his cheeks, and his lips parted in a cry: "Have you come at last, and has the devotion I expected overcome the toilsome path? Is it granted me, my son, to look in your face, and to hear and to answer in the familiar tones? So indeed in fancy I forecast the future, counting the days; nor has my longing misled me. What lands, what broad seas you have traversed to reach me! Through what surging perils, my son! How I feared lest the realm of Libya might work you harm!"

But he: "My father, it was your shadow, your own, that so often met me and drew me to seek out these portals! My fleet is even now standing off the Tyrrhene shore. Give me your hand to clasp, my father—give it, and do not withdraw from my embrace."

So he spoke, his face wet the while with flowing tears. Thrice there he tried to throw his arms around his neck; thrice the phantom, vainly grasped, fled from his hands, light as wind and swift as a fleeing dream.

(703) Meanwhile, in a remote valley, Aeneas sees a secluded grove with rustling forest thickets, and the river of Lethe flow-

ing past these peaceful dwellings. About in it flitted nations
and peoples innumerable, even as in the meadows on clear
summer days the bees light on the bright-hued blossoms and
stream round the snow-white lilies, and all the fields murmur
with their humming. Aeneas is startled by the sudden view,
and, since he does not know, asks the reason—what river it is,
in the distance, and who are those who fill its banks in such
great numbers. Then father Anchises replies: "They are spirits
to whom Fate owes second bodies, and of Lethe's water they
drink a draught that brings freedom from care and long forgetfulness. Of these in truth I have long desired to tell you,
and to show to your face, and to count my children's children,
so that you may the more rejoice with me at finding Italy."

"But, O father, are we to think that any souls travel hence
into the upper air, and return again to sluggish bodies? What
means this dreadful longing for the light?"

"I will tell you, my son," replied Anchises, "and not keep
you in suspense." So he began, and explained each point in
order.

(724) "First of all, heaven and earth and the watery plains,
the moon's shining orb and the Titanian star [the sun], are
nourished by a spirit within them; a mind, which pervades
them as its members, controls their great mass and mingles
with the vast frame. Thence [i.e., from the *anima mundi* or
world soul] come the races of man and of beast, the life of
winged creatures, and those monstrous forms the sea brings
forth beneath its shining floor. Fiery is the energy and celestial
the origin of their seed, as far as they are not clogged by bane-
ful bodies and dulled by earthly limbs and dying members.
From these [i.e., bodies] come fear and desire, sorrow and joy;
nor do they see the sky, shut up in the darkness of their blind
dungeon. No, even when their last day of life is done, and life
and light depart, not even then do all the plagues and deep
evils of the body wholly leave them; for it is inevitable that
many a long-continued evil should take an amazingly deep
root. Hence they are disciplined with punishment, and pay in
suffering for their lifelong sins; some are hung stretched out to

the empty winds; some have their taint of guilt washed away in the seething tides, or burned out with fire. We suffer, each in his own ghost [*Manes*]; then we are sent through the broad spaces of Elysium, some of us to remain in those happy fields; [others] till length of days, completing the cycle of time, removes the inbred taint and leaves unsoiled the ethereal sense and the spirit's pure flame. All these, when they have turned the wheel of a thousand years, God summons in a vast throng to the river Lethe, so that, bereft of memory, they may visit once more the vault above, and desire again to return into bodies."

Anchises ceased, and led his son and the Sibyl into the midst of the assembled murmuring throng, and mounted a hillock from where he could view the whole long procession and study their countenances as they came on.

(756) "Come now, the glory that hereafter shall follow our Dardanian line, and the Italian descendants that await you, illustrious souls and the future heirs of our name—these will I set forth, and teach you your destiny. That youth whom you see yonder, leaning on his unpointed spear, holds by lot the place nearest the light, and will be the first to rise into the air of heaven from the mingling of Italian blood; [he is] Silvius, an Alban name, your youngest child, whom late in your old age your wife Lavinia shall bring forth in the woodland, a king and father of kings; from him our house shall rule in Alba Longa. Next to him is Procas, the glory of the Trojan race, and Capys and Numitor, and the one who shall renew your name, Silvius Aeneas, equally renowned in piety and in arms, if ever he receives his kingdom in Alba. What men! See what strength they display, and their brows shaded by the civic oak. They shall build for you Nomentum and Gabii and the city of Fidena, they shall crown the hills with the fortress of Collatia, with Pometii and the Fort of Inuus, with Bola and Cora; these shall be their names—now they are unnamed districts.

(777) "Even more, a child of Mars shall become a companion to Romulus, likewise his grandsire, even Romulus whom his mother Ilia shall bear, of the blood of Assaracus. Do you see

that twin plumes stand upright on his crest, and that his father even now marks him out for honor in the world above? Under his auspices, my son, that noble city [Rome] shall equal the earth with her empire and Olympus with her spirit, girding her seven hills with a single wall, happy in her breed of men; even like the Berecynthian mother [Cybele] who, turret-crowned, rides in her chariot through the Phrygian cities, glad in her offspring of gods, clasping a hundred of her children's children, all heavenly beings, all dwellers in the heights above.

(788) "Turn now and look with both your eyes: behold this people, your own Romans! Here is Caesar, and all of Iulus's posterity, destined to appear under the mighty vault of heaven. And here is he, the one you have so often heard promised you, Augustus Caesar, the son of a god, who shall once more re-establish the Age of Gold in Latium, over the fields where once Saturn reigned, and carry his empire beyond the Gara-mants and Indians, to the land that lies beyond our stars, be-yond the sun's yearly paths, where Atlas the sky-bearer turns on his shoulder the pole with its glittering stars. Before his coming even now the Caspian kingdoms and the land of Mae-otia shudder over the oracular responses, and the mouths of the sevenfold Nile tremble in terror. Not even Alcides [Hercu-les] traversed such vast spaces of earth, though he pierced the brazen-footed deer, though he silenced the Erymanthian wood-lands and made Lerna tremble at his bow; nor did he who guides his span with reins of vine tendrils, conquering Liber, when he drives his tigers down from Nysa's lofty height.—And do we still hesitate to give full range to valor in deeds, or does fear hold us back from settling on the Ausonian land?

(808) "But who is he who stands apart, crowned with sprigs of olive, bearing a sacrifice? I know the locks and hoary chin of that king [Numa] of Rome who shall first establish the city upon law, called from the poor little land of Cures to the majesty of kingship. To him shall succeed Tullus, who shall break the peace of his country and rouse to arms a settled people, men long unaccustomed to triumphs. Next comes vain-glorious Ancus, even now glorying too much in popular re-

port. Can you see also the Tarquin kings, and the haughty soul of avenging Brutus, and the fasces regained? He shall be the first to obtain a consul's power and the cruel axes, and when his sons stir up fresh war, the father, for fair freedom's sake, will summon them to doom—unhappy man, however much posterity may praise the deed! Love of country, and insatiable passion for honor, will prevail.

(824) "Still further on behold the Decii and the Drusi, Torquatus with his cruel axe, and Camillus bringing back the standards. But those whom you see shining in equal armor, souls harmonious now while buried in Night—alas, what mutual war, if they attain the light, what battle-lines, what carnage will they inspire! The father-in-law [Caesar] descending from the Alpine barrier and the fortress of Monoecus, the son-in-law [Pompey] facing him with the armies to the East! O my sons, do not harden your hearts to such warfare, nor turn your country's might and valor upon her own vitals! And you, be the first to forbear, you who draw your descent from Olympus; cast away the weapons from your hand, O blood of mine!

(836) "That one [Mummius] shall drive his conquering chariot to the Capitoline Mount after triumphing over Corinth, famous for the Achaeans he has slain. That other one [Aemilius Paulus] shall uproot Argos and Agamemnonian Mycenae, and even the Aeacid's own heir [Perseus], descended from Achilles mighty in arms, thus avenging his Trojan ancestors and Minerva's ravaged temple. Who can leave you, great Cato, or you, Cossus, in silence? Who the family of the Gracchi? Or those two sons of the Scipios, the two thunderbolts of war, the bane of Libya? Or you, Fabricius, poor yet powerful? Or you, Serranus [Regulus], sowing the seed in your furrow? Whither do you hurry me on, though weary, O Fabii? You, Maximus, are the one—the greatest— who alone, by his delaying, restores the state. Others, I readily believe, will beat out the breathing bronze in softer lines, and draw the living features from the marble; others may plead their causes more eloquently, or with the [astronomer's] rod mark out the path-

ways of the heavens, and tell the rising of the stars: *but let it be your charge, O Roman, to rule the nations by your authority* (these are to be your arts), *on the foundation of peace to build order, to show mercy to the conquered, and to subdue the proud.*"

(854) Thus father Anchises spoke, and while they marveled he went on: "See how Marcellus advances, glorious with his splendid spoils, and towering as victor high above them all! He, though a knight, shall steady the Roman state when it is disturbed and greatly shaken, and shall ride down the Carthaginian and the insurgent Gaul, and a third time hang up the captured armor before Father Quirinus."

(860) At this Aeneas, for he saw accompanying him a youth of exceptional beauty and in shining armor, though his face was sad and his eyes downcast, [inquired]: "Who, my father, is this one who thus attends him on his way? Is he a son, or some other great one of his descendants? What whispering among his comrades! How noble in presence himself! But dark night hovers round his head with mournful shade."

(867) Then father Anchises with welling tears began: "O my son, do not ask about the deep sorrow of your people [Augustus' nephew and adopted son, Marcellus, died 25 B.C.]. The Fates shall only show him to earth, but will not let him stay longer. Too mighty, O gods, you thought the Roman people would become, had this your gift been made permanent. What mourning of men shall arise from the Field of Mavors [the Campus Martius] and be brought to the imperial city! What a funeral train shall you see, O Tiber, as you flow past the newly heaped tumulus! No boy of the Ilian race shall raise his Latin forefathers' hopes so high, nor shall the land of Romulus ever boast so proudly of any son. Alas for his goodness, alas for his old-style honor, for his hand invincible in war! None would have met him in arms unscathed, whether he met the foe on foot, or drove his spurs into the flanks of his foaming horse. Ah, unhappy boy! if only you can break the hard bonds of Fate, you shall *be* a Marcellus [i.e., another, like

his namesake]! Give me lílies, in full hands; let me strew purple blossoms; these gifts at least let me heap up for my descendant's shade and so perform an unavailing service."

(886) Thus they wandered up and down through the whole region of wide misty plains, and covered it all. And when Anchises had led his son over every scene, one after another, and had kindled his soul with love for the fame that was to be, he tells him then of the wars he must soon wage, and instructs him about the Laurentine peoples and the city of Latinus, and how he is to face or avoid each labor [that confronts him].

(893) "There are two gates of Sleep, one of which is said to be of horn, and through it true shades are given a ready outlet; the other shines with the gleam of polished ivory, but false are the dreams which the shades send upward by it." With these words Anchises then accompanies his son and the Sibyl, and dismisses them by the ivory gate. Aeneas pursues his way to the ships and revisits his comrades; then straight along the shore bears on to Caieta's haven. The anchor is cast from the prow; the sterns lie aground on the beach.

VI. RELIGION UNDER THE EMPIRE

The chief characteristic of religious history in the imperial period was the influx of foreign deities and cults into Rome. Not only the so-called "mystery" religions, but many different cults and schools of religious thought had their votaries and propagandists throughout the empire (see F. C. Grant, HR, pp. 105–149). The scene was described by T. R. Glover under the title *The Conflict of Religions in the Early Roman Empire* (1909); in general this was a true enough description, but such a "joiner" or "pluralist" as Apuleius makes it clear that the conflicts were readily resolved (somewhat as many men today hold simultaneous membership in several fraternal orders). Only in the case of Christianity was such dual or plural membership impossible, as a long line of advocates, from Paul and Tertullian to Ambrose and Augustine, made clear. The general attitude of the Empire toward religious cults was tolerant and friendly, save when there seemed reason to suspect secret purposes of treason, insurrection, or social anarchy. It was a tragedy that neither the Church nor the Empire was capable of recognizing their separate and mutually co-ordinate spheres; the Christians recognized the duty of loyalty to the state, but the state demanded impossible forms for its expression.

See G. Wissowa, RKR, §§ 16–18, 56–60; S. Angus, *Religious Quests of the Graeco-Roman World* (1929); C. Bigg, *Origins of Christianity* (1909); G. Boissier, *La Religion romaine d'Auguste aux Antonins*, 2 vols. (3d ed., 1884); C. Bonner, "Some Phases of Religious Feeling in Later Paganism," *Harvard Theological Review*, XXX (1937), 119–140; J. Carcopino, *Aspects mystiques de la Rome païenne* (1942), *La Basilique Pythagoricienne de la Porte Majeure* (1944), *Daily Life in Ancient Rome* (1940), especially pp. 121–140; F. Cumont, RO; A. J. Festugière and P. Fabre, *Le Monde gréco-romain au temps de notre-seigneur*, 2 vols. (1935); L. Friedländer, *Darstellungen aus der Sittengeschichte Roms* (6th ed., 1890; also Engl. tr.), Vol. III, Pt. III, chs. 4–6; F. C. Grant, HR, pp. 105–149 (on mystery cults in the Hellenistic age); R. M. Grant, *The Sword and the Cross* (1955); W. R. Halliday, *The Pagan Background of Early Christianity*

(1925); M. P. Nilsson, GGR, II, 555–672 (on syncretism); A. D. Nock, "Religious Developments from the Close of the Republic to the Death of Nero," in CAH, Vol. X (1934), ch. 15, with bibliography, pp. 951–953; R. Pettazzoni, *I Misteri* (1923); G. La Piana, "Foreign Groups in Rome during the First Centuries of the Empire," in *Harvard Theological Review*, XX (1927), 183 ff.; N. Lewis and M. Reinhold, RC, II, §§ 167–171; J. Réville, *La Religion à Rome sous les Sévères* (1886); M. J. Rostovtzeff, *Mystic Italy* (1927); N. Turchi, RRA, Pt. II. 4–7, *Le Religioni Misteriche del Mondo Antico* (1948), *Le Religioni di Grecia e di Roma* (1950); J. H. Waszink, W. C. Van Unnik, Ch. de Beus (eds.), *Het Oudste Christendom en de Antieke Cultuur*, Vol. I (1951), ch. 2, with excellent bibliographies; P. Wendland, *Die Helle-nistisch-Römische Kultur* (2d ed., 1912); H. Willoughby, *Pagan Regeneration* (1929). On astrology, see also C. Koch, *Gestirnverehrung im alten Italien: Sol Indiges und der Kreis der Di Indigetes* (1933); F. H. Cramer, *Astrology in Roman Law and Politics* (1954).

A PRAYER FOR THE STATE

Velleius Paterculus, II. 131. Velleius was a historian in the time of Tiberius. His *History of Rome* concludes with a prayer:

I must conclude my volume with a prayer. "O Jupiter Capitolinus, and Thou, O founder and preserver of the Roman name, Mars Gradivus, and Vesta, guardian of the perpetual fire, and whatsoever deity has raised this mighty mass of the Roman Empire to the world's highest peak: You I pray and invoke with public voice. Guard, preserve, protect this present state of affairs, this peace, this ruler, and when he has reached the final station, fixed as the boundary to human life, grant him, at as late a date as possible, to have as successors men who are strong enough to bear upon their shoulders the burden of this empire of the whole earth, as bravely as we have seen it borne by this Prince; and grant that the counsels of all citizens, if they are good, [may be carried out, but if evil, bring them to nothing." This is obviously the sense intended, but the rest of the prayer is missing.]

A DECREE OF HOMAGE AND AN OATH OF
ALLEGIANCE TO THE EMPEROR GAIUS

Dittenberger, Sylloge[2] 364, [3] 797; R. Helbing, *Auswahl aus Grie-chischen Inschriften* (1915), no. 12; *Papers of the American School at Athens,* I (1882–3), pp. 50–53. A bronze tablet found at Assos in 1881. Note that Caesar Augustus (Octavian) is named between Zeus and Athena. Athena's temple stood on the acropolis above the city of Assos. The date of the inscription is A.D. 37. Note that the delegates were to pay their own expenses of travel.

Under the consulship of Gnaeus Acerronius Proclus and Gaius Pontius Petronius Nigrinus.

Decree of the Assians, by Vote of the People

Since the announcement of the coronation of Gaius Caesar Germanicus Augustus, which all mankind had longed and prayed for, the world has found no measure for its joy, but every city and people has eagerly hastened to view the god, as if the happiest age for mankind [the Golden Age] had now arrived:

It seemed good to the Council, and to the Roman business-men here among us, and to the people of Assos, to appoint a delegation made up of the noblest and most eminent of the Romans and also of the Greeks, to visit him and offer their best wishes and to implore him to remember the city and take care of it, even as he promised our city upon his first visit to the province in the company of his father Germanicus.

Oath of the Assians

We swear by Zeus the Savior and the God Caesar Augustus [Octavian] and the holy Virgin of our city [Athena Polias] that we are loyally disposed to Gaius Caesar Augustus and his whole house, and look upon as our friends whomever he favors, and as our enemies whomever he denounces. If we observe this oath, may all go well with us; if not, may the opposite befall.

Delegates announced, at their own cost

Gaius Varius, son of Gaius, of the tribe of Voltinia Castus
Hermophanes son of Zoilus
Ktetos son of Pisistratus
Aeschrion son of Kalliphanes
Artemidorus son of Philomousos

who [pl.] also offered prayers for the welfare of Gaius Caesar Augustus Germanicus, and sacrificed to Jupiter Capitolinus in the name of the city.

SENECA'S CRITICISM OF THE TRADITIONAL RELIGION

From Annaeus Seneca's lost work *On Superstition*, of which one fragment is preserved by St. Augustine in his *City of God*, Bk. VI, ch. 10. After explaining Varro's threefold classification of religion (that of the poets, the philosophers, and the civil administrators) and quoting his criticism of the poetical type, Augustine cites Seneca's criticism of the "civil and urban" religion, which, he says, is far more vigorous than Varro's criticism of the "poetic" or "theatrical." The early Christians made thorough use of the pagan philosophers' criticisms of the traditional mythology and cults, and were quite familiar with their works. Tertullian (*Apology,* 12) also refers to this book by Seneca. See also Seneca, *Natural Questions,* VI. 3. 1. As Augustine says, Seneca "flourished in the times of our apostles," i.e., in the first century. He was the emperor Nero's teacher, confidant, and victim— Nero ordered him to commit suicide in A.D. 65.

In that book which he [Seneca] wrote *Against Superstition* he himself far more extensively and more vehemently censured that civil and urban theology than Varro did the theatrical and fabulous. For when writing about images [of the gods], he says:

"They dedicate images to the sacred and inviolable immortals made of the most vile and inert matter. They make them look like men, beasts, and fish; some make them of mixed sex, and with heterogeneous bodies. They call them deities [*numina*], but if they should draw breath and suddenly meet them, they would be thought monsters."

Then a little later, when praising the natural theology and expounding the views of certain philosophers, he sets himself a question and says: "Here someone will say, 'Shall I believe that the heavens and the earth are gods, and that some are above the moon, and some below it? Shall I bring forward either Plato or Strato the Peripatetic, one of whom made God to be without a body, the other without a mind?'" To this he replies, "Now really, how much truer do the dreams of Titus Tatius, or Romulus, or Tullius Hostilius seem to you? Tatius declared Cloacina to be a goddess; Romulus named Picus and Tiberinus; Hostilius declared Pavor and Pallor, the most offensive afflictions of men, the one an agitation of the mind when terrified, the other an effect upon the body, not a disease but a [change of] color. Will you prefer to believe that these are deities, and receive them into heaven?"

And how freely he wrote about the rites themselves, so cruel and so shameful! "One," he says, "castrates himself, another pierces his own arms. When they honor [in this way] the gods when angry, who will gain their favor when propitious? But gods who desire to be worshiped in this fashion ought not to be worshiped at all. So great is the frenzy of the mind when disturbed and driven from its proper place, that the gods are propitiated in a way in which not even the most ferocious of men, even those described in the myths, are said to vent their cruelty. Tyrants have torn the limbs of some; but no one has ever been ordered to tear his own. For the gratification of royal lust some have been castrated; but no one has ever, at the command of his master, laid violent hands on himself to destroy his own manhood. They cut themselves in the temples; they make supplication with their own wounds and blood. If anyone has the time to look at the things they do and suffer, he will find so many that are unfit for decent men to do, so unworthy of freemen, so unlike the acts of sane men, that no one would doubt they are mad, if they were in a minority; but now it is the multitude of the insane which is the defense of their sanity."

Next he relates those things which are customarily done even in the Capitol, and with complete frankness he asks if anyone would believe they were done except in play or by madmen. For after speaking with derision of the Egyptian sacred rites of Osiris, who after being lost is lamented but presently when found is the occasion of enormous jubilation— for both the loss and the recovery are only make-believe, and only the grief and the joy are real, though they belong to those who have neither lost anything nor found anything—after saying all this, he goes on and confesses the truth as follows: "Nevertheless there is a definite time for this outburst of frenzy. It is permitted to go mad once a year! Go to the Capitol [and what do you see?]: It is shameful to speak of the extravagances which the popular dementia has thought up, and performs as if a duty. One man is calling off names to Jupiter [as if announcing new arrivals!], another is telling the hours to Jupiter; one is washing him; another is anointing him with oil, and with the movement of his arms imitates the action. Some women are arranging the hair of Juno and Minerva, standing off some distance not only from the image but even from the temple, and moving their fingers in the manner of hairdressers; others hold up to her a mirror. There are some who are calling the gods to assist them in court; others are holding up documents and explaining their cases to them. A famous comedian [archimimus], now old and decrepit, gives a daily performance at the Capitol, as though the gods would take pleasure in viewing a play which men had ceased to be interested in. Every kind of artist lives there and works for the immortal gods." A little later he says, "After all, the services which these people render, if useless, are at least not shameful and indecent. There are certain women sitting in the Capitol who think themselves beloved by Jupiter—not in the least frightened by the glance of the (if you can believe the poets) most jealous and wrathful Juno."

This freedom [of speech] Varro never knew. He ventured to criticize the poetical theology, but not the civil, which this man [Seneca] demolished. To tell the truth, the temples where these rites are performed are far worse than the theaters where they are only represented fictitiously. Hence, as to those sacred rites of the civil theology, Seneca chose, as the course for the wise man to follow, to go through with them in act, but not to make them a part of his personal religion. So, he says, "A wise man will observe them as they are prescribed by law, but not as something pleasing to the gods." And a little later he says, "And what about these marriages by which we unite the gods, and not even decently, for we join brothers and sisters? We marry Bellona to Mars, Venus to Vulcan, Salacia to Neptune. Some of the gods we leave celibate, as though for lack of a suitable partner; but this is surely needless when there are certain goddesses who are unmarried, such as Populonia, or Fulgora, or the goddess Rumina—for whom, however, I am not astonished that there have been no suitors. All this ignoble crowd of gods, which the superstition of ages has gathered together, we ought," he says, "to adore, but in such a way as to remember all the while that their worship belongs to custom rather than to reality."

Wherefore neither those laws nor customs have instituted in the civil theology anything which was pleasing to the gods, or which had any real foundation. But this man, whom philosophy apparently had made free, but who was nevertheless an illustrious senator of the Roman people, worshiped what he censured, did what he disapproved, adored what he condemned. Philosophy certainly had taught him something great, viz., not to be superstitious about anything in the world; but on account of the laws of cities and the customs of men, to be an actor, not indeed on the stage, but as scenes were imitated in the temples—an attitude the more to be condemned in that in those things which he was insincerely acting the people thought he was acting sincerely. But an actor on the stage prefers to please people by acting plays rather than by deceiving them.

THE GOOD OLD TIMES

Petronius, *Satyricon*, 44 *ad fin*. Date, about A.D. 64. The work is a satire, especially upon the *nouveaux riches* who have more money than they know what to do with, and grow bored and cantankerous. In § 44 the speaker is Ganymede, who is complaining about the way everything is going downhill; prices are going up, quality down, and the government is rotten. Like many others (not often really religious men), he blames it on the decline in religious faith.

What is the future to be, if neither gods nor men have any pity on this place [Cumae]? As I hope to be happy in my children, I think all these things are managed by the aediles! For no one any longer believes that the gods are gods. No one keeps a fast, no one cares a straw for Jove; they all close their eyes and count up their possessions. In the old days the mothers, wearing their finest gowns, climbed the hill with bare feet, loosened hair, and pure minds, and prayed Jupiter to send them rain. Then it used to rain instantly, in buckets!— for it was either then or never. And they all came home, soaking wet, like drowned rats. But as it is [now], the gods come shuffling along with wool-clad feet, because we have no religion. And so our fields lie [parched and baking]!

WOMEN DEVOTEES OF THE EASTERN CULTS

Juvenal, *Satires*, VI. 511–591. Probably in the time of Hadrian. This satire deals with the foibles and vices of women, and might lead one to think its author a hater of the fair sex, or the society in which he lived, Rome early in the second century, utterly corrupt and degenerate. In fact, many readers have drawn this second inference, and have passed it on as a mature judgment upon the whole of Roman life, or even of paganism generally at the end of antiquity.

But a satirist is not a social historian, and his special interests lead him to present a one-sided picture. This is true also of the other Roman satirists, e.g., Persius and Martial.

The references to religion and the description of rites in Satire VI are apparently those which appealed especially to women. Other passages give us tiny vignettes of religious scenes and conditions, e.g., the drunken *gallus* (a self-emasculated votary of Attis) at a low tavern in Ostia, the festival of the Great Goddess, the sacrifice to the rustic god Silvanus. It must always be remembered in reading satires that as a rule the author disapproves what he describes and, what is more, counts on his readers to join him in disapproving. Some of the fine passages which take a higher view of religion will be found, e.g., in VIII. 254 ff.—the plebeian Decii who died to save the legions were nobler men than those they saved; or X. 346 ff.—the gods know what we need, better than we do: man is dearer to them than he is to himself; or XIII. 8—the desire to sin is as sinful as the deed. See the text and translation by G. G. Ramsay in LCL (1918); Gilbert Highet, *Juvenal the Satirist* (1955).

And now look, here comes the chorus of the raving Bellona and the Mother of the Gods, attended by a giant eunuch [a votary of Attis] to whom his obscene inferiors must offer reverence, one who has only recently cut off his soft genitals. Before him a raucous herd with timbrels give way; above his plebeian cheeks there towers a Phrygian tiara. In majestic, solemn tones he bids the lady beware the parching south wind of September, unless she purifies herself with a hundred eggs, and presents him with some old dark red garments so that if any great and unforeseen calamity threatens, it may pass into the clothes and thus make expiation for the whole year. On a winter morning she will go down to the Tiber, break the ice, and plunge in three times, dipping her trembling head in its whirling waters; then climbing out, naked and shivering, she will crawl on bleeding knees all the way across the proud king's field [i.e., the field of Tarquin the Proud, the Campus Martius]. If the white Io [Isis?] so orders, she will journey to the borders of Egypt and bring home water from hot Meroe with which to sprinkle the temple of Isis which stands right beside the ancient sheepfold. For she believes that she was so commanded by the voice of the goddess herself—what a charming mind and spirit for the gods to converse with at night! So likewise the chief and highest place of honor is given to Anubis [the dog-headed Egyptian god of the dead], who with his linen-clothed, smooth-shaven crew mocks at the wailing crowd as he runs along [i.e., the priest of Anubis, the god of the dead, mocks the worshipers lamenting for Osiris]. He is the one who pleads indulgence for wives who break the law of abstinence on days that ought to be kept holy, and who exacts large penalties when the white bed coverlet has been violated, or when the silver serpent has been observed to nod his head. His tears and his carefully practiced murmurings guarantee that Osiris will not refuse to pardon the fault—bribed, of course, by a large goose and a piece of sacrificial cake.

No sooner has this fellow gone his way than a palsied trembling Jewess, leaving her basket and her bundle of hay, comes begging at her secret ear. She is an interpreter of the laws of Solyma [Jerusalem], a high priestess of the woods [where Jews camped out like gypsies], a faithful messenger of highest heaven. She too fills her hand, but more sparingly; for a Jew will sell you whatever dreams you prefer for even a tiny coin.

Next an Armenian or a Commagenian soothsayer, having examined the lungs of a dove, still warm, will promise [her] either a youthful lover or a huge bequest from some rich and childless old man. He will probe into the breast of a chicken or the entrails of a dog, or sometimes even of a boy. He will even do some things which [under other circumstances] he would be reporting [to the police].

Even more reliance is placed in the Chaldeans. Whatever the astrologer says, they believe as if it had come from Hammon's fountain [the ancient oracle in Libya], for now that the Delphic oracles have ceased, the human race is condemned to blindness as to the future. Chief among these was the one, often an exile, by whose friendship and mercenary predictions the great citizen [Galba] died, the one whom Otho feared. Since those days, the art is believed if the astrologer has chains clanking on his right arm or was once a prisoner in some remote camp. No one believes in his skill unless he has some time been condemned and almost put to death, barely managing to get himself exiled to one of the Cyclades, or to get away at last from tiny Seriphos.

Your own Tanaquil [i.e., your wife!] consults [an astrologer] about the long-delayed death of her jaundiced mother—after previously inquiring about your own [demise]; she inquires when she can expect to bury her sister, or her uncles; and whether her lover is going to outlive her—what greater gift could the gods bestow? Of course she herself does not understand the gloomy warnings of Saturn, or [know] under which constellation Venus will show herself favorable, which months will be profitable, which will not. But watch out if you ever meet a woman clutching a well-worn calendar in her hands, as if it were a ball of oily amber [which Roman ladies carried for scent]; she is the one who now makes no inquiries, but can answer them herself. If her husband is going to the camp, or visiting his homeland, she will not go with him if the numbers of Thrasyllus call her back. If she wishes to drive out as far as the first milestone, she looks up the right hour in her book. If she has a sore in the corner of her eye, she consults her horoscope before asking for salve. If she is ill in bed, she thinks no hour more suitable for taking food than that prescribed by Petosiris.

If the woman is of humble rank, she will parade between the turning-posts of the Circus and [there] have her fortune told, presenting her forehead and her hand to [be studied by] the seer, who asks for many a smack of approval. Wealthy women receive their answers from a Phrygian or an Indian augur well versed in the stars and the heavens, or from one of the old men who bury [or expiate] thunderbolts. But plebeian destinies are read in the Circus or on the walls; the woman who wears a long gold chain about her bare neck inquires before the columns with their groups of dolphins—whether she should toss over the innkeeper and marry the peddler.

PERSONAL PIETY IN THE SECOND CENTURY

Apuleius, *Apologia,* 55–56. Apuleius is defending himself against the charge of practicing magic, and especially of carrying magical objects wrapped up in a handkerchief. On Apuleius, see F. C. Grant, HR, p. 136. Text ed. by J. Van der Vliet (1910); see also the translation by H. E. Butler (1909); A. Abt, *Die Apologie des Apuleius von Madaura und die Antike Zauberei* (RGVV, IV. 2, 1908).

You ask, Aemilianus [the prosecutor], what I had in that handkerchief? Although I might deny that I had deposited any handkerchief whatsover of mine in Pontianus' library— or even supposing I were to admit, at the most, that I did so deposit it—I can still deny that there was anything wrapped up in it. And if I should take this line, you have no evidence or argument by which to refute me; for there is no one who has ever touched it, and there is only one freedman, according to your own statement, who has ever seen it. Nevertheless, for all that, let me say that the cloth was jammed full. Imagine yourself now, if you please, to be on the verge of a great discovery— as when the comrades of Ulysses thought they had found a great treasure when they ran off with the bag full of all the winds! Would you like to have me tell you what it was I had wrapped up in that handkerchief and committed to the care of Pontianus' household gods? You shall have your wish.

I have been initiated into almost all of the Greek mysteries, and I have preserved with the greatest care certain of the emblems and tokens [*signa et monumenta*] of my initiations, which were presented to me by the priests. I am not talking now about anything strange or unheard-of. Even a single initiate [*mystēs*] of the mysteries of Liber Pater who is present here knows what he keeps hidden away at home, safe from all profane touch, the object of his silent veneration. But I, as I have said, moved by religious zeal and a desire to know the truth, have devoted myself to many different mysteries [*sacra*], numerous rites, and various ceremonies relating to the gods. I am not making this up on the spur of the moment. Nearly three years ago, during the first days of my residence at Oea, in a public discourse which I delivered on the majesty of Aesculapius, I made the same statement and recounted the number of the mysteries with which I was familiar. That discourse was thronged, has been read far and wide, is in everyone's hands, and has won the approval of the pious inhabitants of Oea not so much through any eloquence of mine as because it speaks of Aesculapius. Will anyone who happens to remember it repeat the beginning of that particular passage in my discourse?—Do you not hear, Maximus [the presiding magistrate], how many voices are supplying the words? Indeed, they are freely reciting it! Let me now order this same passage to be read aloud, since you show by the gracious expression on your face that you will not be displeased to hear it. [The passage is then read aloud.]

Can anyone who has the slightest recollection of religious rites be surprised that a man who has been a partaker of so many divine mysteries should preserve in his home certain mementos of these sacred ceremonies, or that he should wrap them in a linen cloth, which is the purest covering for holy things? For wool, produced by the most lethargic of animals and stripped off the sheep's back, was accordingly recognized by the followers of Orpheus and Pythagoras as a profane vesture. But flax, the purest of all plants and among the best of the fruits of the earth, is used by the most holy priests of Egypt, not only for clothing and raiment but as a veil to hide sacred things.

And yet I know that some persons, and chiefly this fellow Aemilianus, think it a good joke to deride things divine. For I learn, from certain men in Oea who know him, that up to the present he never has prayed to any god or frequented any temple; if he happens to pass by any shrine, he thinks it wrong to raise his hand to his lips as an act of reverence. He never has given the first fruits of his crops or vines or flocks to any of the rural gods who feed and clothe him; there is no shrine at his villa, no holy place nor sacred grove. But why should I speak of sacred groves or shrines? Those who have been at his place say they never have seen there even one stone where an offering of oil has been made or one bough where wreaths have been hung [*ramum coronatum*]. As a result, two nicknames have been given him: he is called *Charon*, as I already have said, on account of his truculence of tongue and manner, but he is also—and this is the name he prefers—called *Mezentius*, because he despises the gods. For this reason I can easily understand why he should regard my list of so many initiations as something to jest about. It is even possible that, because of his contumacy for things divine, it may never enter his head that what I say is the truth, viz., that I guard most sacredly the emblems and mementos of so many holy rites. But I—for what "Mezentius" thinks of me I would not turn a hand; but to others I would announce in the clearest voice: if any of you who happen to be present have been partakers with me in these same solemn rites, give the sign and you shall hear what it is that I am preserving. For no consideration of personal safety will compel me to declare to the uninitiated [*ad profanos*] what things I have accepted to be kept in secret.

A PERSONAL PRAYER

CIL, VI. 18817 (lines 9 ff.). H. Dessau, ILS, 8006. From the tombstone of Lucius Sempronius Firmus, set up by his wife. Found at Rome. A "sweet" death was a gentle one.

So I pray you, ye most sacred Manes, let my loved one be well received, and be graciously favorable to him [i.e., take care of him], and let me behold him in the [long] hours of the night, and let him even persuade Fate that I may the sweeter and sooner follow him.

DEDICATIONS

CIL, I. 2. 365; cf. XI. 3081. H. Dessau, ILS, 3124. K. Latte, RR, § 4a. E. H. Warmington, ROL, p. 80. A bronze tablet found at Falerii, written right to left in Faliscan letters. The language is a mixture of Latin and Faliscan.

Sacred to Minerva. Lars Cotena son of Lars, the praetor, gave this as avowed, in accordance with a decree of the Senate. When he gave it [i.e., dedicated it], he did so correctly [*rected*, with proper rites].

CIL, I. 2. 20. H. Dessau, ILS, 2989. E. H. Warmington, ROL, p. 68. Inscribed on a small bronze plate from the third century B.C.

Marcus Aemilius son of Marcus and Gaius Annius son of Gaius the praetor on behalf of the people dedicated a twentieth part to Jupiter.

Ephemeris Epigraphica, IX. 608. H. Dessau, ILS, 4016. K. Latte, RR, § 4b. Found at Lanuvium. Dessau dates it in the second century B.C.

Whether to a god or to a goddess, [dedicated by] Florianus the king [of the Sacrifices, *rex sacrificulus*].

CIL, I. 2. 622. H. Dessau, ILS, 8884. E. H. Warmington, ROL, p. 78. A dedication at Delphi, after the battle of Pydna, 168 B.C.

Lucius Aemilius [Paullus] son of Lucius, commander in chief, took [this booty] from King Perseus and the Macedonians.

CIL, I. 2. 804; VI. 3732, 31057. H. Dessau, ILS, 4019. K. Latte, RR, § 4c. Found at Rome. The date is perhaps late second or early first century B.C. Verminus is of course the "god" or numen of vermin.

To Verminus. [Dedicated by] Albus Postumius son of Albus, grandson of Albus, who was Duovir in accordance with the Praetorian Law.

CIL, XII. 3129. H. Dessau, ILS, 4031. K. Latte, RR, § 4d. Found at Nîmes. From the third century of the Christian era. Cf. Juvenal IV. 57. G. Wissowa, RKR, p. 246.

To the Quartan Fever. Byrria Severilla has faithfully kept her vow.

THE CONSECRATION OF A TITHE TO HERCULES

CIL, I. 2. 1531; X. 5708. H. Dessau, ILS, 3411. F. Bücheler, *Carmina Latina Epigraphica*, I. 4. K. Latte, RR, § 19. E. H. Warmington, ROL, p. 82. Found near Sora. Date *ca.* 150 B.C. The poem is in the ancient Saturnian meter.

Marcus and Publius Vertuleius, sons of Gaius

What their father here once vowed
When discouraged, afflicted, and despairing,
His children now gladly devote to Hercules
Who greatly deserves it, they having set aside a tithe
And offering it at a sacred banquet.
As one they pray, Grant them often to be forced to fulfill
a vow!

CIL, I. 2. 632; IX. 4672. H. Dessau, ILS, 3410. F. Bücheler, *Carmina Latina Epigraphica*, 248. E. H. Warmington, ROL, p. 86. A dedication of Lucius Mummius, the destroyer of Corinth in 146 B.C. Found near Reate. It is written in hexameters. The Holy One, the Victor, is Hercules. Cf. G. Wissowa, RKR, p. 272 f.

O Holy One!

From the spoils, O Victor, Lucius Mummius vowed
In accordance with ancient ways to give thee from the
tithe as a payment of interest;
He saw his desires fulfilled [after] asking thee graciously
to make it easy for him to pay the debt.
Grant him to render a true account and pay the tithe;
And for this and other gifts grant thy blessings to a deserving man.

LAW REGARDING THE GROVE AT SPOLETIUM

CIL, I. 2. 366; cf. XI. 4766. H. Dessau, ILS, 4911. K. Latte, RR, § 16a. E. H. Warmington, ROL, p. 154. Date probably about 241 B.C., when Spoletium became a Latin colony.

Let no one damage this grove, nor lead out or carry out anything belonging to it, nor cut down [trees], except on the day of the annual sacrifice; on this day it is permitted, without incurring penalty, to cut down what is necessary for the purpose of the sacrifice. If anyone damages it, he shall offer to Jupiter a bull as an expiatory sacrifice. If anyone knowingly and maliciously violates it, he shall offer to Jupiter a bull as an expiatory sacrifice and pay 300 *asses* [say $3] as a penalty. The collection of sacrifice and fine is the business of the *dicator* [presumably a magistrate of Spoleto].

A FOUNDATION IN THE DAYS OF DOMITIAN

CIL, X. 444. H. Dessau, ILS, 3546. K. Latte, RR, § 23. Found near Caposele in Lucania, about five miles south of Salerno. On the *rosalia,* see Marquardt-Mommsen, *Römische Staatsverwaltung,* III (2d ed., 1885), 311; A. S. Hoey, *Rosaliae Signorum* in *Harvard Theological Review,* XXX (1937), 15–35.

Dedicated to Silvanus in fulfillment of a vow for the preservation of our Emperor Domitian. Lucius Domitius Phaon has permanently made over to the present and future members of the College of Silvanus, for the purpose of cultus, maintenance, and sacrifices, the estates belonging to him [known as] Junianum, Lollianum, Percennianum, and Statuleianum, with their now existing buildings and boundaries; and he specifies that from the income of the above-named properties provision shall be made for a sacrifice to be offered in the presence of the members of the College, who shall come together for a meal, on the 1st of January; on the 11th of February, the birthday of the Empress Domitia; on the 27th of June, the anniversary of the dedication of [the statue of] Silvanus; on the 20th of June, the Festival of Roses; on the 24th of October, the birthday of our Emperor Domitian. The arrangements are to be made each year by the officials then in office. It is obvious that no one will deliberately hinder the carrying out of the purpose of this foundation, as described above, since the properties named have been dedicated and the days of sacrifice have been specified for the preservation of the noblest Prince and Lord. Morover, the place or part of the field is woodland, in the forest preserve, marked off according to the boundary stones which are about [the statue of] Silvanus, and belongs to Silvanus; and the entrance to the Silvanum is by a path through the farm [known as] Quaesicianum, open and free for all to use. Also, wood for the sacrifices may be gathered on the estate [named] Gallicanum, and likewise water may be drawn freely either here or in the forest preserve, without distinction. That this should be given, done, and effected without prejudice or favor, is both commanded and permitted by Lucius Domitius Phaon, to whom the whole region belongs. [There are numerous mistakes in spelling, due either to the stone graver or the one who dictated the inscription.]

CONSECRATION OF AN ALTAR AT SALONA

CIL, III, 1933. H. Dessau, ILS, 4907. K. Latte, RR, § 16b. Date, A.D. 137. The regulations concerning the altar of Diana on the Aventine were the oldest in Rome (Dionysius of Halicarnassus, *Roman Antiquities*, IV. 26). See G. Wissowa, RKR, p. 250.

During the consulship of Lucius Aelius Caesar [Hadrian] for the second time, and of Publius Coelius Balbinus Vibullius Pius, on the 9th of October, the duovir Gaius Domitius Valens formally proclaimed the decree of foundation in the following words, the pontiff Gaius Julius Severus saying the words before him:

Jupiter Optimus Maximus, since today I give and dedicate to thee this altar, I will consecrate it to thee with the rights which I here and now publicly announce, together with the ground upon which it rests. If anyone brings hither a sacrificial offering [*hostia sacrum*], but without the inward parts [which were to be cooked and offered], it shall nevertheless be accepted [as valid]. The other regulations shall be the same for this altar as those governing the altar of Diana on the

Aventine [Mount]. With these rights and these grounds, as I have said, I give, dedicate, and consecrate this altar, O Jupiter Optimus Maximus, that thou mayest be favorable and gracious to me and to my colleagues in office, to the town council, the citizens, and the inhabitants of the settlement of Martia Julia Salona, to our wives and our children.

THE *ACTA* OF THE ARVAL BROTHERHOOD

CIL, VI. 2023–2118; H. Dessau, ILS, 5034–47; K. Latte, RR, § 14; Henzen, AFA, pp. cxxx ff. For more recently discovered inscriptions, see Aelius Pasoli (ed.), *Acta Fratrum Arvalium . . . quae post Annum 1874 reperta sunt,* in *Studi e Ricerche,* VII (1950). One of the "reforms" of the emperor Augustus was the restoration of the old priestly college of the Arval Brothers, which went in solemn procession every springtime about the fields (*arva*) with offerings and prayers for the protection of the seed from harm. Most of the fragments of the *acta* are from the sanctuary at the grove of Dea Dia at the fifth milestone on the Via Campana, southwest of Rome.

THE PROCLAMATION OF THE FESTIVAL

CIL, VI. 2068; H. Dessau, ILS, 5036; Henzen, AFA, p. cxxx. This tablet was found under the apse of the basilica of St. Peter in Rome. For the ancient Arval Hymn, see p. 17.

In the same year [A.D. 91] on the 7th of January, the Arval Brethren announced in the vestibule of the temple of Concord the sacrifice for Dea Dia, under the second chairmanship of Lucius Veratius Quadratus. In the vestibule of the temple of Concord L. Veratius Quadratus, chairman of the Arval Brethren, with washed [purified] hands, veiled head, under the open sky, facing the East, announced on behalf of his colleagues the sacrifice for Dea Dia: "May it be well, favorable, happy, fortunate and salutary for the Emperor Caesar Domitianus Augustus Germanicus, Pontifex Maximus, for Domitia Augusta his wife and their whole household, for the Roman people [of] the Quirites, for the Arval Brothers, and for me.

The sacrifice to Dea Dia this year will take place on the 17th of May at my home, on the 19th of May in [the open] grove and at my home, and on the 20th of May at my home." Present with Lucius Veratius Quadratus were his colleagues Lucinus Maecius Postumus, Quintus Tillius Sassius.

THE FIRST DAY

CIL, VI. 2078=32374; Henzen, AFA, p. clii. The date is May 27, A.D. 118. The *acta* for this year include a request from the emperor Hadrian for the prayers of the Brethren, February 26 (Dessau 5028), and the sacrifice offered, March 6, when a storm blew down a tree in the sacred grove.

While Caesar Trajan Hadrian Augustus was imperator for the second time . . . in the house of the chairman Marcus Valerius Trebicius Decianus, the Arval Brethren, vested in the toga praetexta, offered a sacrifice to Dea Dia with incense and wine. They reclined upon white cushions trimmed with purple, and presented an offering with incense and wine. Youths whose parents were both living, children of senators, clad in the praetexta brought the gifts to the altar, with the help of servants [here follow the names of five young men]. Present were the following members of the College: [five names].

THE SECOND DAY

Henzen, AFA, p. clii f. Two days later, May 29, another convocation was held.

In the grove of Dea Dia the chairman, Marcus Valerius Trebicius Decianus, immolated on the altar two sows as an expiation for the pollution [caused by cutting down of trees] and the doing of certain work. Further, he offered on the sacrificial hearth of Dea Dia a white cow as a freewill offering in her honor. Then the priests sat down in the hall and partook of a meal from the sacrifice. After they had put on the praetexta and the crowns made of spiked ears of grain, they went up to the grove of Dea Dia, while the way was kept open for them; there they offered a fat white sheep, the chairman Marcus Valerius Trebicius Decianus and the Flamen Titus Julius Candidus [performing the rite]. After completing the sacrifice they all poured [libations of] incense and wine. Then the crowns were removed [*inlatis*] and the images of the gods were anointed. Next they appointed Titus Julius Candidus Caecilius Simplex to be chairman from these Saturnalia to the next Saturnalia, reclined [once more] in the hall, and dined with the chairman Trebicius Decianus. After the feast, Trebicius Decianus the chairman, arrayed in a purple toga and wearing sandals, with a woven crown of roses on his head, while the way was kept open, ascended to the barriers. They gave the signal to the charioteers and equestrians [for the races to begin]. Julius Candidus and Antonius Albus presided; to the victors were given palms and silver crowns as prizes. The same members of the College were present as on the first day.

THE THIRD DAY

Henzen, AFA, p. cliii. On this day, May 30, the sacrifice was completed.

The Arval Brethren met at the house of the chairman Marcus Valerius Trebicius Decianus to complete the sacrifice to Dea Dia, and during the meal the following offered incense and wine: Valerius Trebicius Decianus, chairman, Julius Candidus, Julius Alexander Julianus, Antonius Albus, Julius Catus. The service was attended to by youths with both parents living, children of senators, the same as on the first day. The youths serving as acolytes, wearing small veils and praetexta, bore to the altar the fruits that had been brought hither, with the help of the public slaves. Then the torches were lighted, and they filled [?] the Etruscan [baskets?], and sent them home by the youths. Present were the same as on the preceding day. This year the banquet cost 100 denarii.

FROM THE ACTA OF A.D. 240

H. Dessau, ILS, 9522; K. Latte, RR, p. 17. These fragments were found in 1914 under the fifth-century church of S. Chrysogonus in Trastévere, i.e., west of the Tiber.

On the 27th of May, at the home of the vice-chairman Fabius
Fortunatus in the Clivus Capsarius on the upper Aventine.
He began to sacrifice to Dea Dia at dawn, touched green and
dry ears of grain and bread crowned with laurel, anointed the
goddess, while the other priests, arrayed in the praetexta and
with garlands, offered incense and wine, touched green and
dry ears along with bread crowned with laurel, and anointed
the goddess. Then they found seats and received their dues,
each 100 denarii [X is crossed out, and C inserted]. Before
noon, the vice-chairman, after a bath and arrayed now in
white garments, took his place at the triclinium and dined.
Youths whose parents were both living, children of senators,
sat upon the chairs: [two names, apparently sons of an Arval
brother, Lucius Alfenius Avitianus] shared in the meal, and
dined. After the meal the table was removed from before the
vice-chairman and water was brought him for washing his
hands; a purple-trimmed cushion was brought in, and he offered incense and wine; the youths wearing the praetexta had
charge of the service and brought [the offerings] to the altar,
with the help of the public slaves. The vice-chairman [re-
ceived] the dues and the crowns which had been worn at the
meal. . . .

[Here follows a long lacuna. The remainder begins on the
second day.]

[In the grove of Dea Dia, Fabius Fortunatus Victorinus the
vice-chairman offered on the altar piacular sacrifices of swine
for the pollution of the grove and for work done there, and
offered a cow in honor of Dea Dia.] Then he returned and presented at the altar of Dea Dia the viscera of the young pig and
on the silver sacrificial hearth he placed the entrails of the
cow, repeated the felicitous words, and returned to the lounge
in the portico. Here he entered in a book that he had been
present, had sacrificed, and had presented the entrails; then
he laid aside his praetexta, and went into the bath. Coming
back, he welcomed his colleagues as they arrived; when the full

number were present, both groups laid aside the praetexta, gathered in the lounge in the hall and entered in the book that they were present and had offered sacrifice; a small table made without iron was placed before them, and they partook of white wheaten bread, tasted of the blood of the pig, and distributed and ate the pig. In the hall they covered their heads, went up to the grove, and the vice-chairman and the priests brought cakes and offerings for the sacrifice and offered a fat sheep, inspected the entrails in order to satisfy themselves of the acceptance of the sacrifice, and placed them on the altar; then they went into the temple and brought the table of sacrifice, and on the grassy turf before the goddess, thrice, [placed] three clots made of milk, liver, and meal [?], likewise thrice, three . . . [this is totally obscure; see Dessau's note] . . . again thrice three upon the turf. Then they went outside the temple again to the altar, and said prayers, as they presented three clots and three offerings [?]. Then they returned to the [temple] again, prayed, and took up the pots with the pap; and the vice-chairman, the flamen, and two public slaves [*sacerdotes*, deleted by Dessau] took the pots, when they had received them, and tossed them down through the open doors above the cliff [or slope] of the Mother as a meal for the Lares. Then the doors were closed, and they sat on the marble benches and distributed the laurel-crowned white wheaten bread to their servants and domestics. Then they left the temple and gathered before the altar; the vice-chairman and the flamen sent two of their companions to bring ears of grain; the vice-chairman and the priest returned with beakers of wine . . . , passed the cups with their right hand, and received the fruit with their left. Then they chanted the hymn. [See p. 17.] Next they all offered incense at the altar, out of dishes, and wine out of beakers, also honeyed wine, milk, honey and raisin wine; finally they brought baskets of baked goods [?] in lieu of the gold offering. Then they returned to the temple once more and took up the books and recited the [Arval] hymn as they marched about in the three-step. At a given signal they handed back the books to the official servants. Then they anointed the goddesses and lighted lamps, and the middle door of the temple was opened. Gifts of crowns of Dea Dia were brought, while the secretary Arescontus Manilianus read out [the names of] our Lord Gordianus Augustus and the names of the rest of the priests. [And the crowns and other appurtenances] were laid away. Then they produced a book and named the person who was to function [as chairman and flamen] from the coming Saturnalia to the next. Then they spoke felicitous words and went down from the temple, wearing the praetexta, and each entered his tent to change [his apparel] and donned white dinner clothes and went down to the hall to dine. [The last few lines were carelessly done by the stone-graver. The rest of the inscription is missing.]

AN INVITATION TO DINNER IN A TEMPLE

Pap. Oxyrhynchus 1485. A. S. Hunt and C. C. Edgar, SP, p. 400. From the second or third century A.D. See also Adolf Deissmann, *Light from the Ancient East* (rev. ed., 1927), p. 351.

The exegete invites you to dine in the [temple of] Demeter today, which is the 9th, beginning at the 7th hour [1 p.m.].

QUESTIONS ASKED AT ORACLES

Pap. Oxyrhynchus 1148. See A. S. Hunt and C. C. Edgar, SP, p. 436. From the first century A.D. Compare the examples in F. C. Grant, HR, pp. 33 f.

My Lord Sarapis Helios, benefactor! [Tell me] if it is better for my son Phanias and his wife not to agree now with his father but to oppose him and not sign the contract. Tell me this truly. Farewell.

Pap. Oxyrhynchus 1149. See A. S. Hunt and C. C. Edgar, SP, p. 436. From the second century A.D. Note the inconsistent spelling.

To Zeus Helios, great Serapis, and the associated gods [sharing the same temple]. Nikē inquires if it is advisable for me to buy from Tasarapion her slave Sarapion who is also called Gaion. Grant me this.

See also Pap. Oxyrhynchus 1477. A. S. Hunt and C. C. Edgar, SP, pp. 436–438. *Ca.* A.D. 300. It is a list of set questions all numbered for easy reference; e.g., 74. "Am I to be sold?" 77. "Am I to be reconciled?" 79. "Shall I receive the money?" 90. "Shall I change my wife?" 91. "Have I been poisoned?" These were evidently typical questions asked at oracles.

A HOROSCOPE

Pap. Oslo 6. Dated A.D. 140. A. S. Hunt and C. C. Edgar, SP, p. 444. On astrology, cf. F. C. Grant, HR, pp. 60 ff.

Birth [Gk. *genesis*] of Philoe: the thirteenth year of the Lord Antoninus Caesar, between the 15th and the 16th of the month Phamenoth, in the 4th hour of the night. Helios [the Sun] in Pisces, Zeus [Jupiter] and Hermēs [Mercury] in Aries, Kronos [Saturn] in Cancer, Arēs [Mars] in Leo, Aphroditē [Venus] and Selēnē [Moon] in Aquarius. *Hōroscōpos* Scōrpios [Capricorn].

CURSING TABLETS

CIL, XI. 4639. H. Dessau, ILS, 3001. K. Latte, RR, § 37. The first of the following tablets was found at Tuder in ancient Umbria, about sixty miles north of Rome, on the edge of the old Etruscan territory. The date was under the Flavians. In the ancient world, a curse was supposed to possess magical force, especially when written out (and thus made permanent) on some magical substance like lead, which was dark (chthonic) and heavy—its weight would drag one down! They were hidden in the ground, as discovery would render them ineffective. Although curses and magic are not properly a part of religion, they often influenced religious thought and practice. The Attic cursing tablets were edited by R. Wünsch in *Inscrip-*

tiones Graecae (1897) III. 3; the others, so far as discovered at that time, by August Audollent, *Defixionum Tabellae* (1904); Dessau 8746–8757 gives a selection; see also R. Wünsch, *Antike Fluchtafeln* (in Lietzmann's *Kleine Texte*, no. 20; 2d ed., 1912). The language is usually crude and vulgar—as we should expect. On the general subject see S. Eitrem, "Magic," § 8, in OCD; cf. F. C. Grant, HR, pp. 46 ff.; C. Bonner, *Studies in Magical Amulets, Chiefly Graeco-Egyptian* (1950); A. D. Nock, "Greek Magical Papyri," in *Journal of Egyptian Archaeology*, XV (1929), 219–235.

For the welfare of the city [colonia], the Common Council [= the order of decurions] and the people of Tuder, Lucius Cancrius Primigenius, freedman of Clemens, one of the Six, Augustal and Flavial, fulfilled his vow to Jupiter Optimus Maximus, Guardian and Preserver, since through the divine power he was able to find and recover the names of the [members of the] Common Council, which by the unspeakable crime of a dismissed public slave had been placed in graves for [the purpose of] cursing [them]; thus the city and its citizens were set free from fear of peril.

CIL, I. 2. 1013. H. Dessau, ILS, 8747. A rolled-up lead tablet found before the Latin gate at Rome; date, first century A.D. The fact that the tablet was rolled had magical significance.

Danae, the new slave of Capito. Accept her as an offering, and consume this Danae. You already have Eutyche, the wife of Soterichus.

CIL, I. 2. 1012. H. Dessau, ILS, 8749. Another lead tablet found outside the Latin gate; also first century.

As the dead man who is buried here can neither talk nor speak, so let Rhodine who belongs to Marcus Licinius Faustus be dead and unable to talk or speak. As the dead is welcome neither to gods nor men, so shall Rhodine who belongs to Marcus Licinius be as welcome and just as precious as this dead person who is buried here. Dis Pater, I commend to you

Rhodine, that she may be for ever hated by Marcus Licinius Faustus. So also Marcus Hedius Amphion. So also Gaius Popillius Apollonius. So also Vennonia Hermiona. So also Sergia Glycinna.

A. Audollent, DT, 286. H. Dessau, ILS, 8753. A lead tablet from Hadrumetum in Africa; imperial period. The author had a "cockney" pronunciation of Latin and dropped his *h*'s; also he was a poor speller. But he added a picture of the demon—with a human head and a coxcomb, and magic words on his breast; then the names (presumably) of the horses: Night-wanderer, Tiber, Ocean.

I charge you, Demon, whoever you are, from this hour, this day, this moment, torment and destroy the horses of the Green and White; kill and mangle the drivers Clarus, Felix, Primulus, Romanus; let them not breathe [again]. I charge you by the one who set you free in his time, the god of the sea and the air. [Then in Greek letters:] *Iaō Iasdaō ooriō . . . aēia.*

H. Dessau, ILS, 8757. A. Audollent, DT, 270. Another tablet from Hadrumetum in Africa; written in Latin, but in Greek letters, in order to increase the magic by the appearance of a foreign tongue. Note the magical use made of biblical as well as pagan divine titles. Note also the stone-graver's mistake near the end.

I charge . . . by the great god and by the Anterotes, by the one who bears a falcon on his head [Horus or Isis], by the seven stars, that from the hour in which I write this, Sextilius, the son of Dionysia, shall not sleep, but shall be consumed with rage [i.e., madness], not sleeping, not able to sit, nor speak, but in mind have me, Septima, the daughter of Amoena, consumed with rage, with love and longing for me, soul and heart; Sextilius, the son of Dionysia, with love and longing for me, Septima, the daughter of Amoena, [let him burn]. But thou, Abar Barbarie Eloee Sabaoth Pachnouphi Puthipemi, let Sextilius, the son of Dionysia, not find sleep, but let him be consumed with love and longing for me, [in] breath and heart, [and] all the members of the whole body of Sextilius, the son of Dionysia, let him burn up. If not, I shall go down to the hall [underworld] of Osiris and destroy the grave and cast [his remains] in the stream and let it bear them away. For I am the great Decan [Dean] of god, of the great god, the God Achrammachalala.

CIL, XI. 1823. H. Dessau, ILS, 8748. A. Audollent, DT, 129. A lead tablet found near Arretium.

Quintus Letinius Lupus, who is also called Caucadio, the son of Sallustia Veneria or Veneriosa, I deliver up, dedicate, and devote to your deity, who are called Boiling Waters, whether ye wish to be called nymphs or by some other name, that ye may bring down and destroy him within this year. . . .

CIL, VIII. 12505. A. Audollent, DT, 228A. From the proconsular province of Carthage. Written on both sides (A and B), in almost identical terms.

To thee I pray, thou who rulest the realms below, to thee I deliver Julia Faustilla daughter of Marius, that you may carry her off as speedily as possible and gather her to your company in the world below.

CARE FOR THE SANCTUARIES

CIL, VI. 754. H. Dessau, ILS, 4269. K. Latte, RR, § 47b. F. Bücheler, *Carmina Latina Epigraphica*, I. 265. Date, between A.D. 382 and 392. As Professor Latte says, the inscription "shows how the prominent families of Rome, after state support had been withdrawn from the heathen cults, came forward with substantial contributions." Phoebus, the invincible Sun God, is Mithras. The grotto (or cave) was a *mithraeum*. Compare the saying of Jesus quoted in Acts 20:35, and the saying of Libanius, *Epistle* 140: "Giving is sweeter than getting." The hereditary name incised across the sides and top reads: Tamesius Olympius Augentius. For another example of pagan piety from this period see F. C. Grant, HR, pp. xvi and 149.

THE OLYMPII

TT	Once upon a time my grandfather, a Victor, honoring heaven and the stars,		AA
AA	Built at Caesar's command the glorious temple of Phoebus the Sun God.		UU
MM	But his grandson, now named Victor, excelled him in zeal		GG
EE	And built a grotto, without asking thee, O Rome, for any contribution.		EE
SS	It is more blessed for the pious to suffer loss than to gain.		NN
II	For who is richer than the one who shares his lean inheritance with them that dwell on high?		TT
II			II
			II

REPAIR OF PRIESTLY DWELLINGS

CIL, VI. 2158. Cf. VI. 2158. H. Dessau, ILS, 4944. K. Latte, RR, § 47b. Inscription found in the Forum of Augustus, among the ruins of the temple of Mars the Avenger. Date, after A.D. 382. See G. Wissowa, RKR, 555; Cicero, *On Divination*, I. 17 (§ 31).

The dwellings of the Palatine Salii, which their ancestor built for the housing of their mighty weapons, but which fell into disrepair for much too long a time, has been restored at their own expense by the noble pontiffs of Vesta, under the presidency of the noble gentlemen, Plotius Acilius Lucillus and Vitrasius Praetextatus.

VII. THE CHRISTIAN VICTORY AND THE PAGAN REACTION

The religion of the ancient world originated before history began; it ended long after the formal triumph of Christianity under Constantine and his successors in "New Rome." Indeed, it has never ended, for some of the primitive rites, beliefs, and practices are still in vogue, either in combination with Christian rites and beliefs or under a Christian guise. The attitude of the suppressed pagan minority is not often voiced in modern works; therefore we give an extended passage in which it is set forth. See also F. C. Grant, HR, p. 149; H. I. Bell, *Cults and Creeds in Graeco-Roman Egypt* (1953); G. Boissier, *La Fin du paganisme*, 2 vols. (4th ed., 1894); C. N. Cochrane, *Christianity and Classical Culture* (1944); L. Duchesne, *Early History of the Church*, 3 vols. (1922–25); W. W. Fowler, RERP, ch. 20; J. Geffcken, *Der Ausgang des Griechisch-Römischen Heidentums* (1920); R. M. Grant, *Miracle and Natural Law in Graeco-Roman and Early Christian Thought* (1952); S. L. Guterman, *Religious Toleration and Persecution in Ancient Rome* (1951); W. R. Halliday, *The Pagan Background of Early Christianity* (1925); M. L. W. Laistner, *Christianity and Pagan Culture in the Later Roman Empire* (1951); G. J. Laing, *Survivals of Roman Religion* (1931); P. de Labriolle, *La réaction païenne* (8th ed., 1942); H. Lietzmann, *The Beginnings of the Christian Church*, Vols. I–II (1937–38); A. D. Nock, *Conversion* (1933), "The Development of Paganism in the Roman Empire," in CAH, Vol. XII (1939), ch. 12, and bibliography, pp. 764–766, "Early Gentile Christianity and its Hellenistic Background," ch. 3 in *Essays on the Trinity and the Incarnation*, ed. by A. E. J. Rawlinson (1928); J. Seznec, *The Survival of the Pagan Gods* (1953); B. H. Streeter, "The Rise of Christianity," in CAH, Vol. XI (1936), ch. 7; N. Lewis and M. Reinhold, RC, II, §§ 172–180; N. Turchi, RRA, Pt. II. 8. See also the bibliography at the beginning of Chapter Six, and add: C. Bigg, *The Church's Task under the Roman Empire* (1905); W. Ramsay, *The Church in the Roman Empire* (1893).

CHRISTIANITY AND THE PAGAN CULTS

Tertullian, *A Demurrer Against the Heretics' Interpretation of Scripture* (*De Praescriptione Haereticorum*), XL. Tertullian was born of well-to-do and prominent heathen parents at Carthage *ca.* A.D. 150 and lived to *ca.* 220. Trained for the law, he became after his conversion a brilliant apologist for Christianity, attacking chiefly the Marcionite type of Gnosticism; he was an almost fanatical champion of orthodoxy, and toward the end of his life adopted the Montanist doctrines, viz., the belief in the approaching Age of the Spirit and the revival of prophecy inculcated in Phrygia by Montanus and his followers. The present passage illustrates the kind of attack the Church Fathers launched against the pagan cults. It is unfortunate that most of the little we know about these cults comes from such polemical and antagonistic representations. For the Mithraic cultus, see Franz Cumont, *Les mystères de Mithra* (2d ed., 1902), ch. 5 (Eng. tr., 2d ed., 1910, pp. 150–174), *Les Religions orientales dans le paganisme romain* (4th ed., 1929), ch. 6 (Eng. tr. of 2d ed., 1911; 3d ed. of the German tr. of the 4th French ed., 1931); M. J. Vermaseren, *Corpus Inscriptionum et Monumentorum Religionis Mithraicae* (1956); H. R. Willoughby, *Pagan Regeneration* (1929), ch. 6.

The question follows [from the verse, "There must be heresies," I Cor. 11:19], by whom is interpreted the meaning of those passages which make for heresies? By the devil, certainly, to whom belong those tricks which pervert the truth, and who in the mystery rites [*mysteriis*] of the idols even imitates the reality of the divine sacraments. He too [like the Christians] baptizes some—i.e., his own believers and faithful; he promises the removal of sins by the laver; and if my memory is sound Mithras even signs his soldiers right on their foreheads [as the Christians do]; and he also celebrates the oblation of bread, and brings in a symbol of the resurrection, and under the sword wreathes a crown. What does this mean! He even limits his high priest to a single marriage! And he also has his virgins, and likewise his celibates!

Suppose we revolve in our minds the various superstitions of Numa Pompilius, and consider his sacerdotal offices, insignia, and privileges, his sacrificial ministrations, and the instruments and vessels of those sacrifices, and consider the curious rites of expiations and vows: is it not clear that the devil has imitated the [well-known] moroseness of the Jewish Law? Since, therefore, he has shown such emulation of those very things by which the sacraments of Christ are administered, and has thus striven to express them in the practices of idolatry, it certainly follows that the very same being, exercising the same ingenuity, has been able to match the instruments [documents?] of things divine and belonging to the Christian saints with his profane imitation of the faith, words taken from words, parables from parables. Hence no one should doubt either that "spiritual wickedness" [cf. Eph. 6:12], from which even now heresies come, has been brought about by the devil, or that there is any difference between heresies and idolatry, seeing that they belong to the same author and his works to whom idolatry belongs. They either imagine another god opposed to the Creator [so, e.g., do the Marcionites]; or, if they confess the Creator to be unique [i.e., the only God], they speak of him as different from what he is in truth. Consequently every lie they tell about God is really a kind of idolatry.

THE STRUGGLE OF HEATHENISM FOR TOLERATION

Symmachus, *Third Relation* (i.e., letter addressed, as prefect of the City of Rome, to the Emperor), p. 280 ff. (Seeck). K. Latte, RR, § 48. See M. Schanz, *Geschichte der römischen Literatur* (2d ed., 1914), IV. 1, § 819. On the affair of the altar of Victory, see Joh. Geffcken, *Der Ausgang des griechisch-römischen Heidentums* (1920), pp. 146–152; Pierre de Labriolle, *La réaction païenne* (1934; 8th ed., 1942), pp. 335–368, 467 ff.; L. Duchesne, *Early History of the Church*, II (Engl. tr. 1912), ch. 17; H. Lietzmann, *Geschichte der Alten Kirche* (Engl. tr., *The Beginnings of the Christian Church*), III (1938), ch. 9.

In the year A.D. 382, the Emperor Gratian removed the altar of Victory (*Victoria*), which from the time of Augustus had stood in the Curia Julia, the assembly hall of the Senate. A deputation from the pagan party in the Senate, headed by the celebrated orator Quintus Aurelius Symmachus, undertook to present a plan for its restoration; but through the efforts of Ambrose, the bishop of Milan, it was not permitted to do so. After the death of Gratian a new attempt was made under Valentinian II, in 384, and the following petition was presented, which Symmachus quotes. It was formally addressed to the two ruling Caesars.

As soon as the illustrious Senate, which is ever obedient to you, learned that abuses were to be removed by the reassertion of the law, and that [our] pious rulers were determined to blot out the disgrace of the recent unhappy period, it allowed itself, following the example of the propitious present, to give utterance to its long-suppressed sorrow, and commissioned me for a second time to be the messenger of its complaints; for the only reason why, on the former occasion, the :ar of the late prince was deaf to me was that evil men prevented [his hearing me], though I might well have supposed that justice would be done, O most illustrious Caesar. A double responsibility is now mine; as your City Prefect, I represent the public interest, and as their deputy I commend the wishes of my fellow citizens. . . .

To what could it be more advantageous, that we should observe the regulations of the forefathers, and defend the rights and fortune of the Fatherland, than to the fame of your reign ["era"]. It waxes great, if you recognize that you cannot control [i.e., alter] the ancestral customs as you please. For this reason we would promote the status of the public worship [cultus], which has proved an advantage to the state for so long a time. One may recall the list of princes of both religions and of both views: the earlier of them observed the ceremonies of the forefathers; the later ones did not set them aside. If one does not imitate the reverence of the former, at least let him imitate the tolerance of the latter! Who is so lacking in all culture that he does not note the absence of the altar of Victory? We are really concerned for the future, and would guard ourselves against further bad omens. At least let the name [nomen] be honored, even if one denies the numen! Your everlasting reign owes a great debt to Victory; even more will [or may] it owe to her in the future. Let those abandon the worship of this Power, to whom it has not been useful! But you must take care not to give up a protection which deals kindly with military success. This power is the object of all men's desire, and no one should refuse reverence to it, when at the same time he recognizes it as desirable. And it is not in itself a sufficient ground, to avoid these malign forebodings— viz., at least the decorations of the assembly hall ought to be spared. Grant us, I pray you, the right to pass on to our descendants what we ourselves received as children.

The love of tradition is a mighty force; quite rightly, the measures undertaken by the late [emperor] Constantius did not long prevail. May you avoid setting an example which, as you recognize, lasts for so short a time. For our part, the eternity of your fame and name lies upon our hearts; and may the future find nothing to improve in the ordinances which you set forth! Where else can we swear loyalty to your laws and ordinances? What is to shame even the double-minded and keep them from giving false testimony [now that the altar is removed]? Certainly, "everything is full of God," and nowhere is the perjurer safe; but it means a great deal in fostering a fear of committing crime when the immediate presence of the deity is there to threaten [penalties upon perjury]. That altar unites all, that altar guarantees the truth [spoken by] the individual; and nothing gives our deliberations so much weight as the fact that the Senate decides everything under oath, so to speak. Must the secularized place now stand open to perjury? Will my noble princes permit this, who are themselves to defend the true oaths of the people?

But, someone will object, the late-lamented Constantius did so! Let us rather imitate the other decrees of this Prince, who certainly would never have undertaken anything of the kind had there been any other before him to take that false path [and show its error]. For the mistakes of a predecessor teach those who follow, and from the blame heaped upon an earlier example comes improvement. It was permitted the ancestor of your Clemency to make an error; but can we be exonerated if we imitate what we know to be blameworthy? Let your eternal majesty listen to other acts of the same Prince, which are more worthy to be brought forward. He did not take away the prerogatives of the sacred [Vestal] virgins, he filled up the priesthoods with noblemen, he did not refuse the allowance for the Roman cultus rites. Through all the streets of the eternal city he followed the happy Senate and looked with blessed eyes upon the temples, read the names of the gods on the gables, described the foundations of the sanctuaries, marveled at the founders, and, though he himself followed another religion, he supported this one for the sake of the Empire. For each one has his own customs, his own religion, and the heavenly Providence has assigned the cities to various guardians; as the newly born are provided with souls, so spirits of destiny are appointed for the various peoples. Hence come the benefits which the gods chiefly guarantee to men.

Since all the reasons for things are shrouded in darkness, upon what better basis can knowledge of the gods rest than upon the memory and the proof of success? If honorable antiquity gives authority to religions, then we must surely remain faithful to so many centuries and follow our ancestors, who with great good fortune followed theirs. Imagine that Rome stands here beside me and addresses you: "O best of Princes, Fathers of the Fatherland, have reverence for the years, from which have been handed down to me these pious customs. I will retain the rites of the forefathers, for they do not grieve me! I will live in my own way, as long as I am free! This religion has brought the whole round world under my law; these sacrifices drove away Hannibal from before my walls, and forced back the Gauls from the Capitol. Must I survive for so long, only to be despised in my old age? I will see what it is that people believe it a good thing to introduce; but it is too late, and full of shame, for gray hairs to be compelled to unlearn [and learn again]." It is on behalf of the ancestral, the native gods that we plead for tolerance. It is all one and the same, whatever god any particular man adores. We all look up to the same stars; heaven is common to all; the same world surrounds every one of us. Whatever rests above [these] —each in his own wisdom seeks to know the truth. It is not by one single path that we arrive at so great a mystery. Yet all that is idle controversy; what I am presenting is a petition, not a debate.

What benefit is it to your royal exchequer that the Vestals have had to give up their exemptions? Shall that be refused, under the most generous of sovereigns, which once was guaranteed by the most parsimonious? It is only a matter of recognition, more or less as a reward for [their] chastity. As the fillets adorn their heads, so it is a token of honor to the priestly office to be exempt from taxation. They enjoy merely the title of exemption, anyway, since their poverty keeps them from paying any tax. Hence they only increase their fame, they who would reduce their property! For a virginity which is dedicated to the welfare of the state only grows in value, when it is left unrewarded! . . .

Let no one imagine that I am defending only the cause of religion; from such deeds [as the removal of the altar of Victory] stem all the woes of the Roman people. The law of the fathers honored the Vestals and the Ministers of the gods with magnificent emoluments and lawful privileges. These provisions remained inviolate until [the time of] those degenerate thieves who seized the sacred sustenance of chastity in order to hand it out as pay to porters and postmen. Upon this act of violence followed a general famine, while bad harvests dashed the hopes of every province. This was no failure of the soil; we cannot blame the winds; no rust infected the seed; no weeds choked the growing grain; it was the plundering of holy things that destroyed that year. Anything that is refused for the service of the gods is certain to be destroyed. If such a misfortune had happened only once, one might say it was only the difference between one year and another; but some greater cause must be found to account for this [vast] unfruitfulness. People kept alive a little longer only by eating what they could pick up in the woods; famine drove people living in the country to turn once more to the Dodonaean oaks. Did the land ever suffer such misfortunes as long as the ministers of the public cult were honored by provisions for their necessities? When did anyone ever shake down acorns in order to feed men, or pull up the roots of weeds? When did the land ever lose its fruitfulness altogether, and not merely here and there, as long as the people and the sacred virgins shared alike in what it produced? The support of their servants recommended to the gods their care and supervision over the produce of the soil; it was a help to us rather than a gift to them! Can anyone doubt that something ought continually to be given for the welfare of all, when now the poverty of all demands it?

LAWS RELATING TO FORBIDDEN SOCIETIES

Justinian, *Digest*, XLVII. 22. 1; text in Theodor Mommsen (ed.), *Digesta Iustiniani Augusti* (1870), Vol. I, pp. 792 f. The decree shows how earlier legislation was still being enforced, now under Christian rule. At one time the prohibition of "unlawful" societies, i.e., those not recognized by the law, had worked serious hardship to the Christians, with their frequent meetings and their common fund (cf. Tertullian, *Apology*, 39). The *Digest* was published in A.D. 533. It was a compilation and correlation of earlier laws, codes, and commentaries on those laws which were still in force.

[Marcianus in Book III of the *Institutes:*] By princely [i.e., imperial] commands it was prescribed to the governors of provinces that they should not permit social clubs [*collegia sodalicia*] and that soldiers should not have societies in the camps. But it is permitted to the poor to collect a monthly contribution, so long as they gather together only once a month, lest under a pretext of this sort an unlawful society meet. And that this should be allowed not only in the city, but also in Italy and the provinces, the divine Severus ordered. But they are not forbidden to come together for the sake of religion, so long as thereby they do nothing contrary to the *senatus consultum* by which unlawful societies are restrained.

It is furthermore not lawful to belong to more than one lawful society [*collegium licitum*], as this was determined by the divine brothers [Caracalla and Geta]; and if anyone is in two, it is ordered that it is necessary for him to choose in which he prefers to be, and he shall receive from the society from which he resigns that which belongs to him proportionately of what there is of a common fund.